Anju Saxena and Lars Borin

Synchronic and Diachronic Aspects of Kanashi

Trends in Linguistics Documentation 38

Synchronic and Diachronic Aspects of Kanashi

Edited by Anju Saxena and Lars Borin

DE GRUYTER
MOUTON

The research and the results presented in this volume as well as its open-access publication have been supported by funding from the Swedish Research Council, for the projects "Documentation of an endangered language: Kunashi" (grant 2014-00560) and "South Asia as a linguistic area? Exploring big-data methods in areal and genetic linguistics" (grant 2014-00969).

Swedish
Research
Council

ISBN 978-3-11-135566-5
e-ISBN (PDF) 978-3-11-070324-5
e-ISBN (EPUB) 978-3-11-070327-6
DOI https://doi.org/10.1515/9783110703245

Library of Congress Control Number: 2021951796

Bibliographic information published by the Deutsche Nationalbibliothek
The Deutsche Nationalbibliothek lists this publication in the Deutsche Nationalbibliografie; detailed bibliographic data are available on the Internet at http://dnb.dnb.de.

This volume is text- and page-identical with the hardback published in 2022.
The book is published open access at www.degruyter.com.

Printing and binding: CPI books GmbH, Leck

www.degruyter.com

Contents

Synthesis

Kanashi basic vocabulary

Acknowledgements

We would like to express our gratitude for the support, encouragement and help which we received from Kanashi speakers. We especially remember with gratitude our oldest Kanashi language consultant, fondly referred to as Mr. Shukur Kardarji – who sadly passed away at a much too early age – for his enthusiasm for our project as well as for generously sharing his knowledge of Kanashi with us. A special note of thanks to Mrs. Suari Devi and her family for their warm welcome, and in particular to Mrs. Suari Devi for sharing her keen insights on Kanashi and for her patience during long data collection sessions, despite her busy schedule. We would also like to thank Ms. Anita, Mrs. Thakur Dasi, Mr. Inder Dev, Mr. Motiram, Mr. Ganga Ram, Ms. Purba, and other Kanashi speakers for their invaluable help and cooperation.

Thanks also to Ms. Santosh Negi, Dr. Prafulla Basumatay, Dr. Tashi Konchok, and Mr. Lalit Thakur (Chand View guest house in Malana) for their help in the field, as well as to the project assistants Armin Chiocchetti and Giada Falcone at Uppsala University.

We are also grateful to Stig Eliasson for his valuable comments on phonological issues (Chapter 2), to Bettina Zeisler at the University of Tübingen for her detailed and constructive comments on an earlier version of Chapter 3, to Rainer Kimmig, also at the University of Tübingen, for his comments on posited Indo-Aryan origins of the adaptive markers discussed in Chapter 6, and to Barbara Karlson (De Gruyter Mouton) and Charlotte Webster (Konvertus) for their support during the preparation of the camera-ready manuscript.

This volume is based on the linguistic fieldwork data collected as part of the project *Documentation of an endangered language: Kunashi*, funded by the Swedish Research Council, contract no. 2014-00560. The work presented in Chapters 6–8 was conducted in part in the project *South Asia as a linguistic area? Exploring big-data methods in areal and genetic linguistics*, funded by the Swedish Research Council, contract no. 2014-00969. The open access publication of this volume has been supported by the Swedish Research Council through its funding of these projects.

https://doi.org/10.1515/9783110703245-203

Abbreviations

For the phonetic and phonemic transcription conventions used in this volume, see the introductions to Chapters 2, 3, and 4.

The morpheme-by-morpheme glossing conventions used in linguistic examples are as far as possible those of the Leipzig Glossing Rules: https://www.eva.mpg.de/lingua/resources/glossing-rules.php. The following table shows the glossing abbreviations used, where items not provided in the Leipzig Glossing Rules are indicated by a preceding asterisk ("*").

Abbr.	Feature	Abbr.	Feature
1	first person	INTR	intransitive
*1/2o	first/second person object	LOC	locative
2	second person	M	masculine
3	third person	*MDL	middle
ABL	ablative	*m.name	male personal name
ACC	accusative	*N, N	noun
*ADE	adessive	N-	non-, not
Adj	adjective	NEG	negation, negative
Adv	adverb	NMLZ	nominalizer
ALL	allative	NOM	nominative
*ASP	aspect	*NP	noun phrase
Aux	auxiliary	OBL	oblique
*BE	auxiliary (<copula)	PASS	passive
*C	consonant	PFV	perfective
CAUS	causative	PL	plural
COM	comitative	*PLE	plural exclusive
*CX	case suffix	*PLI	plural inclusive
DAT	dative	*p.name	place name
DEM, Dem	demonstrative	POSS	possessive
*DIM	diminutive	*Pro	pronoun
*DIST	distal, distant	PROG	progressive
DU	dual	PROH	prohibitive
*EMP	emphatic	PROX	proximal, proximate
ERG	ergative	PRS	present
EXCL	exclusive	PST	past
F	feminine	Q	question marker
*FIN	finite	*Qnt	quantifier
*f.name	female personal name	REFL	reflexive
FUT	future	*SAP	speech act participant
GEN	genitive	SG	singular
*H	honorific	*TAM	tense-aspect-mood
*HAB	habitual	*TNS	tense
*IA	Indo-Aryan borrowing	TR	transitive
*IDX	index	*v, V	verb
IMP	imperative	*V	vowel
INCL	inclusive	*VIS	visible
INF	infinitive	*VOL	volitional
INS	instrumental	*VVB	vector verb

https://doi.org/10.1515/9783110703245-204

Synchrony: description

Anju Saxena and Lars Borin

1 Introduction: Kanashi, its speakers, its linguistic and extralinguistic context

Abstract: Kanashi is an indigenous language of India spoken by some 2,000 individuals in one single village in the Indian Himalayas. It is a Sino-Tibetan language, separated from the other Sino-Tibetan speaking communities in the region by a girdle of Indo-Aryan speaking villages. In the present volume we contribute to the documentation of Kanashi with a phonological and a grammatical description, as well as a basic vocabulary. We also address questions of genealogical classification of the Sino-Tibetan languages of the Himalayas, as well as their history of contact with other language families.

Keywords: Kanashi, Sino-Tibetan, South Asia, areal linguistics, comparative linguistics, Himalayan region

Chapter overview:

1 Kanashi and Malana

Kanashi (xns; <Sino-Tibetan [ST]) is also known in the literature as Malani and Kanasi, and in the speech of our oldest Kanashi language consultant as Kunashi. It is spoken by some 2,000 individuals in one single village, Malana (coordinates: 32°03′46″N 77°15′38″E) which is situated in the upper regions of the Malana river valley in the northern part of the Kullu district in the state of Himachal Pradesh in India (Figure 1).[1] The Malana village stands alone. Primarily due to its geographical location (at an altitude of 2,652 metres and with access only on foot), until recently Malana was more or less isolated from the rest of the world. Even today, getting there requires a two-hour mountain hike after a long, winding and difficult car ride from Jari, the nearest town. It is also linguistically isolated: the

1 The number of Kanashi speakers given by the Ethnologue (Eberhard et al. 2021) is 1,400, but the source for this information is dated 2001. The population of Malana village as given in the 2011 Indian census was 1,722.

https://doi.org/10.1515/9783110703245-001

inhabitants of all the closest surrounding villages speak Indo-Aryan (IA; <Indo-Iranian<Indo-European) varieties.

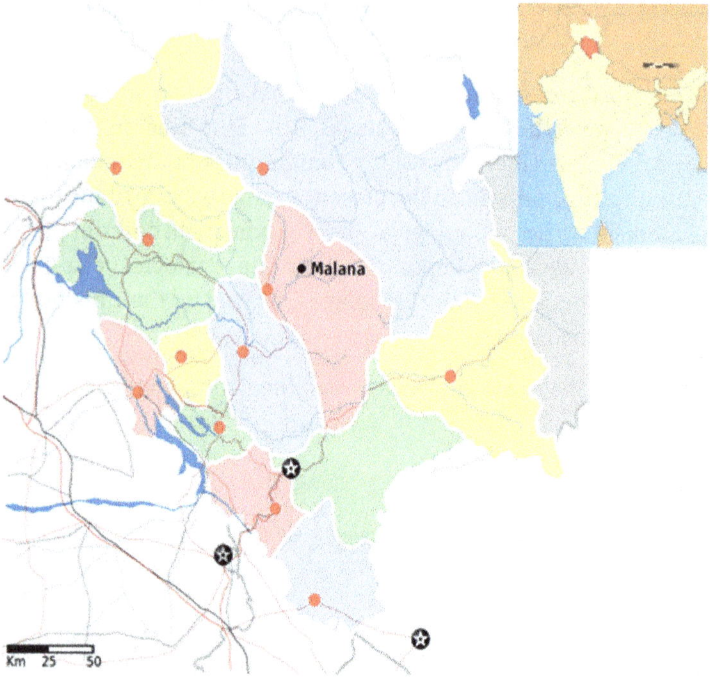

Figure 1: Map of Himachal Pradesh with location of Malana. Map created by Plane-Mad/Wikimedia, reproduced from https://en.wikipedia.org/wiki/File:Himachal_Pradesh_locator_map.svg under a CC-BY-SA license.

Kanashi is an endangered language,[2] for which we, unfortunately, still have very little information available. Like many other languages of this region (and like most of the world's languages), Kanashi is an oral language with no established writing system. The only textual data available in Kanashi come from the few linguistic descriptions made of the language: some short word-lists (Harcourt 1871; Diack 1896; Konow 1909; Tobdan 2011), a short grammatical sketch (6 pages) and 2 short texts in Konow (1909), and linguistic sketches based on secondary data presented by D. D. Sharma (1992: 303–399) and Duttamajumdar (2013; 2015). Sax-

2 Kanashi is "definitely endangered" according to the *UNESCO Atlas of the World's Languages in Danger* (http://www.unesco.org/languages-atlas/) and "threatened" according to the Ethnologue (Eberhard et al. 2021).

ena & Borin (2013) present a comparative Tibeto-Kinnauri study, which includes some Kanashi data.

While Kanashi undisputably is a Sino-Tibetan language, its exact position within ST remains undetermined. Based on a short wordlist, Diack (1896) concluded that Kanashi shows close affiliations to Kinnauri (kfk; Saxena 2017; 2022). Similar suggestions are also made by Bailey (1908), Konow (1909), Glottolog (Hammarström et al. 2018), and in a comparative investigation of a number of ST languages spoken in the Indian Himalayas by Saxena & Borin (2013). Based primarily on basic vocabulary data, Widmer (2017: 44) categorizes Kanashi as a West Himalayish language, closely related to Kinnauri. Figure 2 shows a classification of Kanashi within ST based on the account of Widmer (2017). It also shows the classifications of Kinnauri and Bunan (bfu), which will be used as closely related ST points of comparison in the description of the Kanashi numeral systems in Chapter 5, together with Zhangzhung (xzh), an extinct West Himalayish language.

- Sino-Tibetan
  - Tibeto-Burman
    - Bodic
      - Bodish
        - Tibeto-Kinnauri
          - West Himalayish
            - Eastern branch
              - Central subgroup
                - Zhangzhung (†)
                - Bunan
            - Western branch
              - Kinnaur subgroup
                - **Kanashi**
                - Kinnauri

Figure 2: Genealogical classification of Kanashi (Widmer 2017)

One very characteristic feature of the Kanashi community is that both their language *and* their village are important identity markers, and they have a reputation as forming an extremely secluded community.[3] The physical isolation of Malana finds a parallel in that socioculturally, too, Kanashi speakers make a clear distinc-

3 And this has been the situation for a long time: "[The village of Malauna] is perhaps one of the greatest curiosities in Kooloo, as the inhabitants keep entirely to themselves, neither eating nor

tion between themselves ("the Kanashi community in Malana") and others. There are guidelines as to what a non-Kanashi person can or cannot do. For example, which path in the village the non-Kanashi person should use. Non-Kanashis are prohibited from any type of physical contact with a Kanashi person. Those breaking these rules are liable to punishment in the form of fines. When the Kanashi speakers visit other places in Himachal or elsewhere, they maintain their system of not touching and/or eating with non-Kanashis. Literacy is low and very few Kanashi speakers work outside the village.

P. C. Sharma et al. (1985) investigated the prevalence of endogamy vs. exogamy in Malana. They collected information about all the 141 families residing in Malana at that time, and through personal interviews with the head (or the oldest member) of the family, they recorded their genealogies for up to 3–4 generations back. Their results show that 93.13% of all marriages took place between locals – i.e. exogamy is minimal.

The physical seclusion of the village and the social aloofness of the Kanashi community have contributed to the maintenance of its traditional culture and language, but recent developments are threatening the traditional lifestyle, including the language, where especially contact with Hindi[4] is becoming an integral part of the villagers' daily lives. This is the latest episode in a long history of continuous IA influence on Kanashi, which probably started before the Kanashi speakers settled in Malana, and which is continually reinforced by the circumstance that in all the villages closest to Malana local IA varieties are spoken, collectively referred to as Kullu Pahari.[5]

There are striking differences between the most recent influences and older contacts with IA languages, however. Earlier contacts with non-Kanashi were ritualized and periodical, but now the contacts are more pervasive, also inside the village. In the recent past there have been dramatic socio-economic changes in and around Malana, which have intensified the exposure to and the need to learn Hindi and Kullu Pahari for the Kanashi speakers as never before.

The Malana hydro-electric plant, which was commissioned in July 2001, is being built on the Kanashi people's traditional land. This is destabilizing their traditional lifestyle, including their farming, animal husbandry, and their tradi-

intermarrying with the people of any other village, and speak a language which no one but they themselves can comprehend." (Harcourt 1871: 312).

4 Hindi (hin) is both one of the two national languages of India (together with English) and the official state language of Himachal Pradesh.

5 ISO 639-3 kfx. Also referred to as Kullui/Kulluvi and Inner Siraji.

tional stewardship of the local biodiversity.[6] Suddenly the villagers are finding themselves at the losing end on many fronts at once. The Indian judiciary system relies on written documents, but Kanashi people do not have written documents to prove their traditional ownership of land. During our fieldtrips, many episodes were told where the villagers lost their land to the hydro-electric dam construction company as they lacked written documents to support their claims. This also means that they are losing their traditional livelihood, forcing them to look outside their village to support themselves, where some other language is the lingua franca.

These developments are accompanied by the growing presence and dominance of Hindi. Hindi is the medium of instruction in schools, the language of communication in employment-related situations outside Malana village, and also the language of modern broadcast-media entertainment, which have become an integral part of village life, thanks to the introduction of satellite television, internet and mobile phones in the village, so that even locals who never leave Malana are exposed to Hindi, Kullu Pahari and English on a regular basis. Today we also find many temporary daily wage workers in Malana, many of whom come from Bihar (east India) and Nepal. The lingua franca in such communications is colloquial Hindi. Adding to this, there is a recent influx of younger (Western and Indian) tourists (drawn by trekking, mountain climbing and marijuana) to Malana, introducing the villagers to modern social habits, and bringing with them the need to interact in Hindi and English.

Most Kanashi speakers understand Kullu Pahari and Hindi, and many younger villagers and children speak a mixture of Hindi, Kullu Pahari and Kanashi. Kanashi is not the language of media, education or employment, but it is, at present, the medium of communication among its native speakers in the "in-village" spheres. However, there are already signs of language shift, as will be seen in Chapter 5 in the differences observed in the use of numerals among older and younger Kanashi speakers.

---

6 Villagers depend on the forest for traditional medicine and food, and on the other hand, their local traditions have contributed to the maintenance of the biodiversity in the region. According to their traditional belief, the village god prohibits excessive felling of trees, but this is, unfortunately, changing drastically, as large areas of land are being cleared off to build the dam and the roads needed to bring in heavy construction machinery.

2 Synchronic and diachronic aspects of Kanashi: this volume

In the present volume we present some results of an ongoing long-term substantial research and documentation effort targeting Sino-Tibetan languages spoken in the western and central Himalayas. In this volume the focus will be on Kanashi and its linguistic relatives and neighbors.

As noted above, Kanashi has been underdescribed. For this reason, this volume provides a basic descriptive part: a chapter on the phonology of Kanashi (Chapter 2), a substantial grammar sketch (Chapter 3), and as the last chapter of the volume, a basic vocabulary of Kanashi based on the IDS/LWT list (Borin et al. 2013; Haspelmath & Tadmor 2009), together with Kanashi–English and English–Kanashi versions of the vocabulary (Chapter 9).

Most languages in the world are like Kanashi: small, indigenous languages; about half of the world's languages have less than 10,000 speakers, and only a little over 5% of all living languages have more than one million native speakers (Whalen & Simons 2012: 163). The number of speakers per language follows a power law-like distribution, with a few extremely large language communities at one end and a long tail of very small languages at the other. Many of the approximately 7,000 currently spoken languages have not been described at all by linguists; Seifart et al. (2018: e332f) estimate that about 40% – or about 2,750 – of the languages do not have even a grammar sketch.

At the same time, there is now a fair amount of evidence indicating that the size of a language community correlates inversely with the grammatical – notably morphological – complexity of its language, and investigations are ongoing into the possible causal mechanisms involved (Wray & Grace 2007; Lupyan & Dale 2010; Nettle 2012; Atkinson et al. 2015; Reali et al. 2018; Raviv et al. 2019).

From this follows that we can expect that "almost every new language description still guarantees substantial surprises" (Evans & Levinson 2009: 432), and "there are few signs of our discoveries flatlining" (Seifart et al. 2018: e328). This as-yet far from fully described linguistic diversity – which flies in the face of too categorical a view of what constitutes language and how language universals should be construed (Dryer 1998; Evans & Levinson 2009; Whalen & Simons 2012) – resides mainly in indigenous languages spoken by small, close-knit, often multilingual communities.

There are at least two slightly different consequences for indigenous language description emerging from the above facts. First, we should expect genuinely new,[7] previously unencountered linguistic phenomena to appear as a matter of course. Secondly, because of the sociolinguistic context in which modern (descriptive) linguistics has been developed and is taught, we may also come across linguistic phenomena which actually occur also in more well-described languages, but which have been neglected because of a descriptive bias towards written standard language of speakers similar to the linguists themselves, rather than, e.g., everyday spoken – perhaps multilingual – interaction (Linell 2005; Wray & Grace 2007).

Consequently, in the present volume we also discuss some surprising – to us – phenomena (in particular unexpected variation) encountered in our work on documenting Kanashi. Chapter 4 is devoted to a discussion of the considerable variation exhibited in the phonology of Kanashi and its consequences for the phonological description presented in Chapter 2. In Chapter 5 we turn to a description of the remarkable diversity observed in the Kanashi numerals, and discuss possible reasons for this state of affairs, in particular sociolinguistic factors.

After this, we turn to questions of language diachrony and genealogy. In the course of our work we have come across a number of linguistic features in Kanashi and its ST relatives with potential high relevance for the subclassification of the ST languages of the Himalayas and for uncovering the prehistory of Kanashi. In Chapter 6 we focus on nominal morphology and borrowed nouns and adjectives, while relevant verbal features (verb morphology and stratification of borrowed vocabulary) are investigated and discussed in Chapter 7.

Finally, in Chapter 8, we synthesize and summarize the findings from the diachronic part, attempt to place Kanashi in the ST family tree and draw inferences about the prehistory – including the contact history – of this language community on the basis of the features presented in Chapters 6 and 7.

Note that some information from the descriptive part of the volume may be repeated in the introductory and background sections of individual chapters This is deliberate and has been done in the hope that this will make each chapter reasonably self-contained.

References

Atkinson, Mark, Simon Kirby & Kenny Smith. 2015. Speaker input variability does not explain why larger populations have simpler languages. *PLoS ONE* 10(6): e0129463.

7 New to the field of linguistics, not to the speakers of the described language, of course!

Bailey, Thomas Grahame. 1908. *The languages of the Northern Himalayas, being studied in the grammar of twenty-six Himalayan dialects*. Asiatic Society monographs, Vol XII. London: The Royal Asiatic Society.
Borin, Lars, Anju Saxena & Bernard Comrie. 2013. The Intercontinental Dictionary Series: A rich and principled database for language comparison. In Lars Borin & Anju Saxena (eds.), *Approaches to measuring linguistic differences*, 285–302. Berlin: De Gruyter Mouton.
Diack, Alexander Henderson. 1896. *The Kulu dialect of Hindi: some notes on its grammatical structure, with specimens of the songs and sayings current amongst the people, and a glossary*. Lahore: The Civil & Military Gazette.
Dryer, Matthew S. 1998. Why statistical universals are better than absolute universals. In *Chicago Linguistic Society 33: The panels*, 123–145. Chicago: University of Chicago.
Duttamajumdar, Satarupa. 2013. Reduplication in Kanashi. *The Buckingham Journal of Languages and Linguistics* 6: 95–104.
Duttamajumdar, Satarupa. 2015. Diphthongs in Kanashi. *The Buckingham Journal of Languages and Linguistics* 8: 99–106.
Eberhard, David M., Gary F. Simons & Charles D. Fennig (eds.). 2021. *Ethnologue: Languages of the world*. 24th edn. Dallas: SIL International.
Evans, Nicholas & Stephen C. Levinson. 2009. The myth of language universals: Language diversity and its importance for cognitive science. *Behavioral and Brain Sciences* 32(5): 429–448.
Hammarström, Harald, Robert Forkel & Martin Haspelmath. 2018. *Glottolog 3.3*. Jena: Max Planck Institute for the Science of Human History. Available online at https://glottolog.org.
Harcourt, Alfred Frederick Pollock. 1871. *The Himalayan districts of Kooloo, Lahoul, and Spiti*. London: Wm H. Allen & Co.
Haspelmath, Martin & Uri Tadmor. 2009. The Loanword Typology project and the World Loanword Database. In Martin Haspelmath & Uri Tadmor (eds.), *Loanwords in the world's languages: A comparative handbook*, 1–34. Berlin: Mouton de Gruyter.
Konow, Sten. 1909. *Linguistic survey of India, Vol 3: Tibeto-Burman family. Part I: General introduction, specimens of the Tibetan dialects, the Himalayan dialects, and the North Assam group*. (This and several other volumes of the LSI were edited by Sten Konow, although published as the work of George A. Grierson). Calcutta: Government of India, Central Publication Branch.
Linell, Per. 2005. *The written language bias in linguistics*. First published in 1982 by Dept. of Communication Studies, University of Linköping, Sweden. London: Routledge.
Lupyan, Gary & Rick Dale. 2010. Language structure is partly determined by social structure. *PLoS ONE* 5(1): e8559.
Nettle, Danie. 2012. Social scale and structural complexity in human languages. *Philosophical Transactions of the Royal Society B* 367: 1829–1836.
Raviv, Limor, Antje Meyer & Shiri Lev-Ari. 2019. Larger communities create more systematic languages. *Proceedings of the Royal Society B* 286: 20191262.
Reali, Florencia, Nick Chater & Morten H. Christiansen. 2018. Simpler grammar, larger vocabulary: How population size affects language. *Proceedings of the Royal Society B* 285: 20172586.
Saxena, Anju. 2017. Sangla Kinnauri. In Graham Thurgood & Randy J. LaPolla (eds.), *The Sino-Tibetan languages*, 2nd edn., 756–772. London: Routledge.

Saxena, Anju. 2022. *The linguistic landscape of the Indian Himalayas: Languages in Kinnaur*. Forthcoming 2022. Leiden: Brill.

Saxena, Anju & Lars Borin. 2013. Carving Tibeto-Kanauri by its joints: Using basic vocabulary lists for genetic grouping of languages. In Lars Borin & Anju Saxena (eds.), *Approaches to measuring linguistic differences*, 175–198. Berlin: De Gruyter Mouton.

Seifart, Frank, Nicholas Evans, Harald Hammarström & Stephen C. Levinson. 2018. Language documentation twenty-five years on. *Language* 94(4): e324–e345.

Sharma, Devi Datta. 1992. *Tribal languages of Himachal Pradesh. Part two*. Delhi: Mittal Publications.

Sharma, P. C., V. Bhalla, R. K. Pathak & A. K. Bhalla. 1985. Matrimonial migration in Malaneese: An isolated community of Himachal Pradesh. *Indian Anthropologist* 15(1): 81–86.

Tobdan. 2011. *Exploring Malana: An ancient culture hidden in the Himalayas*. New Delhi: Indus Publishing Company.

Whalen, Douglas H. & Gary F. Simons. 2012. Endangered language families. *Language* 88(1): 155–173.

Widmer, Manuel. 2017. *A grammar of Bunan*. Berlin: De Gruyter Mouton.

Wray, Alison & George W. Grace. 2007. The consequences of talking to strangers: Evolutionary corollaries of socio-cultural influences on linguistic form. *Lingua* 117(3): 543–578.

Anju Saxena, Anna Sjöberg, and Padam Sagar

2 The sound system of Kanashi

Abstract: We present the first systematic description of the sound system of Kanashi. In addition to a thorough investigation and description of the Kanashi phoneme system based on fieldwork data, we also present a comparison of the Kanashi sound system with the phonologies of a number of closely related Sino-Tibetan languages, belonging to the same West Himalayish subgroup of Sino-Tibetan as Kanashi.

Keywords: Kanashi, Sino-Tibetan, phonology, phonetics, comparative linguistics. Himalayan region

Chapter overview:

1 Introduction

The aim of this chapter is to describe the sound system of Kanashi, based on our fieldwork data, collected during a number of field trips to Malana over several years. This is the first systematic description of the Kanashi sound system. In the last section of this chapter (Section 5) we will also compare the Kanashi sound

https://doi.org/10.1515/9783110703245-002

system with some other languages belonging to West Himalayish, the same Sino-Tibetan subgroup as Kanashi.[1]

2 Data collection and processing

This description is based mainly on 2,063 sound files from three Kanashi speakers for 975 words. In addition, our data also include material from other speakers which has been taken into account in this description. The two main etymological sources of the Kanashi vocabulary are Sino-Tibetan (ST) and Indo-Aryan (IA). In the analysis presented in this chapter, we have included all lexical items, regardless of their origin.

The three primary language consultants are one older male Kanashi speaker (older male, "OM" in the following) and two younger speakers – one man (younger male, "YM") and one woman (younger female, "YF"). At the time of the data collection the older speaker was about 50 years old, the younger male speaker around 22 years old and the female speaker around 28 years old. The female speaker had received some formal education. Both male speakers were illiterate; they had not received any formal education. All three speakers were born and brought up in the village. Like other Kanashi speakers, they leave the village occasionally. All three could understand Hindi (hin), the national language of India and Kullu Pahari (kfx), the locally dominant language (both are IA languages). While the female speaker could speak Hindi quite well, the male speakers (especially the younger speaker) spoke a mixed Hindi with strong influence of their mother tongue Kanashi.

Apart from lexical items, we have also collected elicited phrases and sentences and some narratives. The elicitation was done in Hindi. All recordings were done with a general documentary purpose, that is, not with a particular phonetic experiment in mind. This means that in some cases the materials are not optimal for the analyses performed on them (e.g. having list intonation, not having tokens of the same word from all speakers etc.). The sound files were processed using Audacity and Praat (Boersma & Weenink 2018).

1 Our investigations of different aspects of the phonology of Kanashi have been presented at several conferences (Saxena & Sjöberg 2017; Saxena et al. 2018a,b,c). We would like to thank to the participants of these events for their comments and suggestions.

2.1 Transcriptions

Unless otherwise stated,[2] Kanashi examples are provided here in phonemic transcription, using the phoneme inventory presented in Sections 2.2 and 2.3. Stress is not indicated, as at this stage, we are not certain of its phonemic status. In Kanashi lexical items which end in a consonant in the transcription, a short final [ə] is heard when these words are spoken in isolation. Similarly, a short final [h] is heard when words ending in vowels in the transcription are spoken in isolation. In our transcriptions such word-final [ə] and [h] are not marked. Further, vowels preceding a nasal consonant tend to be nasalized. But there is also a restricted set of lexical items with nasal vowels without a following nasal consonant. Nasalization on vowels is only marked when there is no nasal consonant following them. Finally, between vowels and in word-final position, /ŋ/ is often pronounced [ŋg], resulting in variant forms ([ŋ] ~ [ŋg]). This seems to occur more commonly between vowels than word-finally. In some cases where this variation is absent or minimal – only [ŋg] is attested in our data – this is explicitly expressed in our phonemic transcription (e.g. /raŋg/ 'color').

For phonemic analysis, all speakers are considered together and as representing one sound system. This, at times, poses some challenges for describing the phonology of Kanashi. We will discuss some problematic cases below. For phonetic analysis, the transcription of one particular instance of recorded pronunciation is given. Most of the examples come from the female consultant and this is thus normally not indicated. When the transcription represents the speech of one of the male speakers, OM or YM is given in brackets following that transcription.

2 Phonetic transcriptions are given in IPA notation in square brackets "[...]". Even though our transcription conventions for Kanashi are intended as phonemic, whenever we wish to stress that phonemes and phonemic representations are under discussion, we write single phonemes and phoneme sequences surrounded by "/.../". We represent geminate consonants as doubled (biphonemic) rather than long (i.e. we write *daddu* rather than *dad:u*), but we would like to stress that this does not imply a strong preference on our part for the one or the other analysis.

2.2 Consonants

	Bilabial	Alveolar	Postaveolar	Retroflex	Velar	Glottal
Plosive	p b	t d		ʈ ɖ	k g	
Aspirated plosive	pʰ	tʰ		ʈʰ	kʰ	
Fricative		s	ʃ			h
Affricate		ʦ ʣ	ʧ ʤ			
Aspirated affricate		ʦʰ	ʧʰ			
Nasal	m	n		ɳ	ŋ	
Lateral		l				
Rhotics		r		ɽ		
Approximant	ʋ (labiodental)		j (palatal)			

Kanashi exhibits considerable phonetic variation in the realization of consonant phonemes. /ɖ/, /ɳ/ and /ɽ/ in Kanashi are found mostly in words of IA origin, where IA (Western Pahari) languages, too, have the same retroflex consonant. For example, Kanashi: /ka:ɳas/ 'one-eyed person', Kotgarhi: *ka:ɳɔ* 'one-eyed person'; /ba:ɳes/ 'nephew', Kotgarhi: *bʰaɳe* 'nephew').[3] At the same time these retroflex consonants also show a lot of variation in Kanashi. For example, [ɳ] in Kanashi shows variation with [n], [ɽ], [ɻ] and [ʈ]. For example, Kanashi: [kʰa:na] ~ [kʰa:ɳa] 'food';[4] /baniŋ/ [b(ʰ)aniŋ] ~ [b(ʰ)ɔɳiŋ] 'utensil';[5] /baɳaŋ/ 'forest':[6] [baɳaŋ] ~ [baɽaŋ] ~ [baɻaŋ] 'forest';[7] /ʃaɳam/ 'make, do', [kʰa:na/kʰa:ɳa ʃaɳm] ~ [kʰa:na/kʰa:ɳa ʃaʈam] 'to cook'. At times, the retroflex nasal /ɳ/ seems to be realized as a retroflex flap or approximant, with the preceding vowel nasalized, e.g. /ʃaɳaŋ/ 'ice' with variations [ʃãɽaŋ] ~ [ʃãɻaŋ]. The retroflex /ɽ/ also shows variation with [ɖ] in the word-medial position, e.g. /buɽits/ [buɽits] ~ [buɖits] 'old(F)'.

Variation is also observed between [s] and [ʃ]. This variation is found both in the speech of the same speaker (e.g. YF: /aʃi/ [as(s)i] ~ [aʃi] 'eighty') as well as between speakers, e.g. YF vs. OM, where in some lexemes YF has [s] while OM has [ʃ]. For example, /ʃaʈʰ/ 'sixty' YF: [saʈʰ], OM: [ʃaʈʰ] ~ [ʃɔʈʰ]; /sat/ 'seven', YF: [sat], OM: [ʃɑt]; /sadraŋ/ 'autumn' YF: [sadraŋ], OM: [ʃadraŋ]. Note that in all these ex-

3 Source: Hendriksen (1976).

4 Western Pahari *kʰa:ɳ* 'food'. Information provided in this chapter on Western Pahari languages is from Turner (1966) and/or Hendriksen (1976).

5 Jaunsari: *bʰā̃ɖe* [utensil.PL] (Turner 1966: 538).

6 Bhalesi: *baɳ* 'forest'.

7 Variation among /ɽ/, /r/, /l/ is also mentioned by Grierson (1928) (e.g. *chāṛi* 'forty'; *sōṛa* and *sōla* 'sixteen'; *khalas* and *kharas* 'standing').

amples /s/ or /ʃ/ precedes /a/. But at the same time, /a/ is by far the most frequent vowel, therefore it is impossible to say if this is significant.

There is also variation found in our material between [ʣ] and [z] (e.g. /ʣaːm/ [ʣaːm] ~ [zaːm] 'food, to eat'). In general, the voiced fricatives ([z] and [ʒ]) are quite rare in our material. They almost only occur as variants of the affricates (although there are instances where we have [z] and no attested variant with [ʣ], e.g. [zan] 'life' and [dazi] 'doorframe'). This may be a gap in our data. If they should be treated as phonemes, which currently seems unlikely, they appear to have a marginal status in the language.[8]

Similarly, [ʣ] and [ʤ], too, show variation. For instance, /ʤaŋgal/ [ʤaŋgəl] ~ [dzaŋgal] ~ [ʤaŋgal] ~ [ʤaŋgl] 'forest'. However, there are also near minimal pairs for /ʣ/ and /ʤ/, e.g. /ʤab/ 'rain' : /ʣam/ 'to eat'. For this reason they are treated here as separate phonemes.

Variation between aspirated stop and fricative is attested for /pʰ/, which is also realized as [ɸ] or [f]. Example: /kopʰi/ [kɔpʰi] ~ [kɔfi] ~ [kapʰi] ~ [koɸi] 'coffee'), and /kʰ/, which is also realized as [x]. Example, /naʈukʰ/ [naʈukʰ] ~ [naʈux] 'navel'.

Variation is further found in the realization of the rhotics. The alveolar trill /r/ is also realized as a tap or flap [ɾ] and sometimes also as a more approximant-like sound [ɹ] (e.g. /ʤuriŋ/ [ʤuriŋ] ~ [ʤu̟ɹɪŋ] 'glacier'). Further, /r/ is not always clearly audible in the word-final position.

/ʧ/ shows variation with [tsʰ] and [ʧʰ], e.g. /ʧets/ [ʧets] ~ [ʧʰets] ~ [tsʰets] 'wife' and /ʧaːri/ [ʧaːri] ~ [tsʰaːri] 'attic'.

In addition to a more vocalic /ʋ/ that contrasts with /b/ (e.g. /baː/ 'father' /ʋaː/ 'nest'), /b/ is also realized as [ʋ] (e.g. [bais] ~ [ʋais] 'twenty two'). This variation occurs in all positions in our material. In some items (e.g. /naːb/ 'tomorrow') with a final /b/, it is clearly realized as [ʋ] but in other instances it is difficult to tell, whether from listening or from inspecting the waveforms and spectrograms. Further, /b/ sounds at times like a [β] or a [f], as a fricative rather than a stop. This is also the case with /g/. It, too, is often realized as a fricative [ɣ]. Because of the small database, it is not possible to examine the distribution of these variants.

Generally speaking the degree of aspiration in Kanashi consonants is much less than in the corresponding aspirated consonants in IA languages such as Hindi. Voiced aspirates are almost entirely limited to the IA part of the Kanashi lexicon. Hindi is not necessarily – or even most likely – the source language for most IA vocabulary items in Kanashi, but is used here to represent IA. In all such examples we find both variants in our material – with and without aspiration.

8 Grierson (1928) provides the following consonants: *ts, tsh, ʣ, zh*.

They appear to be in free variation, both in the speech of the same speaker and across speakers.[9] IA words beginning with [b^h], [d^h] and [g^h] are realized as [b^h] ~ [b], [d^h] ~ [d] and [g^h] ~ [g] respectively (e.g. /bukamp/ [b^{h}ukamp] ~ [bukamp] 'earthquake'; /daram/ [d^{h}aram] ~ [daram] 'religion'; /ganʈa/ [g^{h}anʈa] ~ [ganʈa] 'hour'). The status of voiced aspirated stops in Kanashi ([b^h], [d^h], [ɖ^h] and [g^h]) is problematic in some respects. There is one potential minimal pair in our materials: [g(^{h})oɽa] 'horse' and [goɽa] 'ankle'. There are, however, two problems with treating this minimal pair as conclusive evidence for their phonemic status. First, the already mentioned free variation: 'horse' is often realized as [goɽa], homophonous with 'ankle'. Postulating voiced aspirated stops as phonemes means that they are only occasionally contrastive on the surface and often have the exact same realization as another phoneme. Additionally, this merger is not rule-bound but completely free. The problem with treating voiced aspirated stops as "allophones" brings a very strange kind of allophony with it. There is free variation, but this free variation occurs only in certain lexical items. Something being lexically restricted is generally taken to be a criterion for phonemicity. This problem complex is discussed in more detail in Chapter 4 in this volume.

Even though retroflex and alveolar consonants have phonemic status in Kanashi, there are also instances of free variation between retroflex and alveolar consonants. The last-mentioned could be due to the fact that the position of the retroflex consonant in Kanashi is closer to alveolar. This has the effect that the retroflex consonant is heard often as a non-retroflex consonant. This variation is heard in the speech of almost all language consultants that we have worked with.

Finally, in the word-final position voiced stops generally exhibit what appears to be free variation between voiced and voiceless consonants. In Section 4 we will discuss this in more detail.

2.2.1 Examples of occurrence

2.2.1.1 Stops

/p/ – a voiceless unaspirated bilabial stop

/pa:n/	[pa:n]	'stone'	/puʥa/	[puʥa] ~ [puza]	'fifty'
/ʈa:pu/	[ʈa:pu]	'island'	/ipiʧ/	[ipɪʤ] ~ [ipɪʧ]	'behind'
/bukamp/	[b(^{h})ukamp]	'earthquake'	/ʃep/	[ʃe̱p] ~ [ʃep]	'foam'

9 There are also instances where the locus of aspiration fluctuates (e.g. [k^{h}akaŋ] ~ [kak^{h}aŋ] 'mouth').

/p^{h}/ – a voiceless aspirated bilabial stop

/p^{h}uts/	[p^{h}u̟ts] (YM), [puts]	‘mouse’	/p^{h}asam/	[p^{h}asəm] ~ [p^{h}asm]	‘to vomit’
/kop^{h}i/	[kop^{h}i] ~ [kɔp^{h}i] ~ [kɔfi] ~ [koɸi] ~ [kap^{h}i]	‘coffee’	/gup^{h}a/	[gup^{h}a]	’cave’

/b/ – a voiced unaspirated bilabial stop

/bi:g/	[bi:g] ~ [bi(:)k^{h}] (YM)	‘ant’	/ba:/	[ʋa:] ~ [ba:] (OM), [ba] (YM)	‘father, uncle’
/bube/	[bube] ~ [bɵbe]	‘father’s sister’	/kuba:r/	[kuba:(r)] ~ [kuʋar]	‘in, inside’
/sura:b/	[sura:b] ~ [sura:ʋ]	‘alcohohol’	/na:b/	[na:b] ~ [na:ʋ] ~ [na:p^{h}]	‘tomorrow’

/t/ – a voiceless unaspirated alveolar stop

/ta/	[ta]	‘nose’	/ti:r/	[ti:r]	‘arrow’
/bitiŋ/	[b(^{h})iti(:)ŋ] ~ [b(^{h})ɪti̟ŋ]	‘wall’	/batak/	[ba̠tak] ~ [ʋatak]	‘duck’

/t^{h}/ – a voiceless aspirated alveolar stop

/t^{h}ar/	[t^{h}ar] ~ [t^{h}a:(r)]	‘lion’	/t^{h}i:d/	[t^{h}i:d] ~ [t^{h}i:t(^{ə})]	‘today’
/matt^{h}a/	[matt^{h}a] ~ [mat^{h}a] (YM)	‘forehead’	/kat^{h}a:/	[kat^{h}a:]	‘story’
/pod/	[pod] ~ [pot^{h}] (YM)	‘dandruff, ash’	/parsed/	[parsed] ~ [pərset^{h}] (YM)	‘sweat (N)’

/d/ – a voiced unaspirated alveolar stop

/dil/	[di̟l] ~ [dɪl] (YM)	‘heart, soul’	/das/	[das]	‘ten’
/gidaɽ/	[gi̟daɽ] ~ [gɪdaɭ]	‘jackal’	/ʥaddu/	[ʥaddu]	‘magic’
/i:d/	[i:d] ~ [i̟d] ~ [it] ~ [i(:)]	‘one’	/bud(d)/	[büdd] ~ [bud(d^{ə})]	‘Wednesday’

/ʈ/ – a voiceless unaspirated retroflex stop

/ʈa:ŋg/	[ʈã:ŋ(g)]	‘leg, foot’	/ʈulem/	[ʈüle̩m] ~ [ʈulem]	‘to sleep’
/beʈiŋ/	[b(^{h})eʈiŋ] ~ [b(^{h})eʈɪŋ] ~ [bɪʈɪŋ]	‘tree’	/gaʈa:ŋ/	[g(^{h})aʈã:ŋ]	‘watermill’
/seʈ/	[seʈ(^{h})]	‘rich’	/ũʈ/	[ũʈ(^{h})]	‘camel’

/ʈʰ/ – a voiceless aspirated retroflex stop

/ʈʰi:k/	[ʈʰi:k]	'right (= not wrong)'	/ʈʰullaŋ/	[ʈʰu̟lla] (OM), [ʈʰullaŋ]	'leg'
/uʈʰras/	[uʈ(ʰ)əras] ~ [uʈ(ʰ)ᵊras] ~ [uʈ(ʰ)aɽas]	'high'	/ka:ʈʰiŋ/	[ka:ʈʰi] ~ [ka:ʈʰiŋ]	'mountain top'
/aʈʰ/	[aʈʰ] ~ [a̠ʈʰ]	'eight'	/paʈ/	[pɔʈʰ] (YM), [paʈ]	'threshing stone'

/ɖ/ – a voiced unaspirated retroflex stop

/ɖeb/	[ɖeb] ~ [ɖep]	'left (direction)'	/ɖugas/	[ɖugas] ~ [ɖugɔ̟s]	'deep'
/goɖiŋ/	[goɖiŋ] ~ [godĩ:(ŋ)]	'foot'	/ɖoɖre/	[ɖɔɖre̟] (YM)	'beehive'
/guɖ/	[guɖ] ~ [gɵʈ] (YM)	'arm, hand'	/ho:ɖ/	[ho:ɖ]	'bread'

/k/ – a voiceless unaspirated velar stop

/ka/	[ka] ~ [kə]	[2SG]	/keb/	[keb] ~ [kep]	'needle'
/bakar/	[ba̠kar] ~ [bɔkar]	'goat'	/tsʰika/	[tsʰi̟ka] ~ [tsʰeka]	'early, soon'
/jak/	[jak] ~ [ja(ʔ)]	'yak'	/ɖe:k/	[ɖ(ʰ)e:k]	'fence'

/kʰ/ – a voiceless aspirated velar stop

/kʰas/	[kʰɔs] (OM), [kʰɵs] ~ [kʰɨs] (YM)	'sheep'	/kʰili/	[kʰi̟li̟] (YM)	'neck'
/bikʰa:rija/	[bi̟kʰa:rijə]	'beggar'	/dukʰe/, /dukʰis/	[du̟kʰe] ~ [dukʰis]	'disease, grief'

/g/ – a voiced unaspirated velar stop

/ga:r/	[ga:(r)] ~ [ga:(ɹ)] ~ [gar] (YM)	'tooth'	/gun/	[gun]	'winter'
/dauga/	[d(ʰ)auga] ~ [d(ʰ)aga]	'thread'	/rigi:n/	[rɪgi:(n)]	'above'
/bi:g/	[bi:g] ~ [bi:kʰ] (YM)	'ant'	/ɖag/	[ɖag] ~ [ɖʰɑ̜g]	'cliff'

2.2.1.2 Fricatives

/s/ – a voiceless alveolar fricative

/sa:t/	[sa:(t)] ~ [ʃɑ:t]	'seven'	/su:ru/	[surṷ] ~ [su:r] ~ [suru]	'pig, swine'
/gasa/	[gasa]	'dress'	/ba:saʈʰ/	[ba:saʈʰ] ~ [ʋa:saʈʰ]	'sixty two'
/ti:s/	[ti:(s)]	'thirty'	/ba:s/	[ba(:)s] ~ [ʋa:s]	'scent, smell'

/ʃ/ – a voiceless postalveolar fricative

/ʃa/	[ʃa]	'skin, hide'	/ʃiŋ/	[ʃi̟ŋ] ~ [ʃɪŋ]	'wood'
/ʤuʃaŋ/	[ʤu̟ʃaŋ] ~ [ʤʉʃaŋ]	'cloudy weather, fog'	/oʃaŋ/	[oʃaŋ]	'dew'
/buʃ/	[bʉʃ] ~ [bɵʃ]	'rope'	/niʃ/	[nɪʃ],[nɪʃ] ~ [nis]	'two'

/h/ – a voiceless glottal fricative

/ha:r/	[ha:r]	'necklace'	/ho:m/	[ho:m] ~ [hom] (YM)	'bear'
/samhetaŋ/	[samhetaŋ]	'get someone ready.FIN'	/ʃeher/	[ʃɛhe̟r] ~ [ʃɛr]	'town'

2.2.1.3 Affricates

/ts/ – a voiceless alveolar affricate

/tsa:m/	[tsã:m]	'wool'	/tsu:mu/	[tsu:mu]	'catch, hold'
/ketsi:/	[kɛtsi:]	'alone'	/tsʰutsurug/	[tsʰʉtsʉrɵg]	'a kind of wild mushroom'
/barits/	[b(ʰ)ɵri̟ts] ~ [b(ʰ)ɔrɪts] ~ [b(ʰ)arits]	'many, more'	/sõts/	[sɔ̃ts]	'place'

/tsʰ/ – a voiceless aspirated alveolar affricate

/tsʰa:m/	[tsʰã:m]	'hear, listen'	/tsʰika/	[tsʰi̟ka] ~ [tsʰeka]	'early, soon, fast'

/dz/ – a voiced unaspirated alveolar affricate

/ʥa:ŋ/	[ʥa:ŋ]	'gold'	/ʥeher/	[ʥɛher] ~ [ʥɛr]	'poison'
/baʥug/	[baʥu(g)] ~ [baʥuk] ~ [bazuk]	'thigh'	/niʥa/	[niʥa] ~ [niza]	'twenty'
/ʋa:ʥ/	[ʋa:ʥ]	'hawk'	/roʥ/	[roʥ] ~ [roz]	'daily'

/ʧ/ – a voiceless unaspirated postalveolar affricate

/ʧara/	[ʧara] (YF, OM)	'child'	/ʧeka/	[ʧeka] (YF, YM)	'back'
/pʰakuʧ/	[pʰakuʧ] ~ [pʰakuʤ]	'small, young, short'	/ʧa:ʧi/	[ʧa:ʧi(:)]	'paternal uncle's wife'

/ʧʰ/ – a voiceless aspirated postalveolar affricate

/ʧʰo/	[ʧʰɔ]	'boy'	/ʧʰets/, /ʧʰetsaŋ/	[ʧʰets] ~ [tsʰets] (YM), [ʧʰetsaŋ]	'wife'
/kaʧʰua/	[kaʧʰua]	'turtle'	/magarmaʧʰ/	[magarmaʧʰ]	'crocodile'

/ʤ/ – a voiced unaspirated postalveolar affricate

/ʤab/	[ʤab]	'rain'	/ʤuʃtʰa/	[ʤuʃtʰa] ~ [ʤɘʃtʰa] ~ [ʤʉʃt(ʰ)a]	'moon'
/aʤaŋ/	[aʤã(ŋ)] ~ [aʤãŋ] (YM)	'intestines'	/ʧuʤaŋ/	[ʧuʤaŋ] ~ [ʧʉʤaŋ] (YM)	'beak'
/hu:ʤ/	[hu̟:ʤ] ~ [hʉ:ʤ]	'cow'	/suraʤ/	[su̟rə(:)ʤ]	'sun'

2.2.1.4 Nasals

In the word-final position, nasals (especially [n] and [ŋ]) are not always clearly articulated; instead the preceding vowel is nasalized and in some cases also lengthened. See Section 4.

/m/ – a voiced bilabial nasal

/mig/	[mig] ~ [mik(ʰ)]	'eye'	/mu:l/	[mu:l]	'silver'
/duma:ŋ/	[d(ʰ)u̟ma:ŋ]	'smoke'	/ʧime/	[ʧi̟me]	'daughter'
/ho:m/	[ho:m] ~ [hom] (YM)	'bear'	/li:m/	[li:m]	'pine (tree)'

/n/ – a voiced alveolar nasal

/na:b/	[na:b] ~ [na:ʋ] ~ [na:pʰ]	'tomorrow'	/niʃ/	[nɪʃ],[nɪʃ] ~ [nis]	'two'
/baniŋ/	[baniŋ] ~ [b(ʰ)anɪŋ]	'pot'	/munuk/	[mu̟nɘk]	'person'
/gun/	[gun]	'winter'	/ʧi:nɖ/	[ʧi:nɖ] ~ [ʧi:n]	'fingernail'

/ɳ/ – a voiced retroflex nasal. There are no instances of /ɳ/ word-initially

/ba:ɳes/	[b(ʰ)a:ɳɛs]	'nephew'	/ʋaɳam/	[ʋaɳᵊm]	'to be hungry'
/kra:ɳ/	[kra:ɳ]	'brain, mind'	/poɳ/	[poɳ] (OM)	'straw shoe'

/ŋ/ – a voiced velar nasal

/ŋa/	[ŋa] (OM), [na]	'five'	/maŋgal/	[maŋgal]	'Tuesday'
/toŋ/	[tɔ̃ŋ]	'face'	/bitiŋ/	[b(ʰ)ti(ː)ŋ] ~ [b(ʰ)ɪti̟ŋ]	'wall'

2.2.1.5 Lateral

/l/ – a voiced alveolar lateral approximant

/luk/	[luk]	'itch'	/laːr/	[laː(r)] ~ [laː(ɹ)]	'rice (uncooked)'
/kʰili/	[kʰi̟li̟] (YM)	'neck'	/sulus/	[suləs] ~ [sulus] ~ [ʃulus]	'slow'
/laːl/	[laːl]	'red'	/ʃeːl/	[ʃeːl]	'medicine'

2.2.1.6 Rhotics

/r/ – a voiced alveolar trill

/rag/	[rag(g)] ~ [rag(g)] ~ [rak(k)]	'green, blue'	/reːt/	[reːt]	'sand'
/aːri/	[aːri]	'dough'	/kʰiraŋ/	[kʰɪraŋ] ~ [kʰiraŋ(g)]	'milk'
/duːr/	[duː(r)] ~ [duː(ɹ)]	'far'	/gaːr/	[gaː(r)] ~ [gaː(ɹ)] ~ [gar] (YM)	'tooth'

/ɽ/ – a voiced retroflex trill. There are no instances of /ɽ/ word-initially

/boɽits/	[boɽɪts]	'butterfly'	/doɽag/	[doɽag] ~ [doɭag]	'twins'
/gidaɽ/	[gi̟daɽ] ~ [gɪdaɭ]	'jackal'	/ʧamgaːdaɽ/	[ʧamgaːdaɽ]	'bat'

2.2.1.7 Approximant

/ʋ/ – a voiced bilabial approximant

/ʋaːʥ/	[ʋaːʥ]	'hawk'	/ʋeraŋ/	[ʋerã(ŋg)]	'evening'
/tʰauʋis/	[tʰauʋis] ~ [tʰauʋi̟s] (OM)	'traditional wooden house builder'	/talaːʋ/	[talaːʋ] ~ [tulaːʋ] (OM)	'pond'

/j/ – a voiced palatal approximant

/jaː/	[jaː] ~ [ja(ː)] (YM)	'mother'	/juʃk/	[juʃk] ~ [jʉʃk]	'old'
/baːjlits/	[baːjlits]	'mad'	/ʋajaŋ/	[ʋəjaŋ] (YM), [ʋaiŋ] (YF)	'honey bee'
/maːj/	[maːj] ~ [mai]	[NEG.BE]	/ettej/	[e̟tte(j)]	[1PLI]

2.2.2 Evidence of contrast

/p/ – /b/	/pi:g/	[pi:g] ~ [pi̟g]	'yellow'	/bi:g/	[bi:g] ~ [bi:kʰ] (YM)	'ant'
/t/ – /d/	/ra:t/	[ra(:)t]	'night'	/ra:d/	[r(ʰ)a:d] ~ [ra:t] ~ [ra:ɖ]	'bull, ox'
/ʈ/ – /ɖ/	/ʈaki/	[ʈaki] ~ [taki] (YM)	'window'	/ɖaggis/	[ɖaggɪs]	'blacksmith'
/k/ – /g/	/ka:r/	[ka:(ɹ)]	'axe'	/ga:r/	[ga:(r)] ~ [ga:(ɹ)] ~ [gar] (YM)	'tooth'
/t/ – /ʈ/	/ra:t/	[ra(:)t]	'night'	/laʈpaʈ/	[laʈpaʈ]	'cloth'
/d/ – /ɖ/	/ru:d/	[ru:d] ~ [rüt(ʰ)] (YM)	'horn'	/muɖ/	[muɖ]	'yesterday'
/p/ – /pʰ/	/pa:n/	[pã:n]	'stone'	/pʰar/	[pʰar]	'shoulder'
/t/ – /tʰ/	/to/	[tö]	'be'	/tʰo/	[tʰo] ~ [tʰɵ]	'up'
/ʈ/ – /ʈʰ/	/ʈulem/	[ʈüle̟m]	'to sleep'	/ʈʰulla/, /ʈʰullaŋ/	[ʈʰu̟lla] (OM), [ʈʰu̟llaŋg]	'leg'
/k/ -/kʰ/	/ka/	[ka] ~ [kə]	[2SG]	/kʰa:/	[kʰa:]	'sheep.PL'
/ʦ/ – /ʦʰ/	/ʦa:m/	[ʦã:m]	'wool, sheep's hair'	/ʦʰa:m/	[ʦʰã:m]	'to listen'
/ʧ/ – /ʧʰ/	/ʧokeʦ/	[ʧɔkɛʦ]	'rotten'	/ʧʰakʦ/	[ʧʰakʦ] ~ [ʧʰɔkʦ]	'boy'
/t/ – /ʧ/	/ti:/, /ti:s/	[ti:(s)]	'thirty'	/ʧiʦ/	[ʧi̟ʦ] ~ [ʧi̟ʧ]	'wet, washed'
/t/ – /ʦ/	/ta/	[ta]	'nose'	/ʦa:m/	[ʦã:m]	'wool, sheep's hair'
/d/ – /dz/	/daddu/	[dadu] (YM), [daddu] (YF)	'paternal grandfather'	/ʣaddu/	[ʣaddu]	'magic'
/d/ – /ʤ/	/dil/	[di̟l] ~ [dɪl] (YM)	'heart, soul'	/ʤil/	[ʤ(ʰ)i̟l]	'lake, lagoon'
/g/ – /ŋ/	/ʧʰog/	[ʧʰög]	'white'	/toŋ/	[tɔ̃ŋ]	'face'
/k/ – /ʧ/	/ka:m/	[ka:m]	'soil, clay'	/ʧa:m/	[ʧã(:)m]	'dance'
/ʦ/ – /dz/	/ʦa:m/	[ʦã:m]	'wool, sheep's hair'	/ʣa:m/	[ʣã:m] ~ [zã:m]	'food, to eat'
/ʧ/ – /ʤ/	/ʧaŋg/	[ʧãŋ(g)] (OM)	'mountain'	/ʤaŋ/	[ʤã(:)ŋg]	'root'

/ʧ/ – /ʦ/	/ʧa:m/	[ʧã(:)m]	‘dance’	/ʦa:m/	[ʦã:m]	‘wool, sheep’s hair’
/ʧ/ – /ʃ/	/ʧa(:)/	[ʧa(:)]	‘tea’	/ʃa/	[ʃa]	‘skin, hide’
/ʤ/ – /dz/	/ʤab/	[ʤab]	‘rain’	/ʥa:b/	[ʥa:b]	‘now’
/s/ – /ʦ/	/saŋ/	[sãŋg]	‘with’	/ʦa:m/	[ʦã:m]	‘wool’
/s/ – /ʃ/	/su:ru/	[surŭ̟] ~ [su:r]	‘pig, swine’	/ʃum/	[ʃüm]	‘three’
/s/ – /h/	/som/	[som]	‘morning’	/ho:m/	[ho:m] ~ [hom] (YM)	‘bear’
/ʃ/ – /h/	/ʃo/	[ʃo̟]	‘hundred’	/ho:m/	[ho:m] ~ [hom] (YM)	‘bear’
/m/ – /n/	/ka:m/	[kã:m]	‘work’	/pa:n/	[pã:n]	‘stone’
/m/ – /b/	/ʥa:m/	[ʥa:m] ~ [za:m]	‘to eat’	/ʥa:b/	[ʥa:b]	‘now’
/n/ – /ŋ/	/ʧi:nɖ/	[ʧi:nɖ] ~ [ʧi:n]	‘fingernail’	/ʃiŋ/	[ʃi̟ŋ] ~ [ʃɪŋ]	‘wood’
/n/ – /ɳ/	/ʋanam/	[ʋan(ᵊ)m]	‘to laugh’	/ʋaɳam/	[ʋaɳᵊm]	‘to be hungry’
/n/ – /ɳ/	/gana/	[gana] ~ [gʰana]	‘flame’	/gaɳa/	[gaɳa]	‘song’
/n/ – /d/	/nid/	[nɪd] ~ [nid]	‘here’	/didd/	[dɪd(d)] ~ [di:t] ~ [ditt]	‘there’
/l/ – /r/	/du:r/	[du:(r)] ~ [du:(ɹ)]	‘far’	/du:l/	[d(ʰ)u:l]	‘dust’
/r/ – /d/	/ri:d/	[ri(:)d] ~ [ri:t]	‘day before yesterday’	/didd/	[dɪd(d)] ~ [di:t] ~ [ditt]	‘there’
/r/ – /ɖ/	/ha:r/	[ha:r]	‘necklace’	/ho:ɖ/	[ho:ɖ]	‘bread’
/r/ – /ɽ/	/a:ri/	[a:ri]	‘dough’	/ta:ɽi/	[ta:ɽi]	‘padlock’
/r/ – /ɽ/	/ʃika:r/	[ʃi̜ka:r]	‘hunting’	/gidaɽ/	[gi̟daɽ] ~ [gɪdaɭ]	‘jackal’
/ɖ/ – /ɽ/	/ro:ɖ/	[ro:ɖ] ~ [rɔ:ɖ]	‘ear’	/ʥoɽ/	[ʥoɽ] ~ [zoɽ]	‘shoe’
/ɖ/ – /ɽ/	/maɖa	[maɖə]	‘mute’	/naɽa/	[nəɽa] ~ [nɜɽa]	‘arm’
/j/ – /ʋ/	/ja:/	[ja:] ~ [ja(:)] (YM)	‘mother’	/ʋa:/	[ʋa:]	‘nest’
/b/ – /ʋ/	/ba:/	[ʋa:] ~ [ba:] (OM), [ba] (YM)	‘father, uncle’	/ʋa:/	[ʋa:]	‘nest’

Table 1: Distribution of consonants

	Initial	Medial	Final		Initial	Medial	Final
Stops							
/p/	+	+	+	/ʈ/	+	+	+
/pʰ/	+	+	(+)	/ʈʰ/	+	+	+
/b/	+	+	+	/ɖ/	+	+	+
/t/	+	+	+	/k/	+	+	+
/tʰ/	+	+	+	/kʰ/	+	+	+
/d/	+	+	+	/g/	+	+	+
Fricatives							
/s/	+	+	+	/h/	+	+	(+)
/ʃ/	+	+	+				
Affricates							
/ʦ/	+	+	+	/ʧ/	+	+	+
/ʦʰ/	+	+	(+)	/ʧʰ/	+	+	+
/ʣ/	+	+	+	/ʤ/	+	+	+
Nasals							
/m/	+	+	+	/ɳ/	(+)	+	+
/n/	+	+	+	/ŋ/	(+)	+	+
Rhotics							
/r/	+	+	+	/ɽ/	(+)	+	+
Lateral							
/l/	+	+	+				
Approximants							
/j/	+	+	+	/ʋ/	+	+	+

2.2.3 Distribution of consonants

/ŋ/ occurs word-initially only in one word (*ŋa* 'five') in the speech of OM and some other older speakers (both male and female: [ŋa]), while the younger speakers use an [n] in 'five' (i.e. [na] 'five').[10]

10 *ŋa* coincides with the reconstructed proto-ST word for 'five', and should consequently be the older variant.

In Table 1, the positions in which the consonant phonemes are attested[11] are indicated. "+" denotes that the phoneme is found in that position, "(+)" indicates that the phoneme rarely occurs in this position (5% or less of its highest number of occurrences in some other position), and "–" that it is not found in this position.

2.3 Vowels

The vowel phonemes in Kanashi are the following.

i, iː		u, uː
e, eː		o, oː
	a, aː	

As was the case with the consonants, Kanashi also exhibits considerable variation in the phonetic realization of its vowel phonemes. For instance, /i/ shows variation between [i] and [ɪ]; /e/ is also realized as [e̹] or [ɛ]. In a similar way /u/ is sometimes realized as more central and closer to [ɵ] or [ʉ]. /a/ and /o/, too, display considerable variation. /o/ is, at times, realized as more central, and, at times, it is realized more like [ɔ]: [ʧʰakts] ~ [ʧʰɔkts] 'boy'; /barʃ/ [barʃ] ~ [bɔrʃ] 'year'; [madras] ~ [mɔdras] 'man'. /a/ is also realized as [ə] or as a variant that is more like [ɑ]. In words such as /barits/ 'many, more, full', the realization of /a/ is more central [ɞ]. Cross-linguistically [r] tends to make the preceding vowel more like a [ɞ], which is also the case in Kanashi.

Finally, at times, [a] in Kanashi words of IA etymology occurs as [u] or [o] especially in OM's speech (e.g. [buzaːr] 'market'; cf. Hindi: [bazaːr]). OM, in some lexemes, has [u] while the younger speakers pronounce [a] (for example, [kunaːʃi] (OM), [kanaːʃi] (YF, YM) 'Kanashi (language name)'). On the other hand, for 'iron' OM and YF have [raɳ], while another young female speaker pronounces it as [roɳ].

2.3.1 Vowel charts

In order to prepare the vowel (non-long vowels) chart, we took into consideration only YF's speech.

11 The information in the table refers to occurrence in lexical citation forms, not in text word types, so it should be taken as indicative only.

The vowels of all recorded monosyllabic words (253 recordings in total with YF)[12] were manually marked in Praat and then the average of formants 1 and 2 for the duration were extracted. At times, Praat had obvious difficulty in getting good formants (for instance, not being able to differentiate two low formants for words with [u]) and as can be seen in the plot of all the items (Figure 1, left-hand panel), there are some that were almost certainly incorrect. Despite this shortcoming, we can still see in this chart that the vowels tend to cluster in the expected way, which suggests that the measurements are largely correct and that averages are useable.

We can also see in this chart that /u/ tends to be centralized. Similarly, /a/ is displaced toward the back, and /i/ and /e/ are quite close to each other. We have not found a phonemic contrast between two central, unrounded vowels.

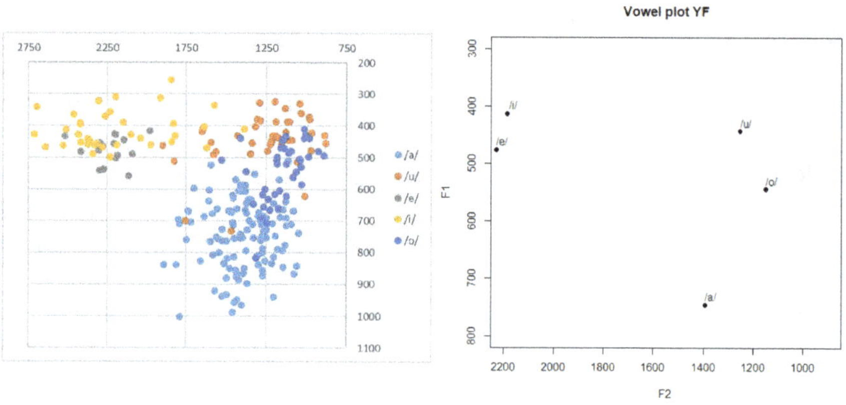

Figure 1: Vowel instance plot (left) and vowel plot (right) for YF

A comparison of the resulting vowel plot (Figure 1, right-hand panel) with corresponding vowel plots (produced in the same way), based on the recordings of OM and YM show some interesting results (Figure 2). For OM the number of words/tokens were 36/43 and for YM the number of words/tokens were 52/137.

To some extent in the speech of all three speakers the realization of /u/ is more central – closer to [ʉ] or [ɵ], but it is more so in the case of YM. In his speech, /u/ is almost always more centralised.

12 As there is a possibility of vowels in unstressed positions behaving differently (e.g. vowel reduction), we have considered here only monosyllabic words.

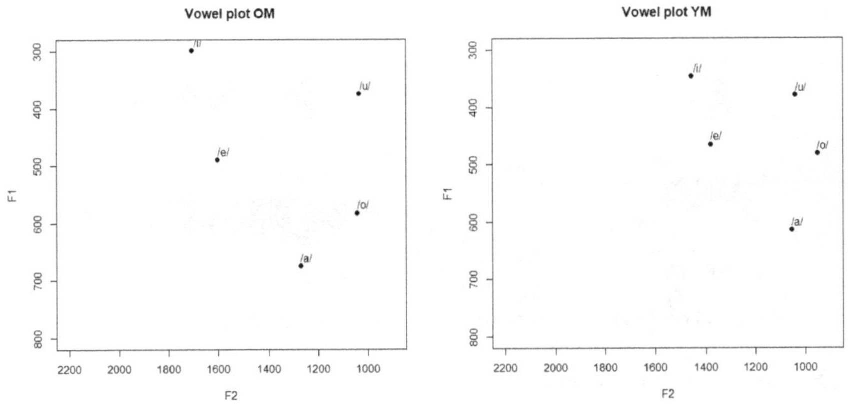

Figure 2: Vowel plot for OM (left) and YM (right)

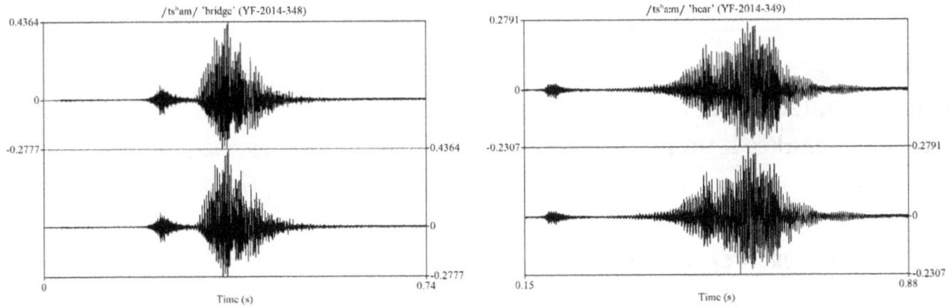

Figure 3: Vowel length minimal pair: /tsʰam/ 'bridge' : /tsʰa:m/ 'hear, listen'

2.3.2 Vowel length

Vowel length appears to be phonemic in our material (*pace* D. D. Sharma 1992). An illustrative minimal pair is shown in Figure 3.

YM's speech diverges also concerning long vowels. In his speech the long vowels tend to be shorter than in YF's speech; see Figure 4.

The average vowel durations are provided in Table 2.[13] This difference in the vowel length between YM and YF can also be seen in the box plots shown in Figure 5 of vowels preceding stops in monosyllabic words. The labels LONG and SHORT refer to the underlying phonological category.

13 The figures in Table 2 are based on a dataset with the following parameters: words (long/short): 8/4 (YM), 13/10 (YF), 6/5 (OM); tokens (long/short): 27/16 (YM), 20/18 (YF), 7/5 (OM).

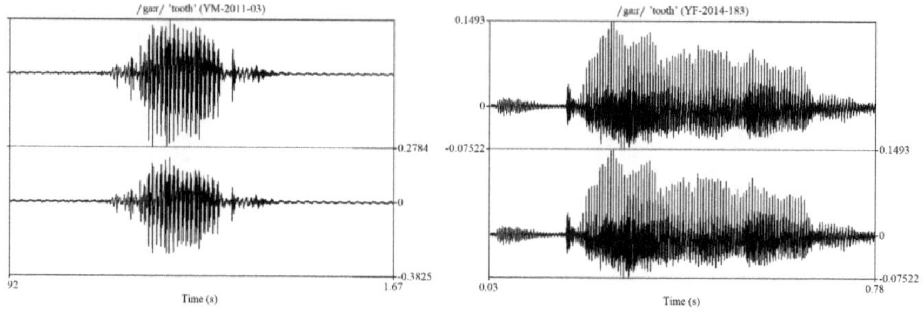

Figure 4: Inter-speaker vowel length realization differences: /ga:r/ 'tooth': YM (left) : YF (right)

Table 2: Vowel duration before stops

Vowels (sec)	YM	YF	OM
LONG	0.136	0.190	0.203
SHORT	0.122	0.149	0.125

While the differences are quite striking between YM and YF/OM, the small size of our dataset makes it premature to draw any strong conclusions.

2.3.3 Examples of occurrence

/i/ – a close front unrounded vowel

/ipidʒ/	[ipɪdʒ] ~ [ipɪtʃ]	'behind'	/ikkatis/	[ɪkkati(s)]	'thirty one'
/kʰissa/	[kʰissa]	'pocket'	/dil/	[di̪l] ~ [dɪl] (YM)	'heart, soul'
/kʰili/	[kʰi̪li̪] (YM)	'neck'	/a:ri/	[a:ri]	'dough'

/i:/ – a close front unrounded long vowel

/i:d/	[i:d] ~ [i̪d] ~ [it] ~ [i(:)]	'one'	/ti:r/	[ti:r]	'arrow'
/li:m/	[li:m]	'pine (tree)'	/mistri:/	[mistᵊri:]	'carpenter'

/e/ – a mid-close front unrounded vowel

/ettej/	[e̞tte(j)]	[1PLI]	/ei/	[e̞i̯]	'four days after today'
/brest/	[b(ʰ)re̞st]	'Thursday'	/bẽʃur/	[bẽʃur]	'flute (wooden)'
/bja:le/	[b(ɦ)ja:lɛ]	'breakfast'	/kʰurke/	[kʰu̞rkɛ]	'wrist'

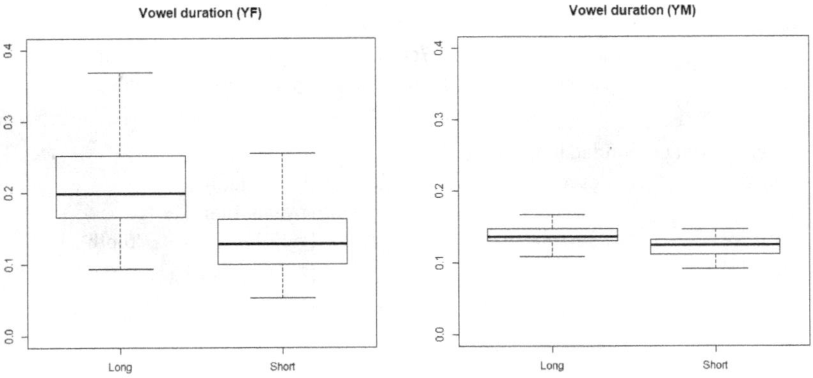

Figure 5: Vowel duration before stops in monosyllables for YF (left) and YM (right)

/e:/ – a mid-close front unrounded long vowel. /e:/ is attested in our data only in medial position

/ɖe:k/	[ɖʰe:k]	'fence'	/ʃe:l/	[ʃe:l]	'medicine'

/u/ – a close back rounded vowel

/unni/	[u̟nni(:)] (OM)	'nineteen'	/uɽug/	[uɽu̟(g)]	'owl'
/arʃuk/	[arʃük] ~ [arʃüg]	'mirror'	/buka/	[b(ʰ)uka] (YM)	'liver'
/daddu/	[dad(d)u]	'paternal grandfather'	/nu/	[nu̟]	[3SG.PROX]

/u:/ – a close back rounded long vowel

/u:nam/	[u:nᵊm]	'take'	/u:/	[u:]	'flower'
/du:r/	[du:(r)] ~ [du:(ɹ)]	'far'	/hu:dʒ/	[hu̟:dʒ] ~ [hʉ:dʒ]	'cow'

/o/ – a mid-close back rounded vowel

/oʃaŋ/	[oʃaŋ]	'dew'	/odʒim/	[odʒim]	'to play'
/boɽits/	[boɽɪts]	'butterfly'	/ba:ro/	[ba:ro] ~ [baro̞]	'outside'

/o:/ – a mid-close back rounded long vowel

/ho:ɖ/	[ho:ɖ]	'bread'	/ho:m/	[ho:m] ~ [hom] (YM)	'bear'

/a/ – an open, central unrounded vowel

/aʈʰ/	[aʈʰ] ~ [a̠ʈʰ]	'eight'	/aŋgu:r/	[aŋgu:r]	'grape'
/bal/	[bal] ~ [ʋal]	'head'	/ʤab/	[ʤab]	'rain'
/ara/	[a(:)ra]	'saw(N)'	/na/, /ɳa/	[na] ~ [ɳa]	'five'

/a:/ – an open central unrounded long vowel

/a:g/	[a:g]	'cave'	/ja:/	[ja:] ~ [ja(:)] (YM)'mother'	
/ba:ro/	[ba:ro] ~ [ba:ro̝]	'outside'	/ga:r/	[ga:(r)] ~ [ga:(ɹ)] ~ [gar] (YM)	'tooth'

2.3.4 Nasal vowels

As mentioned above, there is a restricted set of Kanashi lexical items with nasal vowels, in which there is no nasal consonant following the vowel – at least not synchronically. In the present analysis, nasal vowels are not regarded as phonemes. If they should be regarded as phonemes, they constitute a marginal phenomenon in the Kanashi phonological system.[14]

mĩc	'female'	tẽis	'for the sake of'
[sirãõ]	'vein, artery'	[sõʦ]	'place'
[pũĩ]	'cat'	[ũʈ]	'camel'

2.3.5 Evidence of contrast

/i/ – /i:/	/dil/	[di̟l] ~ [dɪl] (YM)	'heart, soul'	/ti:r/	[ti:r]	'arrow'
/e/ – /e:/	/teg/	[te̝g]	'big'	/ɖe:k/	[ɖʰe:k]	'fence'
/o/ – /o:/	/om/	[om]	'path'	/ho:m/	[ho:m]	'bear(N)'
/u/ – /u:/	/guɖ/	[guɖ] ~ [gɵɖ] (YM), [gɵʈ(ʰ)] (YM)	'hand'	/bu:ʈ/	[bu:ʈ]	'boot, shoe'
/a/ – /a:/	/ʦʰam/	[ʦʰãm]	'bridge'	/ʦʰa:m/	[ʦʰã:m]	'hear, listen'
/i/ – /e/	/ʈʰig/	[ʈʰig] ~ [ʈʰik]	'sweet'	/teg/	[te̝g]	'big'
/i/ – /o/	/ʈʰig/	[ʈʰig] ~ [ʈʰik]	'sweet'	/ʤog /	[ʤog]	'hot'

14 The top two items are from D. D. Sharma (1992: 337, 347). The original transcription is retained.

/i/ – /a/	/a:ri/	[a:ri]	'dough'	/ara/	[a(:)ra]	'saw(N)'
/i/ – /a/	/raunḍa/	[raunḍa]	'stepson'	/raunḍi/	[raunḍi]	'step-daughter'
/e/ – /a/	/seb/	[seb] ~ [se̞ʋ]	'apple'	/sab/	[sab]	'all'
/e/ – /u/	/le/	[le]	'tongue'	/gu /	[gu]	[1SG.NOM]
/u/ – /o/	/-mug /	[mug]	[1PLI]	/mog/	[mog]	'birdseed'
/u/ – /o/	/kum/	[kum]	'pillow'	/kone/	[kone] ~ [kɔne] ~ [koni]	'edge'
/o/ – /a/	/to/	[tö]	[be.FIN]	/ta/	[ta]	'nose'

2.3.6 Distribution of vowels

In Table 3, the positions in which the vowel phonemes are attested are indicated.[15] "+" denotes that the phoneme is found in that position, "(+)" indicates that the phoneme rarely occurs in this position (5% or less of its highest number of occurrences in some other position), and "–" denotes that it is not found in our material.

Table 3: Distribution of vowels

	Word-initial	Word-medial	Word-final
/a/	+	+	+
/a:/	(+)	+	+
/e/	(+)	+	+
/e:/	–	+	–
/i/	(+)	+	+
/i:/	+	+	+
/o/	(+)	+	+
/o:/	–	+	+
/u/	(+)	+	+
/u:/	(+)	+	–

15 The information in the table refers to occurrence in lexical citation forms, not in text word types, so it should be taken as indicative only.

2.3.7 Diphthongs

D. D. Sharma (1992) states that Kanashi lacks diphthongs, but rather has sequences of vowels, but without providing any supporting arguments. Adjoining vowels (in the sound files) in our material are almost always heard as diphthongs and not as two distinct syllables. The diphthongs found in our material are listed in Table 4.[16]

Table 4: Diphthongs in Kanashi

[iu]	/ʥiu/	'living being'	[ue]	/kʰue/	'why'
[ui]	/bui/	'm.name'	[ua]	/ɖabua/	'money'
[ia]	/ʤeʧialga/	'red sweet potato-?PL'	[ai]	/suʧai/	'truth'
[ai]	/ruʤai/	'quilt'	[oa]	/soar/	'monday'
[ei]	/ʧeit/	'a.month.name')	[ao]	/taoli/	'towel (< English)'
[eo]	/deodar/	'cedrus deodara (tree)'	[ũĩ]	/pũĩ/	'cat'
[oi]	/boiʦ/	'younger sibling'	[õũ]	/ʥõũɽi/	'pair'
[ou]	/louk/	'jump(N)'	[au]	/bau/	'o.brother'

[au] is, at times, also heard as [aʋ] and [aʊ] as in /sauda/ [sauda] ~ [ʃaʋda] 'sweets, candy'. Similarly, [ai] is sometimes heard as a vowel–glide sequence (e.g. /bais/ [bais] ~ [bajs] 'twenty two'; /suʧai/ [suʧai] ~ [suʧaj] 'truth'). /oi/ is, at times, phonetically more like [ɔi] or [oj], as in /koile/ [koile] ~ [kɔile] 'charcoal', and /ei/ can be realized more like [ɛi], as in /ei/ [ei] ~ [ɛi] ~ [e̝i̯] 'fourth day after today'. [ue] is also realized as [ʋe].

3 Phonotactics

3.1 Syllable structure

The syllable structures attested in our material are shown in Table 5. CV and CVC are the most frequently occurring syllable structures.

16 Duttamajumdar (2015) includes long vowels in her description of diphthongs in Kanashi. In some cases there is a slight difference in the vowel quality between our materials. The sequences described here as [oi] and [ou] are transcribed by Duttamajumdar (2015) as [ɔi] and [ɔu], respectively.

Table 5: Syllable structures

Syllable structure	Kanashi	Gloss
CV	/ʃa/	'skin, hide'
	/gu/	[1SG.NOM]
CVC	/pod/	'ash, dandruff'
	/kum/	'pillow'
CCV	/kra/	'hair'
	/bjaːle/	'breakfast'
CCVC	/kraːɳ/	'brain, mind'
	/praːd/	'finger, toe'
CVCC	/garts/	'arrow'
	/polk/	'strong (person)'
V	/uː/	'flower'
	/aːri/	'dough'
VC	/aːg/	'cave'

3.2 Consonant clusters

3.2.1 Word-initial consonant clusters

Word-initial consonant clusters are of the form [stop + sonorant]. The following consonant clusters are found in our material.

[gj]	/gjara/	'eleven'	[kr]	/kra/	'hair'
[gl]	/gliŋ/	'barley beer'	[pj]	/pjaːʥ/	'onion'
[gr]	/graːmaŋ/	'village'	[pl]	/plen/	'fill'
			[pr]	/praːd/	'finger, toe'

3.2.2 Word-final consonant clusters

The following consonant clusters are attested word-finally.[17] In addition, at times, the vowel of the word-final syllable is not audible, creating an appearance of a cluster (e.g. /ʤaŋgal/ [ʤaŋgəl] ~ [dzaŋgal] ~ [ʤaŋgal] ~ [ʤaŋgl] 'forest'; /himat/ [himt] ~ [himət] 'courage'. Such instances of apparent consonant clusters are not included here.

17 Clusters in parentheses are attested only once in our material.

[ks]	/ṭeks/ (< English)	'tax'	[nk]	/nenk/	'thus'
([ɳʧ])	/ʤaɳʧ/	'weak'	[nt]	/ʃa:nt/	'calm'
[mp]	/bukamp/	'earthquake'	[rʃ]	/barʃ/	'year'
[nd]	/gund/	'glue'	([rd])	/mord/	'gentleman'
[nɖ]	/kʰanɖ/	'sugar'	[rg]	/sʊarg/	'heaven'
[ŋg]	/raŋg/	'color; paint'	[rk]	/nark/	'bad'
[st]	/brest/ [b(ʰ)ṛest]	'thursday'	([sk])	/rask/	'edge, pointed'

3.3 Geminates

In order to examine the status of geminates in Kanashi, we compared YF's recordings of words with the structure (C*)VCCV(C*) and (C*)VCV(C*). We have 34 words in our materials with geminates, distributed over 70 tokens. For singleton consonants we have 89 words, with 177 tokens. The following geminates are found.

[pp]	/duppe/	'sun'	[bb]	/ɖubbem/	'to be drowned'
[tt]	/ettej/	[1PLI]	[dd]	/didd/	'there'
[kk]	/ikkattar/	'seventy one'	[ll]	/gallas/	'eagle'
[ss]	/massi/	'mother's sister'			

Acknowledging the fact that phonological categories are not directly demonstratable by phonetic measurements, and that we have not found any minimal pairs for consonant length in our material, there is still a measurable difference in their articulation in Kanashi. We examined the measurements of (i) stops, (ii) fricatives and (iii) laterals[18] separately after manually marking the duration. The duration of geminates and singleton consonants was measured using a script. For stops, the boundaries were identified using the beginning/ending of formants and the sharp increase/fall in amplitude. The duration includes burst, if such was present. For fricatives, the boundary was identified using the shape of the formants and the presence of aperiodic turbulence (and also the lack of voicing, as no voiced fricatives were investigated due to their uncertain phonemic status). For laterals, the identification was made mainly using formants and changes in amplitude. The results are provided below with a focus on stops.[19] An illustrative example pair can

18 Since we had only one example of nasal geminates ([mm] in [dumme] 'fog'), we have not included nasal geminates in our present analysis.

19 Words/tokens of stops: total – 89/180, voiced geminates – 13/30, voiceless geminates – 14/24, voiced singletons – 16/33, voiceless singletons – 46/93.

be seen in Figure 6. It shows a significant difference in the duration of articulation of singleton and geminate in the same environment.[20]

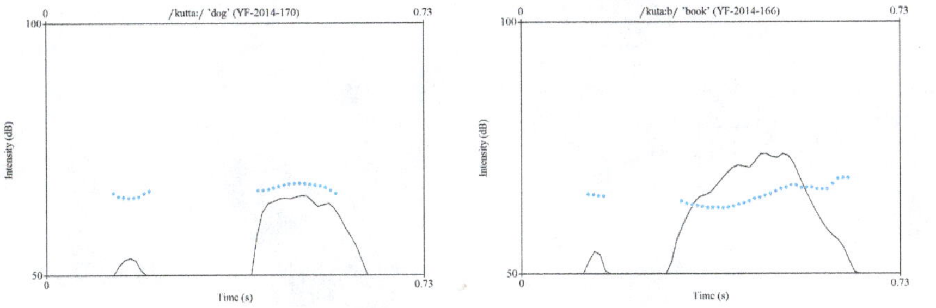

Figure 6: Articulation of double and singleton medial stops ([kutta:] 'dog' ~ [kuta:b] 'book')

The mean values are provided in Table 6 and a box plot of the values in Figure 7. They show that voiceless stops heard as geminates have a considerably longer duration than those of corresponding singleton segments: on average, a geminate is 1.53 times longer than a singleton. The difference is smallest in voiced stops. This is a slightly lower ratio than what is reported for e.g. Hindi (1:1.96 in Hindi for all manners of consonant of singleton and geminates; Ohala 2007), but, on the other hand, it is higher than what is reported for Norwegian (1:1.22–1.38 in non-stops in the medial position; Kawahara 2015). In the box plot in Figure 7 we can also note that there is limited overlap between the two categories. It should, however, be kept in mind that consonant duration is only one of the phonetic correlates of the phonological category of consonant length. A more comprehensive study of other phonetic factors (e.g. the duration of surrounding vowels) should be conducted to determine the phonological status of geminates in Kanashi.

Table 6: Duration of singletons and geminates

Duration (sec)	ALL	VOICED	VOICELESS
Geminate	0.152342	0.119682	0.193167
Singleton	0.121181	0.105545	0.12602
Ratio C:CC	1:1.26	1:1.13	1:1.53

20 The duration of the voiceless segments is shown in Figure 6 by the period of silence between the two vocalic peaks (the latter also coincide with the dotted (blue) line showing the fundamental frequency).

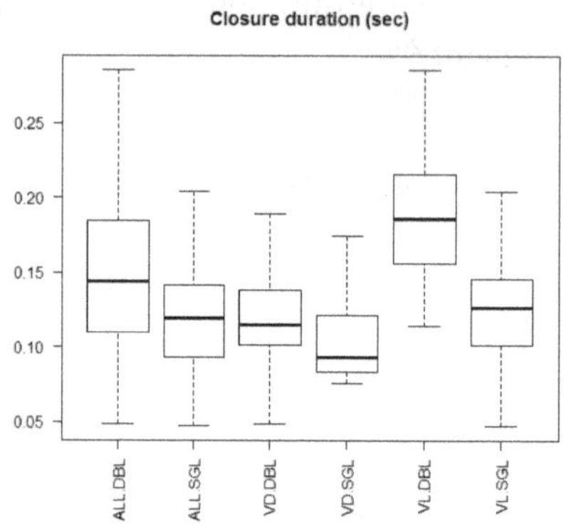

Figure 7: Duration of double and singleton medial stops in the speech of YF

As with voiced aspirated stops, here too, there are some issues complicating the inclusion of geminates into the phonological analysis of Kanashi. The first is that there appears to be a clear difference between speakers. In the speech of YM, consonants that in the speech of YF are heard as geminate are not perceived as geminate. They show no real durational difference in instrumental measurements (Saxena et al. 2018a). Thus, the presence of geminates appears not to be constant across speakers, which brings up the question which language consultant's speech should be taken as the norm. (We do see some intra-speaker variation in our data, but not to the same extent as when it comes to voiced aspirates.) Some examples are given in Table 7.

Table 7: Inter-speaker variation: geminates

YF	YM	
[daddu]	[dadu]	'paternal grandfather'
[ɖubbem]	[ɖubem]	'to be drowned'
[matt^{h}a]	[mat^{h}a]	'forehead'
[haɖɖaŋ]	[haɖaŋ]	'bone'
[duppe]	[dup(p)e]	'sun'

Just as with the voiced aspirated stops, geminates, too, appear to be found mainly in words of IA origin. At this stage it is not possible to state if these variations are found only in IA borrowings, and if so, if only in the older loanwords or also in the more recent borrowings. What we can say is that these features (geminate and voiced aspirated stop) may have originated in IA borrowings.

Here we see three slightly different patterns depending on the nature of the consonants: (i) geminated stops: here both the contours and blue lines are disconnected with separate "pitches"; (ii) geminated sibilants: here while the contours are connected, the blue lines are separated; and (iii) geminated sonorants (nasals and liquids): here the contours for sonorants are more or less one big segment, and the blue lines too are un-interrupted. See Figure 8 for two examples each of the three groups.

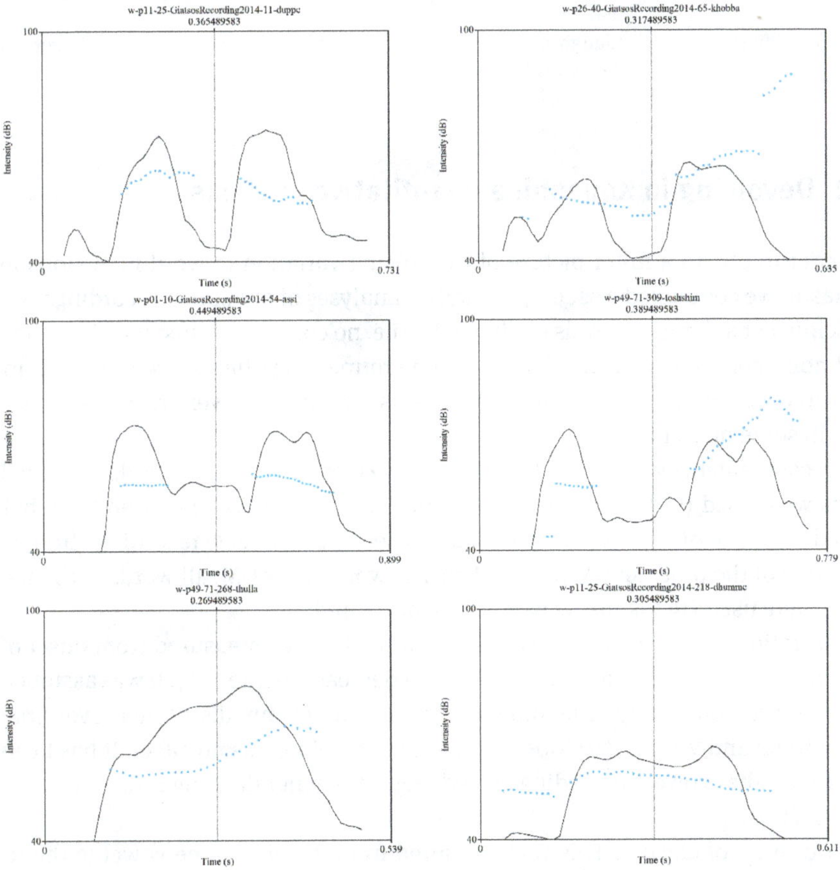

Figure 8: Geminate consonants. Top: stops ([duppe] 'sun' : [kʰobba] 'snowshoe'); middle: sibilants ([assi] 'eighty' : toʃʃɪm 'to fight'); bottom: sonorants ([tʰʊlla] 'leg, foot' : [dʰʊmme] 'fog')

4 On word-final consonants in Kanashi

Kanashi exhibits variation in the realization of (voiced) stops when they occur in the word-final position. For example, voiced stops are often realized as voiceless aspirated stops. And at times, the final stop consonant is not audible at all in fast speech.

/pod/	[pod] ~ [pot^h]	'dandruff, ash'	/parsed/	[parsed] ~ [pərset^h] (YM)	'sweat(N)'
/ʧime/	[ʧi̥me]	'daughter'	/ʧi:nɖ/	[ʧi:nɖ] ~ [ʧi:n]	'fingernail'

4.1 Devoicing in Kanashi: a quantitative analysis

In order to obtain a fuller picture of the voicing variation in word-final stops in Kanashi, we conducted a set of quantitative analyses of our sound recordings. We took into consideration words ending in VC (i.e. no consonant clusters). Aspirated and non-aspirated VOICELESS[21] stops were grouped together, since the latter appear to occur word-finally mainly as variants only in some very restricted cases (e.g. in some numerals).

Measurements were made for all three speakers. For YM, all words with final stops were used (57 tokens, 18 words). For YF, the words were chosen to be balanced for place of articulation plus those where we also have recordings from at least one of the other speakers (38 tokens, 23 words). For OM, all words with final stops were used (14 tokens, 12 words). We measured:

1. Duration of the vowel preceding the stop. This was measured from onset of second and third formants to the abrupt decrease in intensity. It was assumed that phonologically long and short vowels are evenly distributed over final VOICED and VOICELESS stops and that this therefore has no effect. It has been found that vowels preceding voiced stops are generally longer (Dmitrieva et al. 2010).
2. Duration of closure. This was measured from the end of the vowel to the release of the stop, indicated by a sudden spike in intensity. It has been found that voiceless stops are generally longer (Dmitrieva et al. 2010).

21 VOICED and VOICELESS in small caps refer to what we have taken to be the underlying phonological category of the stop.

3. Duration of voicing into closure (absolute and as proportion of total closure time). This was measured as the duration of the periodic waveform into the closure.
4. Number of glottal pulses during the closure (measured using Praat's automatic count).

4.1.1 Analysis results: measurements

Measurements for YM

The average values for these tokens are shown in Table 8.

Table 8: Word-final voicing: YM

	VOICED	VOICELESS
Vowel duration	0.119	0.116
Burst duration	0.066	0.069
Closure duration	0.073	0.087
Voicing duration	0.035	0.027
Voicing proportion	0.500	0.324
Number of pulses	3.275	2.353

There appears to be a difference between VOICED and VOICELESS stops in YM's speech. Vowel duration and total closure duration are shown in Figure 9, and the voicing proportion is shown in Figure 10 (left panel). While there appears to be a difference, the values of VOICED and VOICELESS stops largely overlap.

For comparison, the values for intervocalic stops in YM's speech (tokens = 42) are provided in Table 9.

Table 9: Intervocalic stops: YM

	VOICED	VOICELESS
Vowel duration	0.071	0.065
Burst duration	—	0.030
Closure duration	0.048	0.071
Voicing duration	0.047	0.028
Voicing proportion	0.982	0.414
Number of pulses	5.636	2.581

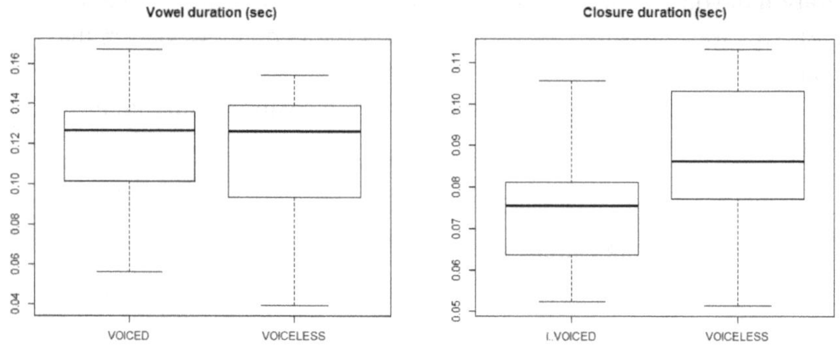

Figure 9: Vowel duration (left) and closure duration (right) for YM

The box plots in Figure 10 show the difference in voicing proportion between final and medial stops in YM's speech.

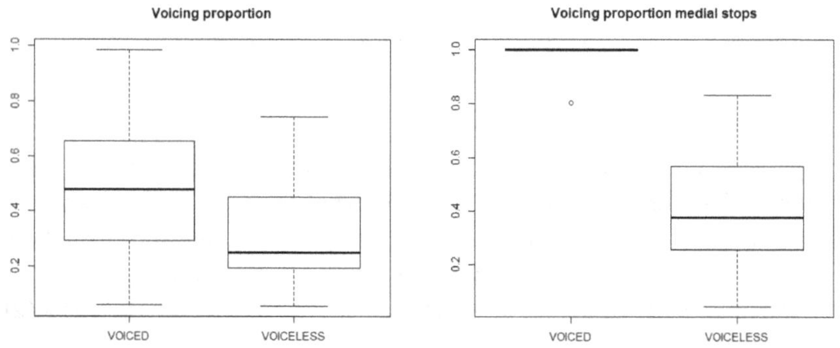

Figure 10: Proportion of voicing during closure in final (left) and medial (right) stops for YM

In short, a comparison of voiced stops word-finally and intervocalically suggests that in intervocalic stops the distinction between VOICED and VOICELESS is robust. VOICED stops retain voicing throughout the closure. Not unexpectedly, the VOICELESS stops have on average a somewhat greater portion of voicing, but are still distinct from VOICED items in always having a portion of voicelessness. On the other hand, in the word-final position, all but one VOICED stop retain voicing throughout the closure phase, although it should be noted that the total number of tokens is quite small. For the VOICELESS tokens, there is considerable variation, but all tokens have at least a portion of voicelessness. The most distinctive feature of intervocalic VOICELESS stops in this sample appears to be that they have a voiceless release phase before voiced onset in the following vowel, which is not the case for VOICED stops.

Measurements for YF

YF sometimes appears not to articulate the final stop at all: it is neither audible nor visible in waveforms or spectrograms (see Section 4.2). Such tokens are not included in the set of tokens measured here. This is since the measurements used here are impossible or difficult to measure here. This happens with both VOICED and VOICELESS stops, though it appears to be more common with VOICELESS stops. The average values for these tokens are shown in Table 10.

Table 10: Word-final voicing: YF

	VOICED	VOICELESS
Vowel duration	0.198	0.137
Burst duration	0.086	0.076
Closure duration	0.094	0.132
Voicing duration	0.057	0.033
Voicing proportion	0.632	0.306
Number of pulses	6.000	5.882

Box plots of the distributions are provided in Figure 11. In general, the difference between VOICED and VOICELESS is greater in these tokens and the overlap is not as great: the values between the first and third quartiles barely overlap at all, although the extreme values do.

In summary, the signs of an ongoing sound change of final devoicing can be seen in YM's speech: words with phonologically VOICED final stops are often realized as voiceless. There is a difference in averages, but as the box plots show us there is also considerable overlap in the phonetic realization of the phonological categories. In the speech of YF, the phonetic difference between VOICED and VOICELESS appears to hold also in the final position, but we can see some signs of devoicing also here. At this stage, the reason for this difference between speakers is not known. A plausible partial explanation may be YF's literacy and greater proficiency in Hindi.

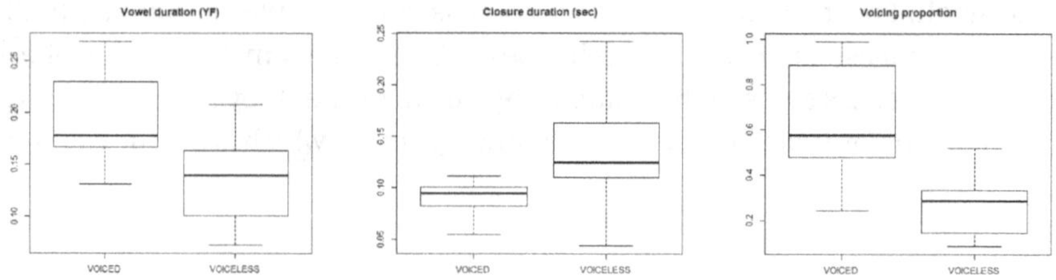

Figure 11: Vowel duration (left), closure duration (middle), and proportion of voicing during closure (right) for YF

4.2 Consonant deletion

Consonant lenition and deletion in the word-final position are widely attested in Kanashi. In this, Kanashi shows a similar development to several other ST languages, where the Proto-ST series of codas /p/, /t/, /k/ have merged into a single glottal stop (Matisoff 2003). This development has been known to also have an influence on tonogenesis (Haudricourt 2018). While fricatives, affricates or /l/ in the word-final position are always audible in Kanashi, we find varying degrees of consonant deletion in: voiceless stops (Section 4.2.1), nasals (Section 4.2.2), and alveolar trill (Section 4.2.3).

4.2.1 Voiceless stops

The omission of final consonants is documented more often with voiceless stops. It occurs most commonly in disyllabic words ending in *-a:t*, though not exclusively. One thing that is noticeable in items where the final consonant is not audible is that they show a higher final pitch than those ending with voiceless final stops words that are phonologically vowel-final. This may indicate that there is some form of glottal gesture involved in the realization of these items.[22]

Figure 12 shows the average pitch of monosyllabic items ending in (from top to bottom at the lefthand side of Figure 12): (1) voiced stops; (2) vowels; (3) voiceless stops; and (4) omitted voiceless stops.[23] The averages are based on mean pitch across successive fifths (1–5) of the duration of the vowel. This is since due to back-

22 Grierson (1928) suggests a possibility of glottalization.

23 Words/tokens: voiced – 18/39; vowels – 26/69; voiceless – 10/23; omitted – 5/8.

ground noise there is sometimes perturbations in Praat's pitch measurements and a mean period across a period of time is therefore likely more accurate.

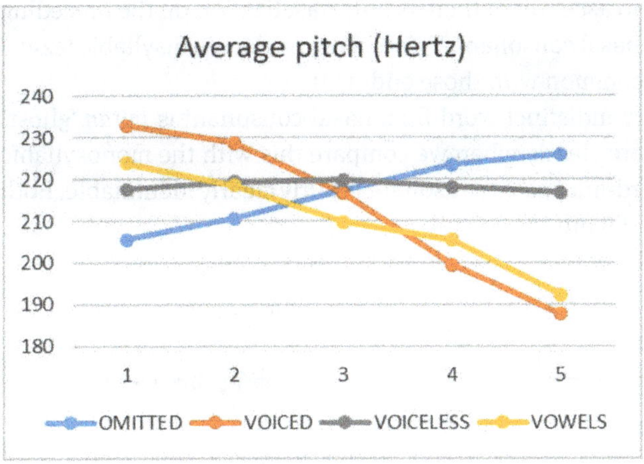

Figure 12: Average pitch

This difference is also illustrated in Figure 13 with the two phonetic realizations of /jaːk/ 'yak' in the speech of the same speaker: the (blue) dotted line shows the pitch (fundamental frequency).

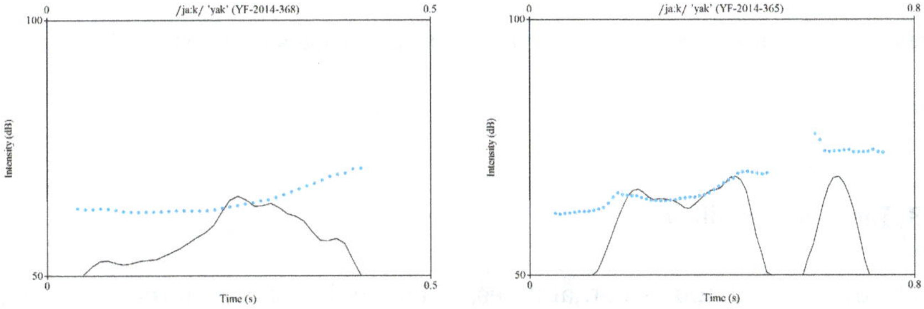

Figure 13: Intra-speaker pronunciation variation (YF: final stops): [jaː(ʔ)] ~ [jaːkᵊ] /jaːk/ 'yak'

4.2.2 Nasals

Nasal consonants are not completely omitted, but they often seem to be very indistinct, making it difficult to ascertain if there is only nasalization on the preceding vowel or if there is also a nasal consonant. This is more evident in disyllabic lexical items, and is especially common with those ending in *-aŋ*.

An example of a very indistinct word-final nasal consonant is *butaŋ* 'ghost'. We see the difference more clearly when we compare this with the monosyllabic *ʥaːŋ* 'gold' where the word-final nasal consonant is fairly clearly identifiable. Both occurred in YF's speech (Figure 14).

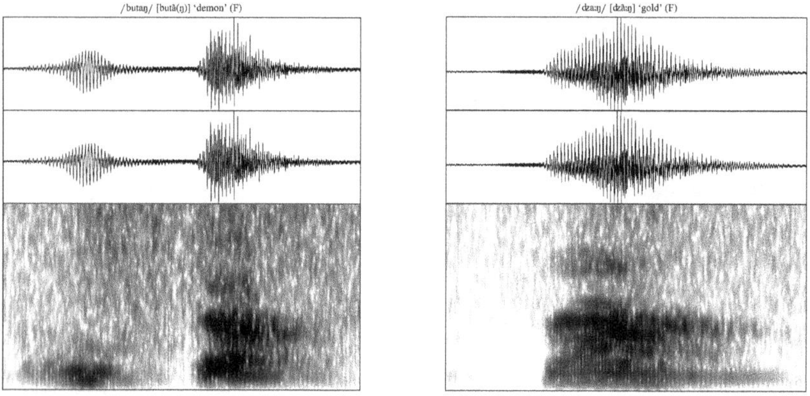

Figure 14: Intra-speaker pronunciation variation (YF: final /ŋ/): [butã(ŋ)] 'ghost' : [ʥãːŋ] 'gold'

4.2.3 The alveolar trill /r/

The alveolar trill /r/, too, is not, at times, articulated explicitly in the word-final position. Examples: /laːr/ [laː(r)] ~ [laː(ɹ)] 'rice (uncooked)' and /duːr/ [duː(r)] ~ [duː(ɹ)] 'far'. This may be compared with, for example, /haːr/ [haːr] 'necklace', where the final /r/ is a clear trill (Figure 15).

Summing up, Kanashi seems to show signs of losing its word-final consonants (stops, alveolar trill and nasals). If true, this change is still at a relatively initial stage as the language consultants, when asked to pronounce the word slowly, provided the form with a word-final consonant.

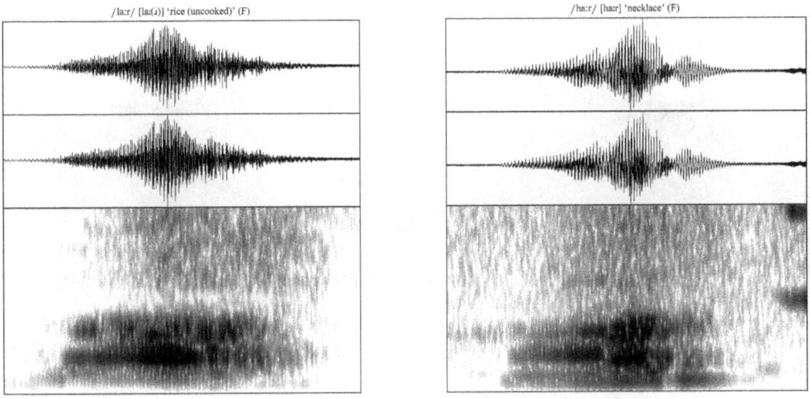

Figure 15: Intra-speaker variation (final /r/): /la:r/ [la:(ɹ)] 'rice (uncooked)' : [ha:r] 'necklace'

5 Placing the Kanashi sound system in its context

In this section we will discuss how the Kanashi sound system relates to the sound systems of some closely related West Himalayish languages: Bunan (Widmer 2017), Darma (Willis Oko 2019), Kinnauri (Saxena 2017; 2022),[24] Pattani (S. R. Sharma 1991) and Lahuli (Singh 1989). All these languages are spoken in Himachal Pradesh (India), except Darma, which is spoken in the easternmost part of the Indian state of Uttarakhand and the adjacent area in western Nepal (see Figure 16).

In its consonant inventory, Kanashi appears to be fairly similar to other West Himalayish languages. Voiceless aspirates – a feature not reconstructable to Proto-Sino-Tibetan (DeLancey 1985) – are shared by most related languages. Voiced aspirates, on the other hand, present a more varied picture. They are found in Lahuli and Pattani, but not in Bunan. In Darma and Kinnauri voiced aspirates are not accorded phonemic status. In both languages they are mainly found in words of IA origin and there is a lot of variation between voiced and voiceless aspirates. As seen above this is the case also in Kanashi. Matisoff (2003) notes that many ST languages of Nepal have developed voiced aspirates due to contact, first restricted to loanwords but later also extended to ST vocabulary.

24 Information provided here on Kinnauri is based on Anju Saxena's fieldwork. See also Saxena (2017; 2022).

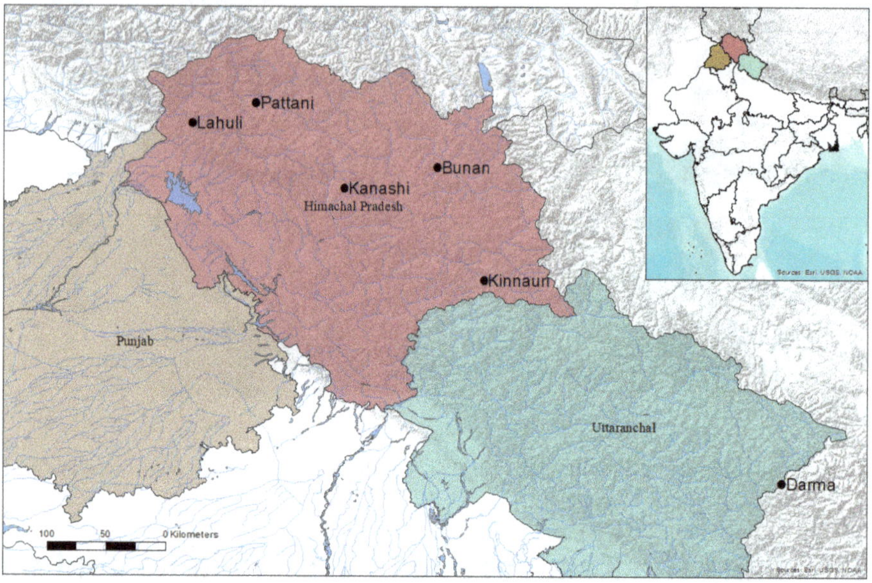

Figure 16: Location of Kanashi and related languages (Uttaranchal is a former name of Uttarakhand)

One difference between Kanashi and Kinnauri concerns nasal consonants. Kanashi has a retroflex nasal consonant phoneme, while Kinnauri has a palatal nasal, but not a retroflex nasal consonant as a phoneme. In both languages this consonant (palatal nasal/retroflex nasal) is rather infrequent.

The West Himalayish languages considered here show variation concerning the number of places of articulation in obstruents and nasals. Most of the languages surveyed here have stops at four to five places of articulation and affricates at two to three. An exception is Darma, which Willis Oko (2019) analyses as lacking affricates but instead having stops at six places of articulation. She notes that previous authors have analyzed the alveolar and palatal stops as affricates and that they are similar in their articulation to affricates (Willis Oko 2019). Retroflex stops are common in all branches of Himalayish (Matisoff 2003). Kanashi seems to differ from the other languages surveyed here in that Kanashi – based on our current knowledge – has sibilants at two places of articulation, while Lahuli, Pattani, and Bunan have three places of articulation. Darma appears to deviate from the other languages in having a uvular fricative. The lack of voiced fricatives that we have observed in Kanashi is also found in several of the related languages.

As for sonorants, the languages surveyed here are fairly similar to Kanashi. Pattani and Lahuli have a retroflex rhotic. For nasal consonants, the places of articulation vary between three and five. However, the (almost) lack of the velar nasal in the word-initial position in Kanashi is not a characteristic of either Bunan or Darma.

Final devoicing is also fairly common in these languages. Bunan only allows /p/, /t/, /k/ in the final position. In Kinnauri the intensity of /b/, /d/, /g/ in the word-final position is either less or the consonant is realized as voiceless. Just as in Kanashi, in Kinnauri too, voiced stops in non-word-initial position are often realized as voiced fricatives. According to Matisoff (2003: 313), "[f]inal stops in Sino-Tibetan, as in virtually all mainland Southeast Asian languages of the Tai-Kadai, Hmong-Mien, and Mon-Khmer families, are unreleased, with no contrasts in voicing or aspiration in that position".

Kanashi is also fairly similar to its genetically related languages concerning its vowel system, with the exception that Darma has the vowel /ɛ/, while Kinnauri, Lahuli, Pattani, and Darma have a /ə/. Unlike Kanashi and Kinnauri, in Darma, length is not distinctive and in Bunan only marginally so, with only two long vowel phonemes /iː/ and /aː/. Nasal vowels exist in several of the languages, but if they have phonemic status, generally they have very low functional load.

The behavior of /u/ observed in Kanashi has similarities in related languages. For example, the fronting of /o/, /u/ to /ø/, /y/ in Bunan in certain environments, e.g. following palatal or alveo-palatal consonants and in the case of /u/ also following /l/. In Darma, /u/ is realized as a high, central unrounded vowel when in closed syllables with nasal codas or following palatal consonants.

When it comes to syllable structures, Kanashi appears to allow for both more complex onsets and codas than Bunan or Darma. In Bunan, the syllable canon is $C_1RVC_2C_3$, where R is a resonant /r/ or /j/ and C_3 is /s/. Darma does not allow final consonant clusters and as onsets only C + /w/, /j/. Kinnauri is more similar to Kanashi here, allowing a wider array of both initial and final clusters. The Proto-ST syllable canon can, according to Matisoff (2003) be reconstructed as $(P_2)(P_1)C_i(G)V(:)(C_f)(S)$, where G is a glide /j/, /w/ and C_f is a restricted set of final consonants. P and S refer to consonantal affixes, where Matisoff notes about the prefixes that "[they], especially those that were stops, and especially when preceding a stop C_i, were undoubtedly vocalized by an epenthetic schwa for ease of pronunciation. Strictly speaking such forms are 'sesquisyllabic' (i.e. 'a syllable and a half' long) rather than simply monosyllabic." (Matisoff 2003: 11).

Many ST languages have phonemic tone and/or voice register distinctions. However, there are differences between the subbranches as well as areal differences. Hildebrandt (2007) surveys the tonal systems of seventeen languages and the distribution along the so called Indosphere and Sinosphere as well as a buffer zone between them, following Matisoff (1999) and Bickel & Nichols (2003). These spheres are to be construed as forming areas of cultural and linguistic similarity. The Sinosphere is east of the Brahmaputra river and is characterized by early influence from the Han culture, monosyllabicity and complex tone systems. The Indosphere lies west of the Brahmaputra and is characterized by Hindu-Buddhist traditions and its languages are atonal (or incipiently tonal) and polysyllabic. The so-called buffer zone lies in-between and is, both culturally and linguistically, a sort of hybrid of the two other spheres. Kanashi lies clearly in the so called Indosphere. Thus, from that point of view, it is not surprising that Kanashi is atonal and polysyllabic.

References

Bickel, Balthasar & Johanna Nichols. 2003. *Typological enclaves*. Presentation at the 2003 Association for Linguistic Typology biennial meeting. http : / / www . uni - leipzig . de / ~autotyp/download/enclaves@ALT5-2003BB-JN.pdf.

Boersma, Paul & David Weenink. 2018. *Praat: Doing phonetics by computer [computer program]*. Version 6.0.42, retrieved 15 August 2018 from http://www.praat.org/.

DeLancey, Scott. 1985. Sino-Tibetan languages. In Bernard Comrie (ed.), *The world's major languages*, 798–810. London: Croom Helm.

Dmitrieva, Olga, Allard Jongman & Joan Sereno. 2010. Phonological neutralization by native and non-native speakers: The case of Russian final devoicing. *Journal of Phonetics* 38(3): 483–492.

Duttamajumdar, Satarupa. 2015. Diphthongs in Kanashi. *The Buckingham Journal of Languages and Linguistics* 8: 99–106.

Grierson, George A. 1928. *Linguistic survey of India, Vol 1, Part II: Comparative vocabulary*. Calcutta: Government of India, Central Publication Branch.

Haudricourt, André-Georges. 2018. *The origin of tones in Vietnamese*. halshs-01678018: https://halshs.archives-ouvertes.fr/halshs-01678018. English translation of: De l'origine des tons en vietnamien, *Journal Asiatique* 242: 69–82 (1954).

Hendriksen, Hans. 1976. *Himachali studies I: Vocabulary*. Copenhagen: Munksgaard.

Hildebrandt, Kristine. 2007. Tone in Bodish languages: Typological and sociolinguistic contributions. In Matti Miestamo & Bernhard Wälchli (eds.), *New challenges in typology: Broadening the horizons and redefining the foundations*, 77–100. Berlin: Mouton de Gruyter.

Kawahara, Shigeto. 2015. The phonetics of sokuon, or geminate obstruents. In Haruo Kubozono (ed.), *Handbook of Japanese phonetics and phonology*, 43–77. Berlin: De Gruyter.

Matisoff, James A. 1999. Tibeto-Burman tonology in an areal context. In Shigeki Kaji (ed.), *Proceedings of the symposium: Cross-linguistic studies of tonal phenomena: Tonogenesis, typology, and related topics*, 3–32. Tokyo: Institute for the study of Languages, Cultures of Asia & Africa, Tokyo University of Foreign Studies.

Matisoff, James A. 2003. *Handbook of Proto-Tibeto-Burman: System and philosophy of Sino-Tibetan reconstruction*. Berkeley: University of California Press.

Ohala, Manjari. 2007. Experimental methods in the study of Hindi geminate consonants. In Maria Josep Solé, Patrice Beddor & Manjari Ohala (eds.), *Experimental approaches to phonology*, 351–396. Oxford: Oxford University Press.

Saxena, Anju. 2017. Sangla Kinnauri. In Graham Thurgood & Randy J. LaPolla (eds.), *The Sino-Tibetan languages*, 2nd edn., 756–772. London: Routledge.
Saxena, Anju. 2022. *The linguistic landscape of the Indian Himalayas: Languages in Kinnaur*. Forthcoming 2022. Leiden: Brill.
Saxena, Anju & Anna Sjöberg. 2017. *On word formation and prosody in Kanashi*. Presentation at the *23rd Himalayan Languages Symposium*. Tezpur University, Tezpur, India. 5-7 July 2017.
Saxena, Anju, Anna Sjöberg & Padam Sagar. 2018a. *Linguistic variation: Challenges for describing the phonology of Kanashi*. Presentation at the *International workshop on Fieldwork: Methods and theory*. University of Gothenburg, Sweden, 13–14 December 2018.
Saxena, Anju, Anna Sjöberg & Padam Sagar. 2018b. *The sound system of Kanashi*. Presentation at the *39th Annual conference of Linguistic Society of Nepal*. Tribhuvan University, Kathmandu, Nepal. 26-27 November 2018.
Saxena, Anju, Anna Sjöberg & Padam Sagar. 2018c. *Typologically interesting features of the Kanashi sound system*. Presentation at the *53rd Linguistics colloquium: Linguistic variation and diversity*. University of Southern Denmark, Odense, Denmark. 24-27 September 2018.
Sharma, Devi Datta. 1992. *Tribal languages of Himachal Pradesh. Part two*. Delhi: Mittal Publications.
Sharma, Suhnu Ram. 1991. *Questionnaire (Manchati)*. Unpublished.
Singh, Jag Deva. 1989. Lahauli verb inflection. *Linguistics of the Tibeto-Burman Area* 12(2): 41–50.
Turner, Ralph L. 1966. *A comparative dictionary of the Indo-Aryan languages*. Available online: http://dsal.uchicago.edu/dictionaries/soas/. Oxford: Oxford University Press.
Widmer, Manuel. 2017. *A grammar of Bunan*. Berlin: De Gruyter Mouton.
Willis Oko, Christina. 2019. *A grammar of Darma*. Leiden: Brill.

Anju Saxena, Lars Borin, Bernard Comrie, and Padam Sagar

3 A linguistic sketch of Kanashi

Abstract: This chapter presents a grammar sketch of Kanashi, covering its main features and contrasting it with its closely related and better described sister language Kinnauri.

Keywords: Kanashi, Sino-Tibetan, Kinnauri, grammar, morphology, syntax

Chapter overview:

https://doi.org/10.1515/9783110703245-003

1 Introduction

In Chapter 2 where we describe the sound system of Kanashi, we saw that the language exhibits a lot of phonetic variation (e.g. between *u* ~ *o*, *a* ~ *o*, *e* ~ *i*, *s* ~ *ʃ*, *ts* ~ *tʃ*, *ts* ~ *tʃ*^{h}). In this chapter we will primarily provide a phonemic transcription (based on our current analysis as presented in Chapter 2) where such variation and certain automatic segmental alternations (e.g. positionally determined devoicing of stops) will not be indicated in the transcription. This phonemic transcription will be rendered in italics without surrounding "/…/". However, our understanding of the sound system of Kanashi is still far from complete. In particular, and primarily due to sparse data, we cannot always determine in individual instances if we are dealing with the mentioned allophonic or morphophonemic variation or not. Consequently, our phonemic transcription may still occasionally contain some "excess" variation. Occasionally we will also provide a phonetic transcription of the actual pronunciation as documented in our field recordings (enclosed in "[…]"). Examples in the text are from our fieldwork notes unless explicitly noted otherwise. Language data from other sources, such as Konow (1909) and Sharma (1992: 305–399) have sometimes been retranscribed and glossed following the conventions used in this volume, and are sometimes left as in the original source.

Within West Himalayish, the subbranch of Sino-Tibetan (ST)[1] to which Kanashi belongs, it is most closely related to a small cluster of languages spoken some 200 km away, in the Kinnaur district of Himachal Pradesh (see Chapters 1 and 8). All these languages are unwritten and largely undocumented. However, one of them, (Standard) Kinnauri (kfk) has been extensively described (e.g. Saxena 2017; 2022), and throughout this chapter we will compare linguistic features of Kanashi with the corresponding Kinnauri constructions whenever appropriate. Similarly, we will occasionally note differences between our description of Kanashi and the brief sketch presented by Konow (1909), and especially the longer treatment by Sharma (1992: 305–399), and also occasionally make comparisons with other ST languages spoken in the same general area.

1 The Sino-Tibetan language family is also referred to by some authors as Tibeto-Burman or Trans-Himalayan. Yet others use Tibeto-Burman for a posited primary branch of Sino-Tibetan. The exact classification of higher-level nodes of ST is not material to our discussion.

2 Noun phrase

2.1 Noun phrase structure

The noun phrase in Kanashi has the following basic structure:

(Dem / NP_{POSS}) (Qnt) ((Adv) Adj((-F/M)-PL)) N(-PL)(-CX)(=EMP)

The head noun may be omitted, in which case a modifier – an adjective or quantifier – will carry the plural and case suffixes. When noun phrases are juxtaposed in apposition – common with quantifiers such as *sab* 'all' – number and case markers may be affixed only to the last NP or to both NPs.

(1) *nu teg kim*
DEM.PROX big house
'this big house'

(2) *du-ga: niʃ mi*
DEM.DIST-PL two man
'those two men'

(3) *bari-ʦ moʈ-a: ʧʰaŋ-ʦ-a:*
much-DIM fat-PL child-DIM-PL
'many fat children'

(4) *bari-ʦ moʈ-eɳ-a: ʧime-ʦ-a:*
much-DIM fat-F-PL girl-DIM-PL
'many fat girls'

(5) *bari-ʦ ʤog bunen-a:*
much-DIM warm sweater-PL
'many warm sweaters'

(6) *pu juʃk-e kim-a:*
four old-PL house-PL
'four old houses'

(7) *tegje himd-a: roʈʰ-a: munuk-a:*
very courageous-PL brave-PL man-PL
'very courageous, brave men'

(8) *du-ga: ʃum tegje himd-a: roṭʰ-a: ʧʰaŋ-ʦ-a:*
DEM.DIST-PL three very courageous-PL brave-PL child-DIM-PL
'those three very courageous, brave children'

The structure of a noun phrase with a pronominal head is:

Pro(-PL)(-CX)(=EMP)

(9) *du-ga:=i tot-ke*
3.DIST-PL=EMP be-PST
'Only they were'

(10) *aŋ-ʥ=i i:d kim la-ge*
1SG-DAT=EMP one house feel-PST
'I, too, wanted a house'

Quantifiers such as *sab* 'all' and cardinal numerals will normally appear after pronouns, in apposition, optionally followed by *lok* 'people' (see Section 2.4.3):

Pro(-PL)(-CX)(=EMP) (Qnt(-CX)) ([lok(-PL)(-CX)])

(11) *ette sab-us an-e-p arʃug-a taŋ-me-muk*
1PLI all-ERG REFL-PL-ACC mirror-LOC look-PST-1PLI
'We all looked ourselves in the mirror'

(12) *du-ga: sab-us ʥa:-ta-ʃ*
3.DIST-PL all-ERG eat-NPST-3PL
'All of them are eating'

(13) *ki niʃ ʧʰub bar-ta-n-e* [bʰəṭṭne]
2PL two when come-NPST-1/2PL-Q
'When will the two of you come?'

2.2 Nouns

Nouns in Kanashi inflect for number and case. Nouns denoting humans, some culturally important animals and mythological beings have inherent gender, shown through adjective agreement and verb indexing (in the imperative; see Section 3.8). There are some Indo-Aryan (IA) nouns in Kanashi which do not inflect, e.g. *taŋ* 'bother', *ʃuru* 'beginning', *pata* 'knowledge'. Such nouns occur as part of a support verb construction, a kind of multi-word lexical unit where the noun carries the semantics of the combination and the verb is one of a small number of items with more or less empty semantics (typically at least the verb 'do'), e.g.:

(14) *raːm-us* *santoʃ-u-p* *tegje* *toŋ* *ʃaɳ-mug*
m.name-ERG f.name-SG-ACC very bother do-PST.3
'Ram bothered Santosh a lot'

These constructions are ubiquitous in IA, and are most likely partial calques in Kanashi. The whole construction has probably been borrowed from an IA language, keeping the semantic part – the IA noun (uninflected also in the donor language) – but replacing the grammatical part – the support verb – with the corresponding native item.

2.2.1 Origin and structure of nouns

2.2.1.1 Derived nouns

Adaptive markers on Indo-Aryan loanwords

A substantial number of Kanashi nouns are borrowings from Indo-Aryan, which means that they may ultimately be also of Persian or English origin. Kanashi together with some related ST languages exhibits a characteristic adaptation mechanism in IA loanwords, where nouns and adjectives often show a final part – an "adaptive marker" *-(V)ŋ* or *-(V)s*, which in many ways behaves formally like a suffix, although no semantics can be assigned to it (except possibly [-SG.NOM]). See the detailed description and discussion in Chapter 6 . Kanashi has been in continuous contact with IA languages for a long time, not only in Malana and Kullu, but during its prehistory presumably also elsewhere (see Chapter 7). This accounts for the fact that the same IA loans are found in several variant forms, e.g. one with the adaptive marker *-(V)ŋ* or *-(V)s*, and another form which is more akin to the form found, e.g., in standard Hindi (e.g. *saːlaŋ* ~ *saːl* 'year'). The latter is more evident among literate language consultants and/or those who have dealings with, for example, Indian judiciary or other governmental agencies.

Diminutive

The most frequent productive nominal derivational category attested in our data is the diminutive, which occurs freely both on nouns and adjectives. The diminutive marker in Kanashi is *-ts*. An identical or similar diminutive suffix occurs in several ST languages, notably in Kinnauri (*-ts*; Saxena 2022), but also in Newar (*-caa*) and

Chepang (*-coʔ*) (STEDT 2016), and a diminutive marker *-tsɛ* is found in some ST languages of Uttarakhand (e.g. Chaudangsi; Krishan 2011: 192).

The diminutive marker is affixed closest to the stem. On noun stems, the plural marker, the case marker and the discourse marker follow the diminutive marker, e.g. *ʧime-ts-u-p* [girl-DIM-SG-ACC]; *ʧʰaŋ-ts-a:-s* [child-DIM-PL-ERG]. It occurs with IA noun stems (e.g. *goʈʰi-ts-a:* [finger-DIM-PL]), with ST noun stems (e.g. *rig-ts-a:* [louse-DIM-PL]) and with nouns of unknown origin (e.g. *ʧʰaŋ-ts-a:* [boy-DIM-PL]). The diminutive marker is also affixed to adjectives (e.g. *buɽi-ts* [old.F-DIM], which then tend to occur without a head noun, *dala-ts* [few-DIM])[2] and to at least one adverb quantifier (*bari-ts* [much-DIM]). There is, however, no instance of the diminutive marker *-ts* with nouns or adjectives ending in an adaptive marker (*-(V)ŋ/-(V)s*) in our material.

Noun-adjective compounds

The placement of adjectives in relation to their modified head nouns is flexible, but with a clear default ordering of constituents, where adjectives precede head nouns. However, we find a number of cases, typically kinship terms, where the adjective follows the head noun. In some such instances the form of the adjective is reduced in shape and the noun-adjective combination has single-word prosody, indicating that we are dealing with a lexeme-formation mechanism, a kind of compounding, where the resulting combination patterns as a noun rather than as an adjective. The plural marker is suffixed to the adjective in such compounds.

(15) (a) *ja: pʰakuʧ* // (b) *ba: pʰakuʧ*
(a) mother small // (b) father small
(a) 'father's brother's wife' // (b) 'father's younger brother'

(16) (a) *ba: kan* // (b) *ja: kan-i*
(a) father step/bastard // (b) mother step/bastard-F
(a) 'step-father' // (b) 'step-mother'

(17) (a) *ba: ʤeʈʰ-a* // (b) *ja: ʤeʈʰ-i*
(a) father senior-M // (b) mother senior-F
(a) 'father's older brother' // (b) 'mother's older brother'

(18) (a) *ba: pʰakuʧ-a:* // (b) *ba: ʤeʈʰ-a-ga:*
(a) father small-PL // (b) father senior-M-PL
(a) 'father's younger brothers' // (b) 'father's older brothers'

2 We do not have any example of [Adj-DIM N-DIM].

Other nominal derivations

The ST feminine prefix *mi(ʧ)-* is attested only in a few lexical items by Konow (1909: 443): *rāng* 'horse' – *mīc rāng* 'mare'; *kui* 'dog' – *mīch kuti* 'bitch' and by Sharma (1992: 338): *jak* 'yak' – *mi-jak* 'yak (female)'. It is not found in our material.

2.2.1.2 Traditional naming strategy

Traditionally, men used to be named after the day of the week that they were born (see Table 1). For example, our oldest language consultant was called *ʃukru* as he was born on a Friday. This strategy is not used for naming women.

Table 1: Traditional Kanashi men's names by weekday of birth

'name of man	born on:	
sũãru	Monday'	(*soar, suãraŋ* 'Monday')
maŋgal	Tuesday'	(*maŋgal* 'Tuesday')
bud^h, bui	Wednesday'	(*bud(d)* 'Wednesday')
bestru, bei	Thursday'	(*brest* 'Thursday')
ʃukru	Friday'	(*ʃukkar* 'Friday')
ʃaniʧaru, ʃẽjĩ	Saturday'	(*ʃuɳiʧare* 'Saturday')
ahuta	Sunday'	(*tʋa:r* 'Sunday')

In modern times, the use of this naming strategy is diminishing. Even though many adult Kanashi speakers are aware of this traditional naming strategy, children and young adults nowadays have names similar to those found elsewhere in India. For example, *indar, anita, dikʃa, monika*. The form of some modern Indian popular names are, at times, slightly modified in Kanashi, e.g. *hari* is called *harja*.

2.2.2 Number

Kanashi makes a two-way number distinction in its nominal morphology. With some exceptions to be noted below, the singular carries no marker. The plural markers on noun stems in Kanashi are: *-ga:*, *-a:* and *-e*. Nouns of ST and IA origin behave alike concerning the choice of the plural marker (including recent borrowings, e.g. *p^hruʈ-a:* [fruit-PL], *frajbin-a:* [frying.pan-PL]).

As elsewhere in Kanashi, phonetic variation is observed even here; we find variation in the phonetic realization of both the consonant and vowel of the plural markers (see Chapters 2 and 4 for details).

As can be seen in examples (19–21), plural marking is optional after cardinal numerals and other quantifiers with plural semantics.

(19) *niʃ ʧʰaŋ-aː*
two boy-PL
'two boys'

(20) *du-gaː niʃ mi*
DEM.DIST-PL two man
'those two men'

(21) *bari-ʦ buraːɽi(-gaː)*
many-DIM cat(-PL)
'many cats'

According to Sharma (1992: 340), "[p]lurality is not marked with case suffixes". This does not find support in our data, where the plural marker occurs with case markers in both nouns and pronouns, e.g.:

(22) *beʈaɽi-gaː-s laʈpaʈ-gaː-p ʧi-ke*
woman-PL-ERG garment-PL-ACC wash-PST
'The women washed clothes'

(23) *nu-gaː-s kʰila-ge*
3.PROX-PL-ERG feed-PST
'They fed (us)'

To a large extent, the distribution of the two most frequently occurring plural markers *-gaː* and *-aː* is phonologically determined.

When a noun stem ends in a vowel, in most cases the noun stem takes the plural marker *-gaː*. This ending is, at times, realized as [g] or as [k], when it occurs word-finally. For example, *laʈpaʈa* 'piece of clothing, garment', *laʈpaʈa-gaː* [laʈpaʈək] [garment-PL].

As the examples in Table 2 show, the plural marker *-gaː* occurs with both monosyllabic and polysyllabic noun stems, with both animate (masculine, feminine) and inanimate noun stems; with both ST and IA nouns. In all these cases the form of the noun stem remains the same in singular and in plural.

The plural marker *-aː* occurs mainly when the noun stem ends in a consonant (see Table 3). As was the case with the plural marker *-gaː*, *-aː*, too, occurs in monosyllabic as well as polysyllabic noun stems, with both animate (masculine and feminine) and inanimate nouns of IA as well as of ST origin. The form of the noun stem remains the same in the plural.

Table 2: The Kanashi plural marker *-ga:*

SG (ST-origin)	PL	SG (IA-origin)	PL
ta 'nose'	*ta-ga:*	*kaʈora* 'bowl'	*kaʈora-ga:*
ba: 'father'	*ba:-ga:*	*ma:mi:* 'maternal uncle's wife'	*ma:mi:-ga:*
ja: 'mother'	*ja:-ga:*	*ʤaɽe* 'day'	*ʤaɽe-ga:*
tso 'thorn'	*tso-ga:*	*ʈʰullaŋ, ʈʰulla* 'leg, foot'	*ʈʰulla-ga:, ʈʰullaŋ-a:*
ʃo 'field, orchard'	*ʃo-ga:*	*bura:ɽi* 'cat'	*bura:ɽi-ga:*
kurti 'shirt'	*kurti-ga:*	*ʈope* 'cap'	*ʈope-ga:*

Table 3: The Kanashi plural marker *-a:*

SG (ST-origin)	PL	SG (IA-origin)	PL
pra:d 'finger'	*pra:d-a:, *pra:d-ga:*	*ʤa:nʊar* 'animal'	*ʤa:nʊar-a:*
kʰas 'sheep, lamb'	*kʰas-a:, kʰ-a:*	*ʤaŋgal* 'forest'	*ʤaŋgal-a:*
mig 'eye'	*mig-a:*	*ʃaɽak* 'road'	*ʃaɽk-a:*
pʰuts 'mouse'	*pʰuts-a:*	*bja:le* 'meal'	*bja:le-ga:*
kim '(traditional) house, home'	*kim-a:*	*seʊ, seb, seo* 'apple'	*seʊ-a:*
om 'path'	*om-a:*	*tsʰol* 'waterspring'	*tsʰol-a:*
ka:g 'crow'	*ka:g-a:*	*ɖibɽiŋ* 'pond'	*ɖibɽiŋ-a:*
ʥimida:r 'farmer'	*ʥimida:r-a:*		

There is a small set of nouns which end in a consonant in their singular form, but still allow the plural marker *-ga:*. In such cases the plural marker *-ga:* is realized as [əga:]. These nouns also permit the default plural marker *-a:*. See Table 4.

As described in Chapter 2, *ŋ* is often realized as [ŋg] between vowels. Hence, the plural forms of words ending in *-ŋ* could be described as involving *-ŋ-a:* or *-ŋ-ga:* (both alternatives pronounced identically as ending in [ŋga:]). As indicated in Chapter 2, we treat the intervocalic realization of *ŋ* as an automatic phonetic process, with the consequence that words ending in *-ŋ* are treated like all other consonant-final words, i.e., if the *-ŋ* is kept (see Table 5), they take the *-a:* plural marker.

Nouns with the adaptive markers *-(V)ŋ/-(V)s* show several different plural formations. As shown in Table 5, the plural marker *-a:* can be suffixed to the full noun form. The adaptive marker can be partially or completely deleted – thus appearing as a kind of (nominative) singular suffix, leaving either a vowel-final stem to which the plural marker *-ga:* is added, or a consonant-final stem to which *-a:* is added to form the plural; see Table 6.

Table 4: Kanashi words with varying or irregular plural markers

SG	PL	SG	PL
ro:ɖ [ro:ɖ], [ro:ʈ(ʰ)] 'ear'	[ro:ɖa:], [ro:ʈ(ʰ)əga:], [rɔʈʰga]	*bu:ʈ* 'shoe, boot'	[bu:ʈa:], [bu:ʈəga:]
binif 'husband'	[binifa:], [binifəga:]	*kar* 'star'	[karo], [karəga:]
barʃ, barʃaŋ 'year'	[barʃa:], [barʃəga:]	*madza:r* 'tenant'	[madza:rəga:]
kim 'house, home'	[kima:], [kiməg(a:)]	*ka:m, ka:maŋ* 'work'	[ka:məga:]

Table 5: Kanashi plural markers with words ending in *ŋ*

SG	PL	SG	PL
jaŋ 'flea'	[jaŋga:]	*na:iŋ* [na:jiŋ] 'river'	[na:jiŋga:]
ʃiŋ 'wood'	[ʃiŋga:]	*ɖa:ɳaŋ* 'penalty'	[ɖa:ɳaŋga:]
goɖiŋ 'foot, leg'	[goɖiŋga:]	*puʧaŋ* 'tail'	[puʧaŋgo]
paʧaŋ 'leaf'	[paʧaŋga:]	*pitaŋ* 'door'	[pitaŋga:]
maɽʃaŋ 'man'	[maɽʃaŋga:]	*kʰa:kaŋ* 'mouth'	[kʰa:kaŋga:]
pakʰiŋ 'wing'	[pakʰiŋga:]	*na:laŋ* 'riverlet'	[na:laŋga:]
haɖɖaŋ 'bone'	[haɖɖaŋga:]	*gitʰaŋ* 'song'	[gitʰaŋ(g)a:]
kukaɽaŋ 'chicken'	[kukaɽaŋga:]	*biʈiŋ* 'wall'	[biʈiŋ(g)a:]
kʰakaŋ 'mouth'	[kʰakaŋga:]	*ɖibɽiŋ* 'pond'	[ɖibɽiŋ(g)a:]
deʃaŋ 'village, world'	[deʃaŋga:]	*laŋ* 'cow'	[laŋ(g)a:], [lã:ga:]

As seen here, there are a total of three possible plural forms of *kʰas* 'cattle (group of sheep or goats)' found in our material: *kʰ-a:*, *kʰas-a:* and *kʰas-ga:* [kʰasəga:]. Since the word *kʰas* 'cattle' does not actually contain the adaptive marker *-(V)s* (all such words are bi- or polysyllabic), its plural form *kʰ-a:* is most likely a result of analogy.

The plural marker *-e*, finally, occurs in a restricted set of nouns. In most of these examples the regular plural marker *-a:* is also permitted; see Table 7. Many nouns in this set are IA loans. In at least some of these examples, the plural/oblique ending is *-e* in IA languages such as Hindi. Consequently it is possible that the plural ending *-e* in Kanashi is an IA borrowing, which entered the language as part of some borrowed IA nouns. It is, however, important to note that not all IA nouns that take the plural/oblique ending *-e* in IA languages such as Hindi take *-e* as the plural marker in Kanashi (e.g. Hindi *kaʈora* 'bowl', *kaʈor-e* [bowl-PL/OBL.SG], but Kanashi *kaʈora-ga:* [bowl-PL]).

Sharma (1992: 339) states that the plural marker *-e* occurs with stems ending in a vowel and the plural marker *-a* occurs with stems ending in a consonant. As can be seen in the examples provided above, this does not hold in our material. Further, according to Konow (1909) and Sharma (1992: 339), when the plural marker *-ga:* is followed by a suffix, it is realized as *-ga:n*. In our material this is

Table 6: Kanashi plural marking with adaptive *-(V)ŋ/-(V)s*

SG	PL	SG	PL
gra:maŋ 'village'	*gra:ma-ga:, gra:maŋ-a:*	*baɽaŋ* 'forest'	*baɽa-ga:, baɽaŋ-a:*
madras 'man'	*madr-a:, *madra-ga:*	*geʈʈʰaŋ* 'oven, fireplace'	*geʈʈʰ-a:*
buɽas 'old (man)'	*buɽ-a:*	*kʰas* 'cattle (sheep, lamb)'	*kʰ-a:, kʰas-a:, kʰas-ga:*
baniŋ 'pot, utensil'	*baniŋ-a:, bani-ga:*		

Table 7: Kanashi plurals in *-e*

SG (IA)	PL	SG (unknown etym.)	PL
ʧammaʧ, ʧamʧi, ʧamʧiŋ 'spoon'	[ʧamtse], [ʧamʧe]	*ʈukor* 'nest'	[ʈukore], [ʈukre]
mobajl 'mobile phone'	*mobajl-e, mobajl-a:*	*rinig* 'snake'	[riniga:], [rinige], [ringa:]
ʧana 'chickpea'	*ʧan-e*	*ʧime(ts)* 'girl'	*ʧimets-e, ʧimets-a:*
tʰepar 'slap'	*tʰepr-e*	*aʤaɽ* 'apricot'	*aʤaɽ-e, *aʤaɽ-a:, *aʤaɽ-əga:*

not always the case. For example, *ʧara-ga:-s* [child-PL-ERG], *ʧara-ga:-p* [child-PL-ACC]. As we will see in the section on case markers below, *-n* in noun phrases in our material has a possessive function. E.g. *paʧa-ga:-n-ka* [leaf-PL-POSS-POSS], *ʤaɽe-ga:-n ba:d* [day-PL-POSS after], *nu-ga: gra:ma-ga:-n na:m* [DEM.PROX-PL village-PL-POSS name] 'the name of these villages'.

As already mentioned, nouns can optionally take the plural marker also in NPs with numerals greater than 'one' and other quantifiers with plural semantics.

(24) *bari-ʦ bura:ɽi(-ga:)*
many-DIM cat(-PL)
'many cats'

(25) *bari-ʦ ʈope(-ga:)*
many-DIM cap(-PL)
'many caps'

(26) *i:d maɽʃaŋ-ka-di niʃ ʧʰaŋ-ʦ-a: to-ʃ*
one man-POSS-ADE two boy-DIM-PL be.PRS-3PL
'One man has two sons'

(27) *ni-ka* *niʃ* *patʃʰiŋ-a:* *to-ʃ*
1PLE-POSS two assembly-PL be.PRS-3PL
'We have two assemblies'

(28) *ʃum* *lok-a:* *bara-ke*
three person-PL go-PST
'Three people went'

2.2.3 Gender

The gender distinction in Kanashi is primarily lexical; there are distinct lexical terms for masculine and feminine human nouns and domesticated animals (e.g. *ba:* 'father : *ja:* 'mother'; *pag* 'ox' : *hu:dʒ* 'cow'). In IA loans the original (i.e., IA) gender distinction is retained in Kanashi. For example, *goɽa* [goɽa] ~ [gʰora] 'horse' : *goɽi* [goɽi] ~ [gʰori] 'mare', *kutta* 'dog' : *kutti* 'bitch'. There are, however, some grammatical constructions (adjective inflection and verb indexing) in which the distribution of the markers reflects a natural gender/sex distinction in noun referents (see Sections 2.4.1 and 3.8).

2.2.4 Case

The case markers in Kanashi are shown in Table 8.[3] The case marker is suffixed only to the last constituent of a noun phrase. Repetition of case markers occurs only in specific structures treated as appositions here (e.g. *ki-n-ka (sab-ka) ba:-ka* [2PL-POSS-POSS (all-POSS) father-POSS] 'your (all's) fathers'). There is more than one layer of case markers in Kanashi nouns; case markers can be stacked. In Table 8 we indicate the combinations that we have found in our data.[4]

3 Konow (1909: 443) provides the following case markers (numbering according to the order in Table 8 and Konow's transcription): Ø: "subject of intransitive verbs"; (2) *-sh*, *-s*: "subject marker with transitive verbs", and -*s*: instrument marker; (3) *-p*: "object" (accusative); (4) *uj, uzh, uz*: dative; (5) *-ka*: possessive; (6) *-a*: "locative and terminative"; (7) *-s*, *-dz*, *-ts*: ablative; (8) *rang*: 'with' (postposition); (9) *di*: "seems to mean 'with'". Additionally, he mentions the following postpositions: *paa* 'on', *kash* 'for the sake of', *hipich* 'behind', *nandris* 'before', *yen* 'under'.

4 In addition to clear (discourse-particle) clitics such as *=i* [=EMP], we also find among the "case suffixes" described in this section some elements which straddle the boundary between suffix and clitic. However, and as indicated in the table, all case markers will be formally treated as suffixes – i.e., preceded by "-" – in analyzed examples and their glosses, while postpositions (not treated in this section) are transcribed as separate (orthographic) words.

Table 8: Kanashi case markers

Case	Case marker(s) // case marker sequence(s)
Nominative	Ø
Ergative/instrumental	*-s, -as, -is, -us*
Accusative	*(-u)-p* [(-SG)-ACC], *(-e)-p* [(-PL)-ACC]
Dative	*-udʒ, -dz, -tʃ*
Possessive	*-n, -u, -ka // -n-ka* [-POSS-POSS]; *-u-ka* [-POSS-POSS]
Locative	*-a, -ŋa, -e* (*-e* occurs only in a few words)
Ablative	*-dz, -ts, -tʃ // -a-ts* [-LOC-ABL]; *-di-ts* [-ADE-ABL]; *-u-di-ts* [-POSS-ADE-ABL]
Comitative	*-raŋ // -u-raŋ* [-POSS-COM]
Adessive	*-di // -ka-di* [-POSS-ADE]; *-n-di* [-POSS-ADE]; *-u-di* [-POSS-ADE]

2.2.4.1 Nominative

The nominative form is the stem of a noun or pronoun without any other case suffixes, although as we have seen, the adaptive markers *-(V)ŋ/-(V)s* are sometimes dropped in other forms than the nominative singular. This form can be used for subjects (intransitive and transitive) – i.e., the NP co-referring with the subject indexing in the verb – and direct objects.

2.2.4.2 Ergative/instrumental

The case marker *-(V)s* functions both as an ergative marker and as an instrumental marker. It has four basic allomorphs: *-s, -us, -is* and *-as*. As elsewhere in Kanashi, in all these cases, -*s* is, at times, realized as *-ʃ* without any difference in meaning (e.g. *nu-ga:-s* [nuga:s] ~ [nuga:ʃ] [3.PROX-PL-ERG]; *beʈaɽi-ga:-s* [beʈariga:s] ~ [beʈaɽiga:ʃ] [woman-PL-ERG]; *ra:m-us* [ra:mus] ~ [ra:muʃ] [m.name-ERG]; *santoʃ-is* [santoʃis] ~ [santoʃiʃ] [f.name-ERG] (see Chapter 2).

Sharma (1992: 343) states that the ergative marker occurs in transitive clauses in the past tense. This is not the case in our material. In our material the ergative marker occurs in all tenses and aspects – in transitive clauses and in active intransitive clauses.

The first and second person singular personal pronouns do not take the ergative marker[5] (see Section 2.3.2). The ergative marker occurs with nouns, with plural personal pronouns, and with third person singular personal pronouns.

5 In Tinani and Pattani (see Sharma 1992), too, the same 1SG pronoun form occurs in nominative and ergative.

The ergative marker *-s* occurs on stems ending in vowels (e.g. *ba:-s* [father-ERG]; *ja:-s* [mother-ERG]; *anʤu-s* [f.name-ERG]; *ʃukru-s* [m.name-ERG]; *du-ga:-s* [3.DIST-PL-ERG]). *-s* can also be added to consonant-final stems (see below).

The remaining ergative markers (*-is, -us, -as*) occur with stems ending in consonants. *-us* occurs only with masculine nouns, *-is* is predominantly found with feminine nouns, although there are also some examples of *-is* with masculine nouns. The distribution of the ergative marker *-as* is unclear. In some instances, more than one of *-s, -as, -is* and *-us* are permitted (see Table 9).

Table 9: Variation in ergative marking

N-ERG	N-ERG
santoʃ-is ~ *santoʃ-as* [f.name-ERG]	*maheʃ-us* ~ *maheʃ-is* [m.name-ERG]
kukaʈaŋ-s ~ *kukaʈaŋ-as* [hen-ERG]	*munuk-s* ~ *munuk-us* [man-ERG]
mohan-as ~ *mohan-s* [m.name-ERG]	*hariʃ-us* ~ *hariʃ-is* [m.name-ERG]
lalit-s ~ *lalit-us* [m.name-ERG]	*ʧiʈa-s* ~ *ʧiʈ-us* [m.name-ERG]

(29) *ra:m-us poʈo-ga: reʈ-ta*
m.name-ERG fruit-PL sell-NPST
'Ram sells fruit'

(30) *ra:m-us sura:b tui-gu-ta*
m.name-ERG alcohol drink-PROG-NPST
'Ram is drinking alcohol'

(31) *ra:m-us ʧʰo-p tog-u-ta* [togut(a)]
m.name-ERG child-ACC hit-PROG-NPST
'Ram is hitting the child'

(32) *sonu-s letu buʈu-mug*
m.name-ERG spit(N) throw-PST.3
'Sonu spat'

(33) *sonu-s vaʈʃu-ke*
m.name-ERG scratch-PST
'Sonu scratched'

(34) *nu huʤ-is tʰi:d kʰiraŋ dalats ken-ke*
DEM.PROX COW-ERG little milk today give.1/2O-PST
'This cow gave (us) little milk today'

(35) *gu* *du-ga:-p* *roʤ* *ta-gu-ta-k*
1SG.NOM 3.DIST-PL-ACC every.day look-PROG-NPST-1SG
'I am watching them every day'

The instrumental markers are the same as the ergative markers. The instrumental marker occurs with concrete nouns (e.g. *tsʰure-s* [knife-INS]) and abstract nouns (e.g. *υakt-us* [time-INS]). The default instrumental marker with stems ending in vowels is *-s*. For example,

(36) *aŋ* *ja:-s* *ɳija-s* *ba:ʤi* *ʧʰul-ku-ʈa*
1SG.NNOM mother-ERG chopper-INS vegetables cut-PROG-NPST
'My mother is cutting the vegetables with the (traditional) chopper'

(37) *ni* *geʈʈʰaŋ-a* *ʃiŋ-a:-s* *mi:* *sut-ta-ŋ*
1PLE stove-LOC wood-PL-INS fire light-NPST-1/2PL
'We light fire in the stove with wood'

(38) *gu* *ɖabaŋ-ts* *ʧamʧi-s* *ma:r* *ɖun-me-k*
1SG.NOM box-ABL spoon-INS butter take.out-PST-1SG
'I took out butter with a spoon from the box'

The default instrumental marker with consonant ending stems is *-as*. For example,

(39) *du-s* *simiʈ-a:* *iʈ-as* *kim* *gaɳ-mug*
3.DIST-ERG cement-PL brick-INS house build-PST.3
'He built a house with cement and bricks'

Similarly to the ergative, some stems allow both variants. This occurs especially frequently with stems ending in a nasal consonant in our material. For example,

(40) *mohan-s/-as* *muʃi:n-s/-as* *laʈpaʈa-ga:* *ʧi-gu-ta*
m.name-ERG/-ERG machine-ERG/-ERG garment-PL wash-PROG-NPST
'Mohan washes clothes in the machine'

There are very few examples of the instrumental markers *-is* and *-us* in our data. The basis for their distribution is unclear since gender is only attributed to animate nouns.

(41) *nu-s* *pen-us* *ʧiʈʈʰi* *likʰ-ja:-mug*
3.PROX-ERG pen-INS letter write-TR-PST.3
'He wrote the letter with a pen'

As with the Hindi instrumental marker *se*, the Kanashi suffix, too, occurs in some other contexts, e.g. with a quantifier to give a superlative interpretation.

(42) *gu* *sab-as* *tsʰeka/tsʰika* *bas* *soara* *boŋ-ta-k*
1SG.NOM all-INS early bus p.name go-NPST-1SG
'I will go to Kullu with the earliest bus'

2.2.4.3 Accusative

-p is the accusative case marker in Kanashi. It does not show any sign of assimilation. It occurs with noun and pronoun stems (e.g. *ʃer-p* [tiger-ACC]; *aŋ-p* [1SG-ACC]).

Kanashi is atypical for a South Asian language in having a distinct accusative case. The most common situation – at least among surrounding languages; see, e.g., the three sketches of languages of Kinnaur in Saxena (2022), including closely related Kinnauri, which does not have a separate accusative – is to have a case called *dative* or *objective*, used both on patient and recipient arguments.[6]

The accusative marker *-p* occurs with animate (masculine and feminine) as well as inanimate head nouns (43).

(43) *om-p* [path-ACC]
kʰiraŋ-p [milk-ACC]
latpaṭ-a:-p [garment-PL-ACC]
ʃer-p [tiger-ACC]
rinig-p [snake-ACC]
monika-p [f.name-ACC]
ra:m-p [m.name-ACC]
ʧara-ga:-p [child-PL-ACC]

Only the emphasis marker *=i* follows the accusative marker. Example, *ʧʰu-p=i* [what-ACC-EMP].

As already seen in some examples above, in some cases there is an *-u* or *-e* between the consonant-ending stem and the accusative marker *-p*. In all such instances nouns with *-u* are singular,[7] while *-e* in the same slot signifies plural. *-u* and *-e* occur with both IA loans (including recent loans) and ST noun and pronoun stems.

6 Typical for this configuration is also that the dative/objective can be replaced by the nominative in some cases. Specifically, if there is both a patient and a recipient argument, only the latter receives dative marking.

7 A (partial) exception is formed by *sabup* (*sab-u-p* [all-SG-ACC]), which arguably has plural semantics.

(44) *du-s* *ʧʰog* *madras-u-p* *taŋ-mug*
3.DIST-ERG fair.complexioned man-SG-ACC see-PST.3
'He saw a fair-complexioned man'

(45) *du-s* *i:d* *ʈʰinɖ-u-p* *a:ɽe-mug* [a:ɽemo]
3.DIST-ERG one servant-SG-ACC call-PST.3
'He called one of the servants' (Konow)

(46) *ra:m-us* *santoʃ-u-p* *tegje taŋ* *ʃaɳ-mug*
m.name-ERG f.name-SG-ACC very bother do-PST.3
'Ram bothered Santosh a lot'

(47) *du-s* *das ʈaka-n* *loʈ-u-p* *ke-ta*
3.DIST-ERG ten money-POSS note-SG-ACC give.1/2O-NPST
'He will give (us) a ten rupee note'

(48) *gu* *ga:ɽiŋ-ʦ beg-u-p* *ɖun-me-k*
1SG.NOM car-ABL bag-SG-ACC take.out-PST-1SG
'I took out my bag from the car'

(49) *sab ʧara-ga:-s* *an-e-p* *arʃuk-a* *ta-ge*
all child-PL-ERG REFL-PL-ACC mirror-LOC look-PST
'All the children looked at themselves in the mirror'

The occurrence of *-u/-e* is, however, not obligatory here. We have instances of the same noun taking *-u-p* in one occurrence and *-p* in another, apparently with no difference in meaning.

(50) *ka* *ʥa:b-a* *ʃer-u-p* *sat-ta-n*
2SG.NOM now-LOC tiger-SG-ACC kill-NPST-2SG
'You now kill a tiger'

(51) *ka* *ʃer-p* *san-me-n*
2SG.NOM tiger-ACC kill-PST-2SG
'You killed a tiger'

The accusative marker does not occur obligatorily.

(52) *gu* *kuta:b-u-p* *ba:le-me-k*
1SG.NOM book-SG-ACC see-PST-1SG
'I saw the book'

(53) *ra:m-us* *kuta:b paʈ-mug*
m.name-ERG book read-PST.3
'Ram read a book'

(54) *ra:m-us* *mohan-uʥ* *kim-p* *ren-mug*
m.name-ERG m.name-DAT house-ACC sell-PST.3
'Ram sold the house to Mohan'

(55) *gu* *kim* *g^ho-ta-k*
1SG.NOM house build.structure.from.foundation-NPST-1SG
'I will build a house (from the ground up)'

2.2.4.4 Dative

The dative case marker with nouns is *-(u)ʤ*. As elsewhere in Kanashi, in the dative case marker too, there is variation in the realization of the consonant and vowel of the dative marker ([ʤ] ~ [z] ~ [ʥ] ~ [ʧ] and [u] ~ [o]). This variation is observed both within the speech of one language consultant as well as across speakers. For example, [aŋʤ] and [aŋʥ] 'to me' were provided by the same consultants. Furthermore, as elsewhere in Kanashi, the consonant of the dative marker is barely audible in the word-final position. For example, [santoʃuʤ] ~ [santoʃu] 'to Santosh'; [mohanuʤ] ~ [mohanu] 'to Mohan'; [ʧarao] ~ [ʧarauʤ] ~ [ʧarauʧ] 'to a/the child'; [sabuʧ] ~ [sabu] 'to all/everybody'). But when asked to repeat, language consultants provided the full dative marker with the final consonant.

The dative case marker *-uʤ* occurs both with noun stems ending in consonants (e.g. *hariʃ-uʤ* [m.name-DAT]; *kusum-uʤ* [f.name-DAT]; *t^ha:r-uʧ* [tiger-DAT]) and with stems ending in vowels (e.g. *ba:-uʤ* [father-DAT]; *ja:-uʤ* [mother-DAT]; *bare-uʤ* [m.name-DAT]; *pratiba-uʤ* [f.name-DAT]). In some instances, however, when the stem ends in a vowel, the stem final vowel is either deleted or it is modified (e.g. [a] > [o], [i] > [j]: *kalpu-uʤ* [kalpuʤ]; *papa-uʤ* [papouʤ]; *nirali-uʤ* [niraljuʤ].

(56) *an* *ja:-s* *aŋ-ʥ* *ʈaka* *ken-ke*
1SG.NNOM mother-ERG 1SG-DAT money give.1/2O-PST
'My mother gave money to me'

The following are all the examples that we have with the dative marker on plural nouns. All three examples are from a text provided by Konow (1909). Unlike the accusative marker, *-u* here occurs with plural stems too.

(57) *mitar-aː-dʑ* [friend-PL-DAT]

ʧʰaŋ-aː-udʑ [child-PL-DAT]

beʈaɽi-gaː-udʑ [woman-PL-DAT]

With the dative case marker too, only the emphasis marker *=i* follows the dative marker:

(58) *aŋ-dʑ=i sauda-gaː ʃobilas lag-e-ta*
1SG-DAT=EMP candy-PL good feel-INTR-NPST
'I for one do like sweets'

The dative marker also occurs in some other grammatical contexts in Kanashi. For example it occurs on the subject of an obligative construction and in the experiencer subject (or dative subject) construction (see Section 4.3).

2.2.4.5 Possessive

The possessive markers in Kanashi are: *-n*, *-u* and *-ka*.[8]

The possessive marker *-n* is used with pronouns and shows a strong preference for plural nouns in our material, With nouns (but not pronouns), it seems that it forces a plural interpretation even in the absence of an overt plural marker.

(59) *du-s das ʈaka-n loʈ-u-p ke-ta*
3.DIST-ERG ten money-PL.POSS note-SG-ACC give.1/2O-NPST
'He will give (me) a ten rupee note'

With singular noun stems ending in vowels, *-ka* is strongly preferred.

(60) *baɽka-ka/*bʰaɽka-u kim* [f.name-POSS house]

*ʃo-ka/*ʃo-u* [field-POSS]

*koʈi-ka/*koʈi-u kim* [m.name-POSS house]

*ʧiʈa-ka kim/*ʧiʈa-u kim* [m.name-POSS house]

but: *svati-u/svati-ka kim* [f.name-POSS house]

The possessive markers *-u* and *-ka* occur freely with singular noun stems ending in a consonant, apparently with no change in meaning. We encountered the possessive marker *-u* with a particular noun stem during one data collection session, while in another data collection session we recorded *-ka* with the same noun stem.

8 As elsewhere in Kanashi, there is variation in the vowel quality ([ka] ~ [ko]) of the possessive marker *-ka*, and the vowel of *-ka* in the word-final position is often not heard. E.g. *radʑa-ka* [radʑok] [king-POSS], *disambar-ka* [disəmbark] [december-POSS], *sonu-ka* [sonug] [m.name-POSS].

(61) *amit-ka/amit-u kim* [m.name-poss house]

kusum-u/kusum-ka kim [f.name-poss house]

anup-ka/anup-u kim [m.name-poss house]

punam-ka/punam-u kim [f.name-poss house]

Further, *-ka* can follow the possessive markers *-u* or *-n*, but there are no instances of the co-occurrence of the possessive markers *-u* and *-n*.

The following examples illustrate that the possessive markers *-n/-u* and *-ka* can occur in a sequence affixed to the same noun stem.

(62) *paʧ-a:-n-ka rokʈʰaŋ*
leaf-pl-poss-poss roof
'roof of leaves'

(63) *mohan-u-ka katab*
m.name-poss-poss book
'Mohan's book'

(64) *buʃ-u-ka raŋg rok to*
rope-poss-poss color black be.prs
'The color of the rope is black'

(65) *nu an-u-ka ʧʰetsaŋ-u-ka ʥa:ŋmamula:-p kʰoɽ-mug*
3.prox refl-sg-poss wife-poss-poss gold.necklace-acc snatch-pst.3
'He snatched my wife's gold necklace'

(66) *santoʃ-u-ka ʧʰo aŋ-raŋ guɖ-a:-p mila-ʃi-ke*
f.name-poss-poss son 1sg-com hand-pl-acc shake-mdl-pst
'Santosh's son shook hands with me'

The distribution of the possessive markers remains the same with alienable and inalienable head nouns, for example:

(67) *mohan-u-ka ta-ʦ kʰui dʋa-ta*
m.name-poss-poss nose-abl blood come.out-npst
'Blood comes out of Mohan's nose'

(68) *mohan-u-ka kuta:b ʈeble-n-ka rigi:n tot-ke*
m.name-poss-poss book table-poss-poss on/above be-pst
'Mohan's book was on the table'

(69) *hu:ʤ-u-ka t^hutre la:mas*
cow-POSS-POSS tail long
'The cow's tail is long'

When the possessive marker is affixed to nouns with an adaptive marker, we find both variants – one with the adaptive marker and another without the adaptive marker, without any difference in meaning. Here we again see variation: in some cases the possessive marker is *-ka*, while in other the possessive marker is *-u*.

(70) *sa:laŋ-u sa:l-ka ba:d*
year-POSS year-POSS after
'year after year'

A predicative possessive in a copular construction is used to render 'have'.

(71) *harija-ka ʃu:m ʧ^haŋ-a: to-ʃ*
m.name-POSS three boy-PL be.PRS-3PL
'Harija has three sons'

The possessive marker *(-u)-ka* also occurs after a nominalized verb. E.g.

(72) *ra:m-uʥ ka:m-a: ʃaɳ-m-u-ka man ma:j*
m.name-DAT work-PL do-NMLZ-POSS-POSS desire(N) BE.NEG.NPST
'Ram does not want to work'

(73) *gu:n-a ri:-ga: bar-am-ka batr to*
winter-LOC glacier-PL come-NMLZ-POSS danger be.PRS
'During winter there is a danger of avalanches'

It is possible that *-u* is the inherited ST possessive marker, while *-ka* could be a relatively recent borrowing from IA. On the one hand, this hypothesis is supported by the ordering of the two possessive markers *-u* and *-ka* on one stem, where *-u* precedes *-ka*. But unlike the IA possessive marker *ka* (for example in Hindi), the possessive marker *-ka* in Kanashi does not inflect for number and gender of its head noun. On the other hand, a complication is that the form *-ka* is typically not found in Western Pahari, where possessive suffixes tend to be r-initial, similar to what is found in Kullui (*ra:*; Grierson 1928: 674) or Kinnauri Pahari (*-rɔ/-ri*; Saxena 2022), although Jaunsari does have *-ko* (Hendriksen 1986: 105). Also, k-initial possessive markers are not unknown in ST: a possessive clitic *=ki* occurs both in Bunan (Widmer 2017) and Navakat (Saxena 2022), and in the cross-linguistic survey of borrowed affixes presented by Seifart (2017), genitive/possessive suffixes do not occur even once, despite the fact that borrowed case morphology is not uncommon in his sample, pointing to the need for more concrete evidence of borrowing in this case.

2.2.4.6 Locative

The locative marker occurs productively in our material with common nouns, place names, and pronouns. The most frequently occurring locative marker in Kanashi is *-a*. It has three allomorphs: [a], [ʋa] and [ja]. [ʋa] and [ja] occur with stems which end in vowels. [ʋa] occurs when the stem ends in a back vowel and [ja] occurs when the stem ends with a front vowel; [a] occurs with stems ending in consonants.

(74) *arʃuk-a* [mirror-LOC]
ʃo-a [ʃoʋa] [field-LOC]
kim-a [house-LOC]
ʈokori-a [ʈokorija] [basket-LOC]
pra:d-a [finger-LOC]

The locative denotes both location at a place (75) and direction or movement to a place (76–77).

(75) *ka mud̪ kim-a ma:j-ge-n*
2SG.NOM yesterday house-LOC NEG.be-PST-2SG
'You were not at home yesterday'

(76) *nu-ga: sab mud̪ kim-a bo-ke-oɳ*
3.PROX-PL all yesterday house-LOC go-PST-?
'They all went home yesterday'

(77) *gu bedʥa kʰaŋ-am-a bo-ke-k*
1SG.NOM seed buy-NMLZ-LOC go-PST-1SG
'I went to buy seeds'

Some adverbs also seem to historically contain the locative suffix: *du:r-a* [far-LOC]; *ʥa:b-a* [now-LOC].

A few place names take the locative marker *-e*. For example, *ʃiml-e* [p.name-LOC], *kulu-e* [p.name-LOC]. *-e* is mostly not permitted with common nouns (e.g. *skul-a* [school-LOC], **skul-e*; *kʰisaŋ-a* [pocket-LOC], **kʰisaŋ-e*; *ʈokri-a* [basket-LOC], **ʈokri-e*). There is, however, one instance where both locative markers *-a* and *-e* are permitted: *boʈuaŋ-a* ~ *boʈuaŋ-e* [purse-LOC].[9] In some cases the locative marker

9 The locative marker *-e* could possibly be due to IA influence. In Hindi, for instance, the noun appears in the non-nominative in *-e* when a locative marker follows (*baʈu-e mẽ* [purse-OBL LOC]).

is realized as [i]. For example, *mala:ɳa-e* [mala:ɳaji] 'in Malana', *ʃum-e-ʦ* [ʃumits] [three-LOC-ABL].[10]

The adaptive marker *-(V)ŋ* is retained when the locative marker is affixed to nouns with an adaptive marker.

(78) *deʃaŋ* 'village' : *deʃaŋ-a*
ga:ɽiŋ, ga:ɽi 'car, bus' : *ga:ɽiŋ-a*
kʰiraŋ 'milk' : *kʰiraŋ-a*
dili, diliŋ 'Delhi' : *diliŋ-a*
gra:maŋ 'village' : *gra:maŋ-a*
najiŋ 'river, ocean' : *najiŋ-a*

Distinct from this, there are some examples of plural nouns where the locative seems to be rendered as *-ŋa*. The following are all the examples of this type in our material. This is possibly due to reanalysis of locative forms of nouns with the adaptive marker *-(V)ŋ* – *-(V)ŋ-a* > *-a-ŋa* – and subsequent analogical extension of this pattern to other nouns.

(79) *mobajl-a* [mobile.phone-LOC] : *mobajl-a:-ŋa* [mobile.phone-PL-LOC]
pra:d-a [finger-LOC] : *pra:d-a:-ŋa* [finger-PL-LOC]

2.2.4.7 Ablative

The ablative case marker is *-ʦ*. It is also realized as *-s*, *-ʧ* and *-ʥ*. In some cases we find the same allomorph in all instances of a particular stem (e.g., [dudits], [duts], [duats] 'from him/her'; [mala:ɳiŋdz] 'from Malana'). But, in other cases, this is not the case, e.g. [aŋdits] ~ [aŋdiʧ] 'from me'.

The ablative case marker *-ʦ* is affixed to stems ending in consonants and those ending in vowels. It can be affixed directly to the noun or pronoun, or it can be affixed to a stem containing a noun or pronoun followed by adessive *-di* or the locative marker *-a*.

(80) *ɖabaŋ-ʦ* [box-ABL]
maŋɖi-ʦ [p.name-ABL]
bitiŋ-a-ʥ [wall-LOC-ABL]
dilli-ʦ [p.name-ABL]

10 The locative marker can occur on numerals when there is no explicit head noun.

mala:ɳiŋ-ʥ [p.name-ABL]

ʧamʧiŋ-a-ʦ [spoon-LOC-ABL]

ga:ɽiŋ-ʦ [river-ABL]

ni-ʧ [here-ABL]

u:-a-ʦ [flower-LOC-ABL]

ham-ʧ [who-ABL]

sa:laŋ-ʥ [year-ABL]

sima-di-ʦ [f.name-ADE-ABL]

kʰisaŋ-ʥ [pocket-ABL]

ta-ʦ [nose-ABL]

kartik-u-di-ʦ [m.name-POSS-ADE-ABL]

As we saw above *-ʦ* in Kanashi also functions as the diminutive marker. The ablative and the diminutive markers occur in two different slots: [N-DIM-PL-ABL]. But when *-ʦ* is suffixed directly to a noun stem (e.g. *ka:ʈʰi-ʦ* [mountain-ABL] or [mountain-DIM]), the word form is ambiguous. We do not have any example of ablative occurring with the diminutive or with plural head nouns.

2.2.4.8 Comitative

The comitative marker is *-raŋ*. The diminutive and plural markers precede the comitative marker (e.g. *ʧʰak-ʦ-raŋ* [boy-DIM-COM][11]). As elsewhere in Kanashi, the word-final consonant (*-ŋ* in the comitative marker *-raŋ*) is not always clearly audible (e.g. *ri:ŋdz-raŋ* [ri:ŋdzra] 'with sister'). *-raŋ* occurs both with proper nouns and with singular and plural animate and inanimate common nouns.

-raŋ as a comitative marker occurs in several ST languages of the Himalayas, but unlike some of these other ST languages (Kinnauri, Navakat), in Kanashi the *-r* in *-raŋ* is not assimilated to the preceding consonant.

(81) *da:l-raŋ* [lentil-COM]

maɽʃaŋ-raŋ [man-COM]

rameʃ-raŋ [m.name-COM]

kulpu-raŋ [m.name-COM]

11 This is the only example in our material of COM preceded by DIM. Note also, that all occurrences of *ʧʰak* 'boy' in our data have the diminutive marker.

pʰul-raŋ [cooked.rice-COM]

ri:ŋdz-raŋ [ri:ŋdzrã] [sister-COM]

lata:-raŋ [f.name-COM]

ra:m-raŋ [m.name-COM]

ʧara-ga:-raŋ [child-PL-COM]

With some proper nouns (masculine as well as feminine) which end in a consonant, the possessive marker *-u* occurs before the comitative marker (82), but there are also instances of consonant-final proper noun stems which occur without an intervening possessive marker *-u*, e.g., *ra:m-raŋ*, *rameʃ-raŋ* in (81). It is unclear what determines the occurrence of *-u* here.[12]

(82) *amar-u-raŋ* [m.name-POSS-COM]
kusum-u-raŋ [f.name-POSS-COM]
santoʃ-u-raŋ [f.name-POSS-COM]
anup-u-raŋ [m.name-POSS-COM]
mohan-u-raŋ [m.name-POSS-COM]
suraʤ-u-raŋ [f.name-POSS-COM]
apa:r-u-raŋ [m.name-POSS-COM]
punam-u-raŋ [f.name-POSS-COM]

As the following example illustrates, a NP may contain more than one comitative marker *-raŋ*.

(83) *gu pʰul-raŋ da:l-raŋ ho:ɖ ʥa:-ge-k*
1SG.NOM cooked.rice-COM lentils-COM roti eat-PST-1SG
'I ate roti with cooked rice and lentils'

-raŋ can sometimes be omitted, without any apparent difference in meaning.

(84) *ʧak-ʦ(-raŋ) ʧimeʦ bo-ke*
boy-DIM(-COM) girl go-PST
'The girl went with the boy'

The comitative marker *-raŋ* also functions as a subordinator where it is suffixed to the bare verb form of a non-final clause.

12 Possibly, we are dealing with IA influence: notice that this construction (N-POSS COM) is similar to the *ke s:atʰ* [POSS along] construction in Hindi. In Hindi too the possessive marker *ke* is optionally deleted.

(85) *dug-udʑ nark-da:n gek kubo:r bu-raŋ ma-ja-g*
3.DIST-DAT bad-temper became inside go-COM NEG-want.PST
'He became angry and refused to go in' (source: Konow 1909)

2.2.4.9 Adessive

In our material the adessive marker *-di* is attached either to a noun (proper and common) or to a pronoun. With common or proper noun stems ending in a consonant, a possessive marker (*-u*, *-ka*, *-n* or *-en*) occurs before the adessive marker. It is unclear what determines its occurrence.

(86) *an-en-di* [REFL-PL.POSS-ADE]
ba:-di [father-ADE]
hendu-di [m.name-ADE]
indru-di-ts [m.name-ADE-ABL]
kartik-u-di [m.name-POSS-ADE]
kartik-u-di-ts [m.name-POSS-ADE-ABL]
maɽʃaŋ-ka-di [man-POSS-ADE]
sima-di-ts [f.name-ADE-ABL]
sipahis-u-di [soldier-POSS-ADE]
tʃʰak-ka-di [boy-POSS-ADE]

As seen in the examples above, *-di* can be followed by the ablative marker *-ts*. In our material *du-di* [3.DIST-ADE] and *aŋ-di* [1SG-ADE] can be replaced in some contexts with *du-ka* [3.DIST-POSS] and *aka* [1SG.POSS] respectively.

2.3 Pronouns

Pronouns do not have inherent gender and honorificity distinctions. Like nouns, they inflect for number (singular and plural) and case.

2.3.1 Demonstrative pronouns

The demonstrative pronouns in Kanashi are: *du* [DEM.DIST], *nu* [DEM.PROX] and their corresponding plural forms (*du-ga:* [DEM.DIST-PL], *nu-ga:* [DEM.PROX-PL]).

(87) *du* *kursi*
DEM.DIST chair
'that chair'

(88) *nu* *kuta:b sastas to*
DEM.PROX book cheap be.PRS
'This book is cheap'

(89) *nu-ga:* *niʃ mi-s* *ʤa:-ge*
DEM.PROX-PL two man-ERG eat-PST
'These two men ate'

The demonstrative pronouns also function as third person personal pronouns.

2.3.2 Personal pronouns

2.3.2.1 The set of personal pronouns

The personal pronouns in Kanashi are the following:

	SG	PL
1	*gu* (NOM) *aŋ* (NNOM/POSS) *aka* (POSS)	*ette* (INCL) *ni* (EXCL.NOM) *niŋ-* (EXCL.NNOM)
2	*ka*	*ki*
3	*du* (3.DIST) *nu* (3.PROX)	*du-ga:* (3.DIST-PL) *nu-ga:* (3.PROX-PL)

An exclusive-inclusive distinction is made in the first person plural pronouns. Further, some personal pronouns have distinct nominative and non-nominative forms. The analysis presented here is consistent with Konow's description (Konow 1909: 444), except that Konow does not mention the inclusive-exclusive distinction. He glosses *ni* as 'first person plural'.

Sharma (1992: 349) provides the following as honorific pronouns: "/ki/ you (pl and hon.)", "/duš/ he (hon.)", "/du gəš/ they (hon.)", "/nu gəš/ those (hon.)". This is not corroborated in our material. Pragmatically, however, the choice of pronoun conveys (dis)respect. The use of the plural pronoun form for a singular referent conveys respect, and the use of a singular pronoun form for a plural referent conveys disrespect.

As shown in the table above, the first person singular pronoun allomorphs in Kanashi are: *gu* (NOM), *aŋ* (NNOM/POSS) and *aka* (POSS). The last-mentioned could conceivably be analyzed as *a-ka* [1SG-POSS], but will be glossed unanalyzed as *aka* [1SG.POSS] in this chapter.[13]

gu occurs in the subject position in copular, transitive and intransitive clauses in all tenses and aspects. It never takes the ergative marker.

(90) *naliŋ gu ʥimida:r tot-ke-k*
last.year 1SG.NOM farmer be-PST-1SG
'Last year I was a farmer'

(91) *gu ʃiml-e tot-k*
1SG.NOM p.name-LOC be.PRS-1SG
'I am in Shimla'

(92) *gu pʰul-raŋ a:l-raŋ ho:ɖ ʥa:-ge-k*
1SG.NOM cooked.rice-COM lentils-COM bread eat-PST-1SG
'I ate bread with cooked rice and lentils'

(93) *gu du-ga:-p roʥ ta-gu-ta-k*
1SG.NOM 3.DIST-PL-ACC daily look-PROG-NPST-1SG
'I am watching them every day'

(94) *gu na:b ka:m-ga: ʃaʈ-ta-k*
1SG.NOM tomorrow work-PL do-NPST-1SG
'I will work tomorrow'

aŋ occurs in non-nominative positions. For example, it occurs with the accusative, dative, ablative and comitative case markers.

(95) *aŋ-ʥ ʃabɽi pasand to*
1SG-DAT meat liking(N) be.PRS
'I like meat'

(96) *pʰakuʧ boi-ʦ aŋ-raŋ soaraŋ bore-ke*
small sibling-DIM 1SG-COM p.name go-PST
'The younger sibling went with me to Kullu'

13 While *-ka* is a bona fide possessive morph in Kanashi, the remainder (*a-*) does not occur anywhere else in the 1SG paradigm. As with other vowel-final words, *aka* is sometimes realized as *ak*, with apocope.

It also occurs in possessive constructions, but without the possessive marker.

(97) *aŋ ja:-s aŋ-ʥ ʈaka ken-ke*
1SG.NNOM mother-ERG 1SG-DAT money give.1/2O-PST
'My mother gave money to me'

aŋ occurs frequently with *-di* [-ADE]:

(98) *aŋ-di iːd kim to*
1SG-ADE one house be.PRS
'I have a house'

(99) *aŋ-di bais kʰ-a: to-ʃ*
1SG-ADE twenty.two sheep-PL be.PRS-3PL
'I have twenty-two sheep'

(100) *indru aŋ-di ʧobbi ʤaʈe-ga: naʃ-ta*
m.name 1SG-ADE twenty.four day-PL stay-NPST
'Indru stays with me for twenty-four days'

While case markers are regularly suffixed to *aŋ* (except possessive markers; see below), there are also instances where there is no overt case marker.[14]

(101) *aŋ som kula:r ken to-ʃ*
1SG.NNOM morning breakfast give.1/2O BE.PRS-3PL
'In the morning (they) give me breakfast'

(102) *om-a santoʃ-is aŋ ʤinɖije pʰon-a ʃed-mug*
path-LOC f.name-ERG 1SG.NNOM much phone-LOC send-PST.3
'On the way Santosh called me many times (she sent me on phone)'

aŋ also occurs in the "dative subject construction", with or without the dative case marker (see also Section 4.3).

(103) *aŋ-ʥ=i sauda-ga: ʃobilas lag-e-ta*
1SG-DAT=EMP candy-PL good feel-INTR-NPST
'I like sweets'

14 These cases coincide with those where we would have expected to see a dative/objective-marked argument in some other South Asian languages, possibly pointing to an earlier stage of Kanashi.

(104) *aŋ* *du* *kamra ʤiŋ lag*
1SG.NNOM DEM.DIST room big feel
'That room felt big to me'

As the following examples illustrate, in possessive constructions both *aka* and *aŋ* are found. They occur in different contexts, however.

(105) *aka* *ba:*
1SG.POSS father
'my father'

(106) *aka* *niʃ kim-a:* *to-ʃ*
1SG.POSS two house-PL be.PRS-3PL
'(I) have two houses'

(107) *aŋ-di* *niʃ kim-a:* *to-ʃ*
1SG-ADE two house-PL be.PRS-3PL
'(I) have/near me there are two houses'

It seems that while both *aka* and *aŋ* can occur with animate head nouns – both *aka ba:* and *aŋ ba:* 'my father' are acceptable – only *aka* is permitted with inanimate head nouns. For example, according to our language consultants, *aka laʈpaʈa-ga:* 'my clothes', *aka bu:ʈ-a:* 'my shoes' *ak beg* 'my bag', *aka ro:ɖ* 'my ear' are acceptable, but not **aŋ laʈpaʈa-ga:*, **aŋ beg* or **aŋ ro:ɖ*.

aka occurs with both singular and plural head nouns, as well as animate and inanimate head nouns.

(108) *aka ba:* 'my father'
aka ja: 'my mother'
ak ʃo 'my field'
ak ʃo-ga: 'my fields'

The NP containing *aka* does not seem to be sensitive to the grammatical relation it occurs in. In the following examples the NP containing *aka* occurs in the subject and direct-object positions as well as in non-agentive constructions.

(109) *aka* *ja:ba* *dilli* *naʃ-is*
1SG.POSS parents p.name sit-PFV
'My parents live in Delhi'

(110) *ka* *aka* *help^h ʃa-ʈ^h*
2SG.NOM 1SG.POSS help do-IMP
'You, (please,) help me!'

(111) *ak parset da-k ??*
1SG.POSS sweat fall-?
'I got sweaty'

(112) *ak battis ga:r-a:*
1SG.POSS thirty.two tooth-PL
'my thirty-two teeth'

(113) *ak bari-ʦ deʃaŋ-a:*
1SG.POSS much-DIM village-PL
'my many villages'

As with *aka*, *aŋ* as a possessive pronoun occurs in NPs in various grammatical relations.

(114) *aŋ ba: ba:saʈʰ sa:laŋ-ʦ to*
1SG.POSS father sixty.two year-DIM be.PRS
'My father is sixty-two years old'

(115) *gu aŋ ja:-uʤ pʰon ʃan-me-k*
1SG.NOM 1SG.POSS mother-DAT phone do-PST-1SG
'I phoned my mother'

(116) *du aŋ na:na:-raŋ naʃi to*
3.DIST 1SG.POSS m.grandfather-COM stay BE.PRS
'S/He lives with my maternal grandfather'

(117) *aka/aŋ-di niʃ kim-a: to-ʃ*
1SG.POSS/1SG-ADE two house-PL be.PRS-3PL
'I have two houses'

The second person singular pronoun is *ka*. It occurs in both subject and non-subject positions. Just as with the first person singular pronoun, the second person singular pronoun, too, never takes the ergative marker. In other non-nominative positions, *ka* optionally takes the relevant case marker.

(118) *ka ʃobilas madras to-n*
2SG.NOM good man be.PRS-2SG
'You are a good man'

(119) *ka muḍ kim-a ma:j-ge-n*
2SG.NOM yesterday house-LOC NEG.be-PST-2SG
'You were not at home yesterday'

(120) *ka ʥa:-mi raɳ-me-n*
2SG.NOM eat-NMLZ give-PST-2SG
'You gave (someone) food'

(121) *ra:m-us ka-ʥ poʈo ken-ke*
m.name-ERG 2SG-DAT fruit give.1/2O-PST
'Ram gave you fruit'

ka sometimes is used for second person plural referents. First, in constructions where it is followed by *sab* 'all'. For example:

(122) *gu ka-p sab-u ta-gu-ta-n*
1SG.NOM 2SG-ACC all-ACC watch-PROG-NPST-?
'I am watching all of you'

Secondly, as mentioned above, the use of the singular pronoun form for plural referents indicates disrespect.

In the possessive construction *ka* obligatorily takes the suffix *-n*, which may then be followed by the additional possessive marker *-ka*. *ka-n* and *ka-n-ka* seem to be in free variation.

(123) *ka-n/ka-n-ka kim*
2SG-POSS/2SG-POSS-POSS house
'your house'

(124) *gu ka-n sa:mna bagʋa:n sa:mna kasu:r ʃaɳ-mug*
1SG.NOM 2SG-POSS in.front god in.front sin do-PST.3
'I have sinned in front of you, in front of god' (Konow)

(125) *ka-n-ka kim ham to*
2SG-POSS-POSS house where be.PRS
'Where is your house'

The demonstrative pronouns *du* and *nu* function as third person singular pronouns, where they retain their semantic distinction: *du* has a distant interpretation, while *nu* has a proximate interpretation.[15] They occur in copula construc-

15 Sharma (1992) describes *nu* as distant and not as proximate.

tions, in intransitive and transitive clauses with both masculine and feminine referents. Unlike the first and second person singular pronouns, third person singular pronouns take the ergative marker.

(126) *du/nu* *daʈʰis ʧara*
3.DIST/3.PROX good child
'S/He is a good child'

(127) *du/nu* *kim-a* *maːj*
3.DIST/3.PROX home-LOC NEG.be.3SG
'S/He is not at home'

(128) *du-di/du-ka* *niʃ=i* *kim-aː* *to-ʃ*
3.DIST-ADE/3.DIST-POSS two=EMP house-PL be.PRS-3PL
'S/He has two houses'

(129) *du* *bo-ke*
3.DIST go-PST
'S/He went'

(130) *nu-s* *an-u-ka* *ʧime-p* *aːɽe-mug*
3.PROX-ERG REFL-SG-POSS girl-ACC call-PST.3
'S/He called her/his daughter'

(131) *nu-p* *sa-t-o*
DEM.PROX-ACC kill-IMP-M
'Kill this one!'

(132) *pʰaːkuʧ boi-ʦ* *nu-raŋ* *soaraŋ* *bo-ke*
little y.sibling-DIM 3.PROX-COM p.name go-PST
'The child went with him/her to Kullu'

The possessive form *du(-n)-k(a)* occurs with both alienable and inalienable head nouns, with both masculine and feminine head nouns and with singular as well as plural head nouns.

(133) *du-n-ka* *daːdi* *baːsaʈʰ* *saːlaŋ-ʥ to*
3.DIST-POSS-POSS p.grandmother sixty.two year-ABL be.PRS
'His/her paternal grandmother is sixty-two years old'

(134) *du-n-ka* *dil-a* *binḍra* *to*
3.DIST-POSS-POSS heart-LOC pain be.PRS
'There is pain in his heart'

(135) *du-n-ka* *kʰas* *voʃ* *to*
3.DIST-POSS-POSS sheep hunger be.PRS
'His sheep is hungry'

The grammatical role of the NP in which POSS occurs does not affect the choice of the POSS markers.

(136) *du-ka* *mig-a:* *pʰak-e* *to-ʃ*
3.DIST-POSS eye-PL small-PL be.PRS-3PL
'His eyes are small'

(137) *du-ka* *pʰa:kuʧ* *ʧʰo* *krab-ku-ta*
3.DIST-POSS small child cry-PROG-NPST
'His younger child is crying'

(138) *nu* *du-ka/du-n-ka* *gaɽi* *to*
DEM.PROX 3.DIST-POSS/3.DIST-POSS-POSS watch be.PRS
'This is his watch'

(139) *du-ka* *ta-ʦ* *kʰui* *dva-ta*
3.DIST-POSS nose-ABL blood come.out-NPST
'Blood comes out of his nose'

ette functions as the 1PLI pronoun. In our material it occurs as subject in copular and transitive clauses, but unfortunately we do not have any examples of an intransitive clause with a first person plural inclusive pronoun subject.

(140) *ette* *naliŋ* *ʥimida:r-a:* *ma:j-ke-muk*
1PLI last.year farmer-PL NEG.be-PST-1PLI
'Last year we were not farmers'

(141) *ette* *kamraŋ-a* *ton-muk* [tonmo]
1PLI room-LOC be.PRS-1PLI
'We are in the room'

(142) *ette* *sab* *beʈiŋ* *ʈaŋ-ta-muk*
1PLI all tree climb-NPST-1PLI
'All of us will climb the tree'

(143) *ette-n-ka ba:*
1PLI-POSS-POSS father
'our father'

(144) *ette-n-ka kim*
1PLI-POSS-POSS house
'our house'

There is one example in our material where *ette* takes the ergative marker:

(145) *na:b ette-s buʃame tam*
tomorrow 1PLI-ERG ? ?
'We will relax tomorrow'

sab 'all' sometimes follows this pronoun. In the following example, *sab* takes the case marker, but not *ette*.

(146) *ette(j) sab-us an-e-p arʃug-a taŋ-me-muk*
1PLI all-ERG REFL-PL-ACC mirror-LOC look-PST-1PLI
'All of us looked at ourselves in the mirror'

The first person plural exclusive pronoun in Kanashi has two main allomorphs: *ni* and *niŋ-*. *ni* occurs in the nominative case as subject in copular, intransitive and transitive clauses. We have no examples of the first person plural exclusive pronoun with an ergative marker.

(147) *ni ʧ^{h}aŋ-ʦ-a: to-ŋ*
1PLE boy-DIM-PL be.PRS-1/2PL
'We are boys'

(148) *ni niraŋ t^{h}epar bo-ku-ta-ŋ*
1PLE p.name p.name go-PROG-NPST-1/2PL
'We are going to Nirang and Thepar'

(149) *ni ka:m-a:/ka:maŋ-a: ʃa-ta-ŋ*
1PLE work-PL do-NPST-1/2PL
'We will do the work'

(150) *ni ʦ^{h}ol-a latpaʈ-a:-p mi-ʧi-me-ŋ*
1PLE waterfall-LOC garment-PL-ACC NEG-wash-PST-1/2PL
'We did not wash clothes in the waterfall'

ni only takes the possessive marker *-ka*. It occurs with animate and inanimate head nouns, singular as well as plural head nouns.

(151) *ni-ka kim*
1PLE-POSS house
'our house'

(152) *ni-ka ba:*
1PLE-POSS father
'our father'

(153) *ni-ka hu:ʤ-u-ka ʈʰuʈʰre tegje la:mas*
1PLE-POSS cow-POSS-POSS tail very long
'Our cow has a very long tail'

(154) *ni-ka ʤaŋ sab-a(s) teg*
1PLE-POSS god all-INS great
'our god is the greatest'

(155) *nu-ga: ni-ka na:ʈa-ga: to-ʃ*
3.PROX-PL 1PLE-POSS relative-PL be.PRS-3PL
'They are our relatives'

In the remaining non-nominative positions, *niŋ-* [1PLE.NNOM] occurs. This is a bound stem form, always followed by a case suffix, as indicated by the "-".

(156) *gopal-us niŋ-p ta-ge-kuk ??*
m.name-ERG 1PLE-ACC look-PST-?
'Gopal saw us'

(157) *gopal-us niŋ-ʥ sab seʋ poʈo keni-ke*
m.name-ERG 1PLE-DAT all apple vegetable/fruit give.1/2O-PST
'Gopal gave us apples'

(158) *niŋ-ʥ ti-ka kam=i*
1PLE-DAT water-POSS shortage=EMP
'We do have a shortage of water'

ki functions as the second person plural pronoun. It occurs in both nominative and non-nominative positions. There are no instances of *ki* in the ergative, even though there are transitive clauses with second person plural subjects in our material.

(159) *ki ʧʰaŋ-ʦ-a: to-ŋ*
2PL boy-DIM-PL be.PRS-2PL
'You (PL) are boys'

(160) *ki mud̪ kim-a ma:j-ge-ŋ*
2PL yesterday house-LOC NEG.be-PST-2PL
'You (PL) were not at home yesterday'

(161) *gopal-us ki-p ta-ge-kuk ??*
m.name-ERG 2PL-ACC look-PST-?
'Gopal saw you'

(162) *gopal-us ki-ʥ sev pot̪o keni-ke*
m.name-ERG 2PL-DAT apple vegetable/fruit give.1/2O-PST
'Gopal gave you apples'

At times, *sab* 'all' follows the pronoun. As the following examples illustrate, the case marker can be suffixed either to each element of an NP or only to the last element of the NP.

(163) *ki-n-ka sab-ka kim*
2PL-POSS-POSS all-POSS house
'the house(s) of all of you'

(164) *du-ga: sab-us ʥa:-ta-ʃ*
3.DIST-PL all-ERG eat-NPST-3PL
'All of them (will) eat'

(165) *ki sab lok-a:-ʃ an-e-p arʃug-a taŋ-me-ŋ*
2PL all person-PL-ERG REFL-PL-ACC mirror-LOC look-PST-2PL
'All you people looked at yourselves in the mirror'

du-ga: and *nu-ga:* function as third person plural pronouns. As in the singular, *du-ga:* has a distant interpretation, while *nu-ga:* indicates proximity. They take the ergative marker.

(166) *du-ga: ʥimida:r-a: to-ʃ*
3.DIST-PL farmer-PL be.PRS-3PL
'They are farmers'

(167) *du-ga: malaɳi-ʦ*
3.DIST-PL p.name-ABL
'They are from Malana'

Table 10: The personal pronouns: attested case forms

SG	**1**		**2**	**3**
NOM	*gu*		*ka*	*nu* (3.PROX), *du* (3.DIST)
ERG(/INS)	*gu*		*ka*	*nu-s*, *du-s*
ACC	*aŋ*, *aŋ-p*, *aŋ-u-p*		*ka-p*	*nu-p*, *du-p*
DAT	*aŋ-ʥ*		*ka-ʥ*	*nu-ʥ*, *du-ʥ*
POSS	*aŋ* (NNOM), *aka*		*ka-n*, *ka-n-ka* (POSS-POSS)	*nu-ka*, *du-ka*, *du-n-ka* (POSS-POSS)
LOC	–		–	*nu-a*
ABL	*aŋ-ʦ*		*ka-ʦ*, *ka-n-ʦ* (POSS-ABL)	*du-ʦ*
LOC-ABL	–		–	*du-a-ʦ*
COM	*aŋ-raŋ*		–	*nu-raŋ*, *du-raŋ*
ADE	*aŋ-di*		–	*nu-di*, *du-di*
ADE-ABL	*aŋ-di-ʦ*		–	*du-di-ʦ*
PL	**1PLI**	**1PLE**	**2**	**3**
NOM	*ette*	*ni*	*ki*	*nu-ga:*, *du-ga:*
ERG(/INS)	*ette-s*	–	–	*nu-ga:-s*, *du-ga:-s*
ACC	–	*niŋ-p*	*ki-p*	*nu-ga:-p*, *du-ga:-p*
DAT	–	*niŋ-ʥ*	*ki-ʥ*	*nu-ga:-uʥ*, *du-ga:-uʧ*, *du-ga:-uʥ*
POSS	*ette-n-ka* (POSS-POSS)	*ni-ka*	*ki-n-ka* (POSS-POSS)	*du-ga:-ka*, *du-ga:-n-ka* (POSS-POSS)
LOC	–	–	–	–
ABL	–	–	–	–
LOC-ABL	–	–	–	–
COM	–	*niŋ-raŋ*	–	–
ADE	–	*niŋ-di*	–	*du-ga:-n-di* (POSS-ADE)
ADE-ABL	–	–	–	–

(168) *nu-ga:* *sab* *muɖ* *kim-a* *bo-ke-oɳ* *??*
3.PROX-PL all yesterday house-LOC go-PST-?
'They all went home yesterday'

(169) *gu* *du-ga:-p* *taŋ-me-k-oɳ* *??*
1SG.NOM 3.DIST-PL-ACC look-PST-1SG-?
'I looked at them'

(170) *du-ga:-s* *ʥa:-gja*
3.DIST-PL-ERG eat-PST.3
'They ate'

du-ga: and *nu-ga:* occur also in the dative subject construction (see also Section 4.3).

(171) *du-ga:-uʥ sardi la-ke*
3.DIST-PL-DAT cold feel-PST
'They had a cold'

With the ergative, accusative and possessive markers, the pronoun form remains the same (i.e., *du-ga:*, *nu-ga:*). But the final vowel of the plural suffix is often deleted when the dative case marker is affixed: *du-ga:-uʧ* ([duguʧʃ] ~ [dugaoʧʃ]) ~ *du-ga:-ʥ* [duguʥ] ~ *du-ga:-ʤ* [duguʤ].

2.3.2.2 Personal pronouns: case forms

Table 10 provides summary paradigms (of forms attested in our data; unattested forms are indicated by "—") for the personal pronouns in Kanashi.

2.3.3 Interrogative pronouns and adverbs

what, which	*ʧʰu*, *ʧʰupe* [which-ACC-PL], *ʧʰuge* [what-?PL] (Konow 1909: 444: "*chhuge*, what?")
where	*ham*
who	*hat(e)* (Konow 1909: 444: "*hate*, who? *hase*, by whom? *hat-ka*, whose? *hate ditse* from whom?")
when	*ʧʰub(a)*
why	*kʰue* (Konow 1909: 444: "*kwe*, why?")
how	*hale(s)* (Konow 1909: 444: "*hole*, how?"), *hane*
how much, how many	*tada*

(172) *ka ʧʰub-a boŋ-ta-n*
2SG.NOM when-LOC go-NPST-2SG
'When will you go?'

(173) *ka ʤo kʰue bara-ke-n*
2SG.NOM down.south why come-PST-2SG
'Why did you come down south?'

(174) *ka ʧa hale-s ʃaŋ-me-n*
2SG.NOM tea how-INS make-PST-2SG
'How did you make tea?'

(175) *ka* *ham-e* *to-n*
2SG.NOM where-LOC be.PRS-2SG
'Where are you?'

(176) *nu* *tʃʰu* *to*
DEM.PROX what be.3SG
'What is this?'

The interrogative pronouns appear *in situ.* While in most instances the WH-interrogative clauses have the same finite verb forms as affirmatives, there is one example in our material where the polar question suffix *-a* is affixed to the verb:

(177) *ka* *ʥa:b-a* *ham* *bo-ku-ta-n-a*
2SG.NOM now-LOC where go-PROG-NPST-2SG-Q
'Where are you going now?'

When the emphatic discourse marker *=i* is affixed to interrogative pronouns they function as indefinite pronouns. For example,

(178) *ɖaba hat=i* *mo-to-ta-ʃ*
then who=EMP NEG-be-NPST-3PL
'Then no-one will be (there)'

IA *koi* also occurs in our material, as an indefinite pronoun 'some', but not as an interrogative pronoun. But unlike IA languages, *koi* can take a plural marker (*-ge*) in Kanashi: *koi-ge naʃi-ge* 'some stayed'

2.3.4 Reflexive pronouns

The reflexive pronoun is *an*. Distinct from the personal pronouns which normally have external reference, the reflexive pronoun co-refers within the current discourse, either to an explicit NP (with a nominal or pronominal head) or a person index on a verb, in the (typically preceding) context. Its main usage is as a reflexive for all persons,[16] although in 1SG the regular personal pronominal form *aŋup*

16 In contrast, Kinnauri and Tinani display the more typical ST pattern: reflexivity in Kinnauri is either expressed by using the detransitivizing morpheme *-ʃ(i)* on the verb, or by means of reflexive pronouns, which inflect for number and person. With regard to the reflexive pronouns in Kanashi, Kinnauri and Tinani, they form a continuum, where Kanashi has almost an invariant form for reflexives, while in Kinnauri we find somewhat more variant forms and in Tinani mostly variant forms.

alternates with *anup*. In almost all instances it either has an *-u* (with singular arguments) or an *-e* (with plural arguments), to which the relevant case marker is suffixed. In reflexive usage it carries the accusative marker *-p* as shown in Table 11 and (179–184).

Table 11: The reflexive pronoun in Kanashi

	SG	PL
1	*an-u-p (aŋ-u-p)*	*an-e-p* (EXCL/INCL)
2	*an-u-p*	*an-e-p*
3	*an(-u-p)*	*an-e-p*

(179) *gu aŋ-u-p/an-u-p taŋ-me-k*
1SG-NOM 1SG-SG-ACC/REFL-SG-ACC look-PST-1SG
'I saw myself'

(180) *ette sab-us an-e(-p) arʃuk-a taŋ-me-muk*
1PLI all-ERG REFL-PL(-ACC) mirror-LOC look-PST-1PLI
'We all looked at ourselves in the mirror'

(181) *ka an-u-p arʃuk-a taŋ-me-n*
2SG.NOM REFL-SG-ACC mirror-LOC look-PST-2SG
'You looked at youself in the mirror'

(182) *ki: (sab) lok-a:-s an-e-p arʃuk-a taŋ-me-n*
2PL (all) person-PL-ERG REFL-PL-ACC mirror-LOC look-PST-2SG
'You (people) looked at yourselves in the mirror'

(183) *monika-s an-u-p arʃuk-a taŋ-mug*
f.name-ERG REFL-SG-ACC mirror-LOC look-PST.3
'Monika looked at herself in the mirror'

(184) *sab ʧara-ga:-s an-e(-p) arʃuk-a ta-ge*
all child-PL-ERG REFL-PL(-ACC) mirror-LOC look-PST
'All children looked at themselves in the mirror'

Reflexivity and reciprocity are also indicated by using the middle voice marker (*-ʃ(i)*) on the verb (see Section 3.1.1).

The other case forms of *an* found in our data are *an-e-n-ka* [REFL-PL-POSS-POSS], *an-e-n-di* [anindi/anendi] [REFL-PL-POSS-ADE], *an-u* [REFL-POSS], *an-u-ka* [REFL-SG-POSS] (or [REFL-POSS-POSS]) and *an-u-ʤ* [REFL-SG-DAT].

(185) *an-u-ʤ lapta-p kʰaŋ-t*
REFL-SG-DAT garment-ACC buy-IMP
'Buy some clothes for yourself!'

(186) *du-s an-u-ka guɖ-as kim gaɳ-mug*
3.DIST-ERG REFL-SG-POSS hand-INS house build-PST.3
'He built his house with his own hands'

(187) *mohan-as an-u ja:-uʧ ʈaka raɳ-mug*
m.name-ERG REFL-POSS mother-DAT money give-PST.3
'Mohan gave money to his (=Mohan's) mother'

There is one instance where *du* occurs in place of the third person singular reflexive pronoun *an*:

(188) *du du-ka ja:-raŋ naʃi-m ʃobilas dan-ta*
3.DIST 3.DIST-POSS mother-COM stay-INF beautiful fall-NPST
'He likes to stay with his mother'

an(-u) also functions as an emphatic pronoun, in apposition to an immediately preceding NP. As usual in this construction, number and case marking can occur either on the last NP (as in 189) or on both NPs.

(189) *ka an-u-s lon-me-n*
2SG.NOM REFL-SG-ERG tell-PST-2SG
'You yourself told (me this)'

2.4 Adjectives

In Kanashi adjectives prototypically occur as modifiers of explicit head nouns (190) or as predicates in adjectival copula constructions (191). In these structural positions they can show agreement inflection, agreeing in number and gender with their head noun.

(190) *jug ba:ʥi / ʃobilas biɳiʃ / pʰakuʧ bakar*
just.cooked vegetable / beautiful husband / small goat
'freshly cooked vegetable' / 'beautiful husband' / 'small/younger goat'

(191) *nu kuta:b sastas to*
DEM.PROX book cheap be.PRS
'This book is cheap'

Adjectives used as modifiers stand before their head noun. A systematic exception to this is exhibited in a (multi-word) noun-formation pattern characteristic of a number of kinship terms showing the order N–Adj (see Section 2.2.1.1), although there are also lexicalized multi-word kinship terms with adjectives preceding the head noun:

(192) *p^{h}akutʃ bau-ts / p^{h}akutʃ ri:ŋ-dʑ*
small brother-DIM / small sister-DIM
'younger brother' / 'younger sister'

(193) *teg bau / teg ri:ŋ-dʑ*
big brother / big sister-DIM
'older brother' / 'older sister'

A noun phrase may contain more than one adjective.

(194) *tegje himt roʈ^{h}as munuk*
very courageous brave man
'very courageous, brave man'

(195) *tegje himt-a:* [himda:] *roʈ^h-a: munuk-a:*
very courageous-PL brave-PL man-PL
'very courageous, brave men'

(196) *jug tʃ^{h}og* [tʃ^{h}ɔk] *kim*
new white house
'new white house'

(197) *jug-e tʃ^{h}og-e* [tʃ^{h}ɔke] *p^{h}akuts-e kim-a:*
new-PL white-PL small-PL house-PL
'new white small houses'

2.4.1 Adjective agreement and independent inflection

In earlier descriptions of Kanashi, Konow (1909: 443) notes that number agreement occurs, while Sharma (1992: 353) classifies adjectives as "belong[ing] to the undeclinable class of words".

On the basis of our fieldwork data, we find that adjectives in Kanashi may agree with their head noun in number (SG–PL) and gender (M–F). We distinguish the following four inflectional classes of Kanashi adjectives:

1. indeclinable (one form);
2. agreeing in number only (two forms: singular and plural);
3. agreeing in number, and in the plural also in gender (three forms: singular, masculine plural, and feminine plural); and
4. agreeing fully in number and gender (four forms: masculine singular, feminine singular, masculine plural, and feminine plural).

As mentioned in Section 2.2.3, the gender system of Kanashi nouns is partial in that only a relatively small number of animate nouns can be said to participate in it. In other cases adjectives in category 3 and 4 will occur in the "masculine" form.

The indeclinable category 1 comprises both mono- and polysyllabic adjectives and both native and borrowed items, e.g. *sust* 'lazy', *polak* 'strong'. It also includes perfective and habitual verb forms used as participles (see below).

Adjectives in category 2 behave like nouns with regard to their plural formation. The attested plural endings are *-(g)aː* and *-e*. It is unclear what determines their distribution. See Table 12. In two instances both plural markers *-aː* and *-e* are possible: *rag-aː*, *rag-e* [green-PL]; *ʧits-aː*, *ʧits-e* [wet-PL].

Table 12: Adjectives in category 2

SG	PL	SG	PL
ʤaŋts ʧimets 'weak girl'	*ʤaŋts-aː ʧimets-aː*	*seʈ munuk* 'rich man'	*seʈ-aː munuk-aː*
ʤaŋts ʧʰakts 'weak boy'	*ʤaŋts-aː ʧʰakts-aː*	*seʈ beʈaɽi* 'rich woman'	*seʈ-aː beʈaɽi-gaː*
juʃk ʧara 'big child'	*juʃk-e ʧara-gaː*	*rok beʈaɽi* 'black woman'	*rok-e beʈaɽi-gaː*

Adjectives in category 3 exhibit different plural forms depending on the gender of the head noun, where *-e* occurs with masculine head nouns and *-aː* occurs with feminine plural head nouns, e.g. *ʧʰog* 'white, fair-skinned'. See Table 13.

In adjectives in category 4, the masculine and feminine plural adjectival forms are built on the gendered singular forms, i.e. if an adjective inflects for feminine singular, the corresponding plural form is made by affixing the plural marker to the feminine (singular) form [Adj-F-PL], and correspondingly for the masculine forms. As can be seen in the examples provided in Table 14, in contrast to ad-

Table 13: Adjectives in category 3

SG	PL	SG	PL
ʧʰog madras 'white man'	*ʧʰog-e madr-a:*	*ʧʰog beʈaɽi* 'white woman'	*ʧʰog-a: beʈaɽi-ga:*

jectives with masculine head nouns, a range of inflectional strategies occur with feminine head nouns. With feminine head nouns, the following strategies are found for adjectives ending in *-as*. It is unclear what determines the distribution of the various feminine suffixes on adjectives.

Table 14: Adjectives in category 4

SG	PL	SG	PL
ka:ɳ-as madras 'blind man'	*ka:ɳ-a: madr-a:*	*ka:ɳ beʈaɽi* 'blind woman'	*ka:ɳ-e beʈaɽi-ga:*
moʈʰ-as ʧʰakts 'fat young man'	*moʈʰ-a: ʧʰakts-a:*	*moʈ-eɳ beʈaɽi* 'fat woman'	*moʈ-eɳ-a: beʈaɽi-ga:*
buɽ-as munuk 'old man'	*buɽ-a: munuk-a:*	*buɽ-its beʈaɽi* 'old woman'	*buɽ-its-a: beʈaɽi-ga:*
roʈʰ-as munuk 'brave man'	*roʈʰ-a: munuk-a:*	*roʈʰ-ar beʈaɽi* 'brave woman'	*roʈʰ-ar-a: ~ roʈʰ-ar-e beʈaɽi-ga:*
ʃobil-as biɳiʃ 'beautiful husband'	*ʃobil-a: biɳiʃ-a:*	*ʃobil, ʃobilas beʈaɽi* 'beautiful woman'	*ʃobil-e beʈaɽi-ga:*
matsl-is ʧaŋts 'lazy boy'	*matsil ʧaŋts-a:*	*matsl-en beʈaɽi* 'lazy woman'	*matsl-en-e beʈaɽi-ga:*

As these examples show, many IA-origin adjectives in Kanashi have the adaptive marker *-(V)s* (as also some nouns; see Section 2.2.1.1). In these adjectives the adaptive marker *-as* is almost always deleted and the plural ending *-a:* is suffixed to the remainder. See Table 15. As they normally also have a distinct feminine form, the *-(V)s* element could be treated as the masculine marker, and has been marked as such in the above examples. There is only one adjective in our material where the *-(V)s* is retained when the plural marker *-a:* is added (*ʥuniŋas-a:* [difficult-PL]).

There are a few adjectives where the gender distinction is made in Kanashi by the choice of the suffix *-a* (M) or *-i* (F). See Table 16. Note that almost all the adjectives of this set are of IA origin. In a number of IA languages, the gender distinction is also made by *-a* and *-i*. This set of adjectives takes the plural marker *-ga:* with masculine and feminine head nouns. These adjectives (frequently) occur without a head noun.

Table 15: Adjectives with the adaptive marker *-(V)s*

SG	PL	SG	PL
la:mas ʧʰakts 'tall y.man'	*la:m-a: ʧʰakts-a:*	*uʈʰras ka:ʈʰi* 'high mountain'	*uʈʰr-a: ka:ʈʰi-ga:*
miʈʰas seʊ 'sweet apple'	*miʈʰ-a: seʊ-a:*	*ma:gas ʧiʤ* 'expensive thing'	*ma:g-a: ʧiʤ-a:*

Table 16: Adjectives with the adaptive marker *-(V)s*

SG	PL	SG	PL
nagɽij-a munuk [poor-M man]	*nagɽij-a-ga: munuk-a:*	*nagɽij-i/-e/-en beʈaɽi* [poor-F woman]	*nagɽij-en-a: beʈaɽi-ga:*
kubek-a munuk [stingy-M man]	*kubek-a-ga: munuk-a:*	*kubek-i beʈaɽi* [stingy-F girl]	*kubek-i-ga: beʈaɽi-ga:*
naɳʈ-a ʧara [naked-M child]	*naɳʈa-ga: ʧara-ga:*	*naɳʈ-i ʧara* [naked-F child]	*naɳʈ-i-ga: ʧara-ga:*

Adjectives in Kanashi are not sensitive to the grammatical relations of the NPs they occur in.

Predicative:

(198) *nu ʧʰog kamɽ to*
DEM.PROX white blanket be.3SG
'This is a white blanket'

Subject:

(199) *ʧʰog-e madr-a: kim-a bo-ke*
fair.complexioned-PL man-PL house-LOC go-PST
'The fair-complexioned men went home'

(200) *ʧʰog-a: beʈaɽi-ga: kim-a bo-ke*
fair.complexioned-PL woman-PL house-LOC go-PST
'The fair-complexioned women went home'

Direct object:

(201) *du-s ʧʰog-a: beʈaɽi-ga: taŋ-mug*
3.DIST-ERG fair.complexioned-PL woman-PL look-PST.3
'S/He saw fair-complexioned women'

(202) *du-s ʧʰog beʈaɽi-p taŋ-mug*
3.DIST-ERG fair.complexioned woman-ACC look-PST.3
'S/He saw the fair-complexioned woman'

(203) *du-s ʧʰog madras-u-p taŋ-mug*
3.DIST-ERG fair.complexioned man-ACC look-PST.3
'S/He saw the fair-complexioned man'

In (204), illustrating a predicative adjective as object complement, the syntactic dependency of the complement on the object is marked by both constituents receiving the accusative suffix.

(204) *ʧa:-p ʤog-i-p tuŋ la-ge*
tea-ACC warm-SG-ACC drink feel-PST
'One should drink tea warm'

The habitual and perfective aspect markers also form participles, e.g. habitual: *pa-ʃ-idz* [cook-MDL-HAB] 'cooked (cauliflower)'; *ʃi:-ʥ maɽʃaŋ* [die-HAB man] 'corpse'; *ʦʰar-ʥ ʃiŋ* [dry-HAB wood] 'fodder, hay'; *ʧi-ʦ ka:m* [wash-HAB floor]; *kiʃ-ʥ* [tame-HAB] 'domesticated' (about animals). Examples of perfective verb forms as participles are *tuŋ~tuŋ madras* [drink~PFV man] 'drunk man'; *naʃ-is* [naʃis] ~ [naʃiʃ] [rest-PFV] 'rested'. Both seem to correspond to past participles in translation.

2.4.2 Degrees of comparison

The instrumental marker is suffixed to the quantifier *sab* 'all' to express the superlative.

(205) *gu sab-as ʦʰeka/ʦʰika bas soara boŋ-ta-k*
1SG.NOM all-INS early bus p.name go-NPST-1SG
'I will go to Kullu with the earliest bus'

(206) *ni-ka ʤaŋ sab-a(s) teg*
1PLE-POSS god all-INS great
'Our god is the greatest'

2.4.3 Quantifiers

Quantifiers in Kanashi can be classified as determiners or pronouns. In the former case they occupy the Qnt slot in the NP structure shown above in Section 2.1, instead of or together with the numerals. As determiners, quantifiers do not inflect, e.g. *bari-ʦ* [borits] [much-DIM]. Some quantifiers can appear in both roles: *sab* 'all' as determiner remains invariant, while as a pronoun it behaves like any NP head, taking number and case suffixes. A salient usage of *sab* and the pronoun-like item *lok* 'people' (from *lokas* 'non-Kanashi person') is in apposition to a (plural) pronoun.

The determiner usage is illustrated in the following examples.

(207) *sab ʧara-gaː-s an-e-p arʃuk-a ta-ge*
all child-PL-ERG REFL-PL-ACC mirror-LOC watch-PST
'All children looked at themselves in the mirror'

The pronominal usage of *sab* can be seen in the following examples, in (208–209) following a pronoun, and in (210–211) as NP head. As we can see in the examples below, the case marker can either be suffixed only to the last constituent of a NP, or to every constituent or only to the pronoun. *sab* 'all' can also be followed by *lok*.

(208) *ette sab-us an-e-p arʃuk-a taŋ-ke-muk*
1PLE all-ERG REFL-PL-ACC mirror-LOC look-PST-1PLE
'We all looked at ourselves in the mirror'

(209) *ki-n-ka sab-ka kim*
2PL-POSS-POSS all-POSS house
'the house(s) of all of you'

(210) *sab-us niʥa ʈaka ka-ku-ta-ʃ*
all-ERG twenty money bring-PROG-NPST-3PL
'All are bringing twenty rupees'

(211) *nu munuk-us sab-ka kim-gaː ʧorig-gaː ʃaɳ-mug*
DEM.PROX man-ERG all-POSS house-PL theft-PL do-PST.3
'This man robbed everybody's houses'

A similar pattern is observed also with *lokas* 'non-Kanashi person'. When it functions as a lexical noun, it behaves like any head noun of a noun phrase. In this role it takes the relevant noun inflectional morphemes.

(212) *nu-gaː lok-aː beiman-aː to-ʃ*
DEM.PROX-PL person-PL dishonest-PL be.PRS-3PL
'These people are dishonest'

Table 17: The Kanashi cardinal numerals 1–20

Gloss	Kanashi	Origin (Source: IA: Turner 1966; ST: STEDT 2016; Matisoff 2003)
'one'	*iːd*	ST: *it
	ek	IA: Turner 2462 ḗka
'two'	*niʃ*	ST: *g-ni-s/*g-nis
'three'	*ʃum*	ST: *gsum; ST: *g-sum
'four'	*pu*	ST: *pwɑ (breadth of four fingers)
'five'	*ŋa, na*	ST: *ŋa
'six'	*ʧʰa*	IA: Turner 12803 ṣáṣ
'seven'	*sat*	IA: Turner 13343 sáptá
'eight'	*aʈʰ*	IA: Turner 941 aṣṭā́
'nine'	*nao*	IA: Turner 6984 náva
'ten'	*das*	IA: Turner 6227 dáśa
'eleven'	*gjara*	IA: Turner 2485 ḗkādaśa
'twelve'	*bara*	IA: Turner 6658 dvā́daśa
'thirteen'	*tera*	IA: Turner 6001 tráyōdaśa
'fourteen'	*ʧoda*	IA: Turner 4605 cáturdaśa
'fifteen'	*pandra*	IA: Turner 7662 páñcadaśa
'sixteen'	*sola*	IA: Turner 12812 ṣṓḍaśa
'seventeen'	*ʃum-is kam niʥa*	[three-INS less twenty]
	sutaːra	IA: Turner 13146 saptádaśa
'eighteen'	*niʃ kam niʥa*	[two less twenty]
	ʈʰara	IA: Turner 946 aṣṭā́daśa
'nineteen'	*iːd-is kam niʥa*	[one-INS less twenty]
	unni	IA: Turner 2411 ūnaviṁśati
'twenty'	*niʥa*	ST: [two:ten] (cf. Kinnauri *nidza* : *niʃ* 'two'; *se* 'ten')
	bi	IA: Turner 11616 viṁśatí

(213) *ʃum lok-aː bara-ke*
three person-PL come-PST
'Three persons came'

lok also has a grammaticalized function, where it exhibits pronoun-like behavior similar to *sab* 'all'.

(214) *ki sab lok-aː-s an-e-p arʃug-aː taŋ-me-n*
2PL all person-PL-ERG REFL-PL-ACC mirror-LOC watch-PST-2/3PL
'All you people looked at yourselves in the mirror'

2.5 Numerals

The structure and remarkable multiplicity of the Kanashi numerals are given detailed treatment in Chapter 5 of this volume. Here we simply list some of the cardinal numbers in Table 17 (reproduced from Chapter 5). Similar to other ST languages of the Himalayas, only a few (synchronically) nondecomposable cardinals are ST in origin (1–5 and 20), while the rest are IA loanwords (Matisoff 1997; Mazaudon 2010). The little data that we have concerning ordinal numbers in Kanashi indicate an even more overwhelming IA influence. Thus, even the lowest ordinals 'first' and 'second' (at least as they are attested in our material) are IA borrowings (*pela* and *duʤa*, respectively).

3 The verb complex

The finite verb complex in Kanashi – except imperatives and prohibitives, which are given separate treatment in Section 3.8 below – exhibits the following structures:[17]

Simplex: (N) (NEG-)V-TAM-IDX(-*oɳ*)(=EMP)
Aux 1: (N) (NEG-)V-ASP (BE-TNS-IDX(-*oɳ*)(=EMP)) (see Section 3.9)
Aux 2: (N) (NEG-)V-ASP (VVB-TNS-IDX(-*oɳ*)(=EMP)) (see Section 3.9)

With the exception of a few monosyllabic verb stems with the phonotactic structure CV(:), (underived) Kanashi verbs stems are consonant-final.[18] Most verb stems in our data are monosyllabic CV(:)C structures, but we also find stems with more than one syllable, especially among the IA loanwords.

In the sections below, verbs will be cited either as stems[19] (e.g., *taŋ-* 'look') or as nominalizations in *-(a)m* (*taŋam* 'to look'), which we will refer to in the text as

17 The initial "(N)" in these structural schemes is the (uninflected) nominal component of a support verb construction; see Section 2.2, especially example (14). The function of the element *-oɳ* is as yet unclear. The 1SG index is, at times, realized as *-g* when it is followed by the suffix *-oɳ*.

18 As another exception, we find some vowel-final disyllabic verb stems of IA origin in our data, e.g. *ba:le-* 'look, see'; *kaʈe-* 'cut'.

19 Specifically: the stem of the infinitive; there is a sizeable group of verbs undergoing morphologically conditioned stem variation.

"infinitives" when used as citation forms.[20] The suffix *-(a)m* has the form *-m* after vowels and *-am* after consonants: *ʃiː-m* 'to die' : *taŋ-am* 'to watch'.[21]

Kanashi has many verbs which have more than one stem allomorph. One prominent such set comprises verbs whose infinitive stem ends in *-n*, *-ɳ* or *-ŋ*, and which we will refer to as "nasal stems" below.[22] As a general rule, the final *-n* and *-ɳ* are dropped in front of a consonant-initial suffix, whereas *-ŋ* is optionally dropped, but there are many special cases depending on the suffix, which we will describe in connection with each suffix below. Additionally, vowel-final verb stems may lose the vowel in certain contexts.

3.1 Valency-changing morphology

Valency-changing morphology is among the main derivational morphological devices available in the Kanashi verbal system. By and large, we find the same valency-changing mechanisms in Kanashi as in Kinnauri. There are three productive valency-changing mechanisms, two which decrease valency and one which increases it. Finally, there is a non-productive historically detransitivizing mechanism which synchronically manifests itself as a stem alternation with no obvious directionality.

3.1.1 Reflexive/middle *-ʃi*

Kanashi has a multifunctional verbal suffix *-ʃi* with cognates in several other ST languages.[23] This suffix is realized as *-ʃ* when the suffix following it starts with a vowel.

20 This ending is glossed as [INF] in the examples, except when it is followed by case morphology, in which case we gloss it as a nominalization: [NMLZ].

21 The infinitive suffix is given as *-(a)m* since the suffix vowel is often barely audible in normal speech.

22 This name is slightly misleading, since infinitive stems ending in the bilabial nasal *-m* do not as a rule participate in the stem alternations characteristic of the nasal stems.

23 Similar morphemes for this function have been reported for several other ST languages, e.g. Kinnauri *-ʃ(ɪ)* (Saxena 2017), Byangsi *-ʃɪ* (Willis Oko 2019), Darma *-si/-xi* (Willis Oko 2019), Thulung Rai *-si* (Lahaussois 2003). LaPolla (1996) also reports similar morphemes with middle voice functions in other ST languages: *x* (Rawang/Dulong), *-siŋ* (Limbu), *(na) ci* (Bantawa), *sit* (Thulung), *si* (Khaling), *-s* (Rongpo), *-su* (Padam-Mishing) and *-s* (Nishi).

(215) *su-* : *su-ʃi-* 'bathe'
taŋ- : *taŋ-ʃi-* 'look, watch'
ʤi-/ʧi- : *ʤi-ʃi-/ʧi-ʃi-* 'wash'
ses- : *ses-ʃi-* 'know, recognize'
sar- : *sar-ʃi-* 'awaken'
ken- : *ke-ʃi-* 'give.1/2O'

Nasal stems drop the stem-final nasal before *-ʃi*, except *-ŋ*, whose deletion is optional (e.g. *ken-* : *ke-ʃi-* above).

(216) *ʧara ka:m ʃa-ʃ-o tʰake~ke*
child work(N) do-MDL-PROG tired~PFV
'The child got tired, working' (cf. *ʃaɳam* 'to do, to make')

(217) *du an-u-ka ʧʰok-adi ʈʰor raɳ-mu bo-ke ʧʰum-ʃi-ge*
3.DIST REFL-SG-POSS son-near run give-NMLZ go-PST catch-MDL-PST
'He ran to his son, he kissed (him)'

The middle marker occurs with both ST and IA verbs as well as with verbs of unknown etymology. But unlike Kinnauri, in Kanashi *-ʃi* is also affixed to IA transitive forms without the transitive marker *-ja:*.

(218) *sesam* (<ST) 'to recognize, to know' : *sesʃim*
tsu:mam (<IA) 'to catch, to hold' : *tsu:mʃim*
saram (<ST) 'to awaken' : *sarʃim*
kʰulam (<IA) 'to open(TR), to peel' : *kʰulʃim*
sum (<unknown origin) 'to bathe' : *suʃim*

While *-ʃi* in Kanashi does express functions which are normally associated with the middle marker, as shown below, it also occurs in some other, distinctly non-middle constructions. For consistency, we will still refer to *-ʃi* as the "middle marker" here.

As described above in Section 2.3.4, Kanashi has a reflexive construction involving a transitive verb and a reflexive pronoun, with the verb form remaining the same as in a regular transitive clause. As in many other ST languages, a reflexive and a reciprocal reading in Kanashi can also be accomplished by adding *-ʃi* to a transitive verb.

(219) *ette taŋ-ʃi-muk*
1PLI look-MDL-1PL
'We looked at ourselves (in the mirror)'

(220) *ka taŋ-ʃi-me-n*
2SG.NOM look-MDL-PST-2SG
'You looked at yourself'

(221) *ʧara-ga:-s arʃuk-a taŋ-ʃi-ge*
child-PL-ERG mirror-LOC look-MDL-PST
'The children looked at themselves in the mirror'

Note that in (221) the subject is in the ergative. This is distinct from Kinnauri, where ergative subjects are not found with verbs showing the middle suffix.

Analogously, there is one example in our material where we have both the reflexive pronoun and the middle voice marker.[24]

(222) *gu aŋ-u-p/an-u-p arʃuk-a ba:le-ʃi-ge-k*
1SG.NOM 1SG-SG-ACC/REFL-SG-ACC mirror-LOC see-MDL-PST-1SG
'I saw myself in the mirror'

We have only two examples of reciprocal constructions in our material. In both examples the verb contains the middle marker *-ʃi*, but there is no reflexive pronoun.

(223) *sagar nita niʃ mi-s ses-ʃi-ge*
m.name f.name two man-ERG recognize-MDL-PST
'Sagar and Nita recognized each other'

(224) *muḍ mi-ga: niʃ mi-s ba:le-ʃi-ge*
yesterday man-PL two man-ERG see-MDL-PST
'Yesterday the men looked at each other'

-ʃi also occurs in transitive clauses where the subject is suppressed, and the interpretation of the clause is that of a general statement. E.g.

(225) *laṭpaṭa-ga:-p ʧi-ʃ-im ʥaruri*
garment-PL-ACC wash-MDL-INF necessary
'Washing clothes is important'

(226) *ra:tiŋ kar-aga: taŋ-ʃi to-ʃ*
night star-PL look-MDL be.PRS-3PL
'Stars are seen in the night'

24 In Kinnauri, the middle marker does not occur together with the reflexive pronoun.

(227) *pa-ʃ-idʑ gobi*
cook-MDL-PFV cauliflower
'cooked cauliflower'

In addition, *-ʃi* in Kanashi occurs also in constructions which are not normally associated with the middle voice.

First, we find a kind of generalization of the reflexive usage of *-ʃi* in Kanashi, where the verb retains an object or other non-subject argument. The *-ʃi* here seems to emphasize the agency or individuality of the subject. This usage has been reported as the primary function of cognate items in the Macro-Tani languages by Modi & Post (2020) under the label "subject autonomy".

(228) *ʧara ka:m ʃa-ʃ-o tʰake~ke*
child work make-MDL-PROG tired~PFV
'The child got tired (after) having done the work himself'

There are some examples of verbs where more than one intransitivizing strategy is found on a single verb: word-initial consonant voicing as well as the middle marker *-ʃi* (for example, *ʧim* 'to wash (e.g. clothes)': *ʧi-ʃi-m* and *ʤi-ʃ* 'to get washed (e.g. in the rain)'. Interestingly, in the following pair of examples, the verb stem is transitive (*ʧim* 'to wash (e.g. clothes)') in one example, but intransitive (*ʤim* 'to get washed (e.g. clothes)') in the other. But both take the middle marker. In both instances there is an explicit object. In our current understanding, the default interpretation of *ʤim* is 'to wash one's own's hand', but the occurrence of the middle marker here, probably is a kind of emphasizer, wash your own hand, not someone else's.

(229) *ʧara ga:r-a: ʧi-ʃ-id tot-ke*
child tooth-PL wash-MDL-HAB BE-PST
'The child was cleaning his teeth'

(230) *sita guɖ ʤi-ʃ-is dʑa:mi raʈ*
f.name hand wash.INTR-MDL-PFV food give.IMP
'Sita, wash your hands and (then) give food'

We also find a kind of generalization of the reflexive usage of *-ʃi* in Kanashi, where the verb retains an object or other non-subject argument, and *-ʃi* indicates that the referent of the latter belongs to the subject; this could be through a kinship relation, or part of one's body part (the subject doing something to/with his body-part) or belongs to the subject (ownership).

(231) *nu: ba: ka-n-ka kim-aj-ʃo-ka hisa-p aŋ-ʥ*
oh father 2SG-POSS-POSS house-and-field-POSS portion-ACC 1SG-DAT
ke-ʃ-a-g
give.1/2O-MDL-?-?
'(The younger son said to his father:) "Oh father, please give me a share of your estate." ' (source: Konow 1909)

In our Kanashi material we do not seem to have any instance of middle where it emphasizes that the action was done collectively. This may be a gap in our material.

3.1.2 Intransitivizing *-e*

The intransitive marker *-e* in Kanashi occurs only with IA verbs (see Chapter 7).

(232) *k^{h}ul-am* [open-INF] : *k^{h}ul-e-m* [open-INTR-INF] 'to open (TR : INTR)'
baɳ-am [make-INF] : *baɳ-e-m* [make-INTR-INF] 'to make (TR : INTR)'

Confusingly, there seem to be some underived disyllabic verb stems ending in *-e* as well (e.g., *ba:le-*'look, see'; *kaʈe-* 'cut'). These are recognized by their occurrence in clear transitive clauses. In some cases there are also intransitive usages in our data, so that the same verb stem receives two different analyses: *ba:le-m* [look-INF] 'to look, see' : *ba:l-e-m* [see-INTR-NMLZ] 'to be visible'.

Kanashi *-e* has a close correspondence in Kinnauri *-ed* (Saxena 2017; 2022). The suffixes are presumably cognate, and in Kinnauri, too, *-ed* occurs only with IA verbs. Distinctly from Kanashi, the Kinnauri suffix appears in the variants *-e*, *-ed* or *-en* depending on the (morphophonological) context. In Kinnauri there is a set of simple (ST) verb stems whose stem-final segments alternate in exactly the same way. The most economical description is one where *-ed* is assumed to be the basic form of the suffix and the other two variants are the results of assimilatory processes. Kanashi *-e* is invariant (except for normal phonetic variation involving the vowel /e/; see Chapter 2). It is reasonable to assume that Kinnauri presents the more original situation, and that Kanashi has lost the final *-d* (or *-n*, since the cognates of the simple ST verb stems exhibiting this variation in Kinnauri end in *-n* in Kanashi, e.g. *lonam* 'to tell'; *sanam* 'to kill'; *ʦunam* 'to tie'). For further details on intransitivizing *-e*, see Chapter 7.

3.1.3 Valency increasing *-ja:*

The suffix *-ja:* functions as a transitivizer/causativizer.[25] It attaches to stems of IA origin and to stems with unknown etymology. Very often, the corresponding intransitive verb has either *-e* or – in some cases – the middle marker *-ʃi*.

(233) *bi:-m* [disappear-INF] : *big-ja:-m* [disappear-TR-INF]
mil-e-m [meet-INTR-INF] : *mil-ja:-m* [meet-TR-INF]
ʈul-e-m [sleep-INTR-INF] : *ʈul-ja:-m* [sleep-TR-INF]
ʥik-e-m [press-INTR-INF] : *ʥik-ja:-m* [press-TR-INF]
roh-e-m [grow-INTR-INF] : *roj-ja:-m* [grow-TR-INF]
siʈ-e-m [cook-INTR-INF] : *siʈ-ja:-m* [cook-TR-INF]
kaʈe-ʃi-m [cut-MDL-INF] : *kaʈ-ja:-m* [cut-TR-INF]
ba:l-e-m [see-INTR-INF] / *ba:le-ʃi-m* [see-MDL-INF] : *ba:l-ja:-m* [see-TR-INF]

Notably, nasal stems do not drop their final consonant before *-ja:* (e.g. *gaŋja:m* 'to count'), which indicates that the *-j-* patterns as a vowel in the phonological system of Kanashi.

For further details on valency increasing *-ja:*, see Chapter 7.

3.1.4 Consonant voicing alternation

Finally, there is a small number of verb stem pairs, where a transitive verb stem beginning with a voiceless obstruent (stop, affricate) has a corresponding intransitive verb stem beginning with the voiced counterpart of this obstruent, e.g. *tʰan* 'drop, fell(TR)' : *dan* 'drop, fall(INTR)'; *ʧi* 'wash(TR)' : *ʤi* 'wash(INTR)'; *ʧuk* 'break(TR)' : *ʤuŋ* 'break(INTR)'. This is, however, not a productive process in Kanashi.

25 *-ja:* is used to derive both transitive and causative verbs from IA items. Despite this, it will be consistently glossed [TR] here.

3.2 Aspect

3.2.1 Perfective aspect

The perfective aspect in Kanashi is formed by adding a suffix *-is* to verb stems ending in *-ʧ* or *-ʃ* (including verbs with the middle suffix *-ʃ(i)*) and by reduplication of the final syllable of the verb in all other cases.

(234) *ka na:mi pʰa:kuʧ bakar me-ken~ken*
2SG.NOM even small goat NEG-give.1/2O~PFV
'You did not give me even a small goat'

(235) *du-s sima-uʧ ʈaka tʋa~tʋa*
3.DIST-ERG m.name-DAT money take.away~PFV
'He sends (out) money to Sima'

The perfective aspect markers also occur in non-final clauses in clause chain constructions, e.g.

(236) *sohan naʃ-is gitaŋ-a: ma-la-gu-ta*
m.name sit-PFV song-PL NEG-sing-PROG-NPST
'Having sat down, Sohan is not singing'

(237) *ʧara-ga: oʤ-is ʈʰak-e-ke*
child-PL play-PFV tire-INTR-PST
'The children got tired, having played (for a long time)'

(238) *sita guɖ ʤi-ʃ-is ʥa:-mi ra-ʈ*
f.name hand wash.INTR-MDL-PFV eat-NMLZ give-IMP.SG
'Sita, wash (your) hands and (then) give food'

Finally, the perfective forms of Kanashi verbs are frequently used adjectivally, as participles (see Section 2.4.1 above).

3.2.2 Habitual aspect

The habitual aspect markers are *-id* and *-ʦ* (the latter as usual with variants *-ʧ* and *-ʤ*), where *-id* occurs with verb stems ending in *-ʧ* or *-ʃ* (including after the middle marker *-ʃ(i)*); and *-ʦ* occurs elsewhere. Nasal stems optionally lose the stem-final nasal before *-ʦ*.

(239) *didd ʧa-ʤ to-ʃ*
there dance-HAB BE.PRS-3PL
'There (they) dance'

(240) *suvari ʤo aŋganva:riŋ-a ka:m ʃa-ʦ to*
f.name down.south p.name-LOC work do-HAB BE.PRS
'Suari works down south in the Anganwadi'

(241) *gu beʈiŋ kaʈe-ʦ tot-k*
1SG.NOM tree cut-HAB BE.PRS-1SG
'I cut trees daily'

(242) *ʧara ga:r-a: ʧi-ʃ-id tot-ke*
child tooth-PL wash-MDL-HAB BE-PST
'The child was cleaning his teeth'

(243) *du bara-ʦ to*
3.DIST come-HAB BE.PRS
'He is coming'

(244) *sattar lokas ʈʰoro-ga: ra-ʦ tot-ke*
seventy person running-PL give-HAB BE-PST
'Seventy people were running'

Similar to the perfective forms, the habitual aspect markers in Kanashi, too, function as participial markers (see Section 2.4.1 above). They are also used in object complementation constructions, as illustrated in examples (245–246).

(245) *gu ʤuʃʈa-p ʦamk-e-ʦ-u-p taŋ-me-k*
1SG.NOM moon-ACC shine-INTR-HAB-SG-ACC see-PST-1SG
'I saw the moon shining'

(246) *gu santoʃ-u ko:ʈ gaʃ-iʣ taŋ-me-k*
1SG.NOM f.name-SG.ACC coat wear-HAB see-PST-1SG
'I saw Santosh wearing a coat'

3.2.3 Progressive aspect

The progressive aspect marker in Kanashi is *-u* (as elsewhere in Kanashi it is, at times, also realized as *-o*). With nasal stems, final *-n* and *-ɳ* are dropped before *-u*, and stem-final *-ŋ* is optionally dropped (with doublet forms as a result).

(247) *bar-am* [come-INF] 'to come' : *bar-u* [come-PROG]
naʃi-m [sit-INF] 'to sit, rest' : *naʃi-u* [sit-PROG]
boʃ-am [forget-INF] 'to forget' : *boʃ-u* [forget-PROG]
raɳ-am [give-INF] 'to give' : *re-u* [give-PROG]
buɽ-am [throw-INF] 'to throw' : *buɽ-u* [throw-PROG]
su-ʃi-m [bathe-MDL-INF] 'to bathe' : *su-ʃi-u* [bathe-MDL-PROG]
kaʈ-e-m [cut-INTR-INF] 'to cut' : *kaʈ-e-u* [cut-INTR-PROG]
ʃaɳ-ʃi-m [make-MDL-NMLZ] 'to be made' : *ʃaɳ-ʃi-u* [make-MDL-PROG]
kʰul-e-m [open-INTR-INF] 'to open' : *kʰul-e-u* [open-INTR-PROG]
ʦamk-e-m [shine-INTR-INF] 'to shine' : *ʦamk-e-u* [shine-INTR-PROG]
mil-e-m [mix-INTR-INF] 'to mix' : *mil-e-u* [mix-INTR-PROG]
ʈul-e-m [sleep-INTR-INF] 'to sleep' : *ʈul-e-u* [sleep-INTR-PROG]

With a small number of verbs, the progressive aspect marker is realized as *-gu/-ku*. After the intransitive marker *-e* and after the middle marker *-ʃi*, the progressive marker is always *-u* (never *-gu/-ku*). Sharma (1992: 364–365) describes the *-k* in the *-ku* variant of the progressive suffix as the first person agreement marker. This is not supported in our material. *-gu/-ku* shows up in all persons.

The choice between *-u* and *-gu/-ku* does not seem to depend on phonological factors. Notably, there are some verbs which can take both markers:

(248) *ʥa:m* 'to eat' : *ʥa:-gu, ʥa:-u*
toŋam 'to beat' : *toŋ-u, to-gu*
nem 'to exist' : *ne-gu, ne-u*

With *-gu* and *-ku*, on the other hand, we find *-gu* after vowels and *-ku* after consonants. The only exception in our data is *bonam* 'to go' : *bo-ku*.

(249) *bon-am* [go-INF] 'to go' : *bo-ku*
puʃ-am [sow-INF] 'to sow' : *puʃ-ku*
ʤab-am [rain-INF] 'to rain' : *ʤap-ku*
su-m [bathe-INF] 'to bathe' : *su-gu*
ʥa:-m [eat-INF] 'to eat' : *ʥa:-gu*
taŋ-am [watch-INF] 'to watch' : *ta-gu*
gual-am [dig-INF] 'to dig' : *gual-ku*
toŋ-am, tog-am [beat-INF] 'to beat' : *to-gu, toŋ-u*
krab-am [cry-INF] 'to cry' : *krab-ku*
tuŋ-am [drink-INF] 'to drink' : *tuŋ-u, tu:-gu*

lan-am [do-INF] 'to do, make' : *la:-gu*
ʧi-m [wash-INF] 'to wash' : *ʧi-gu*

3.3 Tense

Kanashi makes a two-way tense distinction between non-past and past.

3.3.1 Non-past tense

The marker for non-past tense is *-ta*. It appears after any valency changing suffix and the progressive marker. With nasal stems, the final nasal may be kept, dropped or assimilated to the *-t-* of the ending; see, e.g., the verbs *raɳam* 'to give' and *renam* 'to sell' below.

(250) *baɳem* 'to build': *baɳe-ta*
renam 'to sell': *ret-ta*
baram 'to come': *bar(a)-ta*
sanam 'to kill': *sa(t)-ta*
bonam 'to go': *bok-ta, boŋ-ta*
sum 'to bathe': *su-ta*
ʥa:m 'to eat': *ʥa:-ta*
ʃaɳam 'to make': *ʃa(ʈ)-ta*
kanam, kaɳam 'to bring': *ka-ta, kaʈ-ʈ*
ʃenam 'to send': *ʃe-ta*
kenam 'to give.1/2O': *ken-ta, ke-ta*
ʃi:m 'to die': *ʃi:-ta*
k^h^aŋam 'to buy': *^h^aŋ-ta*
taŋam 'to look': *tag-ta*
lanam 'to do, make': *laʈ-ʈ, la-ta*
tuŋam 'to drink': *tuŋ-ta, tug-ta*
lonam 'to tell': *lo-ta*
ʈulem 'to sleep': *ʈul(-e)-ta*
milem 'to meet': *mil-ta*
ʦumam 'to catch': *ʦum-ta*
nem 'to be, exist': *ne-ta*

ʧa:m 'to dance': *ʧa-ta*

raɳam 'to give': *raʈ-a, ra-ta, raɳ-ta*

ʧi:m, ʤim 'to wash': *ʧi-ta*

(251) *gu* *roʥ* *ʈul-e-u-ta-k*
1SG.NOM daily sleep-INTR-PROG-NPST-1SG
'I sleep daily'

(252) *mukeʃ* *dilli* *boŋ-ta*
m.name p.name go-NPST
'Mukesh will go/goes to Delhi'

(253) *gu* *ʥa:b-a* *su-ʃi-u-ta-k*
1SG.NOM now-LOC bathe-MDL-PROG-NPST-1SG
'I am bathing right now'

(254) *gu* *muɖ* *ʃer-p* *san-ta-k*
1SG.NOM yesterday tiger-ACC kill-NPST-1SG
'Yesterday I was killing a tiger'

3.3.2 Past tense

The past tense marker has the allomorphs *-ke*, *-ge* and *-me*, which are used with all persons, optionally signalled by an added person indexing suffix. Additionally, there are some portmanteau past tense markers used with third person subjects (see below).

-ke/-ge are the normal past tense markers Their basic distribution is that *-ge* occurs after vowels and *-ke* after most consonants, although we find a fair number of instances in our material where *-ke* appears after a vowel, e.g.:

(255) *gu* *beddʑa* *k^{h}aŋ-am-a* *bo-ke-k*
1SG.NOM seed buy-NMLZ-LOC go-PST-1SG
'I went to buy seeds'

As elsewhere in Kanashi, the vowel in *-ke/-ge* is realized also as [i] (i.e. [ki/gi]). Also, as elsewhere when the past tense marker occurs word-finally, the final vowel is, at times, not audible (e.g. [bok(e)] '(He) went').

With nasal stems we find a variety of forms:

(1a) The past tense marker is realized as *-me* and the verb-stem final consonant is retained (e.g. *sanam* 'to kill' : *san-me-k* [kill-PST-1SG]; *taŋam* 'to look' : *taŋ-me-k* [look-PST-1SG]).
(1b) The past tense marker is realized as *-me* and the verb-stem final consonant is dropped (e.g. *lanam* 'to do, to make' : *la-me-k* [do-PST-1SG]).
(2) When the verb stem ends in a retroflex nasal (e.g. *raɳam* 'to give'), the past tense marker is *-me* (*raɳ-me* [give-PST]); here we also find the past tense marker *-ke*, but in this case, the stem final consonant loses its nasalization: *raʈ-ke-k*.

These past tense markers occur with all person subjects, and they are the only possibility with first and second person subjects. With third person subjects, Kanashi has two additional past-tense markers: *-mug* and *-gja/-gjo*. They occur only with third person subjects in our data.

(256) *du* *ʥa:-ge* / *nu-ga:-s* *ʥa:-gja* / *ram-us* *an-u-p*
3.DIST eat-PST / 3.PROX-PL-ERG eat-PST.3 / m.name-ERG REFL-SG-ACC
taŋ-mug [taɲmuk]
watch-PST.3
'S/He ate' / 'S/He ate' / 'Ram watched me'

The following list shows some of the past-tense forms attested in our data.

(257) *anam* 'to carry' : *an-me*
milem 'to meet' : *mile-ge, mile-ke*
a:ɽem 'to call' : *a:ɽ-e-me, a:ɽ-e-mug*
pi:m 'to lose' : *pi:-me, pi:-mug*
baɳem 'to build' : *baɳe-k(e)*
raɳam 'to give' : *raɳ-ke, raɳ-me, raʈ-ke, ran-mug, raɳ-mug*
baram 'to come' : *bar(a)-ke*
renam 'to sell' : *ren-mug*
bi:m 'to disappear' : *bi-ge*
sanam 'to kill' : *sat-ke, san-me, san-mug*
bonam 'to go' : *bo(k)-ke*
sum 'to bathe' : *su-me, su-mug*
dvanam, tvanam 'to take out' : *dvat-ke, dvan-me, tvat-ke, tvan-me*
ʃaɳam 'to make' : *ʃaɳ-e, ʃaʈ-ge, ʃaɳ-(e)-me, ʃaɳ-mug*
ʥa:m 'to eat' : *ʥa:-ge, ʥa:-ke, ʥa:-gja*
ʃenam 'to send' : *ʃe-mug*
kanam, kaɳam 'to bring' : *kan-mug*

ʃiːm 'to die' : *ʃiː-g(e), ʃiː-k(e)*
kaʈem 'to cut' : *kaʈe-me, kaʈe-mug*
taŋam 'to look' : *tag-e, taŋ-me*
kenam 'to give.1/2O' : *ken-k(e)*
tuŋam 'to drink' : *tu-ke*
kʰaŋam 'to buy' : *kʰaŋ-me*
ʈulem 'to sleep' : *ʈule-k(e)*
kʰaŋem 'to cough' : *kʰaŋe-k(e)*
tsʰaːm 'to listen' : *tsʰaː-me*
kʰulam 'to open' : *kʰul(i)-mu(g)*
ʧaːm 'to dance' : *ʧaː-ge*
lanam 'to do, make' : *la-k(e), la-me, la-mug*
ʧiːm, ʤim 'to wash' : *ʧi-ge, ʧi-me, ʧi-mug*
lonam 'to tell' : *lon-me, lon-mu(g)*
uːnam 'to take' : *uːn-mug*

3.4 Subject indexing

Kanashi has subject index markers. They are placed after tense, aspect and mood markers. The subject index markers are the following (the corresponding subject pronouns are also provided in the following table):[26]

	SG (pronoun)	(suffix)	PL (pronoun)	(suffix)
1	*gu*	*-k*	*ni* (1PLE) *ette(-s)* (1PLI)	*-ŋ* *-muk*
2	*ka*	*-n*	*ki*	*-ŋ* (and *-n*)
3	*du(-s), nu(-s)*	Ø	*du-gaː(-s), nu-gaː(-s)*	*-ʃ* (and Ø)

Note that the two verbal suffixes *-muk* [-1PLI] and *-mug* [-PST.3] are very similar in form, and due to the phonetic system of Kanashi, *-mug* [-PST.3] is also realized as

26 *-ŋ* will be glossed [1/2PL] in the examples in this chapter. This (along with Tika Ram Joshi's glossing of *ki* as [2PL]) possibly suggests that Kanashi has retained an older stage, while Kinnauri has grammaticalized the 2/3PL pronoun as honorific singular forms/markers. In Kinnauri *-ŋ* indexes 2SG.H and *-ʃ* 3SG.H. It is, however, interesting to note that in Kanashi we have a retroflex nasal consonant [ɳ] in *raɳ*, while Kinnauri has an [n] – a possible influence of the neighboring IA languages.

[muk], and both *-mug* and *-muk* are also realized as [mu] and [mo] word-finally (see Chapter 2 for details). But *-muk* and *-mug* occur in two different slots, *-muk* [-1PLI] in the IDX slot and *-mug* [-PST.3] in the TNS slot. The verb index marker *-muk* [mu(k)] [-1PLI] occurs with both past and non-past tense markers, while *-mug* [-PST.3] is a past tense marker.

Other authors have noted (Konow 1909; Sharma 1992), and we also find in our material, that the attested verb forms in actual language data are not the expected ones; we often see "first person" forms with explicit third person subjects, and vice versa. We do not have enough data to formulate an explanation for this.

3.5 Object "indexing" – the verb *ken/raɳ* 'give'

Unlike Kinnauri, Kanashi does not show an inflectional marker indexing an affected SAP on the verb, but it does have the same kind of suppletive paradigm for the verb 'give'[27] that we find in Kinnauri: *ken-* [give.1/2O] occurs with affected speech act participants (first or second person beneficiaries) and *raɳ-* 'give' occurs elsewhere. Further, just as in Kinnauri, both *raɳ-* and *ken-* have two stem variants each: *ken-* and *ke-* and *raɳ-* and *ra-/re-*, respectively.[28]

(258) *me-ken~ken*
NEG-give.1/2O~PFV
'did not give me/you'

(259) *du-s das ʈaka-n loʈ-u-p ke-ta*
3.DIST-ERG ten money-POSS note-SG-ACC give.1/2O-NPST
'He will give (me/you) a ten rupee note'

In our material *raɳ-* 'give' and *ken-* [give.1/2O] occur in the following forms (except imperatives and prohibitives which are described below in Section 3.8):

	NPST	PST	HAB	PFV
raɳ-am 'to give'	*raɳ-ta, raʈ-ta, ra-ta*	*raɳ-me, raʈ-ke, raɳ-ke*	*raɳ-ts, ra-ts*	*re~re*
ken-am 'to give.1/2O'	*ken-ta, ke-ta*	*ken-ke*		*ken~ken*

27 Sharma (1992: 361) states that Pattani too has two verb forms for 'give': *raɳ* and *ke*, the latter occurs with first person indirect object and *raŋ* with third person indirect object.

28 Even if there is no doubt that the Kanashi and Kinnauri verbs are cognates, this behavior of the verb 'give' in particular is attested in a number of languages across the globe (Comrie 2003).

As we can see here, both have several allomorphs. As a nasal stem, when *raɳ-* 'give' is followed by a morpheme which begins with a *t-*, in some cases there is assimilation: [raʈʈa]. The past tense marker appears as *-me* with *raɳ-* 'give'.

ken- 'give.1/2O' does not show any signs of assimilation. The past tense marker here is realized as *-ke*. Similarly, as mentioned above, the verb final consonant (*-ɳ/-n*, respectively) of *ran-* and *ken-* is not always realized.

This person-based distinction in the choice of the verb for 'give' is maintained in non-finite clauses. For example, in a clause chain construction.

(260) *ka na:mi pʰakuʧ bakar me-ken~ken dug-uʥ*
2SG.NOM even small goat NEG-give.1/2O~PFV 3.DIST-DAT
an-u-ka mita:r-a:-uʥ kʰuʃi ʃo-ta-ŋ
REFL-SG-POSS friend-PL-DAT happy do-NPST-1PLE
'Yet you never gave me even a young goat so that me and my friends could celebrate'

Unlike Kinnauri, in Kanashi we find some occurrences of *raɳ-* with affected speech act participants. This typically happens when the interpretation of *raɳ-* is something else than 'give', as in (261–263),[29] which could be taken to indicate that these usages are no longer perceived as representing the same verb.

(261) *du-s aŋ-p raʈ-ke-guk*
3.DIST-ERG 1SG-ACC give(bite)-PST-?
'He bit me'

(262) *gopal-us niŋ-p sab raɳ-mug*
m.name-ERG 1PLE-ACC all give(hit)-PST.3
'Gopal hit all of us'

(263) *gopal-us ki-p raɳ-mug*
m.name-ERG 2PL-ACC give(hit)-PST.3
'Gopal hit you (PL)'

Finally, the IA verb *de-* 'give', too, occurs in our material. It shows an interesting combination of IA and ST elements. Unfortunately we don't have any examples of *de* 'give' with an affected SAP.

	NPST	PST	PROG
de- 'give'	*de-ta*	*de-ke*	*de-u*

29 These usages represent a semantic change similar to that hinted at in the English idiom *to **give** as good as one gets.*

3.6 The verb 'be'

The verb *to* 'be' functions both as copula and as verb of location or existence. In addition, in the non-past there is a distinct lexical verb of location *nem* 'to be, to exist' which does not appear to have copular usage.

As opposed to other verbs, where, as we have seen, the main dividing line in the tense system runs between non-past and past, both *to* and *ne-m* [be-INF] show a three-way present–past–future opposition in their tense inflection. The paradigm of *to* is shown in the following table.

	PRS	PST	FUT
1SG	*tot-k*	*tot-ke-k(-e), tot-ke*	*hoʃ-ta-k*
2SG	*to-n*	*tot-ke-n, tot-ko-ŋ*	*hoʃ-ta-n*
3SG	*to*	*tot-k(-oŋ)*	*hoʃ-ta*
1PLE	*tot-ki-ŋ/to-ŋ*	*tot-ke-ŋ*	*hoʃ-ta-ŋ*
1PLI	*ton-muk*	*tot-ke-muk*	*hoʃ-ta-muk*
2PL	*to-ŋ*	*tot-ke-ŋ, tot-ko-ŋ*	*hoʃ-ta-ŋ*
3PL	*to-ʃ*	*tot-k(-oŋ), tot-k(-on)*	*hoʃ-ta-ʃ*

The copula is not obligatory in Kanashi. For example, *ʤuʃaŋ tʰi* [cloud today] 'It is cloudy today'.

It is also used as auxiliary verb in the second of the two finite verb structures described above (see the beginning of Section 3). This is described in more detail below in Section 3.9.

The verb of location/existence *nem* is inflected as shown in the following table. Note that there are no distinct past-tense forms; instead, forms of *to* are used. Formally, the forms glossed as 'future' are non-past forms (with *-ta* [-NPST]) and the 'present' forms contain *-u-ta* [-PROG-NPST].

	PRS	(PST)	FUT
1SG	*ne-u-ta-k*	*tot-ke-k(-e), tot-ke*	*ne-ta-k*
2SG	*ne-u-ta-n*	*tot-ke-n, tot-ko-ŋ*	*ne-ta-n*
3SG	*ne-u-ta*	*tot-k(-oŋ)*	*ne-ta*
1PLE	*ne-u-ta-ŋ*	*tot-ke-ŋ*	*ne-ta-ŋ*
1PLI	*ne-u-ta-muk*	*tot-ke-muk*	*ne-ta-muk*
2PL	*ne-u-ta-ŋ*	*tot-ke-ŋ, tot-ko-ŋ*	*ne-ta-ŋ*
3PL	*ne-u-ta-ʃ*	*tot-k(-oŋ), tot-k(-on)*	*ne-ta-ʃ*

The corresponding forms of *to* can always be used instead of *nem*, and according to one of our language consultants, there is no difference between the two alternatives. According to him, both are used by all, both older as well as younger speakers, although *to* is more frequent. Sharma (1992: 359), too, suggests that there does not seem to be any difference.

3.7 Negation

Verbal negation is formally expressed by adding a prefix *mV-* to the verb. Unlike some other ST languages, the form of the negative marker in Kanashi is not sensitive to tense/aspect. However, the vowel of the prefix is assimilated to the vowel quality of the first vowel of the verb stem. Thus we find that it appears as *ma-*, *mi-*, *mo-*, and *mu-*, depending on the vocalism of the verb stem.[30]

(264) *gu nu kaːm-aː ma-ʃaɳ-me-k*
1SG.NOM DEM.PROX work-PL NEG-do-PST-1SG
'I did not do those tasks'

(265) *gu didd mo-bo-ke-k*
1SG.NOM there NEG-go-PST-1SG
'I did not go there'

(266) *svari-s laʈpaʈ-gaː-p mi-ʧi-mug*
f.name-ERG garment-PL-ACC NEG-wash-PST.3
'Suari did not wash clothes'

(267) *lugɽi mu-tu-gu-ta-ŋ*
rice.beer NEG-drink-PROG-NPST-1/2PL
'We are not drinking rice beer' (Konow)

A similar pattern is observed in non-final clauses.

(268) *ka naːmi pʰakuʧ bakar me-ken~ken dug-uʥ*
2SG.NOM even small goat NEG-give.1/2O~PFV 3.DIST-DAT
an-u-ka mitaːr-aː-uʥ kʰuʃi ʃo-ta-ŋ
REFL-SG-POSS friend-PL-DAT merry do-NPST-1PLE
'Yet you never gave me even a young goat so that me and my friends could celebrate' (Konow)

30 Pattani (Sharma 1989) has two negative prefixes *ma-* and *tha-*. They do not show correlation with tense/aspect or vowel harmony. Darma (Willis Oko 2019) may have vowel harmony in the vowel of the negative marker (Willis 2007: 369), similar to that of Qiang and Dolakha Newar. In Darma the distribution of verb-indexing markers (1SG) in negative clauses is dependent on PST vs. NPST.

(269) *ma-taŋ-m=i mufkil to*
NEG-see-INF=EMP difficult be.PRS
'Not seeing is difficult'

3.7.1 Negation of the verb 'be'

The copula *to* and the verb of location/existence *nem* have a common suppletive negated stem *ma:j-* [NEG.be-]. It is used in all persons and numbers in all tenses. The same form is also used in negated auxiliary constructions (*ma:j-* [NEG.BE-]).

(270) *gu dzimida:r ma:j-k*
1SG.NOM farmer NEG.be.PRS-1SG
'I am not a farmer'

(271) *gu naliŋ dzimida:r ma:j-ge-k*
1SG.NOM last.year farmer NEG.be-PST-1SG
'Last year I was not a farmer'

(272) *nu-ga: / du-ga: dzimida:r-a: ma:j-ʃ*
3.PROX-PL / 3.PROX-PL farmer-PL NEG.be.PRS-3PL
'They are not farmers'

(273) *naliŋ nu-ga: / du-ga: (sab) dzimida:r-a: ma:j-ge*
last.year 3.DIST-PL / 3.PROX-PL (all) farmer-PL NEG.be-PST
'Last year they were not farmers'

(274) *ette kim-a ma:j-muk / mai-ŋ* [mãĩ]
1PLI house-LOC NEG.be.PRS-1PLI / NEG.be.PRS-1/2PL
'We are not at home'

(275) *ette muḍ kim-a ma:j-ge-ŋ*
1PLI yesterday house-LOC NEG.be-PST-1/2PL
'We were not at home yesterday'

3.8 Imperative and prohibitive

The imperative can be expressed with the bare verb stem, e.g. *naʃ* 'sit!'. Additionally, Kanashi has specific optional imperative suffixes expressing number and gender. Together with an optional prohibitive prefix, they define the following structure:

(PROH-)V-IMP(-SG/PL)(-M/F)
tʰV- V (*-t/-ʈ/Ø*)(*-u/-o*) [(-SG)(-M)]
(*-t/-ʈ/Ø*)(*-e*) [(-SG)(-F)]
(*-ŋ/-n*)(*-o/-u*) [(-PL)(-M)]
(*-ŋ/-n*)(*-e*) [(-PL)(-F)]

The distribution of the imperative singular suffix allomorphs is determined by the stem-final segment. Ø (null) occurs after vowel-final stems[31] and *-t* after consonant-final stems. In nasal stems, the stem-final consonant is deleted and *-t* or *-ʈ* is affixed to to the stem, the latter with stems ending in *-ɳ*. The plural imperative suffix is *-ŋ* in all contexts except after verb stems ending in a velar nasal, where *-n* appears instead, a case of dissimilation. The masculine marker *-u* in imperative constructions is frequently realized as *-o*.

INF	[-SG-M]	[-SG-F]	[-PL-M]	[-PL-F]
san-am 'to kill'	*sa-t-o*	*sa-t-e*	*sa-ŋ-o*	*sa-ŋ-e*
ren-am 'to sell'	*re-t-o*	*re-t-e*	*re-ŋ-o*	*re-ŋ-e*
an-am 'to carry'	*a-t-o*	*a-t-e*	*a-ŋ-o*	*a-ŋ-e*
lan-am 'to make'	*la-o*	*la-je*	*la-ŋ-o*	*la-ŋ-e*
raɳ-am 'to give'	*ra-ʈʰ-u*	*ra-ʈ-e*	*ra-ŋ-o*	*ra-ŋ-e*
ʃaɳ-am 'to do'	*ʃa-ʈʰ-u*	*ʃa-ʈʰ-e*	*ʃa-ŋ-o*	*ʃa-ŋ-e*
bon-am 'to go'	*boŋ-t-o*	*boŋ-t-e*	*boŋ-n-o*	*boŋ-n-e*
tuŋ-am 'to drink'	*tuŋ-t-u*	*tuŋ-t-e*	*tuŋ-n-o*	*tuŋ-n-e*
ʥa:-m 'to eat'	*ʥa:-u*	*ʥa:-je*	*ʥa:-ŋ-o*	*ʥa:-ŋ-e*
tsʰa:-m 'to listen'	*tsʰa:-o*	*tsʰa:-e*	*tsʰa:-ŋ-o*	*tsʰa:-ŋ-e*
ʧi-m 'to wash'	*ʧi-u*	*ʧi-e*	*ʧi-ŋ-o*	*ʧi-ŋ-e*
tuʃ-ja:-m 'to wipe'	*tuʃ-ja:-u*	*tuʃ-ja:-ve*	*tuʃ-ja:-ŋ-o*	*tuʃ-ja:-ŋ-e*

The subject (i.e., the second person pronoun *ka/ki*) may also explicitly occur together with the imperatives: *ka nid naʃ* 'you sit here!'. If the imperative clause has a direct object, the object takes the regular inflectional endings:

(276) *ti:* *tuŋ-n-e*
water drink-IMP.PL-F
'Drink water!'

[31] This also happens with at least one consonant-final verb in our data (*tog-am* 'to beat, hit'): *to-u* [hit.IMP.SG-M], *to-e* [hit.IMP.SG-F], *to-ŋ-o* [hit-IMP.PL-M], *to-ŋ-e* [hit-IMP.PL-F].

(277) *suma:n-a:-p a-t-o*
thing-PL-ACC carry-IMP.SG-M
'Carry (the) things!'

The verb 'come' has a suppletive imperative form *ʤar* [come.IMP] [ʤar] ~ [ʥar] (the non-imperative infinitive stem 'come' is *bar-*). The regular imperative markers are not suffixed to *ʤar*.

As discussed above in Section 3.5, the verb 'give' has two distinct stems (*ken-*, *raɳ-*), where *ken-* occurs with affected speech act participants. However, in imperative clauses *raɳ-* 'give' occurs also with speech act participants in our material.

The prohibitive prefix *t^ha-* that we find in Kanashi also occurs in many other ST languages. It is prefixed to the imperative verb form, including the suppletive imperative form of 'come' (*t^ha-ʤar* [PROH-come.IMP] 'don't come!'). In Kanashi, unlike in Kinnauri, but analogously to the negative prefix (see Section 3.7), the vowel of the prohibitive marker *t^ha-* assimilates to the first vowel of the verb stem, except when this is *e*. In the last-mentioned case the prohibitive prefix remains *t^ha-*. In our material there is no instance of prohibitives where the first verb stem vowel is *i*.

(278) *ʈuʃ-ja:-u* [wipe-TR-IMP.SG.M] : *t^hu-ʈuʃ-ja:-u* [PROH-wipe-TR-IMP.SG.M]
ʈuʃ-ja:-ŋ [wipe-TR-IMP.PL] : *t^hu-ʈuʃ-ja:-ŋ* [PROH-wipe-TR-IMP.PL]
ʥa:-u [eat-IMP.SG.M] : *t^ha-ʥa:-u, t^ha-ʥa:-o* [PROH-eat-IMP.SG.M]
ʥa:-ŋ-o [eat-IMP.PL-M] : *t^ha-ʥa:-ŋ-o* [PROH-eat-IMP.PL-M]
ʥa:-e [eat-IMP.SG.F] : *t^ha-ʥa:-e* [PROH-eat-IMP.SG.F]
ʥa:-ŋ-e [eat-IMP.PL-F] : *t^ha-ʥa:-ŋ-e* [PROH-eat-IMP.PL-F]
ka boŋ-t [you come-IMP.SG] : *t^ho-boŋ-t* [PROH-come-IMP.SG]
boŋ-n-o [come-IMP.PL-M] : *t^ho-boŋ-n-o* [PROH-come-IMP.PL-M]
boŋ-t-e [come-IMP.SG-F] : *t^ho-boŋ-t-e* [PROH-come-IMP.SG-F]
boŋ-n-e [come-IMP.PL-F] : *t^ho-boŋ-n-e* [PROH-come-IMP.PL-F]
bedʥa puʃ-t [seed sow-IMP.SG] : *bedʥa t^hu-puʃ-t* [seed PROH-sow-IMP.SG]

3.9 Complex verb forms

Kanashi has two types of grammatical complex verb constructions – as opposed to the more lexical support verb constructions described above in Section 2.2, especially example (14) – labeled "Aux 1" and "Aux 2" in the verb complex schemas given above in Section 3.

The verb 'be' (see Section 3.6) is used as an auxiliary (glossed [BE-] in this usage) in (Aux 1) constructions with the general structure

V-ASP BE-TNS-IDX

For example:

(279) *gu* *dʑa:-ʦ* *tot-k*
1SG.NOM eat-HAB BE.PRS-1SG
'I am eating'

(280) *ʧara* *ga:r-o* *ʧi-ʃ-id* *tot-ke*
child tooth-PL wash-MDL-HAB BE-PST
'The child was cleaning his teeth'

The compound verb (Aux 2) construction is another grammatical complex verb construction in Kanashi. Here the main verb (its stem or its perfective form) is followed by a *vector verb*.[32] In our data we have attested *ʃaɳ-* 'do' and *bon-* 'go' as vector verbs (glossed [DO-] and [GO-], respectively):

(281) *harija-s* *rinig-p* *tupkʰ-s* *raɳ* *ʃaɳ-mug* [saɳmuk]
m.name-ERG snake-ACC gun-INS give DO-PST.3
'Harija killed the snake with a gun'

(282) *indr-us* *raŋ-a* *bo-ke* *sap* *saɳ* *ʃaɳ-mug* [saɳmuk]
m.name-ERG summit-LOC go-PST snake kill DO-PST.3
'Indra went to the summit and killed the snake'

(283) *nu-s* *ʧara-ga:-p* *tʰepr-a:* [tʰepre] *re~re* *ʃaɳ-mug* [saɳmuk]
3.PROX-ERG child-PL-ACC slap-PL give~PFV DO-PST.3
'S/He slapped the children'

(284) *sonu* *malani* *buɖ~buɖ* *bo-k*
m.name p.name leave~PFV GO-PST
'Sonu went, leaving Malana (forever)'

32 Kinnauri has a parallel construction, where the lexical main verb in the perfective is combined with one of a small number of auxiliary-like "vector verbs" – such as *nimu* 'to stay', *rannu/kemu* 'to give', *bjɔmu* 'to go', *tamu* 'to keep', *ʃɛnnu* 'to send' – each of which adds a specific semantic dimension to the main verb (and serves as the carrier of finite verb morphology).

4 Clauses and sentences

4.1 Word order

The default and the most frequent constituent order in direct elicitation is SOV, where the subject (both noun and pronoun) normally occurs in the first position.

(285) *harija-s rinig-p tupk^{h}-s raɳ ʃaɳ-mug* [saɳmuk]
m.name-ERG snake-ACC gun-INS give DO-PST.3
'Harija killed the snake with a gun'

(286) *nu huʤ-is t^{h}iːd k^{h}iraŋ dalats ken-ke*
DEM.PROX COW-ERG little milk today give-PST
'This cow gave (us) little milk today'

(287) *du-s ʧ^{h}og madras-u-p taŋ-mug*
3.DIST-ERG fair.complexioned man-SG-ACC see-PST.3
'He saw a white/fair-complexioned man'

(288) *gu du-gaː-p roʥ ta-gu-ta-k*
1SG.NOM 3.DIST-PL-ACC every.day look-PROG-NPST-1SG
'I am watching them every day'

4.2 Alignment

For core expressions, Kanashi noun phrases (other than first and second person singular pronouns) have three cases available, though their distribution leads to a complex alignment pattern. The ergative is used for some, but not all, transitive subjects, and also for some more agentive intransitive subjects. The accusative is used for some, but not all, direct objects. In both cases, subjects and direct objects can appear in the nominative instead. Kanashi thus has both differential subject marking and differential object marking, combined with semantic alignment (agentive versus patientive).

First and second person pronouns (except 1PLI) lack an ergative case, using the nominative instead, but generally take accusative marking.

4.3 Experiencer subjects

Like many other languages of South Asia, Kanashi has oblique – or dative, or experiencer – subjects. The dative marker occurs on the "subject" of an obligative construction and in the dative subject construction.

(289) *aŋ-ʥ=i sauda-ga: ʃobilas lag-e-ta*
1SG-DAT=EMP candy-PL good feel-INTR-NPST
'I like sweets'

(290) *aŋ du kamra ʤiŋ lag*
1SG.NNOM DEM.DIST room big feel
'That room felt big to me'

(291) *niŋ-ʥ ti:-ka kam=i*
1PLE-DAT water-POSS shortage=EMP
'We do have a shortage of water'

(292) *du-ga:-uʥ sardi la-ke*
3.DIST-PL-DAT cold(N) feel-PST
'They had a cold'

4.4 Clause chaining

Kanashi makes use of clause chaining, whereby any number of non-final clauses (including zero) are followed by a final clause. Non-final clauses use (at least) the perfective form(s) of the verb (see Section 3.2.1). Non-final clauses differ from final clauses in that only final clauses take tense and subject index marking. Hence, non-final clauses are normally interpreted to have the same subject as the final clause. It is very likely that such coreferentiality is a preference rather than an absolute constraint; cf. (293) from Kinnauri.

(293) Kinnauri (kfk) (Saxena 2022):

gə-s gitʰaŋ lan-ʦ mi-pəŋ taŋ-o-k
1SG-ERG song make-HAB man-DAT observe-PST-1SG
'I looked at the man while he (= the man) was singing'
'I looked at the man while I was singing'

4.5 Content and polar questions

In our data, we have only attested polar questions with second person singular subject. Just as in Kinnauri, in Kanashi too, *-a* ([a] ~ [e]) is suffixed to the finite verb in polar questions. This *-a* also occurs in WH-questions, but its occurrence in WH-questions is not obligatory.

(294)	*ka-ʥ*	*pata*	*to-a*
	2SG-DAT	knowledge	be.NPST-Q
	'Do you know (X)?'		

(295)	*ka*	*nu-p*	*rat̪-ta-n-a*
	2SG.NOM	3.PROX-ACC	strike-NPST-2SG-Q
	'Will you beat him?'		

(296)	*tuŋ-a*
	drink-Q
	'May I drink?' (Sharma 1992: 377)

(297)	*ki*	*niʃ*	*ʧʰub*	*bar-ta-n-e* [bʰət̪t̪ne]
	2PL	two	when	come-NPST-1/2PL-Q
	'When will the two of you come?'			

4.6 Honorificity

Distinct from some of its linguistic relatives and geographical neighbors, Kanashi does not mark honorificity grammatically, neither in the choice of pronouns nor in verb indexing. There is also no lexical expression of honorificity, e.g., by using different noun, verb, or adjective stems based on mutual interlocutor status relations in discourse. Honorificity is, however, indicated by using a plural pronoun form for a singular referent, and vice versa (see Section 2.3.2).

References

Comrie, Bernard. 2003. Recipient person suppletion in the verb 'give'. In Mary Ruth Wise, Thomas N. Headland & Ruth M. Brend (eds.), *Language and life: Essays in memory of Kenneth L. Pike*, 99–164. Dallas: SIL International & The University of Texas at Arlington.

Grierson, George A. 1928. *Linguistic survey of India, Vol 9, Part IV: Indo-Aryan languages, Central group: Specimens of Pahari languages and Gujuri*. Calcutta: Government of India, Central Publication Branch.

Hendriksen, Hans. 1986. *Himachali studies III: Grammar*. Copenhagen: Munksgaard.

Konow, Sten. 1909. *Linguistic survey of India, Vol 3: Tibeto-Burman family. Part I: General introduction, specimens of the Tibetan dialects, the Himalayan dialects, and the North Assam group*. (This and several other volumes of the LSI were edited by Sten Konow, although published as the work of George A. Grierson). Calcutta: Government of India, Central Publication Branch.

Krishan, Shree. 2011. A sketch of Chaudangsi grammar. In Randy J. LaPolla (ed.), *The Tibeto-Burman languages of Uttar Pradesh*, 185–206. Osaka: National Museum of Ethnology.

Lahaussois, Aimée. 2003. Thulung Rai. *Himalayan Linguistics Archive* 1: 1–25.

LaPolla, Randy J. 1996. Middle voice marking in Tibeto-Burman. In *Proceedings of the Fourth International Symposium on Languages and Linguistics: Pan-Asiatic Linguistics, volume 5*, 1940–1954. Bangkok: Mahidol University at Salaya.

Matisoff, James A. 1997. *Sino-Tibetan numeral systems: Prefixes, protoforms and problems*. Series B, Volume 114. Canberra: Pacific Linguistics.

Matisoff, James A. 2003. *Handbook of Proto-Tibeto-Burman: System and philosophy of Sino-Tibetan reconstruction*. Berkeley: University of California Press.

Mazaudon, Martine. 2010. Number-building in Tibeto-Burman languages. In Stephen Morey & Mark Post (eds.), *North East Indian linguistics, volume 2*, 117–148. New Delhi: Cambridge University Press India.

Modi, Yankee & Mark W. Post. 2020. *Trans-Himalayan "middle voice" and the case of Macro-Tani languages*. Presentation at the Societas Linguistica Europaea conference.

Saxena, Anju. 2017. Sangla Kinnauri. In Graham Thurgood & Randy J. LaPolla (eds.), *The Sino-Tibetan languages*, 2nd edn., 756–772. London: Routledge.

Saxena, Anju. 2022. *The linguistic landscape of the Indian Himalayas: Languages in Kinnaur*. Forthcoming 2022. Leiden: Brill.

Seifart, Frank. 2017. Patterns of affix borrowing in a sample of 100 languages. *Journal of Historical Linguistics* 7(3): 389–431.

Sharma, Devi Datta. 1989. *Tribal languages of Himachal Pradesh. Part one*. Delhi: Mittal Publications.

Sharma, Devi Datta. 1992. *Tribal languages of Himachal Pradesh. Part two*. Delhi: Mittal Publications.

STEDT. 2016. *James A. Matisoff et al. The Sino-Tibetan etymological dictionary and thesaurus*. Available online at: http://stedt.berkeley.edu/search. Berkeley: University of California.

Turner, Ralph L. 1966. *A comparative dictionary of the Indo-Aryan languages*. Available online: http://dsal.uchicago.edu/dictionaries/soas/. Oxford: Oxford University Press.

Widmer, Manuel. 2017. *A grammar of Bunan*. Berlin: De Gruyter Mouton.

Willis, Christina M. 2007. *A descriptive grammar of Darma: An endangered Tibeto-Burman language*. Austin: University of Texas. (PhD thesis).

Willis Oko, Christina. 2019. *A grammar of Darma*. Leiden: Brill.

Synchrony: variation

Anju Saxena, Anna Sjöberg, Padam Sagar, and Lars Borin

4 Linguistic variation: a challenge for describing the phonology of Kanashi

Abstract: Kanashi exhibits a great deal of variation on several linguistic levels, which raises questions of a theoretical and methodological nature relevant to the formulation of useful and faithful linguistic descriptions of Kanashi. In this chapter, we address such questions in connection with working out a description of the phonology of Kanashi as part of a larger language documentation effort. Specifically, we discuss two aspects of the sound system of Kanashi where we have noted considerable variation among our language consultants, and which consequently necessitate reflection and discussion over their place – if any – in the phonology of Kanashi: aspirated voiced stops and geminated (long) consonants.

Keywords: Kanashi, Sino-Tibetan, phonology, phonetics, variation

Chapter overview:

1 Introduction

In this chapter, we will describe some challenges we have faced in preparing a description of the phonology of Kanashi as part of a more extensive language-documentation effort among whose main results are the descriptions presented in Chapters 2 and 3 in this volume. The challenges are primarily caused by the

† The following notational conventions are used in this chapter. Phonetic transcriptions are given in IPA notation in square brackets "[...]". Even though our transcription conventions for Kanashi are intended as phonemic, whenever we wish to stress that phonemes and phonemic representations are under discussion, we write single phonemes and phoneme sequences surrounded by "/.../". We represent geminate consonants as doubled (biphonemic) rather than long (i.e. we write *daddu* rather than *dadːu*), but we would like to stress that this does not imply a strong preference on our part for the one or the other analysis.

https://doi.org/10.1515/9783110703245-004

amount of inter- and intra-speaker variation evidenced in our recordings. We will discuss the following two phonological phenomena to illustrate our case, both concerning the phoneme inventory of Kanashi:

1. the status of aspirated voiced stop consonants (Section 4.1)
2. geminate ~ singleton consonant variation (Section 4.2)

2 Data collection

The following description is based mainly on the speech of three Kanashi speakers (2,063 sound files for 975 words): one older male Kanashi speaker (older male, "OM" in the following) and two younger speakers, one man (younger male, "YM") and one woman (younger female, "YF"). At the time of the data collection OM was about 50 years old, YM around 22 years old and YF around 28 years old. The female speaker had received some formal education. Both male speakers were illiterate; they had not received any formal education. All three speakers were born and brought up in the village. Like most other Kanashi speakers, they leave the village occasionally. All three could understand Hindi (hin), the national language of India, and Kullu Pahari (kfx),[1] the locally dominant language, both Indo-Aryan (IA) languages. While the female speaker could speak Hindi quite well, the male speakers (especially YM) spoke a mixed Hindi with strong influence of their mother tongue Kanashi.

The Kullu Pahari data in this chapter is from our fieldnotes;[2] Hindi data is from McGregor (1993).

Apart from lexical items, we have also collected elicited phrases and sentences and some narratives. The elicitation was done in Hindi. All recordings were done with a general documentary purpose, that is, not with a particular phonetic experiment in mind. This means that in some cases the materials are not optimal for the analyses conducted on them (e.g. having list intonation, not having tokens of the same word from all speakers etc.). The acoustic phonetic analysis of the sound files was done using Praat (Boersma & Weenink 2018).

1 It is also referred to as Kullui/Kulluvi/Inner Siraji.

2 Thanks to our language consultants Mrs Kanta Devi and Mrs Meena Bodh for their input.

3 Linguistic variation in Kanashi

Even with the limited data available on Kanashi, the language exhibits a great deal of variation, at several linguistic levels. For instance, there are no less than four different ways of forming composite numerals in Kanashi for each cardinal in the range 21–99, and in addition the corresponding Hindi numerals can also be freely used instead. The Kanashi numerals are described and discussed in more detail in Chapter 5 of this volume.

IA loanwords are found in the language in both an older and a more recent form, showing different degrees of integration into the linguistic system of Kanashi. Lexical items belonging to the older loanword stratum have undergone various adaptation processes, not only in their pronunciation, but notably also addition of the adaptive suffixes *-es/-aŋ/-iŋ* to IA noun and adjective stems (see Table 1 and Chapter 6).

Table 1: Older IA loanwords in Kanashi

Gloss	Kanashi	Kullu Pahari
'traditional guesthouse'	*marhaŋ*	*marh*
'treasury'	*banɖa:raŋ*	*bʰanɖa:r*
'cattleshed'	*kʰuɽaŋ*	*kʰuɽ*
'name'	*na:maŋ*	*na:m*
'wall'	*bitiŋ*	*bi:t*
'bucket'	*ba:lʈiŋ*	*ba:lʈi*
'thief'	*ʧoras*	*ʧor*

Distinct from this, more recently borrowed IA nouns and adjectives occur without these adaptive markers, and also retain the phonological structure of IA to a greater extent than in the older loanword stratum, e.g. *dahi* 'yoghurt'; *laɽi* 'wife'.

This now leads to situations where we find lexical doublets going back to the same IA item in our data, e.g. *gra:maŋ* ~ *gra:m* 'village'; *na:maŋ* ~ *na:m* 'name'; *diliŋ* ~ *dilli* 'Delhi'. This, too, contributes to variation – both in phonological realization and in creating lexical and morphological variants. In such cases it is not easy to draw a line between borrowings and instances of code mixing. For the most part, we have treated these cases as borrowing, with one main exception. In instances where we have pronunciation variants of a certain lexical item with IA etymology, e.g. [puʥa] ~ [puʧas] 'fifty' (cf. standard Hindi *pacās* 'fifty'), we examined if the more standard IA form is found only in the speech of the literate speaker(s), and in those instances where this turned out to be true we chose the other variant as our phonemic representation of that lexical item, e.g. *pudza* 'fifty'. Such variation is not unique to Kanashi, but instances of variation which cannot be correlated with some linguistic/socio-cultural factors, pose a challenge to the linguist, especially when the phoneme inventory is often seen as a closed set.

In this chapter we will describe some challenges we have faced in describing the phonology of Kanashi in the face of the variation found. It is likely that several factors contribute to the variation that we find in Kanashi. Kanashi is an oral language. It is in the early days of documentation, so that uncertainties about the phonemic status of segments may possibly translate into variation in transcriptions. Some of the variations that we see in our data may be due to variation among speakers correlating with demographic and sociocultural factors, e.g. literacy and increasing intrusion of Hindi (one of the two national languages of India and the official state language of Himachal Pradesh, as well as the medium of instruction in schools).

Another suggested factor contributing to variation in descriptions of lesser-known languages is (inadvertent) inclusion of more than one geographical variety into the description. This does not seem to be a relevant factor in the case of Kanashi, however, as Kanashi is spoken only in one village (Malana), and the physical structure of the village is rather compact with houses close to one another.

Further, there is the observation made about many endangered languages that there may be variation without any apparent explanation – no stylistic differences, no social variables such as age or class correlating with the variation (Cook 1989; Palosaari & Campbell 2011). This may be the result of previously obligatory phonological processes being lost, giving rise to free variation. The mechanisms behind these changes in phonology in endangered languages are probably multifarious. It has been suggested that a pivotal role is played by so-called semi-speakers, i.e. speakers who have not learnt the language fully (Cook 1989). In the case of Kanashi, children still acquire the language, there are no semi-speakers and the language is used in everyday life in the village. Thus, the role of imperfect learning or semi-speakers in any variation found in Kanashi should be negligible.

Others stress the influence of language contact, e.g. Andersen (1982), who proposes the generalization that contrasts are maintained that exist both in the target language and the language with which it is in contact and also contrasts that carry a high functional load. As Malana village where Kanashi is spoken has neighboring villages where IA languages are spoken, one assumption could be that linguistic variation in Kanashi can possibly be due to contact with speakers of neighboring villages. This, however, is not a major contributing factor, as Kanashi speakers, in their everyday life, maintain a clear distinction between Kanashi and non-Kanashi people.

The effects of language contact, however, cannot be discounted, as most Kanashi speakers are bilingual. Despite the focus on maintaining distance from non-locals, there is regular interaction for religious and economical purposes between Malana and the neighboring IA-speaking villages. As mentioned above, the Kanashi lexicon in fact contains a large share of IA loanwords. In recent times, with the advent of (satellite) television, mobile phones and the internet, the influence of Hindi has become an integral part of the linguistic environment of Kanashi speakers.

Finally, we should perhaps also not overlook the circumstance that we have from an early age been prescriptively exposed to our own standard language with its concomitant normative conceptual framework connected to language standardization, which easily could be unreflectingly carried over into language description conducted by us in our capacity of academic linguists, arguably a special case of "written language bias in linguistics" (Linell 2005). It is well recognized that a central aspect of the creation of standard languages is reduction of variation; some variants are simply excluded from the standard (Joseph 1987: 126ff). This means that a language like Kanashi would be expected to exhibit more variation simply by virtue of not being standardized.[3]

The fact remains that we find a great deal of variation in Kanashi, and more research is definitely needed in order to ascertain how (if at all) this variation correlates with demographic and other factors. Whatever its causes, the variation has consequences for the linguistic description of Kanashi, and as a concrete illustration of this we now turn to a discussion of two instances of variation in the sound system of Kanashi which have forced us to think about what should be counted as evidence for phonemic status of a phonetic segment or feature.

4 Two instances of variation in the sound system of Kanashi

Kanashi exhibits several kinds of variation in its sound system. For example, degree of final devoicing of voiced stops, aspirated voiced stops alternating with their unaspirated counterparts, varying vowel and consonant length, and some

3 The kinds of observations that we make here about Kanashi are far from new: "Variation in Navajo pronunciation had long disturbed Haile (to Sapir, 30 March 1931: SWL): 'Sometimes I do wish that the informants would be more careful in pronunciation and follow some system which would conform to theory. ... Apparently no excuse, excepting that informants are too lazy to use it correctly.'" (Darnell 1990: 257)

aspects of vowel quality (in particular the presence of a vowel in the space between /a/ and /o/ in OM and a more centralized /u/, often approaching [ɵ], in YM).

Below, we will focus on two of these instances of variation, namely voiced aspirates and geminate consonants.

4.1 Phoneme inventory: aspirated voiced stops

For each place of articulation, many IA languages exhibit four series of oral stop phonemes with respect to their manner of articulation, characterized by presence or absence of voicing and aspiration. Thus, oral stop phonemes can be voiceless and unaspirated, voiced and unaspirated, voiceless and aspirated, and voiced and aspirated, e.g. /p/, /b/, /p^{h}/, and /b^{h}/.

Kanashi has stop phonemes at four places of articulation: bilabial, alveolar, retroflex and velar. For each of these places of articulation, there is an incontestable basic three-way distinction between unaspirated voiced stop, unaspirated voiceless stop and aspirated voiceless stop, as demonstrated by the near minimal triplet /du/ [3SG.DIST], /to/ 'be' and /t^{h}o/ 'up'. The aspirated voiceless stops are somewhat limited in their distribution and are almost only found in word-initial position, with a few exceptions, but since they contrast with the other two stop series in that position, their phonemic status seems incontrovertible.

In our data we also find aspirated voiced stops – [b^{h}], [d^{h}], [ɖ^{h}] and [g^{h}]. However, their distribution is such that it is unclear if they are to be considered parts of the Kanashi phoneme inventory. Voiced aspirates are not a characteristic feature of ST languages, although Matisoff (2003) notes that many Himalayish ST languages that are in close contact with IA languages borrow them, first in loanwords and then extending their use to the entire lexicon.

In Kanashi voiced aspirated stops are predominantly found in the IA part of the lexicon, see Table 2. Hindi is not necessarily the source language, but is here taken to represent IA. As we can see here, in all these examples we find both variants in our material – with and without aspiration.[4] They appear to be in free variation. That is, lexical items which are realized with aspirated voiced stops are also realized with plain voiced stops, by the same speakers.

4 The second point is that voiced aspirates are, similarly to voiceless aspirates, limited in their distribution. They are almost only found in word-initial position (examples of exceptions to this in our data: [gind^{h}i] 'ball' and [prad^{h}aːn] 'chieftain'). This, however, is a minor point, especially since several consonant phonemes in Kanashi that are clearly supported also show some distributional limitation.

Table 2: Aspiration alternation in voiced stops

Kanashi	Hindi	Gloss
[b^{h}ukamp] ~ [bukamp]	*bhūkamp*	'earthquake'
[b^{h}au] ~ [bau]	*bhāi*	'brother'
[g^{h}ari] ~ [g^{h}aɽi] ~ [gari]	*ghaṛī*	'clock, watch'
[g^{h}oɽa] ~ [goɽa]	*ghoṛā*	'horse'
[d^{h}auga] ~ [dauga]	*dhāgā*	'thread'

If we would like to maintain that a morpheme should normally have *one* unitary underlying shape (a sequences of phonemes), this raises the question of which phoneme should be taken as being present in the underlying form of these lexical items: the aspirated voiced stop, contrasting with the voiced unaspirated stop, or the voiced unaspirated stop, or possibly some underspecified segment or (equivalently) an archiphoneme? These three alternatives are represented below, together with the resulting underlying representation for the word for 'brother'.

Alternative 1	Alternative 2	Alternative 3
/b/ → [b]	/b/ → [b], [b^{h}]	/B/ → [b], [b^{h}]
/b^{h}/ → [b^{h}], [b]		[..., +voiced, ?aspirated]
/b^{h}au/	/bau/	/Bau/

The problem with the first alternative (i.e. postulating two phonemes /b/, /b^{h}/), is that it means positing a phoneme that is only occasionally contrastive on the surface and often has the exact same realization as another phoneme. Additionally, this merger is not rule-bound but completely free. The problem with the second alternative is that it brings a very strange kind of allophony with it. There is free variation, but this free variation occurs only in certain lexical items. Something being lexically restricted is generally taken to be a criterion for phonemicity. The third alternative sneaks in lexical restriction through an underspecified underlying representation of unclear status vis-à-vis the empirical language data.

Finally, we may note one potential minimal pair in our materials: [g^{h}oɽa] 'horse' and [goɽa] 'ankle'. There are, however, two problems with treating this minimal pair as conclusive evidence for phonemic status. The first is the already mentioned free variation: 'horse' is just as often (probably more often, though it is hard to quantify precisely from our data) realized as [goɽa], homophonous with 'ankle'.

4.2 Phoneme inventory: geminate consonants

We analyze Kanashi as having phonemic geminates for all stops and fricatives and for /l/. Our material contains no minimal pairs, but pairs such as /batak/ 'duck' and /battis/ 'thirty-two' demonstrate the difference. Instrumental measurements show a difference in duration between geminates and singletons (Saxena et al. 2018). See Table 3 for some examples.[5]

Table 3: Geminate consonants in Kanashi

Kanashi (YF)	Gloss
/didd/	'there'
/ʥikke/	'anger'
/massi/	'mother's sister'
/tʰulla/	'leg, foot'

As with the aspirated voiced stops, there are, however, some issues complicating the incorporation of geminates into the phonological analysis of Kanashi.

The first is that there appears to be a clear difference between speakers. In the speech of YM, consonants that in the speech of YF are heard as geminate are not heard as geminate and show no significant durational difference in instrumental measurements (Saxena et al. 2018); see Figures 1 and 2.

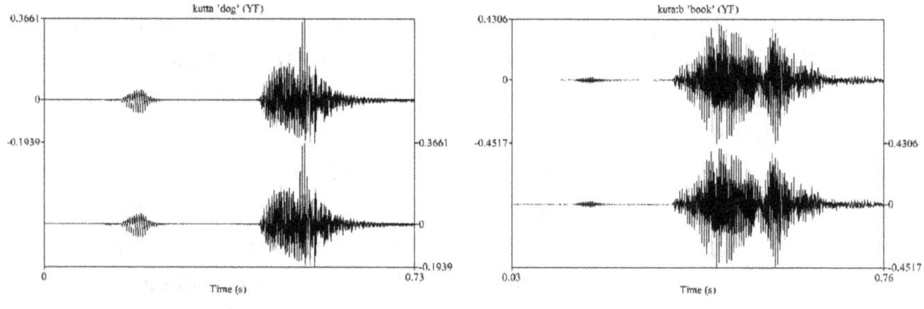

Figure 1: geminate (left: /kutta:/ 'dog') : singleton (right: /kuta:b/ 'book') (YF)

5 Approximately 110 items are found in our material that contain geminates. The number varies, depending on how we count items that appear both with and without a geminate, e.g. /suk(k)ar/ 'Friday'.

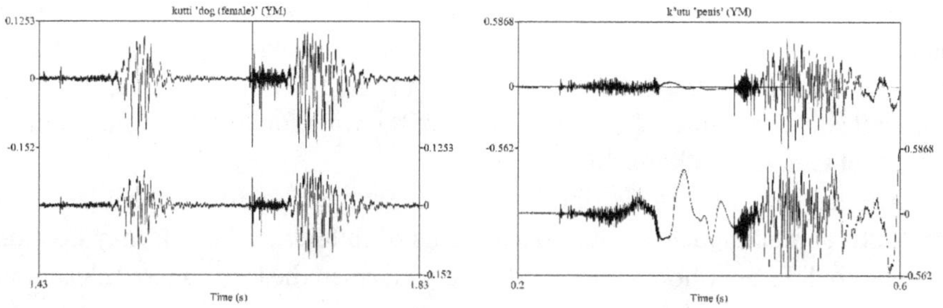

Figure 2: geminate (left: /kutti/ 'bitch') : singleton (right: /k^{h}utu/ 'penis') (YM)

Thus, the presence of geminates appears not to be constant across speakers, which brings up the question which speakers' variety should be taken as the basis for the phonology. We see some intra-speaker variation in our data, but not to the same extent as when it comes to voiced aspirates. Some examples are given in Table 4.

Table 4: Variation in consonant gemination

YF consultant	YM consultant	Gloss
[daddu]	[dadu]	'paternal grandfather'
[ɖubbem]	[ɖubem]	'to be drowned'
[matt^{h}a]	[mat^{h}a]	'forehead'
[haɖɖaŋ]	[haɖaŋ]	'bone'
[duppe]	[dup(p)e]	'sun'

Secondly, just as in the case of the aspirated voiced stops, geminates appear to be found mainly in IA items, so that the observed variation may simply be due to the more educated speakers showing less integration of IA items in their Kanashi.

5 Discussion

As we have seen, several factors appear to play a role in the phonetic variation found in Kanashi. The details of their interplay and which factors are responsible for what is as of yet not entirely clear.

One of these factors is sociolinguistic aspects. As mentioned, we find regular differences between our consultants, such as with the geminates, described above. It is of course tempting to draw sociolinguistic conclusions from this, such as connecting the literacy of YF with the features she exhibits. However, this is risky to do without first collecting more data from other speakers, representing different social variables. This, then, is one of the ways forward to gaining a fuller picture of variation in Kanashi.

Another factor is the distribution of these features across different language strata. In some languages with lexical items of different origin, it may be motivated with different phonologies for different layers in the languages. An example of where such an analysis has been suggested is Japanese, see e.g. Ito & Mester (1995). We have already hinted at why such an analysis seems less desirable for Kanashi. As already mentioned, none of the features discussed are strictly limited to words of IA origin. This sets these features apart from, for instance, the cluster /ks/, which is very clearly limited to a handful of IA/English loans.

It should also be noted that we occasionally find one of these features in items where they do not exist in Kullu Pahari or Hindi. It is currently not clear if this is due to internal change in Kanashi (for instance, by analogy with other borrowed items) or if the items where borrowed in that form.

A final factor to be considered is the possibility that even with comprehensive data, the status of some features in Kanashi will remain unclear, or at least less clearly phonemic than some others. Scobbie & Stuart-Smith (2008: 106) write, regarding some problematic features of Scottish Standard English, that "[i]t must not be thought that these difficulties arise due to sociolinguistic or stylistic variation, and that they can be dismissed as just so much 'noise' by researchers whose focus is exclusively phonological theory. We think that any variation presented above is relevant to phonology in the narrowest sense". They suggest treating phonemicity as a graded property. An overview of similar problems and suggested solutions can be found in Hall (2013), where she refers to them as "intermediate phonological relationships". That is, relationships that are not clearly either phonemic or allophonic but seem to lie somewhere in between, either because the traditional criteria for phonemic status conflict or because some other factors are felt to affect their status. The notion is intuitively appealing, but as usual the devil is in the details. Gradient phonemic status requires a way of calculating how much of a phoneme a particular segment is, or the notion risks becoming vacuous. While Hall (2013: 259–262) discusses at some length various proposals for calculating degree of phonemicity, no immediately practical procedure for doing this is presented. In the absence of such, observations about phoneme gradience or marginal phonemes may be enlightening, but with limited utility, and in reality the only reasonable practical descriptive solution may be a binary phoneme ~ allophone distinction.

We will here point out some ways in which the Kanashi features discussed here make a classical binary divide into phonemic and allophonic status problematic.

With regard to the variations observed concerning geminates and aspirated voiced stops, our preliminary analysis is as follows: aspirated voiced stops cannot be considered fully part of the phoneme inventory of Kanashi; their rarity, their limited distribution strata-wise and the fact that they are always in free variation with plain voiced stops make this clear. Of these, the last one is the strongest argument. However, they also cannot be considered merely allophones of their plain voiced stop counterparts either: the main piece of evidence for this is that they are lexically conditioned, and not phonologically conditioned or in completely free variation. They seem to be examples of so-called marginal phonemes, a time-honored, seemingly unavoidable concept in actual language descriptions (e.g. Ferguson & Chowdhury 1960; Suomi et al. 2008). Returning to the three alternatives discussed above in Section 4.1 (repeated here for convenience), we note the following.

Alternative 1	Alternative 2	Alternative 3
/b/ → [b]	/b/ → [b], [b^h]	/B/ → [b], [b^h]
/b^h/ → [b^h], [b]		[..., +voiced, ?aspirated]
/b^hau/	/bau/	/Bau/

The amount of information that needs to be captured in any language description is determined by attested language phenomena and equal regardless of the particular linguistic model adopted.[6] That said, there are better and worse models, of course. Model-internal parsimony – Occam's razor – is a desirable goal. But in principle there are many different models which will capture the same information equally economically, and the choice among these must be made according to some other criterion or criteria, e.g. relating aspects of the linguistic model to findings from neuro- or psycholinguistics. The main point we wish to make here is simply that the attested facts of the (lexically conditioned) distribution of aspirated and unaspirated voiced stops in Kanashi must be accounted for in our description, and there are several ways in which this can be done.

6 "Information" is understood here in the technical sense of mathematical information theory (Shannon & Weaver 1949), which defines a lower bound on the number of symbols needed to faithfully express a certain set of distinctions.

Our general preference – at least at this stage of description – is to make as few assumptions as possible necessitating the postulation of underlying, 'invisible' entities. Hence, morphemes should be realized as (one or more) phoneme sequences without underspecified segments (such as archiphonemes). Phonemes should in principle correspond to one of their actually occurring allophones. This rules out alternative 3. Further, allophone selection should preferably be determined only by phonological (or phonetic context). This rules out alternative 2, since, as mentioned above, the allophone selection must be lexically determined in our case. The remaining option, alternative 1, is in some sense the mirror image of alternative 2. However, if there are any nonalternating instances of aspirated voiced stops, this alternative will overgenerate, unless we again introduce the possibility of lexical triggering of a phoneme realization rule.[7]

A relevant consideration, and one that Hall (2013) does not mention as such, although it is implicit in some of her argumentation, has to do with what we could call "model-internal consistency". Some modelling assumptions logically restrict other aspects of our model. In fact, if we take the segmental representation(s) of a morpheme to be made up of phonemes, as above, this logically means that any allophony must be computable from this representation (since the representation itself is made up from phonemes). If we further require the conditioning factors for selecting allophones to be strictly phonological, we are forced to accord the aspirated voiced stops phoneme status in Kanashi, and assume that the relevant morphemes have two allomorphs listed, whose precise selection criteria remain to be elucidated, however.

Against this background, the safest route making the fewest assumptions would be to assume that a lexical item like 'brother' will be realized by two possible phoneme sequences: /b^{h}au/, /bau/. Note that alternative 1 and this solution both require that aspirated voiced stops be recognized as phonemes (although marginal).

As for geminates, we have pointed out that the difference in realization here seems mainly to be between speakers. If this turns out to hold, it may be that we can in the future define geminates as sociolinguistically determined. Whether geminates are to be considered a part of the Kanashi sound system as a whole is another question, and must presumably depend on how many and which speakers have it.

7 Since we cannot in principle demonstrate non-occurrence of variation in an individual case, this alternative still seems as the preferable one.

6 Conclusions

We have shown in this chapter that several factors, many of which are perhaps not foremost in the researcher's mind when doing early-stage fieldwork, can be relevant in describing the variation and phonology of a language. Such variation poses additional challenges when it comes to describing the language (sound system) for the first time for a language where the available language data as well as the access to native speakers are very limited. The examples from Kanashi show that we must take into account both potential sociolinguistic factors as well as the etymology of lexical items. Additionally, it should be considered that the conventional criteria for phonemic status might not give a clear answer, regardless of how thorough the coverage of the materials is of the phenomenon under investigation.

References

Andersen, Roger W. 1982. Determining the linguistic attributes of language attrition. In Richard D. Lambert & Barbara F. Freed (eds.), *The loss of language skills*, 83–118. Rowley: Newbury House.

Boersma, Paul & David Weenink. 2018. *Praat: Doing phonetics by computer [computer program]*. Version 6.0.42, retrieved 15 August 2018 from http://www.praat.org/.

Cook, Eung-Do. 1989. Is phonology going haywire in dying languages? Phonological variations in Chipewyan and Sarcee. *Language in Society* 18(2): 235–255.

Darnell, Regna. 1990. *Edward Sapir: Linguist, anthropologist, humanist*. Berkeley: University of California Press.

Ferguson, Charles A. & Munier Chowdhury. 1960. The phonemes of Bengali. *Language* 36(1): 22–59. DOI: 10.2307/410622.

Hall, Kathleen C. 2013. A typology of intermediate phonological relationships. *The Linguistic Review* 30(2): 215–275.

Ito, Junko & R. Armin Mester. 1995. Japanese phonology. In John A. Goldsmith (ed.), *The handbook of phonological theory*, 817–838. Oxford: Blackwell.

Joseph, John Earl. 1987. *Eloquence and power: The rise of language standards and standard languages*. London: Pinter.

Linell, Per. 2005. *The written language bias in linguistics*. First published in 1982 by Dept. of Communication Studies, University of Linköping, Sweden. London: Routledge.

Matisoff, James A. 2003. *Handbook of Proto-Tibeto-Burman: System and philosophy of Sino-Tibetan reconstruction*. Berkeley: University of California Press.

McGregor, R. S. 1993. *The Oxford Hindi-English dictionary*. Oxford: Oxford University Press.

Palosaari, Naomi & Lyle Campbell. 2011. Structural aspects of language endangerment. In Peter Austin & Julia Sallabank (eds.), *Cambridge handbook of endangered languages*, 100–119. Cambridge: Cambridge University Press.

Saxena, Anju, Anna Sjöberg & Padam Sagar. 2018. *Linguistic variation: Challenges for describing the phonology of Kanashi*. Presentation at the *International workshop on Fieldwork: Methods and theory*. University of Gothenburg, Sweden, 13–14 December 2018.

Scobbie, James M. & Jane Stuart-Smith. 2008. Quasi-phonemic contrast and the indeterminacy of the segmental inventory: Examples from Scottish English. In Peter Avery, B. Elan Dresher & Keren Rice (eds.), *Contrast in phonology: Perception and acquisition*, 87–113. Berlin: Mouton de Gruyter.

Shannon, Claude E. & Warren Weaver. 1949. *The mathematical theory of communication*. Champaign: University of Illinois Press.

Suomi, Kari, Juhani Toivanen & Riikka Ylitalo. 2008. *Finnish sound structure: Phonetics, phonology, phonotactics and prosody*. Oulu: Oulu University Press.

Anju Saxena and Lars Borin

5 And then there was one: Kanashi numerals from borrowed superdiversity to borrowed uniformity

Abstract: Despite a long history of physical and social isolation from its surrounding communities, Kanashi exhibits several layers of borrowing from genealogically unrelated Indo-Aryan languages, which contribute substantially to the phenomenon described and discussed in this chapter, Kanashi's surprisingly rich array of mechanisms for forming numerals. The Kanashi numerals form a linguistic subsystem which holds both borrowed items and borrowed structures, and which also shows great variation, with up to four alternative ways of forming most complex numerals, a remarkable fact which deserves attention. This variety is now being displaced by wholesale adoption of Hindi numerals. On the basis of cross-linguistic data we discuss the quite different outcomes of borrowing from the same kind of source languages, but at different times.

Keywords: Kanashi, Kinnauri, numerals, numeral systems, Sino-Tibetan, Indo-Aryan, language contact

Chapter overview:

https://doi.org/10.1515/9783110703245-005

1 Introduction

An intriguing fact which emerged when documenting Kanashi, a phenomenon which we have not seen much mention of in the literature, is that there are – at least traditionally – several alternative ways of forming numerals in the language, and further that the numeral systems exhibit many items and structures borrowed into Kanashi, a Sino-Tibetan (ST) language, from – genealogically unrelated – Indo-Aryan (IA) languages.

This is the topic of this chapter, the rest of which is organized as follows. In Section 2 we present a description of the Kanashi numeral systems based on our own fieldwork data, followed by an investigation into their historical origins and a comparison to closely related or geographically close languages in Section 3. Section 4 is devoted to a discussion of possible reasons why so much borrowed material is found in a language whose speakers are well-known for keeping a clear distance to all outsiders. In Section 5 we address the question of the variation exhibited by Kanashi numerals, and summarize our conclusions in Section 6. Appendix A contains a listing of all Kanashi numerals found in our fieldwork data.

2 The Kanashi numeral systems

The presentation in this section is based mainly on the speech of three Kanashi speakers: one older male Kanashi speaker and two younger speakers, one man and one woman. At the time of the data collection the older speaker was about 50 years old, the younger male speaker around 22 years old and the female speaker around 28 years old. The female speaker had received some formal education. Both male speakers were illiterate; they had not received any formal education. All three speakers were born and brought up in Malana, the single village where Kanashi is spoken. Like other Kanashi speakers, they leave the village occasionally. All three could understand Hindi and Kullu Pahari, the locally dominant language, both IA languages. While the female speaker could speak Hindi quite well, the male speakers (especially the younger speaker) spoke a mixed Hindi with strong influence of their mother tongue Kanashi.

The data elicitation was done in Hindi. In addition to lexical items, we have also collected elicited phrases and sentences and some narratives. The following description of the Kanashi numerals is based on our fieldwork data, and also draws on the scant previous descriptions of Kanashi available in the literature. As can be seen in Appendix A to this chapter, not all numerals are attested in our material.[1] Unless otherwise stated, Kanashi examples are provided here in phonemic transcription based on the description provided in Chapter 2 in this volume.[2]

Among older Kanashi speakers, several alternative systems for forming numerals up to 100 are in use, in addition to wholesale borrowing of the Hindi numerals. The concrete indication of this great variety is that we find up to three different ways of expressing the same amount in our data (four ways if we also reckon with the Hindi numerals), and if we extrapolate from attested combinations, there should be a maximum of four ways (five ways including the Hindi numerals). This variety comes from a set of partly independent choices both in constructing complex numerals and in selecting their components, to be further described below.

First, some terminology. Except for the lowest numerals, which tend to be monomorphemic, numerals in many languages are constructed according to the general pattern[3]

a×n *op* b

where "op" is some arithmetical operation, typically addition or subtraction. Note however, that there may, but need not, be elements in numerals explicitly expressing "×" ('times', '-fold', or the like) and the arithmetical operation ('on', 'and', 'from', 'less', etc.), but often the pattern is implicit, e.g., positionally indicated, as in Swedish *sextiotre* (*sex-tio-tre* [six-ten-three] '6 (×) 10 (+) 3') 'sixty-three'.

E.g.: a×10±b or a×20±b
(thus: 42 = 4×10+2 or 2×20+2 or 5×10−8 or 3×20−18)

1 Note that this overview covers only cardinals. The little data that we have concerning ordinals in Kanashi point to overwhelming IA influence. Thus, even the lowest ordinals 'first' and 'second', at least as they are attested in our material, are IA borrowings (*pela* and *duʤa*, respectively).

2 We have noted much phonetic variation across speakers in our data, where we find various degrees of adaptation of IA items – *puʤa* ~ *puʧas* 'fifty'; *saʈʰ* ~ *ʃaʈʰ* ~ *ʃɔʈʰ* 'sixty' – and also other differences, e.g., *a* ~ *u*, so that the name of the language itself appears both as *kunashi* (with older speakers) and *kanashi* (among younger speakers). See Chapter 4. Where we have recorded more than one variant of a certain IA numeral, we examined if the more standard IA pronunciation is found only in the speech of the literate speaker(s), in which case we chose the other variant, e.g. *ʧalis* (literate speaker) ~ *ʧali* (speaker without any formal education; illiterate) 'forty'. Another guiding principle was frequency, where we have chosen the form which was provided by the majority.

3 Note that we must allow the quantities *a*, *n* and *b* to be atomic or (recursively) composite numerals for this pattern to work as a general characterization of the structure of (recursively binary-branching) numeral systems. Since we are dealing only with numbers in the range 1–100 here, this pattern serves us well in practice.

The actual order of the elements may vary among languages. The quantity *n* is known as a base of the numeral system, so that numbers are built from some multiple of the base modified by "op b", where *b* then ranges from 0 to *n–1*, or, in other words: quantities are counted in groups of *n*. Two common numeral bases in the languages of the world, as well as the two bases encountered in the languages discussed here, are 10 – decimal numeral systems – and 20 – vigesimal systems (Comrie 2005). Numeral systems may exhibit more than one base, e.g. French, with both decimal and vigesimal structures.[4] If more than one base is present, their distribution can be complementary (as in French or Danish), or they may be in free variation (as in Kanashi).

Below, we will refer to the multiples of the numeral base – "a×n" above – as the "major part", and the additive or subtractive elements – "*op* b" – as the "minor part" of the numeral expression.[5]

2.1 Nondecomposable numerals

The numerals in Kanashi which are not (synchronically) decomposable into simpler parts – "atoms" in the sense of J. H. Greenberg (1978) – are those for 1–20, some of the words for multiples of 10, and the numerals for 'hundred' and 'thousand'. Etymologically, the numerals 1–5 and one of the two alternative terms for 20 are ST in origin, and all the others are IA borrowings. IA numerals for 1–5 and 20 also occur in Kanashi, but there is no simple ST numeral for 6 and above (except for 20, which is etymologically, but not synchronically, composite). Table 1 shows the Kanashi numerals 1–20, giving the origin for nondecomposable items and an analysis for composite numerals.

The great diversity in numeral formation patterns in Kanashi which we describe in detail below is characteristic of higher, composite numerals, not the nondecomposable lower numerals. Among the latter, 1–5 (and 20) have at most two variants (ST and IA), and for expressing the numerals 6–16 we have only found one term per item, IA in origin. The diversity in numeral formation starts with the

4 Here we are not referring to the common case where we find successively larger bases expressing powers of some lower base, as when $100 = 10^2$, $1000 = 10^3$, etc., but a situation where alternative bases are used as "paradigmatic alternatives" in positions where the other base would be expected.

5 There are other (rarer) systems which do not conform to this pattern, e.g. systems without any base (Comrie 2005; Hammarström 2010), or the "numeral system!overcountingovercounting" systems mentioned by Comrie (1999) and Mazaudon (2010), referring back to Menninger (1969: 76–80) as the scholar who first introduced this term, e.g., Finnish *kuusitoista* (*kuusi-tois-ta* [six-second-PARTITIVE] 'six of second (ten)') 'sixteen'.

Table 1: Kanashi numerals 1–20

Gloss	Kanashi	Origin (Source: IA: Turner 1966; ST: STEDT 2016; Matisoff 2003)
‘one’	*iːd*	ST: *it
	ek	IA: Turner 2462 ḗka
‘two’	*niʃ*	ST: *gnyis; Sino-Tibetan (ST): *g-ni-s /*g-nis
‘three’	*ʃum*	ST: *gsum; ST: *g-sum
‘four’	*pu*	ST: *pwɑ (breadth of four fingers)
‘five’	*ŋa, na*	ST: *ŋa
‘six’	*ʧʰa*	IA: Turner 12803 ṣáṣ
‘seven’	*sat*	IA: Turner 13343 sā́pta
‘eight’	*aʈʰ*	IA: Turner 941 aṣṭā́
‘nine’	*nao*	IA: Turner 6984 náva
‘ten’	*das*	IA: Turner 6227 dáśa
‘eleven’	*gjara*	IA: Turner 2485 ḗkādaśa
‘twelve’	*bara*	IA: Turner 6658 dvā́daśa
‘thirteen’	*tera*	IA: Turner 6001 tráyōdaśa
‘fourteen’	*ʧoda*	IA: Turner 4605 cáturdaśa
‘fifteen’	*pandra*	IA: Turner 7662 páñcadaśa
‘sixteen’	*sola*	IA: Turner 12812 ṣṓḍaśa
‘seventeen’	*ʃumis kam niʥa*	[3:is less 20]
	sutaːra	IA: Turner 13146 saptádaśa
‘eighteen’	*niʃ kam niʥa*	[2 less 20]
	ʈʰara	IA: Turner 946 aṣṭā́daśa
‘nineteen’	*iːdis kam niʥa*	[1:is less 20]
	unni	IA: Turner 2411 ūnaviṁśati
‘twenty’	*niʥa*	ST: [two:ten] (cf. Kinnauri *niʥa* < *niʃ* ‘two’ + *se* ‘ten’)
	bi	IA: Turner 11616 viṁśatí

numeral 17, which exhibits one nondecomposable (*sutaːra*; IA) and one composite variant (*ʃumis kam niʥa* [3:is less 20]).

Konow (1909) and Sharma (1992) provide brief descriptions of the Kanashi numerals. Both note that higher numerals (except 20) are of IA origin, and that Kanashi uses both the IA decimal system and a vigesimal system. Konow suggests a gender-based tendency in the use of the IA decimal system and numerals based on the vigesimal system: “Higher numbers are counted in twenties, though the Aryan method of reckoning in tens is also commonly used by men, while the women stick to the other way.” (Konow 1909: 444). This gender-based distribution of the decimal and the vigesimal system is not found in our material. As we will seen below, both the IA decimal system and the vigesimal system were provided by an older male speaker, along with some other numeral systems. Konow (1909) also notes a variation between [n] and [ɲ] in ‘two’ (*nish*, *nyish*). This is also not found in our material. We consistently got [niʃ] from both older and younger speakers.

2.2 Structure of the Kanashi numeral systems

As opposed to some modern IA numeral systems, which are characterized by extreme irregularity, so that, e.g., the Hindi numerals 1–100 are in effect synchronically unanalyzable (Berger 1992: 243–245), all the Kanashi structures found in our data are quite regular. The choices characterizing the different ways of composing numerals in Kanashi are choice of[6]

(a) numeral base: 20, 10 or transitional 20>10 (see Section 2.2.2.1)
(b) language of origin for major parts of numerals: ST or IA
(c) operation performed on minor parts of numerals: addition or subtraction

Theoretically, this would yield 3×2×2=12 possible numeral systems, but the choices are not completely independent, and on the whole only four different combinations are found in our material. They are:

(A1) base 20 + ST + addition
(A2) base 20 + IA[7] + addition
(S1) transitional base 20>10 + IA + subtraction
(S2) base 10 + IA + subtraction

6 Interestingly and even unexpectedly – and with one minor exception involving the item ***saɽe*** '+half' – the linear order among components is not variable; multiplication has smaller before larger (3×20), as has subtraction, while with addition the order is larger before smaller (20+3). On the one hand, this seems to be a common parameter for variability in languages (see Section 5), which makes its absence remarkable in a numeral system with so much variation in other respects. On the other hand, in the cases of multiplication and addition the orderings attested in Kanashi are the most frequent across languages, according to J. H. Greenberg (1978).

7 IA 'twenty' as the base is not found at all in our material. All numerals involving the vigesimal system use ST *nidza* 'twenty'. However, Grierson (1928: s.v. *Hundred (13)*) has *ṅa* **biya** [five (×) twenty] 'hundred' (*nabeeha* in Harcourt 1871: 378).

Examples:[8]

(1) (1a) A1: 'fifty five' *niʃ nidzau dʒe* **pandra** [2 (×) 20:u plus 15]

(1b) A1: 'thirty two' *nidzau dʒe* **bara** [20:u plus 12]

(1c) A2: 'seventy six' **saʈʰu** *dʒe* **sola** [60:u plus 16]

(2) (2a) S1: 'sixty nine' *iːdis* **kam saɽe saʈʰ** [1:is less +half 60]

(2b) S2: 'fifty five' *ŋais* **kam saʈʰ** [5:is less 60]

(2c) S2: 'fifty five' **pãtʃ kam saʈʰ** [5 less 60]

Another way of (partly) expressing this would be to say that ST major parts imply addition (A) of minor parts, while subtraction (S) of minor parts implies IA major parts (except 'twenty'; see below). Note that addition occurs with both ST and IA major parts, hence the (one-way) implication.

Regarding choice (b) above (the language of origin), it concerns specifically the major parts of numerals (see 1c and 2b). As for the minor parts, the numerals 1–5 can be both ST and IA (see 2b and 2c), and the numerals 6–19 are only IA. The choice of language of origin for those minor parts where this is an option does not influence the structure of numerals. In numerals of type (A1), the major parts are expressed using ST elements (see 1a and 1b). In type (A2) these are simply replaced by the corresponding IA elements, i.e., 20, 40, 60 and 80, preserving a basically vigesimal system (see 1c).

In numerals of type (S1), base 10 is introduced – or the values half-way between multiples of 20 are given special treatment – using the (IA) expression **saɽe** '+half', i.e., 70 is expressed as [60 +half] or [+half 60] in example (2a). As shown in (2b), in type (S2) the IA words are used for all multiples of 10,[9] making it a pure base-10 system (i.e., decimal).[10]

Exceptionally, subtraction also occurs with the ST numeral *nidza* '20' in our data, where the numerals 17, 18 and 19 are formed as

8 Here and below IA elements will be indicated in examples in **bold with underlining** and inferred – unexpressed – instances of multiplication and addition between separate words will be shown in the glossing of numerals by "(×)" and "(+)", respectively. Even though the element *dʒe* is glossed as 'plus' in the examples, so far we do not actually know its meaning or its origin. For a discussion of this and of the suffixes *-(i)s* and *-u*, see Section 3.

9 These IA items are borrowed from some IA language with a decimal numeral system, and not one whose numeral system is vigesimal, as is the case in several Western Pahari languages. Kullu Pahari has both systems (see also Section 2.3 below).

10 Some modern IA numeral systems – notably that of Hindi – are such that the structure of major parts is not synchronically obvious (because of sound changes), so that these systems are classified as decimal only by virtue of their minor parts cycling through 1–9 rather than 1–19.

(3) 'seventeen' *ʃumis* ***kam*** *niʣa* [3:is less 20]
'eighteen' *niʃ* ***kam*** *niʣa* [2 less 20]
'nineteen' *iːdis* ***kam*** *niʣa* [1:is less 20]

With the pure base-20 numerals (types A1 and S1), intermediate quantities are formed by the operation of addition, i.e., the formula is [a × 20 + b], where a is in the range 2–4, and b ranges from 1 to 19. With types S1 and S2, the pattern is [b subtracted from a], where a is on the form either [IA.multiple.of.10] or [IA.multiple.of.20 +half]/[+half IA.multiple.of.20].

2.2.1 Major part formation with minor part addition

2.2.1.1 Base 20 ST major part

ST major parts are built from the expression *niʣa* 'twenty', which is presumably etymologically compound [two+ten] but synchronically monomorphemic, since the ST word for 'ten' is not attested in Kanashi, but has been replaced by the IA word ***das*** 'ten'.[11] Cf. Kinnauri *niʣa* 'twenty' < *niʃ* 'two' + *se* 'ten' (Saxena 2017: 762). Hence: *niʃ niʣa* [2 (×) 20] 'forty', *ʃum niʣa* [3 (×) 20] 'sixty', *pu niʣa* [4 (×) 20] 'eighty'. Minor parts in the range 1–19 are added to the major parts according to a pattern described below. Thus, 'thirty' is, for example, expressed by *niʣau ʤe* ***das*** [20:u plus ten], and 'fifty-nine' is *niʃ niʣau ʤe* ***unni*** [2 (×) 20:u plus 19].

2.2.1.2 Base 20 IA major part

The only difference from the preceding pattern is that the ST major part is replaced by the corresponding IA numeral. Practically, this means that the IA expressions for 'thirty', 'fifty', 'seventy' and 'ninety' do not appear here, but are instead expressed as, e.g., ***saʈʰu*** *ʤe* ***das*** [60:u plus 10] 'sixty and ten'. Consequently, this pattern is at heart vigesimal, even if the IA numerals substituting for ST major parts have a decimal etymology.

---

11 Although according to Hodson (1913: 329), "Dārmiyā [Darma], Kanawri [Kinnauri], Kanashi, Chamba Lahuli [Tinani], and Rangkas have forms sai or sā" for 'ten'. This may be a mistake, since the stated source of Hodson's data, LSI vol. 3 (Konow 1909), does not list such a form for Kanashi, neither in the Kanashi grammar sketch (Konow 1909: 444) nor in the standard word list (Konow 1909: 532).

2.2.2 Major part formation with minor part subtraction (only IA)

2.2.2.1 Transitional base 20>10

As with the pure base 20 IA major part, only the IA terms for 'twenty', 'forty', 'sixty', and 'eighty' appear in this pattern. However, instead of expressing 'thirty', etc., as 'twenty and ten', etc., these are formed using the (IA) expression ***saɽe*** '+half'.[12] The order of the elements seems to be free; **saɽe** can be placed before or after the multiple of 20: ***saɽe sat***^{h} [+half 60] '70' ~ ***aʃi saɽe*** [80 +half] '90'.

2.2.2.2 Pure base 10

In this pattern, the major parts are simply the IA numerals for the decades: *iːdis* ***kam puʥa*** [1:is less 50] '49'; *sat* ***kam puʥa*** [7 less 50] '43'.

2.2.3 Minor part addition (only base 20)

The pattern here is

major.part(-*u*) (*ʤe*/*ke*) minor.part

The (base-20) major part can be ST or IA as described above; examples:

(4) 'twenty three' *niʥa-u ʤe ʃum* [20.ST.base.20-u plus 3]
'sixty five' *ʃum niʥa-u ʤe ŋa* [3 (×) 20.ST.base.20-u plus 5]
'sixty seven' *ʃum niʥa-u ʤe* ***sat*** [3 (×) 20.ST.base.20-u plus 7]
'sixty seven' ***saʈ***^{h}*-u ʤe* ***sat*** [60.IA.base.20-u plus 7]
'seventy' ***saʈ***^{h}*-u ʤe* ***das*** [60.IA.base.20-u plus 10]

While our language consultant provided most of these numerals with *ʤe*, he said that *ʤe* here can always be replaced by *ke* without any apparent difference. Furthermore, *ʤe/ke* can also be omitted altogether. There is also one instance in our data (*niʥa ʤe ŋa* [20 plus 5] 'twenty five') where -*u* does not appear.

12 [sa:ɽe] (Hindi) or a similar form for '+half' occurs in many IA languages. For example: Punjabi *sādhe*, Bengali *sāɽe*, and Gujarati *sāɽa* (Berger 1992); Kotguru (Koṭgurū), Cameali (Camealī), Bhateali (Bhaṭeālī), Curahi (Curāhī), and Bhadrawahi (Bhadrawāhī) *sāḍhē* (Bailey 1908). It occurs with the numerals 3 and above, where it has the interpretation '+half'. According to Berger (1992: 279), it "has developed from Sanskrit sārdha (< *sa-ardha 'provided with a half')".

2.2.4 Minor part subtraction (transitional base 20>10 or pure base 10)

The pattern here is

minor.part-*(i)s* ***kam*** major.part

The element ***kam*** 'less' is IA; examples:[13]

(5) 'nineteen' *iːdis* ***kam*** *nidza* [1:is less 20]

'twenty eight' *niʃis* ***kam derbija*** [2:is less 1.5:20]

'sixty seven' *ʃumis* ***kam sare sath*** [3:is less +half 60]

'eighty one' ***unnis kam ʃo*** [19:is less 100]

This pattern mixes base 20 and base 10. The minor part consequently ranges between one and 19, but we see both cases where the major part is a multiple of 20 and those where the major part is an odd multiple of 10. The minor part could be ST (e.g. *ʃumis* ***kam*** *nidza* [3:is less 20]) or IA (e.g. ***sat kam pudza*** [7 less 50] '43'). It would be reasonable to assume that a minor part 10 or larger would only be used with a major part that is a multiple of 20, whereas odd multiples of 10 should allow only minor parts with the value nine or less. However, there are only a few examples of this pattern among our fieldwork data, making it hard to confirm or reject this assumption.

The suffix *-is* on the minor part occurs when it ends in a consonant and *-s* occurs when it ends with a vowel, but there is one instance (*ŋais* ***kam sath*** [5:is less 60] '55') where *-is* occurs with a numeral ending in a vowel (*ŋa* 'five'). Further, the occurrence of *-(i)s* seems optional, as we have instances of the same numeral both with and without *-(i)s* before **kam**; for example:

(6) 'twenty eight' *niʃis* ***kam derbija*** [2:is less 1.5:20]

'eighteen' *niʃ* ***kam*** *nidza* [2 less 20]

2.3 Numeral system 5: Modern Hindi numerals

Apart from the four numeral systems described above, the regular modern Hindi numerals are increasingly gaining ground. Examples of some Hindi numerals in Kanashi are provided below. Table 2 contains a comparison of these Kanashi numerals with those in Hindi, in Kullu Pahari (ktx; the dominant regional language)

13 *der* '1.5' is an IA borrowing.

and Mandeali (mjl). Both the latter are Western Pahari IA languages presumably representative of the donor language for the older IA elements in Kanashi numerals.[14] The older borrowed IA words for 'thirty', 'fifty', 'seventy', and 'ninety' have clear base-10 etymologies. Their shape together with linguistic geography points to some Western Pahari language as the source (see Section 3). Equally clearly, the shape of the recent items listed in the "Kanashi" column in Table 2 indicates that their source is not Kullu Pahari or some other Western Pahari language, but Hindi.

Table 2: Some borrowed modern Hindi numerals in Kanashi (Hindi, Kullu Pahari, and Mandeali numerals from <https://mpi-lingweb.shh.mpg.de/numeral/>)

Gloss	Kanashi	Hindi (IA)	Kullu Pahari (IA)	Mandeali (IA)
'five'	*pãʧ*	*pāch* [pã͡tʃ]	*pan͡dʒ*	*pan͡dʒ*
'twenty one'	*ikkis*	*ikkais* [ɪkːis]	*ikki*	*ɪkki*
'twenty two'	*bais*	*bais* [bais]	*bai*	*bai*
'twenty three'	*teis*	*teis* [t̪eis]	*tirei*, *trei*	*t̪ei*

The four numeral strategies described above (A1, A2, S2, S2), were provided primarily by older Kanashi speakers. According to our primary older language consultant, the four patterns are interchangeable, i.e., they are not functionally or situationally differentiated, and he very happily provided more and more examples of Kanashi numerals using the four numeral systems, while younger Kanashi speakers (both males and females) used only Hindi numerals, and when specifically asked about their judgements of the four numeral strategies, they did not recognize the higher numerals formed with *ʤe/ke*, and just laughed and said that they do not know what this is. They provided instead the Hindi numerals.

3 Kanashi numerals in comparison

Kinnauri and Bunan are two other ST languages of Himachal Pradesh which are closely related to Kanashi (see Chapter 1). Comparing the numeral systems of these languages to that of Kanashi will hopefully help to throw light on the

14 We know too little about the prehistory of Kanashi to say which IA language would be the most likely donor language for the older stratum of borrowed IA numerals. Kullu Pahari is geographically closest at the present time, and Mandeali is spoken in an area in-between the present locations of Kanashi and its closest ST relative Kinnauri.

somewhat unexpected situation in Kanashi and also provide some additional information about the structural elements of the Kanashi numeral systems.

As opposed to Kanashi, both Bunan and Kinnauri preserve an inherited ST numeral system, at least up to and including 'one hundred'. In both cases the common inherited ST system is vigesimal.[15]

Additionally, and similarly to Kanashi, in both Kinnauri and Bunan the Hindi numerals can be freely used, since both communities are in effect at least bilingual, with Hindi as the prestige language and the language of wider communication for interacting outside the own language community.

According to Widmer (2017: 309–311), in the case of Bunan, the traditional numerals are nowadays used almost exclusively for lower numbers up to 20. The main numeral system in daily use is a decimal system borrowed from Tibetan, which was the culturally dominant language until the mid-20th century.

Traditional Bunan numerals are vigesimal with minor part addition, i.e., they correspond to the Kanashi A1 pattern. Examples (Bunan [Widmer 2017: 307–308]):

(7) 'four' *piː*

'twenty' *nidza*

'ten' *tɕuj*

'twenty-four' *nidza=ki pi* [twenty=GEN four]

'fourteen' *tɕupi* [ten:four]

'thirty-four' *nidza=ki tɕupi* [twenty=GEN ten:four]

'eighty' *piː nidza* [four (×) twenty]

Kinnauri also shares some features with Kanashi in the way numerals are formed. Kinnauri exhibits basically two strategies for forming complex numerals:

(A) Base 20 major part with minor part addition

(S) Transitional base 20>10 major part with minor part subtraction

Examples (Kinnauri [Saxena 2022]):

(8) A: 'sixteen' *sorug* [ten:o:six]

'thirty-seven' *nidzo sostiʃ* [twenty:o ten:o:seven]

'sixty-nine' *ʃum nidzo gui* [three (×) twenty:o nine]

(9) S: 'thirty-seven' *ʃum maːts niʃnidza* [three is.not two:twenty]

'fifty-seven' *ʃumindza paŋ ʃum maːts* [three:twenty DAT three is.not]

15 Proto-ST is reconstructed as having a decimal numeral system, however.

'seventy-seven' *ʃum kam pa nidza* [three less four (×) twenty]

'eighty-seven' *ʃum ma:ts panidzo se* [three is.not four:twenty:o ten]

'ninety-seven' *ra paŋ ʃum ma:ts* [hundred DAT three is.not]

'ninety-seven' *ʃum ma:ts ra* [three is.not hundred]

The A pattern in Kinnauri corresponds to that seen in traditional Bunan numerals as well as to the Kanashi A1 construction.

The Kinnauri S pattern represents a decimal overlay on the basic vigesimal numeral system, since the minuend is the next multiple of 10 (not 20), as can be seen in the item 'eighty-seven' above, which means that the subtrahend will always fall in the range 1–9. Apparently the element glossed 'less' in the S structures can always be expressed either with the negated ST copula *ma:ts* or with the borrowed IA item *kam*, the latter being the same as in the Kanashi S1 and S2 structures. There are two variants of the S structure, one where the minuend comes first followed by the dative marker *paŋ*, after which the subtrahend and *ma:ts/kam* follow, i.e. 'to X is not Y' or 'X does not have Y'. The ordering of elements in the other variant corresponds to the Kanashi S1 and S2 patterns, i.e., [subtrahend less minuend].

While it is clear that *kam* 'less' is an IA borrowing in Kanashi, the etymology of *-(i)s* normally appearing before it on the subtrahend is unknown. Possibly it is to be identified with the instrumental (and ergative) marker *-(i)s*, which some authors have suggested goes back on an older ablative (Zeisler 2011), making the gloss something like x-*is kam* y 'y from x'.

The *-u* linking major and minor parts in Kanashi could tentatively be identified as the possessive suffix (see Section 2.2.4.5 in Chapter 3). In that case, it has a counterpart in Kinnauri *-o*, a possible genitive suffix allomorph also in Kinnauri (although the same Kinnauri suffix can also be an allomorph of the dative or locative morpheme in certain contexts; Saxena 2017: 759–760).

As mentioned above, the origin of the element *ʤe/ke* in Kanashi numerals is unknown. The following observations seem relevant here.

In the corresponding Bunan numerals an element *ki* appears between the two parts, which is identified as the genitive clitic in Bunan (Widmer 2017: 307); see the Bunan examples presented above. Similarly, in Kinnauri addition of parts of numerals is expressed with an element which can be identified as a genitive suffix. Additionally, the extinct ST language Zhangzhung, a West Himalayish language according to most authors (see Chapter 1), is reported to have a suffix *-ži/-ci* expressing a "Genitive or Causal value" (Thomas 2011: 229). One explanation for the Kanashi construction could be that it is an instance of multiple exponence, where the same content is expressed by two different adjacent morphs. This forms one of the four multiple exponence patterns described by Harris (2017) as being cross-linguistically dominant. A weakness with this analysis of the Kanashi construction is that we have not found the item *ʤe/ke* used as a genitive clitic elsewhere in the language. On the other hand, Kanashi does show instances of stacked genitives, e.g., *buʃ-u-k(a)* [rope-POSS-POSS] (see Chapter 3).

Zhangzhung also has another suffix *-tse/-ce* with "Ablatival or Causal sense" which may be identified with the "Ablatival *che (ce)* of Kunāwarī [Kinnauri]" (Thomas 2011: 23). Relevant in this context is that the modern form of the Kinnauri ablative suffix *-ʧ* is often combined with locative *-o* into *-o-ʧ* [-LOC-ABL] (Saxena 2017: 760). In addition to expressing a concrete spatial sense of 'from inside', the Kinnauri [-LOC-ABL] combination is used to mark the basis of comparison in comparative constructions (Saxena 2017: 762), which semantically is close to 'plus'/'in addition to'. Kanashi has a corresponding structure: *-a-ʦ* [-LOC-ABL], e.g. *ʧamʧiŋ-a-ʦ* [spoon-LOC-ABL], but the differences in form between *-a-ʦ* and *-u ʤe/ke* are non-trivial.

As a third possible origin of this construction, we note that Kanashi has a dative ending *-uʤ*, e.g., *ʧara-uʤ* [child-DAT]. Given that there are clear cases of [-POSS-CX] as alternatives to [-CX] in the Kanashi case system (e.g., *-raŋ* [-COM] ~ *-u-raŋ* [-POSS-COM] and *-di* [-ADE] ~ *-ka-di* [-POSS-ADE] ~ *-n-di* [-POSS-ADE] ~ *-u-di* [-POSS-ADE]; see Chapter 3), a promising hypothesis would be that *-u ʤe* represents a frozen earlier stage in the diachronic development which led to the present-day dative marker in Kanashi, i.e. a parallel to the Kinnauri use of dative in complex numerals, e.g. 'fifty-seven' and 'ninety-seven' in (3).

Further investigation is clearly needed before we can say anything more certain about the origin of *-u ʤe/ke* in Kanashi.

All in all, the Kanashi and Kinnauri numeral systems are quite similar. There are differences in details, but the main difference is the almost complete absence of IA elements in the Kinnauri numerals as opposed to their ubiquitousness in Kanashi. Impressionistically, Kanashi exhibits a heavily "relexified" ST numeral system very close to the one seen in Kinnauri, notably including both the A and S variant structures. The greater commonalities that we have seen between Kanashi and Kinnauri compared to Kanashi and Bunan serve to further support a closer genealogical classification as presented in Chapter 1 above.

As for the origin of the IA elements in the Kanashi numeral systems, the following observations can be made. There are at least three layers of IA borrowing discernible in Kanashi. Firstly, for other items than numerals, Kanashi shares a particular set of unique loanword adaptation mechanisms with Kinnauri. In both languages, many borrowed IA nouns have a suffix-like element not present in any of the modern IA languages spoken in the area, nor in related ST languages (see Chapter 6). This indicates that the borrowing has occurred in their common protolanguage, but not earlier. On the other hand, we have seen that Kinnauri still preserves an essentially ST numeral system without much IA influence. Hence, and secondly, the massive replacement of ST numerals by IA elements in Kanashi has taken place sometime after the split-up of Kanashi and Kinnauri. This older layer of borrowed items and structures in the Kanashi numerals probably originates in some local IA – Western Pahari or possibly Dardic – variety. The forms of IA items on the whole coincide with those given in descriptions of some of these languages (e.g., Bailey 1908), e.g., *ʃo* 'hundred' rather than (Hindi) *sɔ*, and *bi* 'twenty' rather than *bis*, etc. The borrowed IA numerals in Kanashi reflect a decimal system, even though many local IA languages have vigesimal systems. The order of units and decades found in the numerals in local IA varieties is typically the same as in Hindi, and opposite to that of Kanashi (or Kinnauri). The Kanashi numerals thus arguably represent a case of IA lexical replacement in ST structures. Thirdly, we are now observing wholesale replacement of this older borrowed system by freshly borrowed Hindi numerals, as shown above in Table 2.

4 Why are there IA borrowings in Kanashi at all?

Given the traditional degree of isolation of the Kanashi community as described above, one is surprised to find a large number of IA lexical items and some non-ST grammatical patterns in Kanashi. As described in Section 2, even the traditional numeral systems contain a large number of IA elements.

At least in the case of the traditional numerals, the original reason should not have been a need to fill lexical gaps, since, as we have seen, the closely related languages Kinnauri and Bunan have full-fledged indigenous ST numeral systems, whose elements in many instances are reconstructible all the way back to Proto-Sino-Tibetan (Matisoff 1997). Hence, the reason for Kanashi borrowing so heavily from IA in this area must be sought elsewhere.

4.1 Background: Contact opportunities with IA speakers

To account for this massive presence of IA loanwords in Kanashi, we will now present some relevant economic and religious aspects of this community, which suggest that Kanashi speakers have had regular, almost ritualized contacts with the members of some surrounding villages in Kullu (all IA speaking), even though in their day to day life the contact has traditionally been minimal (Tobdan 2011).

4.1.1 Religion

The Malana village god – referred to as *Jamlu devta* – is revered both in Malana and in several other villages in Kullu. According to the legend, Jamlu devta is kin to village gods of other villages in Himachal Pradesh (both IA speaking villages and ST speaking villages). Such a village is referred to as a *deoghar* (an IA word meaning 'god-home') of Jamlu devta. These villages show a number of similarities in how they perform the rites and also in the names of the office-bearers. For example, Jana village is a deoghar of Jamlu devta, whose ritual procedures as well as the names of the office-bearers for the Jamlu devta are the same as in Malana. In the Pulag village (which is geographically closest to Malana), in addition to the similarities in the religious rites and the names of the office-bearers, their administrative system as well as the division of the village in an upper and a lower part is the same as in Malana. Festivals are organized both in Malana and in the various deoghars. The dates of these festivals in the various deoghars are decided in consultation with Malana. The members of the Malana community visit many of these villages at regular intervals. Similarly, the members of other villages come to Malana once or twice each year, staying in Malana for a week or so where they interact closely with the locals. The visits of IA speaking guests from deoghars is such an integral part of the Kanashi community that there is a designated large house in Malana to provide lodging for the visiting members of other deoghars. There is also a community food storeroom which is used for preparing food for these visiting guests and a group of four functionaries is selected each year from among the Malana families to take care of the needs of the guests during various village festivals, which are held several times each year. Such contacts provide regular and perodically intensive opportunities for language contact between the IA languages of Kullu and Kanashi. As often in language contact situations, the contacts are linguistically asymmetrical, in that all interactions will be in some IA language and not in Kanashi.

4.1.2 Collecting revenues

In modern times, the sources of income for most Kanashi families are agriculture, forestry and animal husbandry. Earlier, they used to barter clarified butter, honey, game and herbs with people of the lower Himalayan region, in exchange for rice, corn, rock salt and iron for tools. In modern times they also buy modern amenities. The Kanashi community as a whole generates income by collecting revenues from other villages and deoghars, according to their traditional practices. It is said that Jamlu devta owns land in some deoghars outside Malana, from which it gets part of the yield. To take care of collecting revenues from outside Malana, there is an organized administrative body in Malana. A group of five officials is elected each year in Malana, whose main function is to visit villages and deoghars of Jamlu devta to collect revenue which is provided in kind. For this purpose, they are away from Malana for longer periods of time, visiting various parts of Kullu where they interact with IA speakers. Revenue collection naturally involves discourse where (higher) numerals are used, meaning that the knowledge of IA numerals receives constant reinforcement among the Kanashi speakers.

4.1.3 Seasonal migration

There are two groups of Kanashi speakers who migrate to the plains in lower Himalayan regions during winter. First, since not much grows in and around Malana during the winter months, some practice transhumance, i.e., they take their herds and move to lower regions for the winter. Second, some members of Malana families, including women and children, spend a month or so in the deoghar villages of the lower regions. These situations also provide ample opportunities for language contact between IA languages and Kanashi.

5 Why so many numeral systems?

The many different ways in which a given quantity can be expressed in Kanashi struck us as worthy of investigation. We have not come across any systematic broader treatment of this topic in the linguistic literature. Somewhat paradoxically, numeral systems in languages seem to be both well-studied and under-researched at the same time. The components and structures making up numeral systems are generally well-known, both majority patterns attested across many languages (Comrie 1999; 2005), and rarer or even unique structures (Hammarström 2010). The range of possible systems has been thoroughly explored and described, in terms of number of items (none, few, many, infinite), bases, structures (how items can be combined and how the combinations are interpreted in arithmetical terms).

The kind of intra-language variation that we find in traditional Kanashi numerals has received much less attention, however, and in fact seems to be under-documented. Perhaps this is because of the doubly peripheral position of numerals in language: as is well-recognized, they straddle the boundary between grammar and lexicon, in that they exhibit both grammatical – closed-class – and lexical – open-class – behavior at the same time. As a case in point, Wintu (wit; Wintuan) exhibits alternative ways of forming decades, but this cannot be found out from Pitkin's *Wintu grammar* (1984). Instead, information about the numerals is provided under the entries for 'ten' and 'twenty' in his *Wintu dictionary* (1985: s.v. *tiqeles* and *ḱetewintʰuh*), where we learn that "valuables were subject to vigesimal rather than decimal count", and some alternative formations are listed: "ḱetewintʰuh tiqeles ƛomi thirty (also panuƛ tiqeles)" (Pitkin 1985: 695, s.v. *ḱetewintʰuh*).

Going through numerous individual language descriptions, we have come up with some cases where alternative numeral systems live side by side. Thus, Moghol (mhj; Mongolic) is reported as having four parallel sets of cardinals (Weiers 2003; Blažek & Schwarz 2016), if the use of Persian numerals is taken into account.

Further, several IA and ST languages of the Himalayan region (as non-dominant languages elsewhere) have more than one parallel numeral system. Often there are two systems, one more indigenous and the second a borrowing from a surrounding dominant language, local, regional or national. In each of these cases, the dominant language's numeral system is increasing in use, and the role of the indigenous numeral system is becoming more restricted (see Matisoff 1997: 12–16). Mazaudon (2010: 124–131) notes that Dzongkha uses two systems: a decimal system borrowed from Tibetan which is used in formal contexts and in writing, and a vigesimal system used elsewhere. As mentioned in Section 3, Bunan has three parallel systems. Yliniemi (2019) reports that Denjongke (sip; also referred to as Sikkimese; ST) has a parallel vigesimal and decimal numeral system. Both systems are made up entirely of inherited (ST) elements, and they seem to have complementary application domains: "some initial observations[:] the vigesimal system is used at least when talking about prices of items […], age of people […] and number of people[, while t]he decimal system is used for pointing out the year when something took place […], the number of years since something happened […] and dates" (Yliniemi 2019: 124). It may well be that the presence of multiple numeral systems is a common feature in languages, but this is difficult to find out since language descriptions generally seem to assume one numeral system by default, as it were (Mazaudon 2010).

The few more general discussions that we have found of such situations seem to conclude that a single numeral system is the normal situation: parallel numeral systems reflect a transitory language stage, where a borrowed system from a dominant language is ousting an original indigenous system (e.g., Matisoff 1997; Ahlers 2012). This certainly happens: Eurén's Finnish grammar (1851: 36) lists as the only structure an overcounting formation, e.g., *kaksikolmatta* (*kaksi-kolm-at-ta* [two-three-ORDINAL-PARTITIVE] 'two of the third') 'twenty-two', whereas the most recent modern reference grammar (Hakulinen et al. 2004) provides only the formation of the type *kaksikymmentäkaksi* (*kaksi-kymmen-tä-kaksi* [two-ten-PARTITIVE-two] 'two (×) ten (+) two') (basically the same as in Swedish, which was the dominant language in Finland for several hundred years), and characterizes the pattern described by Eurén as obsolete.

The alternative that more than one numeral system is in stable use in a language, either as free or context-dependent variants, is not generally assumed in the literature, but this is perhaps at least in part an effect of the general paucity of sociolinguistic investigations in language documentation (see the papers in Hildebrandt et al. 2017).

For many of the earlier stages of modern standard languages we find descriptions of variant numeral systems. Some Slavic languages historically in contact with German used to have parallel alternative orderings of tens and ones in the numerals 21–99, according to de Bray (1969). This applied to Czech, Slovak, Slovene, and (Upper and Lower) Sorbian. Consulting more recent grammars of these languages, we find that generally only one ordering is given, with decades preceding 1–9 in Slovak, and units preceding decades in Slovene (M. L. Greenberg 2006: 57), Upper Sorbian (Šewc 1968) and Lower Sorbian (Jenč et al. 1978). However, Czech still allows both orderings (Naughton 2005: 116), and Janaš (1976) notes that in Lower Sorbian the alternative ordering still lingers on "[i]n älteren Schriften und vereinzelt in den Dialekten" (Janaš 1976: 146). A similar situation obtains in Norwegian, where both orderings are possible, the ordering with ones coming before tens due to Danish influence. Pre-Classical and Classical Latin allow both orders between tens and units, with or without a conjunction, making four possibilities, and complex numerals need not be contiguous, but allow other parts of the sentence to be interposed between their components, which is interpreted by de la Villa (2010: 221–222) as an indication that Latin numerals are considered as compositional phrases rather than lexical(ized) items. This could of course be true also in the case of Kanashi, that number building is felt by native speakers to be phrase building rather than strictly regimented word building. Note, however, that – as already mentioned – the Kanashi variation does not include alternative orders of components,[16] with one small exception, viz. the construction where major parts of numerals are formed with the element ***saṛe*** '+half', which may precede or follow a multiple of 20.

According to Noreen (1904: 381), Old Swedish (1225–1526) composite numerals were formed according to the pattern "*en* (*twēr, þrīr* u.s.w.) *ok tiughu, en ok þrætigi* u.s.w." (i.e., [one (two, three, etc.) and twenty], [one and thirty]) and oc-

16 Although since both phrase- and clause-internal word order are generally fixed in Kanashi, this is not so surprising.

casionally "*fiughurtān ok tiughu* 34, [...] *siūtān ok tiughu* 37" (i.e., [fourteen and twenty], [seventeen and twenty]). Modern Standard Swedish has as the only pattern the opposite order between tens and units (the same as English), and the vigesimal variant is completely unknown. A change must have occurred at some point between the Old Swedish period and today. Since language change is not instantaneous, there will presumably have been an interval with variation.

Comparing numeral structures across Indo-European languages, the most reasonable conclusion – given that we find varying structures but also that the atomic elements of these structures are by and large cognate – must be that Proto-Indo-European exhibited a good deal of variation in numeral formation (Winter 1992), not unlike what we see in present-day Kanashi.

Given that we find so many instances of parallel numeral systems even in a small and opportunistic survey of language descriptions – almost exclusively grammars, and not lexicons – why do we typically find one system in grammars of modern standard languages, and what are the impact of this on language documentation, if any?

We suspect that this may have to do with a normative conceptual framework connected to language standardization and unconsciously carried over into language description conducted by academic linguists, a special case of "written language bias in linguistics" (Linell 2005). It is well recognized that a central aspect of the creation of standard languages is reduction of variation; some variants are simply excluded from the standard (Joseph 1987: 126ff). Modern standard languages generally do not seem to recognize alternative numeral systems, for whatever reason.

First we note that, as a general rule, variation in the form of (near) synonymy is not a rare thing, even in modern standard languages, and part of the richness of the traditional numeral systems in Kanashi is due to the availability of alternative expressions – ST and IA – of the components of complex numerals. This can be seen as analogous to lexical synonymy. The existence of variant "synonymous" constructions – such as the parallel A and S patterns for forming Kanashi (and also Kinnauri) numerals – is also commonplace in languages, e.g. possession expressed using an ending or clitic vs. using an adposition, as in English *Mary's mother* ~ *the mother of Mary*.

One reason for having synonyms seems to be variety for its own sake, and in the case of full or almost-full denotational synonyms, the alternatives may have different stylistic value or belong in different registers. In the case of numerals, the latitude for near-synonymy seems minimal, because the semantics of numerals are so narrow, and in a language standardization setting perhaps they may then be perceived more as something like spelling than grammar or even lexicon, meaning that variation will tend not to be normatively tolerated, and will also for this reason tend not to be recognized if it does occur outside of a normative setting, such as documenting an indigenous language.

If we do recognize that a language has alternative ways of expressing the same numeral and we think of this as a form of synonymy, the choice of variant may be dependent on stylistic factors or context of use, as with the Denjongke numeral systems mentioned above.[17] Thus, Bender & Beller (2007) report that Tongan complements a general, unrestricted decimal numeral system with a number of different vigesimal systems used for counting specific objects, typically different natural products of high cultural value in traditional Tongan society. Unfortunately, we are not in a position to say this about the Kanashi numeral variants attested in our material. All we have at the moment is the older language consultant's statement reproduced above to the effect that the alternative Kanashi numerals are interchangeable in all contexts,[18] but this would need independent confirmation, preferably from a large body of natural-interaction data. Given that the younger language consultants were not familiar with any other numeral system than the Hindi-derived one, the prospects of acquiring such data are anything but bright.

6 Discussion, summary and outlook

As we have seen, despite their culturally isolationistic attitude, Kanashi speakers have traditionally had many and frequent opportunities for contact with IA speakers, and the language of interaction in such contacts has invariably been some IA language, traditionally "the language of Kullu" – Kullu Pahari – and now increasingly Hindi, as seen in the most recent Kanashi numeral system, where the elements are recognizable as having their origin in Hindi rather than Kullu Pahari.

One of the reasons for traditional regular interactions between Kanashi speakers and IA speakers is economic in nature, viz. that of collecting revenue and making offerings to the village gods. In such situations counting and numerals would be present at every turn, and these activities would always be conducted in an IA language, as they have been dominant languages in the region. At the same time everyday life in Malana – naturally conducted in Kanashi – by its nature did not

17 For example: for two of its cardinals, Swedish has two fully synonymous variants: *två* ~ *tvenne* 'two' and *tre* ~ *trenne* 'three'. However, the second member of each pair very clearly belongs to a formal, even slightly archaizing style and would be encountered in everyday (written or spoken) language only used jokingly.

18 Relevant in this context, Bender & Beller (2007: 229–230) note that present-day Tongans tend to mix up and overgeneralize the traditional specific counting systems.

provide many opportunities for counting beyond the lower numerals, so we may have at least part of the explanation for the massive borrowing of IA numerals in all the traditional numeral systems and the abandonment of all but the lowest ST numerals. See also Matisoff (1997: 12–16) and Matras (2011: 212–213).

The large variety of parallel numeral systems found in Kanashi may not be so rare among languages, but simply underreported, perhaps both because the relevant data are rare and difficult to come by, and because of an ideological bias introduced by language standardization, potentially distorting data collection procedures (Mazaudon 2010). At the same time, the language standardization mindset is gaining ground in the world, which means that this kind of variety in numeral systems is probably on its way out. In Kanashi this process happens through wholesale borrowing of Hindi numerals, rather than by selection of one of the extant variants, which serves to reinforce our impression that IA influence on Kanashi is increasing.

Finding out more about the history and current usage of the Kanashi multitude of numeral systems could certainly contribute to this neglected area of lexical typology, but – since numerals are easily borrowed, especially in unequal language contact situations (Matisoff 1997; Matras 2011) – time is running out, as both Comrie (2005) and Mazaudon (2010) remind us.

References

Ahlers, Jocelyn C. 2012. Two eights make sixteen beads: Historical and contemporary ethnography in language revitalization. *International Journal of American Linguistics* 78(4): 533–555.

Bailey, Thomas Grahame. 1908. *The languages of the Northern Himalayas, being studied in the grammar of twenty-six Himalayan dialects*. Asiatic Society monographs, Vol XII. London: The Royal Asiatic Society.

Bender, Andrea & Sieghard Beller. 2007. Counting in Tongan: The traditional number systems and their cognitive implications. *Journal of Cognition and Culture* 7: 213–239.

Berger, Hermann. 1992. Modern Indo-Aryan. In Jadranka Gvozdanovic (ed.), *Indo-European numerals*, 243–288. Berlin: Mouton de Gruyter.

Blažek, Václav & Michal Schwarz. 2016. Numerals in Mongolic and Tungusic languages – with notes to code-switching. *Altai Hakpo – Journal of the Altaic Society of Korea* 26: 131–155.

Comrie, Bernard. 1999. Haruai numerals and their implications for the history and typology of numeral systems. In Jadranka Gvozdanović (ed.), *Numeral types and changes wordwide*, 81–94. Berlin: Mouton de Gruyter.

Comrie, Bernard. 2005. Numeral bases. In Martin Haspelmath, Matthew Dryer, David Gil & Bernard Comrie (eds.), *The world atlas of language structures*, 530–533. Also in: Matthew S. Dryer and Martin Haspelmath (eds), The world atlas of language structures online.

Leipzig: Max Planck Institute for Evolutionary Anthropology. http://wals.info/chapter/131. Oxford: Oxford University Press.

de Bray, Reginald George Arthur. 1969. *Guide to the Slavonic languages*. 2nd edn. London: Dent.

de la Villa, Jesús. 2010. Numerals. In Philip Baldi & Pierluigi Cuzzolin (eds.), *New perspectives on Latin historical syntax 3. Constituent syntax: Quantification, numerals, possession, anaphora*, 175–238. Berlin: De Gruyter Mouton.

Eurén, Gustaf Erik. 1851. *Finsk språklära i sammandrag* [A synopsis of Finnish grammar]. Turku: J. W. Lillja & Co.

Greenberg, Joseph H. 1978. Generalizations about numeral systems. In Joseph H. Greenberg, Charles A. Ferguson & Edith A. Moravcsik (eds.), *Universals of human language. Vol. 3*, 249–295. Stanford: Stanford University Press.

Greenberg, Marc L. 2006. *A short reference grammar of Standard Slovene*. Online publication: https://slaviccenters.duke.edu/projects/grammars. Durham: Duke Slavic Centers.

Grierson, George A. 1928. *Linguistic survey of India, Vol 1, Part II: Comparative vocabulary*. Calcutta: Government of India, Central Publication Branch.

Hakulinen, Auli, Maria Vilkuna & Irja Alho. 2004. *Iso suomen kielioppi* [Large Finnish grammar]. Helsinki: Suomalaisen Kirjallisuuden Seura.

Hammarström, Harald. 2010. Rarities in numeral systems. In Jan Wohlgemuth & Michael Cysouw (eds.), *Rethinking universals: How rarities affect linguistic theory*, 11–60. Berlin: Mouton de Gruyter.

Harcourt, Alfred Frederick Pollock. 1871. *The Himalayan districts of Kooloo, Lahoul, and Spiti*. London: Wm H. Allen & Co.

Harris, Alice C. 2017. *Multiple exponence*. Oxford: Oxford University Press.

Hildebrandt, Kristine A., Carmen Jany & Wilson Silva. 2017. *Documenting variation in endangered languages*. Language Documentation & Conservation Special Publication No. 13. Available online: http://nflrc.hawaii.edu/ldc/sp-13-documenting-variation-endangered-languages/. Honolulu: University of Hawaii, Manoa.

Hodson, Thomas C. 1913. Note on the numeral systems of the Tibeto-Burman dialects. *Journal of the Royal Asiatic Society of Great Britain and Ireland* 45: 315–336.

Janaš, Pětr. 1976. *Niedersorbische Grammatik*. Bautzen: Domowina.

Jenč, Helmut, Irena Šěrakowa & Horst Petrik. 1978. *Grammatische Tabellen niedersorbisch. Gramatiske tabele dolnoserbski*. Bautzen: Domowina.

Joseph, John Earl. 1987. *Eloquence and power: The rise of language standards and standard languages*. London: Pinter.

Konow, Sten. 1909. *Linguistic survey of India, Vol 3: Tibeto-Burman family. Part I: General introduction, specimens of the Tibetan dialects, the Himalayan dialects, and the North Assam group*. (This and several other volumes of the LSI were edited by Sten Konow, although published as the work of George A. Grierson). Calcutta: Government of India, Central Publication Branch.

Linell, Per. 2005. *The written language bias in linguistics*. First published in 1982 by Dept. of Communication Studies, University of Linköping, Sweden. London: Routledge.

Matisoff, James A. 1997. *Sino-Tibetan numeral systems: Prefixes, protoforms and problems*. Series B, Volume 114. Canberra: Pacific Linguistics.

Matisoff, James A. 2003. *Handbook of Proto-Tibeto-Burman: System and philosophy of Sino-Tibetan reconstruction*. Berkeley: University of California Press.

Matras, Yaron. 2011. Universals of structural borrowing. In Peter Siemund (ed.), *Linguistic universals and language variation*, 204–233. Berlin: De Gruyter Mouton.

Mazaudon, Martine. 2010. Number-building in Tibeto-Burman languages. In Stephen Morey & Mark Post (eds.), *North East Indian linguistics, volume 2*, 117–148. New Delhi: Cambridge University Press India.

Menninger, Karl. 1969. *Number words and number symbols: A cultural history of numbers*. Cambridge: MIT Press.

Naughton, James. 2005. *Czech: An essential grammar*. London: Routledge.

Noreen, Adolf. 1904. *Altschwedische Grammatik mit Einschluss des Altgutnischen*. Halle: Niemeyer.

Pitkin, Harvey. 1984. *Wintu grammar*. Berkeley: University of California Press.

Pitkin, Harvey. 1985. *Wintu dictionary*. Berkeley: University of California Press.

Saxena, Anju. 2017. Sangla Kinnauri. In Graham Thurgood & Randy J. LaPolla (eds.), *The Sino-Tibetan languages*, 2nd edn., 756–772. London: Routledge.

Saxena, Anju. 2022. *The linguistic landscape of the Indian Himalayas: Languages in Kinnaur*. Forthcoming 2022. Leiden: Brill.

Šewc, Hinc. 1968. *Gramatika hornjoserbskeje rěče. 1. zwjazk: fonematika a morfologija* [A grammar of Upper Sorbian. Vol. 1: Phonetics and morphology]. Budyšin: Domowina.

Sharma, Devi Datta. 1992. *Tribal languages of Himachal Pradesh. Part two*. Delhi: Mittal Publications.

STEDT. 2016. *James A. Matisoff et al. The Sino-Tibetan etymological dictionary and thesaurus*. Available online at: http://stedt.berkeley.edu/search. Berkeley: University of California.

Thomas, Frederick W. 2011. Research notes on the Zhangzhung language by Frederick W. Thomas at the British Library. In Tsuguhito Takeuchi, Burkhard Kessel & Yasuhiko Nagano (eds.), *Senri ethnological reports 99*, 1–246. Osaka: National Museum of Ethnology.

Tobdan. 2011. *Exploring Malana: An ancient culture hidden in the Himalayas*. New Delhi: Indus Publishing Company.

Turner, Ralph L. 1966. *A comparative dictionary of the Indo-Aryan languages*. Available online: http://dsal.uchicago.edu/dictionaries/soas/. Oxford: Oxford University Press.

Weiers, Michael. 2003. Moghol. In Juha Janhunen (ed.), *The Mongolic languages*, 248–264. London: Routledge.

Widmer, Manuel. 2017. *A grammar of Bunan*. Berlin: De Gruyter Mouton.

Winter, Werner. 1992. Some thoughts about Indo-European numerals. In Jadranka Gvozdanovic (ed.), *Indo-European numerals*, 11–28. Berlin: Mouton de Gruyter.

Yliniemi, Juha. 2019. *A descriptive grammar of Denjongke (Sikkimese Bhutia)*. Helsinki: University of Helsinki. (PhD thesis).

Zeisler, Bettina. 2011. Kenhat, the dialects of Upper Ladakh and Zanskar. In Mark turin & Bettina Zeisler (eds.), *Himalayan languages and linguistics: Studies in phonology, semantics, morphology and syntax*, 235–301. Leiden: Brill.

A Attested Kanashi numerals in our fieldwork data

The following list shows those Kanashi numerals which occur in our fieldwork data, except Hindi numerals.[19] Elements of IA origin in the Kanashi column are set in **boldface with underlining.**

1	*i:d*	
	ek	
2	*niʃ*	
3	*ʃum*	
4	*pu*	
5	*ŋa*	
	na	
	pãʧ	
6	***ʧʰa***	
7	***sat***	
8	***aʈʰ***	
9	***nao***	
10	***das***	
11	***gjara***	
12	***bara***	
13	***tera***	
14	***ʧoda***	
15	***pandra***	
16	***sola***	
17	***suta:ra***	
	ʃumis ***kam*** *niʥa*	[3:is less 20]
18	***ʈʰara***	
	niʃ ***kam*** *niʥa*	[2 less 20]
19	***unni***	
	i:dis ***kam*** *niʥa*	[1:is less 20]
20	***bi***	
	niʥa	
21	***ikki***	
	niʥau ʤe i:d	[20:u plus 1]
22	*niʥau ʤe niʃ*	[20:u plus 2]
23	*niʥau ʤe ʃum*	[20:u plus 3]
	teis	
24	***ʧob(b)i***	
25	*niʥa ʤe ŋa*	[20:u plus 5]
	paʧ(ʧ)i	
26	***ʧʰab(b)i***	
	ʧʰabbis	
27	*niʥau ʤe* ***sat***	[20:u plus 7]
	ʃumis ***kam deɽbija***	[3:is less 30]
28	*niʥau ʤe* ***aʈʰ***	[20:u plus 8]
	niʃis ***kam deɽbija***	[2:is less 30]
29	*niʥau ʤe* ***nao***	[20:u plus 9]
	i:dis ***kam deɽbija***	[1:is less 30]
30	***deɽbija***	[1.5:20]
	ti:(s)	
	niʥau ʤe ***das***	[20:u plus 10]
31	*niʥau* ***gjara***	[20:u 11]
	ikkatis	
32	*niʥau ʤe* ***bara***	[20:u plus 12]
	aʈʰ*is* ***kam ʧali***	[8:is less 40]
	batti	
33	*niʥau ʤe* ***tera***	[20:u plus 13]
	teti	
	tetu	
37	*niʥau ʤe* ***suta:ra***	[20:u plus 17]
	ʃumis ***kam ʧali***	[3:is less 40]
38	*niʥau ʤe* ***ʈʰara***	[20:u plus 18]
	niʃis ***kam ʧali***	[2:is less 40]
39	*niʥau ʤe* ***unni***	[20:u plus 19]
	i:dis ***kam ʧali***	[1:is less 40]
40	***ʧali***	
	niʃ niʥa	[2 (×) 20]
43	***ʧali****u ʤe ʃum*	[40:u plus 3]
	sat kam puʥa	[7 less 50]
	niʃ niʥau ʃum	[2 (x) 20:u (+) 3]
44	***ʧali****u ʤe pu*	[40:u plus 4]
	ʧʰas kam puʥa	[6:s less 50]
	niʃ niʥau pu	[2 (×) 20:u (+) 4]

19 We exclude only such IA numerals which are identical to the corresponding Hindi items while not found in Kullu Pahari.

45	***ʧali**u ʤe ŋa*	[40:u plus 5]
	niʃ niʥau ʤe ŋa	[2 (x) 20:u plus 5]
	niʃ niʥau ŋa	[2 (×) 20:u (+) 5]
46	***ʧali**u ʤe **ʧ^{h}a***	[40:u plus 6]
	*niʃ niʥau ʤe **ʧ^{h}a***	[2 (×) 20:u plus 6]
	*niʃ niʥau **ʧ^{h}a***	[2 (×) 20:u (+) 6]
48	***ʧali**u ʤe **aʈ^h***	[40:u plus 8]
	*niʃis **kam pudʑa***	[2:is less 50]
	*niʃ niʥau **aʈ^h***	[2 (×) 20:u (+) 8]
49	***ʧali**u ʤe **nao***	[40:u plus 9]
	*iːdis **kam pudʑa***	[1:is less 50]
	*niʃ niʥau **nao***	[2 (×) 20:u (+) 9]
50	***pudʑa***	
	ʧali**u ʤe **das	[40:u plus 10]
55	*niʃ niʥau ʤe **pandra***	[2 (×) 20:u plus 15]
	*ŋais **kam saʈ^h***	[5:is less 60]
	pãʧ kam saʈ^h	[5 less 60]
59	*iːdis **kam saʈ^h***	[1:is less 60]
	*niʃ niʥau ʤe **unni***	[2 (×) 20:u plus 19]
60	*ʃum niʥa*	[3 (×) 20]
	ʃaʈ^h	
	saʈ^h	
61	***ikaʈ^h***	
62	***saʈ^h**u ʤe niʃ*	[60:u plus 2]
	ʃum niʥau ʤe niʃ	[3 (×) 20:u plus 2]
64	***saʈ^h**u ʤe pu*	[60:u plus 4]
65	*ʃum niʥau ʤe ŋa*	[3 (×) 20:u plus 5]
	ʃum niʥau ŋa	[3 (×) 20:u (+) 5]
67	***saʈ^h**u ʤe **sat***	[60:u plus 7]
	*ʃum niʥau ʤe **sat***	[3 (×) 20:u plus 7]
	*ʃumis **kam saɽe saʈ^h***	[3:is less +half 60]
68	***saʈ^h**u ʤe **aʈ^h***	[60:u plus 8]
	*ʃum niʥau ʤe **aʈ^h***	[3 (×) 20:u plus 8]
	*niʃis **kam saɽe saʈ^h***	[2:is less +half 60]
69	*ʃum niʥau ʤe **nao***	[3 (×) 20:u plus 9]
	ʃaʈ^h**u ʤe **nao	[60:u plus 9]
	saʈ^h**u ʤe **nao	[60:u plus 9]
	*iːdis **kam saɽe saʈ^h***	[1:is less +half 60]
70	***saʈ^h**u ʤe **das***	[60:u plus 10]
	saʈ^h**uke **das	[60:u:ke 10]
	saɽe saʈ^h	[+half 60]
74	***ʧ^{h}a kam aʃi***	[6 less 80]
	ts^{h}a kam aʃi	[6 less 80]
76	***saʈ^h**u ʤe **sola***	[60:u plus 16]
	*ʃum niʥau ʤe **sola***	[[3 (×) 20:u plus 16]
80	***aʃi***	
	pu niʥa	[4 (×) 20]
81	***aʃi**u ʤe iːd*	[80:u plus 1]
	unnis kam ʃo	[19:s less 100]
	pu nidzau ʤe iːd	[4 (×) 20:u plus 1]
82	***aʃi**u ʤe niʃ*	[80:u plus 2]
	ʈ^{h}arais kam ʃo	[18:is less 100]
	pu niʥau ʤe niʃ	[4 (×) 20:u plus 2]
85	***aʃi**u ʤe ŋa*	[80:u plus 5]
	pu niʥau ʤe ŋa	[4 (×) 20:u plus 5]
87	***aʃi**u ʤe **sat***	[80:u plus 7]
	teras kam ʃo	[13:s less 100]
	*pu niʥau ʤe **sat***	[4 (×) 20:u plus 7]
88	***aʃi**u ʤe **aʈ^h***	[80:u plus 8]
	baras kam ʃo	[12:s less 100]
	*pu niʥau ʤe **aʈ^h***	[4 (×) 20:u plus 8]
89	***aʃi**u ʤe **nao***	[80:u plus 9]
	gjaras kam ʃo	[11:s less 100]
	*pu niʥau ʤe **nao***	[4 (×) 20:u plus 9]
90	***aʃi saɽe***	[80 +half]
	aʃi**u **das	[80:u (+) 9]
	nabbe	
99	*iːdis **kam ʃo***	[1:is less 100]
	*pu niʥau ʤe **unni***	[4 (×) 20:u plus 19]
100	***ʃo***	
101	***ʃo** iːd*	[100 (+) 1]
	*iːd **ʃou** iːd*	[1 (×) 100 (+) 1]
500	*na**ʃo***	[5(×)100]
	*ŋa**ʃo***	[5(×)100]

Diachrony

Anju Saxena, Lars Borin, and Bernard Comrie

6 Clues to Kanashi prehistory 1: loanword adaptation in nouns and adjectives

Abstract: In this chapter we focus on a shared innovation of Kanashi and Kinnauri, the addition of characteristic suffixes – or adaptive markers – to Indo-Aryan loan nouns and adjectives. The distribution of this adaptive mechanism in related and unrelated languages in the western Himalayas is investigated, and we also discuss possible sources for the adaptive markers, with the goal of increasing our knowledge about the genealogical composition and structure of the West Himalayish subbranch of Sino-Tibetan.

Keywords: Kanashi, Kinnauri, Sino-Tibetan, Indo-Aryan, language contact, comparative linguistics, nominal morphology

Chapter overview:

https://doi.org/10.1515/9783110703245-006

1 Introduction

There are several layers of Indo-Aryan (IA) borrowings in the two Sino-Tibetan (ST) languages Kanashi and Kinnauri. More recently borrowed IA nouns and adjectives in Kanashi and Kinnauri tend to have (almost) the same form as in the IA donor languages (e.g. *ma:p^{h}i* 'apology', *seb* 'apple'), while there is an older loanword stratum in both languages, of borrowings with an additional ending (*-(V)ŋ* or *-(V)s*) which we refer to in this volume as "adaptive markers" (e.g. Kanashi *kasaŋ* 'bronze'; cf. Hindi *kās, kā̃sā*; Nepali *kā̃so* 'bronze, pewter, white metal').[1] The resulting stems have at least two syllables, while inherited ST noun and adjective stems ending in *-ŋ* or *-s* in Kanashi and Kinnauri are generally monosyllabic.[2]

This is not a straightforward case of "necessary" adaptation of foreign elements to native phonotactics, since the adaptive markers in Kinnauri and Kanashi are added also to those IA loans which already conform to Kanashi or Kinnauri word structure. Also, we find a number of doublets, the same IA item both with and without the adaptive marker.

It is also not an obvious case of an original element present in some borrowed items which has been reinterpreted as a marker of "IA-ness" and subsequently introduced into other borrowings, since there is no evident IA source for the adaptive markers, as we will see below. There is also no obvious ST source for the adaptive markers, making this an intricate and interesting investigation.

Typically, in both Kanashi and Kinnauri nouns are borrowed as nouns, adjectives as adjectives, and verbs as verbs. However, occasionally we find that IA nouns such as *ba:t* 'talk' can form the basis of both nouns and verbs in the target language, which when they function as nouns in Kinnauri and Kanashi take the adaptive marker *-aŋ* (Kinnauri *ba:taŋ* 'talk (N)'), but when they function as verbs take either the transitive marker *-ja:* or the intransitive marker *-e(d)* (Kinnauri: *ba:t-ja:-mu* [talk-TR-INF]; *ba:t-en-nu* [talk-INTR-INF]) (see Chapter 7). Once the part of speech has been established in this way, the IA loans take the regular nominal or verbal inflectional endings of the recipient language.

1 The three recognized distinct historical stages of IA are referred to in the literature as *Old Indo-Aryan* (OIA), *Middle Indo-Aryan* (MIA) and *New Indo-Aryan* (NIA). Kanashi and Kinnauri are closely related members of the West Himalayish (WH) subbranch of ST; see Figure 1 in this chapter.

2 Most of the loanwords containing these adaptive markers are disyllabic, which seems to be preferred: When *-(V)ŋ* and *-(V)s* are affixed to a di- or polysyllabic IA noun/adjective, the vowel of the stem-final syllable often undergoes syncope in both Kanashi and Kinnauri. e.g. *kulut* '(historical) Kullu kingdom' > Kanashi *kultaŋ* 'Kullu region'.

In this chapter we will first describe the adaptive markers on nouns and adjectives in Kanashi and Kinnauri. Next we will examine if other ST languages of the western Himalayas show any traces of this phenomenon. We will see that with the exception of the ST languages of Lower/Middle Kinnaur – which are closely related to Kanashi and Kinnauri – none of the ST languages of Himachal Pradesh and Ladakh show any traces of the adaptive markers. However, we find traces of similar adaptation strategies in some ST languages of the Uttarakhand region in India and in the adjoining Tehri region in western Nepal, raising questions regarding the prehistory of these languages and their genealogical classification. In order to gain a better understanding of the phenomenon, we will also examine if similar elements are attested in the Indo-Aryan, Dravidian and Munda languages spoken in this region (i.e. Himachal Pradesh, Uttarakhand in India and in the Tehri region in Nepal).

We begin with an examination of the adaptive markers in Kanashi and Kinnauri.

2 Nouns and adjectives ending in *-(V)ŋ/-(V)s* in Kanashi and Kinnauri

2.1 Background and overview

The Kanashi and Kinnauri lexicons contain a large number of borrowed IA nouns and adjectives.[3] In both languages a subset of these IA nouns take an adaptive marker (*-(V)ŋ* or *-(V)s*). Similarly, a subset of the IA adjectives in both languages take the adaptive marker *-(V)s*. In Kinnauri some IA adjectives, too, take the adaptive marker *-(V)ŋ*. The adaptive marker in Kinnauri and Kanashi occurs on IA simple (i.e., non-compound) noun and adjective loans, never on a verb. In the IA languages these nouns and adjectives occur without the adaptive markers (*-(V)ŋ* or *-(V)s*).[4] See Table 1.

3 In the tables in this section, the following notational conventions are used. For etymologies, when given in the "Etymology" column, "T*nnnn*" refers to entry number *nnnn* in Turner (1966). Most Kanashi and Kinnauri items are from our own fieldwork data. A few of the Kinnauri items are from B. R. Sharma (1976). These are indicated as follows: *item*†.

4 One important characteristic of Kinnauri, according to Cunningham (1854: 223–224), is that nouns end in *-aŋ* or *-iŋ*, *-uŋ*. He further points out that Kinnauri is known as *Milchân* in the speech of Rampur (where an IA language is spoken), while the Kinnauri speakers themselves use the term *Milchanang* to refer to their language.

Table 1: Adaptive markers on IA noun and adjective loans in Kanashi and Kinnauri

Kanashi	Kinnauri	Gloss	Etymology
da:ɳaŋ	*ɖa:naŋ*	'penalty, punishment'	T6128 daṇḍá m. 'punishment'
sargaŋ	*sorgaŋ*	'sky'	T13910 svargá m. 'heaven'
lokas	*lokas*	'non-Kanashi people' / 'people'	T11119 lōká- m. 'world, people'
laʈʰas	*laʈas*	'dumb' / 'dumb (male)'	T10917 laṭṭa m. 'bad man'
ka:ɳas	*ka:nes, ka:naŋ*	'blind'	T3019 kāṇá 'one-eyed'
piʈʰas	*piʈʰas*	'flour'	T8218 pistá 'crushed, ground; flour'

Appendix A presents some more examples of nouns and adjectives in Kanashi and Kinnauri which show a similar pattern of adaptation (including the choice of the adaptive marker).

In our material there are many more instances of nouns and adjectives with the adaptive markers in Kinnauri than in Kanashi. This may simply be due to the fact that we have more Kinnauri data,[5] but on the other hand, names of months and weekdays as discussed in Section 2.2.2, where we do have comparable data in the two languages, also show more adaptive markers in Kinnauri than in Kanashi. In both newer vocabulary (cf. Saxena 2022) and in the older Kinnauri lexicon (cf. Gerard 1842) the adaptive marker *-(V)ŋ* occurs much more frequently than the adaptive marker *-(V)s*.

2.2 Adaptive markers on nouns

2.2.1 Distribution and inflectional behavior

The distribution of the adaptive markers *-(V)ŋ* and *-(V)s* in Kanashi and Kinnauri is not morphophonologically conditioned, as can be observed in the examples provided here and in Appendix A, except that the vowel-less variants (*-ŋ* and *-s)* are added to items that end in a vowel in the donor language (e.g. Kanashi / Kinnauri *bitiŋ* 'wall', etymology: T9494 bhittí f. 'panel, partition, wall'). There are, however, traces of a semantically-based distribution of the two adaptive markers *-(V)ŋ* and *-(V)s* when used with nouns in both Kanashi and Kinnauri, where *-(V)s* shows a preference for attaching to animate nouns and *-(V)ŋ* to inanimate nouns; see Table 2.

5 We have collected Kinnauri data over several decades in a number of previous projects and there are also more published materials on Kinnauri (Saxena 2022).

Table 2: Animacy sensitivity in the adaptive markers

Kanashi	Kinnauri	Gloss	Etymology
	ɖomaŋ	'name of a social subcaste'	T5570 ḍōmba m. 'man of low caste living by singing and music'
ɖaggis	*ɖagis, ɖomes*	'male member of this subcaste'	T5524 *ḍagga 'defective', 'term of contempt for a blacksmith'
	ʧamaŋ	'name of a social subcaste'	T4698 carmakāra m. 'leatherworker'
ʧama:ras	*ʧama:res*	'male member of this subcaste'	
ʤejʃtʰaŋ		'Malana parliament upper house'	T5285 jyḗṣṭa 'first, chief'
	ʤeʈʰras†	'a committee of three persons appointed for 5 or 6 years to lead the work on the Dewaal festival'	
kaniʃʈʰas	*kanisʈʰas*	'member of an IA subcaste'	T2718 kaniṣṭhá 'youngest'
kaniʃʈʰaŋ		'Malana parliament lower house'	
	kənoriŋ	'Kinnaur (place name)'	
	kənoras	'people/man of Kinnaur'	
dukʰis	*dukʰis*	'disease, ill (person)'	T6375 duḥkhá n. 'difficulty, pain'
(*dukʰ*)	*dukʰaŋ*	'misery, grief, sadness'	
	ʧa:ras†	'a group of four men who carry the devta'	T4655 catvā́raḥ m. pl. 'four'
tisraŋ		'third'	T6018 *triḥsara 'triple'
gitaŋ	*gitaŋ*	'song'	T4167 gītá n. 'singing'
	gitkaras	'singer'	Hindi *gitka:r* 'singer, the one who sings'
hal	*halaŋ*	'plough'	T14000 halá m.n. 'plough'
	ha:les†	'one who ploughs'	
laʈʰas	*laʈas*	'dumb'	T10917 laṭṭa m. 'bad man'
ka:ɳas	*ka:naŋ, ka:nes*	'blind, one-eyed'	T3019 kāṇá 'one-eyed'

While the data presented so far suggest an original semantically-based distribution of *-(V)ŋ* and *-(V)s*, there are also many counterexamples to this. For example, Kinnauri *piʈʰas* 'flour', Kanashi *jaras* / Kinnauri *ãjares* 'darkness'. Similarly, there are some animate nouns which take the adaptive marker *-(V)ŋ*. E.g. Kanashi *bandraŋ* / Kinnauri *bandres* 'monkey'; Kanashi *ʃokkuraŋ* / Kinnauri *ʃokraŋ* 'orphan'; and Kanashi *maɽʃaŋ* / Kinnauri *morʧʰaŋ* 'man'.

In inflection, the adaptive marker generally behaves as part of the stem, so that inflectional suffixes are added after it, e.g. Kanashi *ga:ɽiŋ* 'river' : *ga:ɽiŋ-u* [river-POSS], but there are also instances where the adaptive marker is partly integrated in the grammar of the language, and treated as some kind of suffix. Both in Kanashi and Kinnauri the plural ending or a case marker may sometimes replace the adaptive marker, e.g. Kinnauri *gitaŋ* 'song' : *git-a:* [song-PL]; Kinnauri *k^h^akaŋ* 'mouth' : *k^h^ak-o* [mouth-LOC]. However, we also find instances of two forms of a noun, one where the plural and/or case marker is affixed to the full noun stem (i.e., including the adaptive marker), and another one where the same noun occurs without the adaptive marker when the plural/case marker is affixed, e.g. Kinnauri *bo:ʈ^h^aŋ-o:-nu* ~ *bo:ʈ^h^-a:-nu* [tree-PL-DAT.PL]. Kanashi shows the same general pattern as Kinnauri, although with a much more pronounced preference for attaching number and case suffixes to the full noun stem, e.g. Kanashi *baniŋ-a:-p* [pot-PL-ACC]; *pitaŋ-a:-p* [door-PL-ACC]. See Chapter 3 for more details.

2.2.2 An example: names of months and weekdays

A striking illustration of the role of the adaptive marker *-(V)ŋ* in the linguistic systems of Kanashi and Kinnauri is offered by words for time periods, in particular names of months and weekdays.

Both Kanashi and Kinnauri use the Hindu calendar, according to which the year begins on the vernal equinox (21st or 22nd of March) and then proceeds through 12 months with 30 or 31 days each. A consequence of this arrangement is that the Hindu months do not coincide with the Gregorian months, but overlap them. Table 3 shows the names of the months in Kanashi and Kinnauri in comparison to some neighboring IA languages of the same region and also the corresponding Sanskrit names (from Turner 1966).

Even though Kinnauri and Kanashi use the Hindu calendar and the forms of the month names are, to a large extent, similar to those found in IA languages, Kanashi and Kinnauri differ from IA languages in that in Kinnauri, all month names end with an *-aŋ*. In Kanashi, too, all month names, except three (*ʧeit, buʃa:k, ka:te*) end in *-aŋ*. Distinct from this, none of the month names in Sanskrit, Kullu Pahari and Kotgarhi have a word-final *-aŋ*.

Kinnauri and Kanashi differ more noticeably from the IA languages Kotgarhi and Kullu Pahari regarding two of the month names (*ma:ŋ* 'Jan–Feb'; *indramaŋ* 'Sep–Oct').

In the latter case, Kanashi and Kinnauri – and Kinnauri Pahari, but this is most likely a borrowing from Kinnauri – simply reflect a different item. The closest original form is the Sanskrit *índra*; *índramaha* 'festival for (the god) Indra during

Table 3: Month names in Kanashi, Kinnauri and neighboring IA languages

	Kanashi	**Kinnauri**	**Kinnauri Pahari**	**Kotgarhi**	**Kullu Pahari**	**Sanskrit (Turner 1966)**
Mar–Apr	*ʧeit*	*ʧetraŋ*	*ʧɛta:r*	—	*ʧet(ə)r*	caitraḥ; caitrá
Apr–May	*buʃa:k*	*bɛʃakaŋ*, *bʰaiʃakʰaŋ*	*ba:ʃa:*	*bəśn/a;* Koci: *bəśā*	*beʃakʰ*	vaiśākhá
May–Jun	*ʤeʃtaŋ*	*ʤeʃtaŋ*	*dzeʃth*	*dzēṭ:h*	*ʤeʃt(ʰ)*	jyaiṣṭhaḥ
Jun–Jul	*aʃlaŋ*	*a:ʃaraŋ*	*a:ʃa:r*	*ʃāɽ*	*ʃaɽ*	āṣāḍhaḥ
Jul–Aug	*ʃauɳaŋ*	*ʃa(u)naŋ*	*ʃa:ma:n*	*ʃāuɳ*	*ʃauɳ*	śrāvaṇaḥ
Aug–Sep	*badraŋ*	*bʰadraŋ*	*ba:drɔ*	*bhɔ̃ddər*	*bʰad(ə)r*	bhādra
Sep–Oct	*indramaŋ*	*indramaŋ*	*ɪndrɔma:ŋ*	*sɔ̃:ɟ*	*(?) ʃoʤ*	índra; T1579a. índramaha 'festival for (god) Indra during this month'; T1472 āśviná
Oct–Nov	*ka:te*	*ka:tiaŋ*	*ka:tɪ*	*kat:ɪ*	*ka:ti*	kārtiká
Nov–Dec	*mokʃiraŋ*	*mokʃeraŋ*	*mɔgʃrɪ*	*maŋgʃər*	*mɔkʃar*	mārgaśirāḥ
Dec–Jan	*poʃaŋ*	*poʃaŋ*	*poʃ*	*pōʃ*	*poʃ*	pauṣaḥ
Jan–Feb	*ma:ŋ*	*ma:ŋ*	*maŋ*	*māg:*	*mag*	māgha
Feb–Mar	*pʰagɽaŋ*	*pʰagnaŋ*	—	—	*pʰagaɳ*	phálguna

this month' (Turner 1966: T1579a), and we probably see the outcome of a change *índramaha-aŋ* > *indramaŋ* in present-day Kanashi and Kinnauri.

In the case of 'Jan–Feb', we posit a similar process, i.e. OIA (Sanskrit) *māgha* > MIA (Prakrit) *māha* > *māha-aŋ* > *ma:ŋ*. This is confirmed by the name for this month provided by Gerard (1842): *mahang* 'January'.

As shown in Table 4, the month names in the WH languages Tinani and Bunan are quite different from those of Kanashi and Kinnauri and similar to each other, but still different from the forms found in Tibetic languages, such as Navakat.

The names of the weekdays are also IA loans in Kinnauri and Kanashi, in some of which we also find the adaptive marker *-aŋ*. This is also the case in Chhitkuli (D. D. Sharma 1992: 197–304). See Table 5. Interestingly, *-es* is attested in Kinnauri only in 'Saturday'. Furthermore, the form for 'Thursday' does not contain any adaptive marker in any of the three languages (Kinnauri, Kanashi and Chhitkuli).

To summarize this section:

- The calendar system as well as the month names in Kinnauri and Kanashi differ strikingly from those found in Tinani,Bunan and Navakat.
- Both Kanashi and Kinnauri use the IA calendar system as well as the month names; some (Kanashi) or all (Kinnauri) month names contain the adaptive marker *-(V)ŋ*.

Table 4: Month names in Tinani, Bunan and Navakat

	Tinani	Bunan	Navakat
First month of the calendar (='Mar–Apr')	*ts^{h}ukzu la*	*tsukskisla*	*ndàʋa tàŋbo*
Second month of the calendar (='Apr–May')	*kunzu la, kunzla*	*kunsla*	*ndàʋa ɲíʋa*
Fourth month of the calendar (='Jun–Jul')	*puɳa la, puɳla*	*punasla*	*ndàʋa ʒìʋa*
Eighth month of the calendar (='Oct–Nov')	*surla*	*sursla*	*ndàʋa gétpa*
Tenth month of the calendar (='Dec–Jan')	*k^{j}ur la*	*k^{h}ujsla*	*ndàʋa ʧúʋa*
Eleventh month of the calendar (='Jan–Feb')	*minɖug la, mindzugla*	*tondʑuksla*	*ndàʋa ʧúkʃikpa*

Table 5: Names of weekdays in Kanashi, Kinnauri and Chhitkuli

	Kanashi	Kinnauri	Chhitkuli
'Monday'	*soar, suãraŋ*	*suãraŋ*	*somarəŋ*
'Tuesday'	*maŋgal*	*maŋgla:raŋ*	
'Wednesday'	*bud(d)*	*buda:raŋ*	
'Thursday'	*brest*	*brespot*	*bresət*
'Friday'	*ʃukkar*	*ʃukaraŋ*	*šukarəŋ*
'Saturday'	*ʃuɳiʧare*	*ʃonʃeres*	
'Sunday'	*ʋa:r*	*tʋa:r, tʋa:raŋ*	*itwarəŋ*

– The Kinnauri and Kanashi forms (especially for the two months 'Jan–Feb' and 'Sep–Oct') are more similar to each other than they are to any other IA and ST languages examined here.

It seems highly unlikely that the similarities that we have observed here in Kanashi and Kinnauri relating to the month names (or at least their introduction in the two languages), especially 'Jan–Feb' and 'Sep–Oct', are independent developments in the two languages. It is more likely that this adaptation of the month names took place in their common linguistic variety – before the two communities diverged. The pattern that we have observed here concerning month names is similar to the patterns observed regarding the adaptive markers *-(V)ŋ*/*-(V)s* on IA loans in general in Kanashi, Kinnauri and some other ST languages, as discussed above. This raises the question regarding the etymologies of the adaptive markers *-(V)ŋ* and *-(V)s*.

Table 6: Kanashi and Kinnauri adjectives in *-(V)s*

Kanashi	Kinnauri	Gloss	Etymology
ḍugas	*ḍuges*	'deep'	T6368 dīrghá 'long, tall, deep'
sulus	*mesaŋ, sulus*	'slow'	T13512 sulabha 'easy, trivial'
katʃas	*katʃas, katʃes*	'unripe, uncooked'	T2613 *kacca 'raw, unripe'
kʰulas	*kʰulas*	'wide'	T3945 *khōll 'to open', *khull 'to be open'
sastas	*sosta(s)*	'cheap, less expensive'	

Table 7: Kanashi and Kinnauri adjectives with head nouns

Kanashi	Gloss	Kanashi [Adj N]	Etymology
la:mes, la:mas	'long'	*la:mas kurti* 'long shirt' *la:m-a: kurti-ga:* [long-PL shirt-PL] *la:mas tʃʰakts* 'tall boy' *la:m-a: tʃʰakts-a:* [tall-PL boy-PL] *la:mas tʃimets* 'tall girl' *la:m-a: tʃimets-a:* [tall-PL girl-PL]	T10951 lamba 'long'
uṭʰras	'high'	*uṭʰras ka:ṭʰi* 'high mountain' *uṭhr-a: ka:ṭhi-ga:* [high-PL mountain-PL]	T1783 *uttāḍa 'high'
bellis	'wide'	*bellis bitiŋ* 'wide wall' *bellis bitiŋ-a:* [wide-PL wall-PL]	T11798 vipula 'wide, extensive'
garkas	'heavy'	*garkas baniŋ* 'heavy pot' *gark-a: baniŋ-a:* [heavy-PL pot-PL]	T4209 gurú 'heavy'
Kinnauri	**Gloss**	**Kinnauri [Adj N]**	**Etymology**
la:mes	'long'	*la:mes mi* 'tall man' *la:m-a: mi-go:* [tall-PL man-PL] *la:mes-a: mi-go:* [tall-PL man-PL] *la:mes mi-go:* [tall man-PL] *la:mes tshetsats* 'tall girl' *la:mes tshetsats-o:* [tall girl-PL] *la:m-a: tshetsats-o:* [tall-PL girl-PL]	T10951 lamba 'long'
solḍes	'straight'	*solḍes om* 'straight path' *solḍes om-o:* [straight path-PL]	

2.3 Adaptive markers on adjectives

Next, we will examine the adaptive marker *-(V)s* on IA-origin adjectives in Kanashi and Kinnauri. Some examples are given in Table 6.

As the examples in Tables 6 and 7 illustrate, the occurrence of *-(V)s* in Kanashi and Kinnauri adjectives is not sensitive to formal or semantic characteristics of the head word (except that they may optionally inflect for plural in the same way as nouns, i.e. replacing *-(V)s* with the plural suffix).

Distinct from this, as shown in the Kanashi examples in Table 8 (reproduced from Chapter 3), there is a set of adjectives which end in *-(V)s*, where the adaptive marker appears only with masculine head nouns, while feminine head nouns show a number of different endings.

Table 8: Kanashi adjectives in *-(V)s*

SG	PL	SG	PL
ka:ɳ-as madras 'blind man'	*ka:ɳ-a: madr-a:*	*ka:ɳ beʈaɽi* 'blind woman'	*ka:ɳ-e beʈaɽi-ga:*
moʈʰ-as ʧʰakts 'fat young man'	*moʈʰ-a: ʧʰakts-a:*	*moʈ-eɳ beʈaɽi* 'fat woman'	*moʈ-eɳ-a: beʈaɽi-ga:*
buɽ-as munuk 'old man'	*buɽ-a: munuk-a:*	*buɽ-its beʈaɽi* 'old woman'	*buɽ-its-a: beʈaɽi-ga:*
roʈʰ-as munuk 'brave man'	*roʈʰ-a: munuk-a:*	*roʈʰ-ar beʈaɽi* 'brave woman'	*roʈʰ-ar-a: ~ roʈʰ-ar-e beʈaɽi-ga:*
ʃobil-as biɳiʃ 'beautiful husband'	*ʃobil-a: biɳiʃ-a:*	*ʃobil, ʃobilas beʈaɽi* 'beautiful woman'	*ʃobil-e beʈaɽi-ga:*
matsl-is ʧaŋts 'lazy boy'	*matsil ʧaŋts-a:*	*matsl-en beʈaɽi* 'lazy woman'	*matsl-en-e beʈaɽi-ga:*

2.4 Kanashi–Kinnauri mismatches

If both languages exhibit an adaptive marker, we generally find the same marker in Kanashi and Kinnauri with a particular IA noun or adjective (either *-(V)ŋ* or *-(V)s*). This holds for the majority of this set of IA nouns/adjectives in Kanashi and Kinnauri. Table 9 shows the only mismatches that we have found concerning the choice of the adaptive marker in the two languages.

There are also some instances where we find both *-(V)ŋ* and *-(V)s* as alternatives on the same item, without any apparent change in meaning (Table 10).

Table 9: Nominal adaptive marker mismatches between Kanashi and Kinnauri

Kanashi	Kinnauri	Gloss	Etymology
bakras	*bəkʰaraŋ*	'goat' / 'she-goat'	T9153 bárkara m. 'kid, lamb'
bandraŋ	*bandres*	'monkey'	T11515 vānara m. 'monkey'
kukaɽaŋ	*kukkras*	'cock, rooster'	T3208 kukkuṭá m. 'cock'
sa:mnas	*somaŋ*	'flat, straight'	T13346 sāmaka '*even, *level'
agraŋ	*a:gles*	'beyond' / 'first'	T68 ágra n. 'top, summit'

Table 10: Nominal adaptive marker variation in Kanashi and Kinnauri

Kanashi	Kinnauri	Gloss	Etymology
	galiŋ, gales	'abuse'	T4145 gāli f. PL 'abusive speech'
baniŋ	*baniŋ, banes*	'dish, pot, cooking utensil'	T9440 bhāṇḍa n. 'pot, dish, vessel, ornament, wares'
ka:ɳas	*ka:nes, ka:naŋ*	'one-eyed, blind'	T3019 kāṇá 'one-eyed', Pa. Pk. kāṇá 'blind of one eye, blind'
padras, padraŋ	*podres*	'smooth, plain' / 'plain (land)'	T7767 *paddhara 'straight, level'

3 Adaptive markers in ST and non-ST languages of the region

It is conceivable – even likely (see below in this chapter and Chapter 8) – that *-(V)ŋ* and *-(V)s* represent separate borrowing processes, thus possibly were active at different times and with different donor languages. This might also account for the variation that we observe (e.g. Kinnauri *baniŋ, banes* 'pot'; see Section 2.4).

In order to understand the introduction of the adaptive markers in Kinnauri and Kanashi and to throw light on the prehistory of Kanashi and Kinnauri, we need to explore the following two interrelated questions:

1. Do we find these adaptive markers in other languages in the region?
2. What is the source of the two adaptive markers? Is this a genealogical or an areal phenomenon?

In this section we will examine the distribution of the adaptive markers in other ST and non-ST languages of the region.

3.1 The linguistic neighborhood of Kanashi and Kinnauri

The surrounding Himalayas – depending on how wide we cast our net – are the home of three major language families which all have been present in the region for several millennia, Sino-Tibetan, Indo-Aryan (< Indo-European) and Dravidian, and marginally also a fourth major family: Munda (< Austroasiatic). The last-mentioned may have had a larger presence here in prehistoric times, as indicated by suggested Munda loans in Vedic (Witzel 1999; Southworth 2005). In addition, there are at least two language isolates, Burushaski to the northwest and Kusunda to the east. See Figure 4.[6]

Those languages where we have not been able to find evidence in the consulted sources that adaptive markers are used are listed in Table 11 (possibly apart from a sporadic instance, which is then given under "Comment" in the table).

3.2 Sino-Tibetan languages

The language contact between ST and IA in this region – with IA mostly in the dominant position – goes back at least two and a half to three millennia. Hence, all ST languages of the Indian Himalayas have IA loans – some languages – e.g. Darma, Kanashi, Kinnauri, Pattani, Raji, and Rongpo – have relatively more, while others – e.g, Bunan, Tinani, Darma, Byangsi, and Chaudangsi – relatively fewer.

In order to examine the spread of the phenomenon under investigation more systematically, we will examine the ST languages listed in Figure 1, which are spoken in this part of the Himalayas. We include at least one language of each recognized subbranch. The selection of languages included here is constrained by the availability of relevant data.

3.2.1 Sino-Tibetan languages of Himachal Pradesh and Ladakh

As we will see in this section, with the exception of the ST languages of Lower and Middle Kinnaur: Kinnauri, Chhitkuli and Shumcho (Labrang variety), none of the ST languages of Himachal Pradesh and Ladakh take the adaptive marker on IA loans, except for at most a few isolated examples.

6 The sources of the data presented in this section are various. For Kanashi, Kinnauri, Navakat and Kinnauri Pahari we have drawn upon our own fieldwork data. For other languages we have relied on secondary data sources, texts reflecting extremely varying degrees of editorial rigor, often in digital versions with differing legibility resulting from varying scanning conditions.

Table 11: Languages without adaptive markers

Language	Source	Comment
Sino-Tibetan		
Purik	(Bailey 1915)	–
Ladakhi	(Bettina Zeisler p.c.)	*balṭin* 'bucket' (with *-n*, and not *-ŋ*)
Navakat	(Saxena 2022)	*péraŋ* 'family' (Kinnauri *peraŋ* 'family, clan')
Nyamkad	(D. D. Sharma 1992: 98–196)	–
Pattani/Manchad	(Konow 1909; S. R. Sharma 1987)	–
Tinani	(Konow 1909: Chamba Lahuli)	–
Bunan	(Widmer 2017)	*pitaŋ* 'door' (Kanashi and Kinnauri *pitaŋ*); many village names end in *-(V)ŋ* (Widmer 2017: 20)
Chaudangsi	(Konow 1909; Krishan 2001a)	*morong* 'door'
Rangkas	(D. D. Sharma 1989b: 195–254)	–
Yakkha	(Schackow 2015)	–
Thangmi	(Turin 2006)	*maṇa* ~ *maṇiŋ* 'bread'
Baram	(Kanasakar et al. 2011)	–
Gurung	(Trail 1973)	–
Dravidian		
Brahui	(Andronov 1980)	–
Language isolate		
Burushaski	(Klimov & Èdel'man 1970; Munshi 2006)	–
Indo-Aryan		
Kullu Pahari	(Anju Saxena's fieldwork notes; Diack 1896; Hendriksen 1976; 1986)	–
Kotgarhi	(Hendriksen 1976; 1986)	–
Jaunsari	(Matthews 2008)	–
Kangri (Kángṛī)	(Bailey 1908)	–
Chinali	(S. R. Sharma 1991)	–
Kumaoni	(Apte & Pattanayak 1967; D. D. Sharma 1987)	–
Garhwali	(Chandola 1966)	–
Nepali	(Acharya 1990)	–
Bajjika	(Roy 2010)	–

ST				
	Bodish			Gurung
		W.Archaic Tibetan		Ladakhi
				Purik
		Late Old Tibetan	Lahuli-Spiti	Navakat
				Nyamkad
			Spiti-Jad	Jad
	West Himalayish	Western	Kinnauric	Chhitkuli
				Kinnauri
				Kanashi
				Shumcho
			Lahaulic	Pattani
				Tinani
		Eastern	Central	Bunan
				Rongpo
			Pithauragarh	Chaudangsi
				Byangsi
				Darma
				Rangkas
	Himalayish	Mahakiranti	Newaric	Dolakha Newar
				Kathmandu Newar
			Thangmi-Baram	Thangmi
				Baram
			Kham-Magar-Chepang	Magar
			Eastern Kiranti	Yakkha
	Raji-Raute			Raji
				Raute
				Rawat

Figure 1: Sino-Tibetan languages included in this study (classification [with some internal nodes omitted] according to Glottolog; Hammarström et al. 2021)

3.2.1.1 Western West Himalayish and Tibetic languages of Kinnaur

In Saxena & Borin (2013) we examined the linguistic distance among "Kinnauri dialects", a cover term we used about ST varieties spoken in Lower, Middle and Upper Kinnaur (in the locations shown in the map in Figure 2). Relevant in the present context is that it is not only the Kinnauri variety of Sangla that shows adaptation of IA nouns/adjectives by adding *-(V)ŋ/-(V)s*, but also several other ST varieties of Lower and Middle Kinnaur, while no varieties of Upper Kinnaur – those of Poo, Kuno and Nako (Navakat, already mentioned above) – use the adaptive markers. See Table 12.

This grouping of the languages of Kinnaur according to the prevalence of *-(V)ŋ/-(V)s* in is visualized in the map in Figure 2 (based on data and calculations presented in Saxena & Borin 2013).

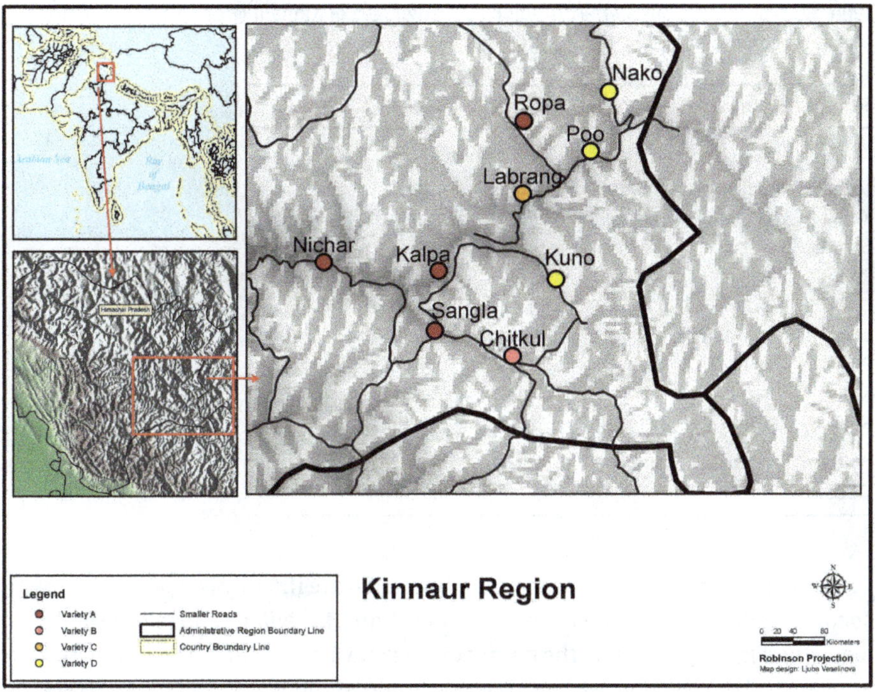

Figure 2: Sino-Tibetan language varieties in Kinnaur

Chhitkuli (Chitkul village)[7] (Philippe Martinez p.c.; D. D. Sharma 1992: 107–304) and Shumcho (Gerard 1842: 548–551) are especially relevant in this regard. Both are spoken in Lower/Middle Kinnaur. In Shumcho (Gerard 1842: 548–551) we find examples of both adaptive markers, *-(V)s* and *-(V)ŋ*. For example, *oris* 'carpenter', *chamung* 'shoemaker', *domung* 'blacksmith', *golung* 'neck', *beeshung* 'poison', *shakrung* 'fine sugar', *palis* 'shepherd', *chorus* 'thief', *soorus* 'hog', *bundrus* 'monkey'. There are a few examples of the adaptive marker in the Shumcho data reported by Huber (2014) too (*meʈɐŋ* 'earth', *deɕɐŋ* 'village', *pɪtɐŋ* 'door'). Chhitkuli has many instances of the adaptive marker *-(V)ŋ* (e.g. *sowarəŋ* 'Monday'; *dukhəŋ* 'pain'; *canəŋ* 'basket'; *bošəŋ* 'year' (all from D. D. Sharma 1992: 107–304), but no occurrence of the adaptive marker *-(V)s* is attested in Chhitkuli.

In Gerard's (1842) vocabularly both the adaptive markers (*-(V)ŋ* and *-(V)s* occur also in T,heburskud (Shumcho). The following examples of words appearing

7 In English-language official documents the name of the village is given as "Chitkul", whereas the language variety is normally written "Chhitkuli". We will adhere to this convention here.

Table 12: Distribution of *-(V)ŋ*/*-(V)s* among ST languages of Kinnaur (written Tibetan items added for comparison)

Sense:	**'snake'**	**'ear'**	**'seed'**	**'night'**
Variety				
Nichar	*sapɔs:*	*kanɔŋ*	*bijaŋ*	*ratıŋ*
Kalpa	*sapas*	*kanaŋ*	*bıjɔŋ*	*ratıŋ*
Sangla	*sapes*	*kanaŋ*	*bijaŋ*	*ratıŋ*
Ropa	*saʋas:*	*kanaŋ*	*bıjaŋ*	*ratıŋ*
Chitkul	*sapa*	*rɔcts*	*bıjaŋ*	*mʊnima*
Labrang	*saʋasəs*	*repaŋ*	*pʊdzad*	*mʊɲəɲa*
Poo	*kʰalʋa*	*nam ɟɔk:*	*saŋon*	*goŋmo*
Kuno	*ʈʊl:*	*nam ɟɔk:*	*saŋɔn*	*tʃamo*
Nako	*(n)ɖul*	*namɟɔ(k)*	*saŋon*	*goemo*
Written Tibetan	*sbrul*	*rna*	*sa sṅon*	*dgoṅ no ~ dgoṅs mo, mtshan*

in his vocabulary in both Kinnauri and Shumcho are illustrative: *palis* 'shepherd'; *sonarus* 'goldsmith'; *chorus* 'thief'; *gulung* 'throat'; *galing* 'abuse'; *deshung* 'village'; *burshung* 'year'. Note the names of weekdays in Kinnauri and Shumcho (Gerard 1842: 511): *aeetwarung* 'Sunday'; *soarung* 'Monday'; *munglarung* 'Tuesday'; *shookarung* 'Friday'; *shunsheerus* 'Saturday'.

Based on what we have seen so far, Lower/Middle Kinnaur could be the home of a posited common Kanashi-Kinnauri proto-language (see Chapter 8 for a discussion). We still need to take a look at the ST languages spoken further east, in the Indian state of Uttarakhand and in the neighboring regions in Nepal.

3.2.1.2 Eastern West Himalayish

Pattani (Francke 1917)

Francke (1917: 13) states that Lahaul was a much-travelled pathway, linking Tibet/Ladakh and Kullu. This continued up until the Sikhs took control over Lahaul. This probably explains a large number of Tibetan and IA loans in Pattani (the lingua franca of this region, the largest population group among Pattani, Tinani and Bunan speech communities). Despite this long-standing contact with IA, none of Bunan (Widmer 2017: 129–130), Tinani or Pattani show any signs of adaptation strategies on nouns and verbs which we have observed in Kanashi and Kinnauri.

3.2.2 Sino-Tibetan languages of Uttarakhand and Nepal

Traces of the adaptive marker *-(V)ŋ* are found in some ST languages of Uttarakhand and Nepal, and in some of them – the Raji-Raute languages – even more than just traces. On the other hand, *-(V)s* is found only exceptionally (one instance in Jad and possibly a few instances in Dolakha Newar).

3.2.2.1 Late Old Tibetan

Jad (S. R. Sharma 2001c):

Jad is spoken in Jadang, Nilang and a few other villages in Uttarakhand (India). Note that the village name Jadang (and possibly also Nilang) seems to have the adaptive marker *-aŋ*. If so, this is consistent with place names found in Kinnauri and in Kanashi. The only nouns which end in *-(V)ŋ* in Jad are shown in Table 13.

Table 13: Adaptive markers in Jad

Jad	Gloss	Jad	Gloss
piriŋ, pi-tiŋ	'baby'	*ghəsiŋ*	'good, better'
ciŋiŋ	'bell'	*padraŋ, (padras)*	'flat, plain (surface)'

In Jad we also find one item with the adaptive marker *-as*: *padras* 'flat' (Kanashi *padras*, Kinnauri *podres*; Etymology: T7767 *paddhara 'straight, level'; Turner 1966).

Table 14: Adaptive markers in Rongpo

Rongpo	Gloss	Etymology
phiṭiŋ, phəṭ	'ashes'	T11348 *varta 'roundstone'
jəbaŋ, jəmən	'meal, food'	T10431 yắya m. 'barley'
kənu:ŋ, kənu:ŋ	'ear'	T2830 kárṇa m. 'ear'
ḍasa:ŋ	'bed'	T6896 dhvámsati 'falls to pieces'
gəṭəm, gərəm	'river'	T3981 *gaḍḍa 'hole, pit'
pijag	'seeds'	T9250 bī́ja n. 'seed, semen'

3.2.2.2 Eastern West Himalayish

Rongpo (S. R. Sharma 2001b; Zoller 1983):

Rongpo has a large number of IA nouns and adjectives, e.g. *os* 'dew'; *des* 'country'; *pʰul* 'flower'; *bɔɳ* 'forest'; *bʰiti* 'wall'; *muskil* 'difficult'; *kʰara:b* 'bad'; *nilo* 'blue'. As seen in these examples, most of the IA loans in Rongpo do not have any adaptive marker.

However, there are some IA loans in Rongpo, which end in *-ŋ*, *-n*, *-m* or *-g*, which may possibly be related to the Kinnauri/Kanashi adaptive marker *-(V)ŋ*, as shown in Table 14.[8]

There are no clear adjective examples with an adaptive marker in Rongpo.

Darma (Willis Oko 2019; Krishan 2001b; S. R. Sharma 2001c):

As shown in Table 15, Darma exhibits a small number of nouns ending in *-(V)ŋ*, at least some of which seem to contain the adaptive marker.

Table 15: Adaptive markers in Darma

Darma	Gloss	Etymology
homaŋ	'darkness'	
ceejaŋ	'pot, kettle'	
khoyang	'pot, copper'	
paləŋ	'spinach'	T8126 pālakyā f. 'Beta bengalensis'
kibaŋ	'meeting place, temple'	
marong	'door'	T10160 *mukhaghāṭā 'entrance frame'
lasəŋ	'goat'	
kolaŋ	'bell'	T12580 śr̥ṅkhalam. n. 'chain'
bəyəŋ	'nest'	T11591 vāsá m. 'abode'
khuyəŋ	'plait'	

Byangsi (S. R. Sharma 2001a):

Byangsi has relatively few IA loans overall. All the words with the final syllable *-(V)ŋ* found in the wordlist are listed in Table 16.

8 *-niŋ* is suffixed to kinship terms as a marker of honorificity. *a:pa>apniŋ*, *ɛnɪŋ* 'father', *a:ma* > *amniŋ* 'mother', *byəd* > *byəniŋ* 'brother'. This is the case in several ST languages of the Himalayas. This *-niŋ* is not the same as the adaptive marker *-(V)ŋ*.

Table 16: Adaptive markers in Byangsi

Byangsi	Gloss	Byangsi	Gloss
serɔŋ, saro, saru	'forest'	*mithaŋ*	'mother's younger brother'
mayaŋ	'basket'	*lasaŋ*	'male goat'
duklaŋ	'food'	*kacaŋ*	'pubic hair'
maːsaŋ	'meat, sheep'		

3.2.2.3 Raji-Raute

The Raji-Raute ST subgroup consists of a small cluster of closely related varieties spoken in Uttarakhand in India and in western Nepal. Glottolog and Ethnologue classify these into three languages ("languoids" in Glottolog): Raji (rji), Raute (rau), and Rawat (jnl). Looking at descriptions of Raji of India (e.g. Krishan 2001c) and Raji of Nepal (e.g. Dhakal 2019), it is clear that the differences between these varieties are significant. Since it is equally clear, and agreed in the literature (e.g. Fortier 2019), that all the varieties form a distinct ST subgroup, their exact number and the precise genealogical relations among them are not crucial for our particular purposes here, where the position of Raji-Raute as a whole in relation to Kanashi and Kinnauri is the primary focus.

Raji (D. D. Sharma 1990; Krishan 2001c; Rastogi 2012; Dhakal 2019; Fortier 2019):

Raji has many instances (about one hundred) of nouns and adjectives ending in *-(V)ŋ*, many of which are obvious IA loans, both older (e.g. *xunəŋ* 'gold') and newer loanwords (e.g. *pjaloŋ* 'cup'; *taliŋ* 'plate').[9] See more Raji examples in Appendix B.1 to this chapter. In some nouns, the adaptive marker is realized as nasalization of the final vowel (e.g. *kəjã* 'body'). As the examples in Table 17 show, Raji is very similar to Kanashi and Kinnauri regarding the use of the adaptive marker *-(V)ŋ*.

Raute (Bista 1978; Khadka 2006; Fortier 2019):

Raute, too, has many instances of the adaptive marker *-(V)ŋ*.

Bista (1978) provides a list of Raute words (the Swadesh 100 concept list). In the following Raute words there seems to be an adaptive marker *-m/-w*, occurring

9 This has been previously noted by Rastogi (2012), who refers to the element *-əŋ* in Raji as one of "a few markers of nativization [of Kumauni and Hindi words]" (Rastogi 2012: 4).

Table 17: Adaptive markers in Raji

Raji	Kanashi	Kinnauri	Gloss	Etymology
haḍəŋ	*haḍḍaŋ*	*haraŋ*	'bone'	T13952 haḍḍa n. 'bone'
uhəŋ	*oʃaŋ*	*oʃaŋ*	'dew'	T855 avaśyā f. 'frost, dew'
manəŋ	*baɳaŋ*	*boniŋ, baunaŋ*	'forest'	T11258 vána n. (once m.R.) 'single tree', RV. 'forest, timber'
bisəŋ	*biʃaŋ*	*biʃaŋ*	'poison'	T11968 viṣá n. 'poison'

where Kinnauri and Kanashi (and also other varieties of Raute) show the adaptive marker *-(V)ŋ*: *ha·řəm* 'bone'; *sikkəm* 'horn'; *mȟwɔm* 'tongue'; *gȟɔnɔw* 'hot'.[10]

Raute is spoken mainly in the mid-western and far-western region of Nepal. Some Rautes are hunter-gatherers, while other groups are settled communities, and some dialectal differences are noted between the hunter-gatherer and settled communities (Khadka 2006). The description by Khadka (2006) seems to be based on the speech of the settled Rautes of Dudeldhura, but he also provides a small core vocabulary comparison between the two varieties. As we can see in Table 18, both varieties use the adaptive markers.

Table 18: Adaptive markers in Raute varieties

Settled Raute/Boto Boli	Hunter-gatherer Raute	Gloss
dudʰʌŋ	*dəduŋ, dudəu*	'milk'
gamʌŋ	*monaŋ, gamaŋ*	'hot'
gaɽoŋ	*garum*	'girl, daughter'
geŋ	*(bəsaha)*	'clarified butter, ghee'
gumʌŋ	*(dʰum)*	'wheat'
haḍḍʌn	*harʌm*	'bone'
manaŋ	*manaŋ*	'forest'

A cumulative list based on the descriptions by Bista (1978), Khadka (2006) and Fortier (2019) of the Raute and Rawat items containing the adaptive marker *-(V)ŋ* is given in Appendix B.2 to this chapter.

Fortier (2019) provides a comparative Raji-Raute Swadesh list (100 concepts) with two Raute varieties of Nepal, two Raji varieties of India and three Raji varieties of Nepal. From this comparison we see that: (1) Raji has more instances

10 There seems to be variation among – or even within – Raute varieties, where word-final *-ŋ* alternates with *-m* or *-u/-w*; cf. the item 'milk' in Table 18.

overall of the adaptive marker *-(V)ŋ* than Raute (which is also the picture given by Appendix B.1 to this chapter); and (2) the Raji varieties of Nepal show many more instances of *-(V)ŋ* than the varieties spoken in India.

3.2.2.4 Mahakiranti

Magar (Beames 1870; Bhattari 2011):
In the description of Magar by Bhattari (2011), there is a large number of IA loanwords (including kinship terms), but none of them shows any adaptive marker.

Newar (Genetti 2007; Hargreaves 2017):
As far as characteristic adaptation of IA nouns and adjectives is concerned, Kathmandu Newar does not have /ŋ/ in its phoneme inventory (Hargreaves 2017). It exists in Dolakha Newar (Genetti 2007), and in the word list provided by Genetti (2007) (about 1,100 entries), there is a handful of items ending in *-ŋ/-s* (see Table 19). Except for those marked as Nepali by Genetti (see below), we could only find similar IA forms for two: *caukos* 'doorframe' (Hindi: *caukhaṭ*) and *dupās* (Hindi: *dhūp*). If it is true, then Dolakha Newar has some examples of the adaptive marker *-(V)s*.

Table 19: Possible adaptive markers in Newar

D. Newar	Gloss	D. Newar	Gloss
bajaŋ	'hookah'	*lāŋtā, laiŋtāŋ*	'naked' (Nepali: *nāŋgo*)
bārpāŋ	'tomato'	*māŋas*	'dream' (Nepali: *sapnā*)
bujiŋ	'housefly'	*nakas*	'first' (Nepali: *pahilo, pratham*)
caukos	'doorframe'	*nimtiŋ*	'benefit' (Nepali: *fāida, lābh*)
dupās	'wick' (for puja)	*pāŋ, paiŋgu*	'fruit'
gāntāŋ	'thin; emaciated'		

3.2.3 Summary

The above description shows that only a few ST languages of Uttarakhand/Nepal show some plausible traces of adaptive markers akin to the Kinnauri and Kanashi adaptive markers. There is, however, one crucial difference: With the possible exception of Dolakha Newar and Jad, these ST languages do not show any instance of the adaptive marker *-(V)s*. This means that items that take *-(V)s* in Kinnauri and Kanashi, will have the adaptive marker *-(V)ŋ*. This is exactly what we find in Raji, e.g. Kanashi *katʃas*; Kinnauri *katʃas, katʃes* : Raji *kətsuŋ* 'raw, unripe, uncooked'.

3.3 Munda languages

Santali (Macphail 1983):
Santali is spoken mainly in Central India, but it also has a fair-sized speaker community in Nepal (about 50,000 speakers, according to both the 2011 Census of Nepal and Eberhard et al. 2021). We find a small number of items ending in *-ŋ* (see Table 20), some of which can be assigned plausible IA etymologies (e.g. 'voice'; T1309 ārava m. 'cry, howl'; 'front' T12982 saṁmukhá 'facing, present').

Table 20: Adaptive markers in Santali

Santali	Gloss	Santali	Gloss
alaŋ	'tongue'	*rabaŋ*	'cold'
aṛaŋ	'voice'	*samaŋ*	'front'
hoḷoŋ	'flour'	*setoŋ*	'heat'
maraŋ	'big, old'	*tetaŋ*	'thirst'

3.4 Dravidian languages

Two Dravidian languages are spoken in or close to the Himalayas: Brahui to the west in Pakistan, Kurukh (also Kurux, Dhangar) in Nepal (the last-mentioned is also spoken in Jharkhand, India). As noted in Table 11, Brahui shows no evidence of the adaptive markers.

Kurukh (Dhangar) (Hahn 1911; Gordon 1973; Yadava 2001):
Kurukh does not seem to possess the adaptive marker *-(V)ŋ*, even though there are many IA loans in the language. But interestingly, in Kurukh *-s* occurs with masculine human nouns: *mabus, babus* 'boy'; *kukuwas* 'son'; *engris* 'younger brother' (cf. *engri* 'younger sister'). This *-s* is also affixed to IA loans (*co:ras* 'thief'; *ra:jas* 'king'; *laṛkas, laṛka* 'boy'; as well as IA male proper nouns which end in a vowel). Plural and case markers are affixed to the full noun stem (e.g. *babus-uthir* [boy-PL]). *-s* does not occur with feminine or inanimate nouns (e.g. *bo:ra* 'sack'; *cuṭṭi* 'hair'). Hahn (1911) describes *-as* as a masculine definite marker affixed to nouns, originally identical to the masculine third person singular pronoun.

3.5 Language isolates

Kusunda (Watters 2006):
There are some Kusunda nouns and adjectives (some of them recognizably IA) which end in *-(V)ŋ*, but none in *-(V)s* (Tables 21 and 22).

Table 21: Adaptive markers in Kusunda nouns

Kusunda	Gloss	Kusunda	Gloss
əubaŋ	'nostril'	*dibaŋ*	'mountain, cliff'
ataŋ	'footprint', 'track'	*eyəŋ*	'upper back'
dibʰaŋ	'crowd'	*haŋnuŋ*	'shadow'
gidaŋ	'water, sap'	*iŋ, inəŋ*	'eye'
gidzaŋ	'body'	*ihəŋ, ehəŋ*	'Newar'
gilaŋ, gelaŋ	'forest'	*idaŋ*	'hunger'
gitaŋ	'sweets'	*hugyaŋ*	'spade, shovel'
gotoŋ, gotəŋ	'soup'	*hilaŋ*	'a kind of tree'
iŋdzũ, idziŋ, idzəŋ	'tongue'	*məŋ, maŋ, maŋlaŋ*	'song'
ipi gidzaŋ	'horn'	*oɴʕtaŋ*	'smoking pipe'
kəbdzaŋ, kəpdzaŋ	'gold'	*pʰeladəŋ*	'lentil' (Nep: *gəgət*)
kəpaŋ	'turmeric, besar'	*sidzaŋ*	'beer', brew'
katəŋ	'itch'	*yuŋsũ, gusuŋ*	'tail'
laɢʕan, laŋ	'village'		

Table 22: Adaptive markers in Kusunda adjectives

Kusunda	Gloss	Kusunda	Gloss
olaŋ	'sweet', tasty'	*paŋdzaŋ*	'five'
dzaŋ, (a)dzəŋən	'new'	*kya.aŋ*	'thin', skinny'
pʰelaŋ	'flat'	*guluŋ*	'round' (Nep. *gulu*)
pʰurluŋ	'red'		

3.6 Indo-Aryan languages

Since the adaptive markers occur on IA loans in Kinnauri and Kanashi, we will now examine nouns/adjectives in IA languages of this region as well as forms attested in Sanskrit with relevance to the adaptive markers to examine if any of these languages could be the source of the adaptive markers in Kanashi and Kinnauri.[11] Again, the selection of languages is constrained by the data available to us; see Figure 3 for IA languages examined here. See the map in Figure 4 for their geographical distribution.

IA					
	NorthernIA zone	Central Pahari			Kumaoni
		Eastern Pahari			Nepali
		Himachali			Jaunsari Mandeali
			Nuclear		Kinnauri Pahari Kullu Pahari Sirmauri
				Mahasu Pahari	Kotgarhi Kiunthali
				Kangric- Chamealic- Bhattiyali	Bhadrawahi Chambeali Gaddi Kangri
		[and others (Bailey 1908; 1915)]			
	Northwestern zone	Sindhi-Lahnda			Lahnda Eastern Panjabi Rambani
		Kohistani			Torwali
		Kashmiri			Poguli
	Bihari	Maithili-Magahi	Maithilic	Maithili	Bajjika Standard Maithili
	Unclassified IA	Chinali-Lahul Lohar			Chinali

Figure 3: Indo-Aryan languages included in this study (classification according to Glottolog; Hammarström et al. 2021)

Kinnauri Pahari (Saxena 2022):

Kinnauri Pahari is very similar to Kinnauri in this regard: We find the same adaptive markers as in Kinnauri, and we find them on the same items (see Table 23). Until recent times, Kinnauri has been the language of wider communication in Lower and Middle Kinnaur, as well as the sociolinguistically dominant language in interactions between speakers of Kinnauri and speakers of Kinnauri Pahari, with the latter being bilingual as a matter of course, but not the former. Thus, it is very likely that these items are loans from Kinnauri rather than original inherited words, despite their clear IA etymology.

11 For ease of exposition, we will continue to refer to these elements as "adaptive markers" even outside ST, although they may not function as such in other language families (in particular IA).

Table 23: Adaptive markers in Kinnauri Pahari

Kinnauri Pahari	Kinnauri	Gloss	Kinnauri Pahari	Kinnauri	Gloss
multʰaŋ	*məltʰaŋ*	'roof'	*si:maŋ*	*simaŋ*	'boundary'
kuaŋ	*kuaŋ*	'well (N)'	*ʥolaŋ*	*ʥolaŋ*	'twin'
ʧʰodaŋ	*ʧʰodaŋ*	'waterfall'	*masaŋ*	—	'meat'
lɛmkaŋ	*ləpəŋ*	'flame'	*ʃiʈaŋ*	*ʃəʈaŋ*	'snot'
mɛsaŋ	*meʃiŋ*	'match(stick)'	*patraŋ*	*patʰraŋ*	'leaf'
dusraŋ	*dusraŋ*	'chimney'	*ʋa:maŋ*	*ʋamaŋ*	'wrong, fault'
joʤaŋ	*joʤaŋ*	'tool'	*tsuʈkaŋ*	*tsuʈkaŋ*	'quiet'
kʰoʤaŋ	*kʰoʤaŋ*	'left'	*ʃiŋga:raŋ*	—	'proud'
pa:les	*pa:les*	'herdsman'	*ʧikas*	*ʦisaŋ*	'flour'

Kullu Pahari (Anju Saxena's fieldwork notes; Diack 1896; Hendriksen 1976; 1986):

As noted in Table 11, Kullu Pahari does not have any instance of the adaptive markers. Kullu Pahari is the IA language of the villages surrounding Malana (where Kanashi is spoken), and the language in which historically Kanashi speakers have interacted with the outside world. Hence, we provide some examples to illustrate this difference between the Kullu Pahari and Kanashi vocabularies (Table 24).

Table 24: Absence of adaptive markers in Kullu Pahari

Kullu Pahari	Kanashi	Kinnauri	Gloss
haʈke	*haɖɖaŋ*	*haraŋ*	'bone'
os	*oʃaŋ*	*oʃaŋ*	'dew'
baṇ, bŏṇ	*baɳaŋ*	*boniŋ, baunaṅ*	'forest'
dhār	*da:raŋ, da:ɽaŋ*	*da:raŋ*	'mountain edge, mountain top'
śākhrā	*ʃakras*	*ʃakras*	'kid (M)'
kʰuɽ	*kʰuɽaŋ*	*kʰuraŋ*	'cattleshed'
na:li	*na:liŋ*	*na:liŋ*	'chimney'
njara	*jaras*	*ãjares*	'darkness'
moʈa	*moʈas*	*moʈʰes*	'fat'
ʃora	*ʃoras, ʃores*	*ʃores*	'father-in-law'

Other Indo-Aryan languages of the region

In two volumes, Bailey (1908; 1915) presents grammar sketches and wordlists of a number of IA varieties spoken in the northwestern Himalayan region (e.g. Himachal Pradesh). These varieties are classified by Bailey (1908; 1915) as belonging to the Himachali (Glottolog; also called Western Pahari) and Northwestern-zone (Glottolog; including Dardic and Sindhi-Lahnda) subbranches of IA. None of the IA languages described in Bailey (1915) show any trace of nouns with the adaptive markers.

In Bailey (1908) and Grierson (1928), the picture is a bit more complex. In Table 25 we list some possible instances of adaptive markers (from Bailey 1908).

Table 25: Possible parallels to the adaptive markers in IA languages of the northwest

Language	Word	Gloss	Etymology
Bhagati	*juāṇas (< jaṇā)*	'woman' (< 'man')	T5098 jána m. 'race, person'
Inner Siraji	*kutt-an*	'dog'	T3275 *kutta 'dog'
Gaddi	*bā́ṅ, bā́ṅ*	'covered well'	T11529 vāpī f. 'pond, tank', WPah. ktg bā (obl..i), bai f. 'tank, stonebuilt reservoir fed by spring'
	chū́ṛā́ṅ	'parched rice'	
	dhī́ū́ṅ	'a kind of tree'	
	ghuṅganī́ā́ṅ	'parched wheat'	
	hiū́ṅ	'snow'	T14096 himá 'cold, frost, snow', WPah bhal. heũ, N. hyũ 'snow, ice'
	kī́ū́ṅ	'common bean'	
	kunnū́ṅ	'stack of rice'	
	mā́hnū́ṅ	'man'	T9827 mánusa m. 'man', cur. mēhṇũ
	manchā́ṅ	'flying fox'	
	bhittā́ŋ	'(shut the) door'	T9493 bhitta n. '*split timber', 'fragment'
Rambani	*babbaṇ*	'father'	T9209 *bāba 'father'
Torwali	*pashiin*	'bird'	T7636 pakṣin 'winged' m., bird'
Poguli	*pachhaṇ*	'bird'	T7627 pakṣá 'wing, feather, fin'

4 Summary thus far: distribution of the adaptive markers

As we have seen in this chapter, the *-(V)ŋ* element attached to IA loans in Kanashi and Kinnauri is attested to various degrees in some other languages in this region. Generalizing somewhat, we can classify these languages into three subsets (see the map in Figure 4):

1. languages with many clear instances[12] of *-(V)ŋ*: Kanashi, Kinnauri, the various Raji-Raute varieties (with increasing incidence of *-(V)ŋ* as we move east) and Kusunda (marked by enclosing circles in the map in Figure 4);
2. languages with a handful (around five) of clear instances of *-(V)ŋ*: Darma, Rongpo, Byangsi, Kinnauri Pahari, Gaddi (marked by enclosing squares in Figure 4);
3. languages with none or an occasional clear instance of *-(V)ŋ*: the remainder (no special marking in Figure 4).

The other adaptive marker (*-(V)s*) is far less frequent than *-(V)ŋ* even in Kanashi and Kinnauri. There are a few isolated instances in some ST languages of this region. The Dravidian language Kurukh has an *-s* element characteristic of masculine nouns, which is also added to IA loans. A closer look at Dolakha Newar, Shumcho and Jad is needed.

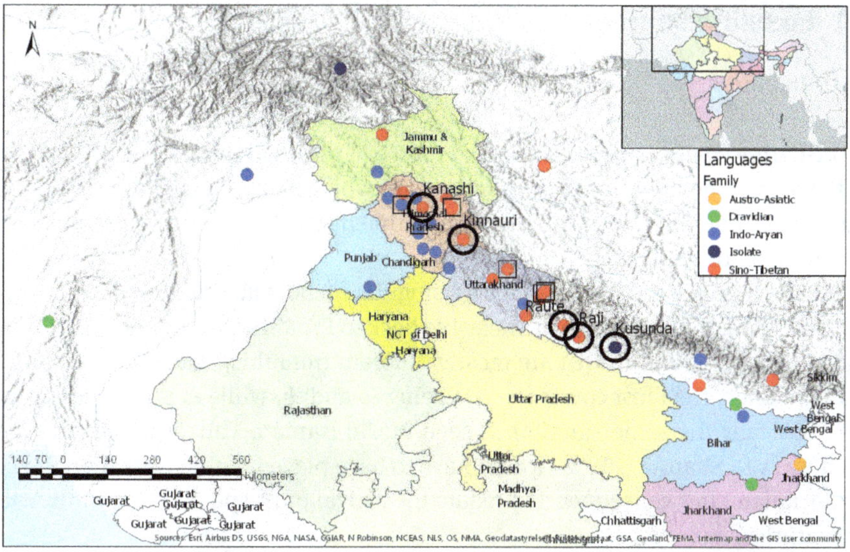

Map design by Anna Sjöberg

Figure 4: Locations of all languages examined in this study with indication of presence of adaptive markers

12 By "clear instances" we mean instances where an IA etymology is likely.

5 Possible origins of the adaptive markers: *-(V)s* and *-(V)ŋ*

We will now explore what could be the source of the adaptive markers *-(V)ŋ* and *-(V)s*.

The two markers, when they appear in ST languages, are similar in that they only attach to (IA) loanwords, and are not as far as we can ascertain found in inherited ST vocabulary items. However, and as noted already above, they are likely to have different histories. Hence, they are treated separately in the following sections.

Wichmann & Wohlgemuth (2008: 97) note that whenever the etymology is known of a loan verb accommodating affix, it turns out to have been borrowed from another language as part of a loan verb. It is not inconceivable that the same could hold for the adaptive markers in the nominal domain discussed here.

5.1 Possible sources of *-(V)s*

5.1.1 In Indo-Aryan

D. D. Sharma (1989a) proposes that the source of the adaptive marker *-(V)s* could be the masculine nominative singular marker which occurred in Old Indo-Aryan, but he does not provide any supporting arguments. This proposal is problematic for a number of reasons.[13]

While it is true that the nominative singular of most masculine nouns in OIA had an ending that ultimately is traceable back to Proto-Indo-European *-s*, the actual exponents found in OIA are mostly different from this, due to the effects of sound change, the most common ones being *-o* and *-ḥ*, while *-s* is comparatively rare. Basically the same situation is seen in Old Iranian. Thus, the scenario implied by D. D. Sharma (1989a) would have to have played out no later than Proto-Indo-Iranian, and consequently predate the arrival of IA speakers in South Asia by centuries.

Further, even the few remaining instances of OIA *-s* had changed into *-e* and *-o* already in the earliest attested MIA (3rd century BCE), while the IA loanwords in Kanashi and Kinnauri exhibit clear New Indo-Aryan phonetics, which makes such a scenario even more unlikely.

13 We would like to thank Rainer Kimmig (University of Tübingen) for his detailed comments on D. D. Sharma's proposal.

Another, more plausible suggestion for an IA source of the adaptive marker *-s* could be that it is related to the dative marker *-as/-is* found in some IA languages. In Bailey (1908) there are several IA languages which have *-as* as the dative marker. In Kishtawaarii and in Poguli the singular dative marker is *-is* (Bailey 1908). Further, as in Kanashi (see Chapter 3) and to some extent in Kinnauri, Poguli too seems to exhibit free variation between *-as*, *-us* and *-is*. In the various Romani languages, which show some affinities with Northwestern IA, masculine nouns have an oblique singular form in *-es*/*-as*, i.e. the form which is used by itself to indicate animate direct objects and some other syntactic roles, and which is also the basis for secondary case inflection (Matras 2002).

5.1.2 In Dravidian

Another plausible source of the adaptive marker *-(V)s* could be the Kurukh masculine singular nominative marker *-(a)s*, which occurs with both indigenous and IA nouns. In Malto its corresponding form (for [M.SG.NOM]) is *-h*. Both the form and its function are reminiscent of the function of *-(V)s* in Kinnauri. However, Kurukh and Malto (which belong to the same subgroup) do not seem to show any sign of the noun adaptation marker *-aŋ*, despite there being a lot of IA nouns in Kurukh.

When contemplating a likely historical scenario and a possible direction of borrowing, the following two facts are relevant.

First, *-as* [M.SG.NOM] is attested in both the Nepal variety and in the Jharkand variety of Kurukh. This suggests that *-as* in the Kurukh variety of Nepal is not the result of borrowing after it split either from the common-Malto-Kurukh language or from the Kurukh of central India.

Second, according to van Driem (2001: 1028), "[t]he Kurukh language communities in Nepal are splinter groups which migrated relatively recently to Nepal and settled near the Kośi river".

Together, these two facts make Kurukh fairly improbable as the source of the adaptive marker *-(V)s* in ST.

5.1.3 In Sino-Tibetan

We find no plausible family-internal source of the adaptive marker *-(V)s* (which of course does not rule out this alternative). A number of ST languages spoken in the area have an ergative (/agentive) suffix *-(V)s*,[14] including Kanashi (see Chapter 3), as well as Kinnauri and Navakat (Saxena 2022). On the one hand, an origin as a repurposed ergative marker would fit with the observed preference of *-(V)s* to attach to animate nouns, but on the other hand, the ergative suffix attaches freely after the adaptive marker *-(V)s* in Kanashi and Kinnauri, and does not replace it. All in all, this hypothesis does not seem likely.

5.2 Possible sources of *-(V)ŋ*

5.2.1 In Indo-Aryan

Similarly to the suggestion cited above about an source of the adaptive marker *-(V)s*, both Thomas (2011: 140) and D. D. Sharma (1984) suggest that the *-(V)ŋ* element found in IA loans in Kanashi and Kinnauri has its origin in OIA *-ṁ*, a nominative singular ending of thematic neutral nouns (*-aṁ*), and also an accusative ending common to several different declensions.[15] The neuter ending appearing in some IA loanwords would have been reanalyzed as a suffix signalling non-animacy, a development which has parallels in Dravidian loans from OIA:

> [...] numerous loanwords in Dravidian languages with the Neuter ending *-am*, *-amu* referring to inanimates, which are not Neuter in proper Sanskrit: e.g., Telugu *ankam* 'number', *tapamu* 'heat, hot season', *deśamu* 'country' = Skt *ankaḥ*, *tapaḥ*, *dēśaḥ*. (Masica 1991: 220f)

But while the shape of the Telugu words cited in the quote clearly reflects their OIA origin (e.g. *tapaḥ*, which corresponds to MIA *tāva* and NIA *tāu*, *tā*, etc.), again the nouns and adjectives in Kanashi and Kinnauri which take the adaptive marker *-(V)ŋ* exhibit NIA phonetics. This excludes also the possibility that *-aŋ* goes back directly to OIA (or MIA) *-aṃ*, which in NIA had already lost nasalization and turned to *-u* (except for languages like Gujarati and Marathi – spoken far away from the Himalayas – which preserved the old neuter gender and nasalization).

In Bailey (1908), some nouns are provided with citation forms that end in *-aŋ* in the word list. Gaddi and some other IA languages of the northwestern region in Bailey (1908) have *-aŋ* as the oblique inflectional marker on nouns (e.g. *bhittáŋ* '(shut the) door'). See Table 25. Since the oblique is an object case and since prototypical objects are inanimate, this would fit with the adaptive marker *-(V)ŋ* originally being used on inanimate loan nouns.

14 Which in some of the languages also expresses the instrumental.

15 Again we are grateful to Rainer Kimmig for his comments on D. D. Sharma's proposal.

5.2.2 In Munda

D. D. Sharma (2003) notes that both Kinnauri and some Munda languages use a similar suffix to "naturalize" borrowed stems. In Mundari it is *-ŋ* and *-m*; in Sora it is *-n*. Notably, Kinnauri has *-ŋ* and *-s*, where the former occurs with inanimate nouns and the latter with animate nouns, but in Munda languages a distinction between animate and inanimate with regard to noun adaptation is not made. This is surprising, since Munda languages generally make this distinction. D. D. Sharma (2003) speculates that could this be a sign that Munda languages have borrowed this from Kinnauri rather recently. According to him the adaptation marker occurs only in Kinnauri.

He provides some examples of putative parallels to the adaptive markers found in the Munda languages Mundari and Sora (see Table 26). According to him, there are parallel formations in Mundari both in *-(V)ŋ* and in *-m*. However, the formations in *-m* have corresponding items in Dravidian (illustrated by Telugu in Table 26), and are most likely Dravidian loans,

Table 26: Putative parallels to adaptive markers in Mundari and Sora

Mundari	**Gloss**	**Mundari**	**Gloss**	**Telugu**
gotoŋ	'clarified butter (ghee)'	*bhārom*	'load'	*bhāramu*
ḍhilaŋ	'loose'	*desum*	'countryside'	*dēṣamu*
diriŋ	'horn'	*jālom*	'fishing net'	*jālamu*
dumaŋ	'drum'	*ka?som*	'cotton'	—
duraŋ	'song'	*kaṛkom*	'crab'	*karkaṭamu*
halaŋ	'brain'	*sutam*	'thread'	*sūtramu*
Sora	**Gloss**			
man(d)rā-n	'a person'			
pe-sij-an	'a child'			
on-lid-an	'a bird'			
sorōn	'a grain'			

He also points out that there is a borrowed IA noun which takes the same adaptive marker in both Kanashi/Kinnauri and Mundari, with the same meaning at least in Mundari and Kinnauri: Mundari *samundrang* 'river', Kanashi *samudra, samudraŋ* 'sea; ocean', Kinnauri *somodraŋ* 'sea, ocean, river'.

According to Ramamurti (1931: 16), as reported in D. D. Sharma (2003: 25), Sora nouns in the nominative case have the ending *-(ə)n*, while to Anderson & Harrison (2008: 307–309) this is not a case marker, but a "multipurpose noun suffix".

It behaves somewhat similarly to the adaptive marker *-(V)ŋ* in Kanashi and Kinnauri in that it may be replaced by some other suffixes. However, a similar suffix has not been noted for Mundari (Osada 2008; Kobayashi & Murmu 2008), which would have made more geographical sense: There are some Mundari speakers in eastern Nepal, according to Anderson (2008: 2, Map 1.1),[16] while Sora is spoken much further away from the region of interest here.

5.2.3 In Sino-Tibetan

In the Raji dictionary by Dhakal (2019), most verb entries end in *-ŋ*, which is obviously a suffix, seen if we compare these entries with verb entries in other Raji or Raute word lists, where verbs are listed in their stem form. If we make the reasonable assumption that this suffix is intended to express the infinitive, it is most likely some kind of nominalizer. In Khatri (2012), the Raji verbal suffix *-tinʌŋ* is glossed as NFNT (non-finite) and NMLZ (nominalizer). Fortier (2019: 47) identifies the Raute and Rawat suffix *-aŋ(a)* as a nominalizer glossed as 'that which is' and suggested deriving it from PTB **kaŋ* 'which, like, deictic' (Matisoff 2003: 488). Recall that among the languages that we have investigated, Raji and Raute have the largest number of IA loanwords with the adaptive marker *-(V)ŋ* apart from Kanashi and Kinnauri.

The Raute-Rawat suffix cited by Fortier appears in both indigenous and borrowed vocabulary: "*nå khåm**aŋa** gunåka*, listen to [that which is] my speech. RW: *phul**aŋ***, flower ("that which blooms")" (Fortier 2019: 47), where "**khåma** RT n., adj. language, speech, talk; Raute language" is of ST origin (Fortier 2019: 123), while "**phul, phulaŋ** RW, DR n. flower" is a Nepali loanword (Fortier 2019: 152).

This may indicate that the adaptive marker *-(V)ŋ* in fact is of ST origin – even in other ST languages where it only occurs on borrowed items – but more research is needed.

16 According to Ethnologue (Eberhard et al. 2021), the number of Mundari speakers in Nepal is about 8,000 (2006). The 2011 Census of Nepal does not list Mundari in the mother tongue statistics. Interestingly, the 2011 Census of India shows 684 speakers of Mundari and 403 speakers of "Munda" in Himachal Pradesh. However, these have presumably come from other parts of India to work on the many large construction projects going on in the state.

6 Conclusion

To conclude, the shared innovation studied in this chapter – the distribution of adaptive markers on borrowed IA nouns and adjectives in languages of the western Himalayas – has hopefully given us better grounds for an investigation of the prehistory of Kanashi and Kinnauri, as well as of the genealogical relationships among the ST languages of this part of the Himalayas. This will be the topic of Chapter 8, but before that we now turn to a similar description of adaptation mechanisms for borrowed verbs, in the next chapter.

References

Acharya, Jayaraj. 1990. *A descriptive grammar of Nepali and an analyzed corpus*. Washington: Georgetown University. (PhD thesis).

Anderson, Gregory D. S. 2008. Introduction to the Munda languages. In Gregory D. S. Anderson (ed.), *The Munda languages*, 1–10. London: Routledge.

Anderson, Gregory D. S. & K. David Harrison. 2008. Sora. In Gregory D. S. Anderson (ed.), *The Munda languages*, 299–380. London: Routledge.

Andronov, Mikhail Sergeevich. 1980. *The Brahui language*. Moscow: Nauka.

Apte, Mahadeo L. & D. P. Pattanayak. 1967. *An outline of Kumauni grammar*. Durham: Duke University.

Bailey, Thomas Grahame. 1908. *The languages of the Northern Himalayas, being studied in the grammar of twenty-six Himalayan dialects*. Asiatic Society monographs, Vol XII. London: The Royal Asiatic Society.

Bailey, Thomas Grahame. 1915. *Linguistic studies from the Himalayas: Studies in the grammar of fifteen Himalayan dialects*. Asiatic Society monographs, Vol XVIII. London: The Royal Asiatic Society.

Beames, John. 1870. On the Magar language of Nepal. *The Journal of the Royal Asiatic Society of Great Britain and Ireland* 4(1): 178–228.

Bhattari, Govinda Raj. 2011. *A trilingual dictionary of the Magar language (Athāra Magarāt)*. Rukum: Jitman Pun Magar.

Bista, Dor Bahadur. 1978. Encounter with the Raute: The last hunting nomads of Nepal. *Kailash* 4(4): 317–327.

Chandola, Anoop Chandra. 1966. *A syntactic sketch of Garhwali*. Chicago: The University of Chicago. (PhD thesis).

Cunningham, Alexander. 1854. *Ladák, physical, statistical, and historical; with notices of the surrounding countries*. London: Wm. H. Allen & Co.

Dhakal, Dubi Nanda. 2019. *A Raji-English lexicon*. Munich: LINCOM.

Diack, Alexander Henderson. 1896. *The Kulu dialect of Hindi: some notes on its grammatical structure, with specimens of the songs and sayings current amongst the people, and a glossary*. Lahore: The Civil & Military Gazette.

Eberhard, David M., Gary F. Simons & Charles D. Fennig (eds.). 2021. *Ethnologue: Languages of the world*. 24th edn. Dallas: SIL International.
Fortier, Jana. 2019. *A comparative dictionary of Raute and Rawat: Tibeto-Burman languages of the central Himalayas*. Boston: Harvard University Press.
Francke, August Hermann. 1917. Vokabular der Manchadsprache [Vocabulary of the Manchati language]. *Zeitschrift der deutchen morgenlandischen Gesellschaft* 71: 137–161.
Genetti, Carol. 2007. *A grammar of Dolakha Newar*. Berlin: Walter de Gruyter.
Gerard, Alexander. 1842. A vocabulary of the Kunawar languages. *Journal of the Asiatic Society of Bengal* 11: 485–551.
Gordon, Kent H. 1973. Clause patterns in Dhangar-Kurux. In Ronald L. Trail (ed.), *Patterns in clause, sentence and discourse in selected languages of India and Nepal. Part II: Clause*, 37–122. Kathmandu: Tribhuvan University.
Grierson, George A. 1928. *Linguistic survey of India, Vol 9, Part IV: Indo-Aryan languages, Central group: Specimens of Pahari languages and Gujuri*. Calcutta: Government of India, Central Publication Branch.
Hahn, Ferdinand. 1911. *Kurukh grammar*. Calcutta: Bengal Secretariat Press.
Hammarström, Harald, Robert Forkel, Martin Haspelmath & Sebastian Bank. 2021. *Glottolog 4.4*. Jena: Max Planck Institute for the Science of Human History. Available online at https://glottolog.org. DOI: 10.5281/zenodo.4761960.
Hargreaves, David. 2017. Kathmandu Newar (Nepāl Bhāśā). In Graham Thurgood & Randy J. LaPolla (eds.), *The Sino-Tibetan languages*, 2nd edn., 453–467. London: Routledge.
Hendriksen, Hans. 1976. *Himachali studies I: Vocabulary*. Copenhagen: Munksgaard.
Hendriksen, Hans. 1986. *Himachali studies III: Grammar*. Copenhagen: Munksgaard.
Huber, Christian. 2014. Subject and object agreement in Shumcho. In Nathan Hill & Thomas Owen-Smith (eds.), *Trans-Himalayan linguistics*, 221–274. Berlin: Mouton de Gruyter.
Kanasakar, Tej R., Yogendra P. Yadava, Krishna Prasad Chalise, Balaram Prasain, Dubi Nanda Dhakal & Krishna Paudel. 2011. *A grammar of Baram*. Kathmandu: Tribhuvan University.
Khadka, Bir Bahadur. 2006. *A sketch grammar of Boto boli*. Kathmandu: Tribhuvan University. (PhD thesis).
Khatri, Ramesh. 2012. Negativization in Raji. *Nepalese Linguistics* 27: 82–84.
Klimov, Georgij Andreevič & Džoj Iosifovna Èdel'man. 1970. *Jazyk burušaski* [The Burushaski language]. Moscow: Nauka.
Kobayashi, Masato & Ganesh Murmu. 2008. Keraʔ Mundari. In Gregory D. S. Anderson (ed.), *The Munda languages*, 165–194. London: Routledge.
Konow, Sten. 1909. *Linguistic survey of India, Vol 3: Tibeto-Burman family. Part I: General introduction, specimens of the Tibetan dialects, the Himalayan dialects, and the North Assam group*. (This and several other volumes of the LSI were edited by Sten Konow, although published as the work of George A. Grierson). Calcutta: Government of India, Central Publication Branch.
Krishan, Shree. 2001a. A sketch of Chaudangsi grammar / Chaudangsi-English, English-Chaudangsi glossary. In Yasuhiko Nagano & Randy J. LaPolla (eds.), *Bon studies 3: New research on Zhangzhung and related Himalayan languages* (Senri Ethnological Reports 19), 401–448. Osaka: National Museum of Ethnology.
Krishan, Shree. 2001b. A sketch of Darma grammar / Darma-English, English-Darma glossary. In Yasuhiko Nagano & Randy J. LaPolla (eds.), *Bon studies 3: New research on Zhangzhung and related Himalayan languages* (Senri Ethnological Reports 19), 347–400. Osaka: National Museum of Ethnology.

Krishan, Shree. 2001c. A sketch of Raji grammar / Raji-English, English-Raji glossary. In Yasuhiko Nagano & Randy J. LaPolla (eds.), *Bon studies 3: New research on Zhangzhung and related Himalayan languages* (Senri Ethnological Reports 19), 449–497. Osaka: National Museum of Ethnology.

Macphail, R. M. 1983. *An introduction to Santali*. Calcutta: KLM.

Masica, Colin P. 1991. *The Indo-Aryan languages*. Cambridge: Cambridge University Press.

Matisoff, James A. 2003. *Handbook of Proto-Tibeto-Burman: System and philosophy of Sino-Tibetan reconstruction*. Berkeley: University of California Press.

Matras, Yaron. 2002. *Romani: A linguistic introduction*. Cambridge: Cambridge University Press.

Matthews, John. 2008. *Jaunsari: A sociolinguistic survey* (SIL Electronic Survey Reports 2008-013). Dallas: SIL International.

Munshi, Sadaf. 2006. *Jammu and Kashmir Burushaski: Language, language contact, and change*. Austin: University of Texas. (PhD thesis).

Osada, Toshiki. 2008. Mundari. In Gregory D. S. Anderson (ed.), *The Munda languages*, 99–164. London: Routledge.

Ramamurti, G. V. 1931. *A manual of the So:ra: (or Savara) language*. Madras: Government Press.

Rastogi, Kavita. 2012. *A descriptive grammar of Raji*. Delhi: Aviram Prakashan.

Roy, Ram Rekha. 2010. *Verbal morphology in Bajjika*. Kathmandu: Tribhuvan University Masters thesis.

Saxena, Anju. 2022. *The linguistic landscape of the Indian Himalayas: Languages in Kinnaur*. Forthcoming 2022. Leiden: Brill.

Saxena, Anju & Lars Borin. 2013. Carving Tibeto-Kanauri by its joints: Using basic vocabulary lists for genetic grouping of languages. In Lars Borin & Anju Saxena (eds.), *Approaches to measuring linguistic differences*, 175–198. Berlin: De Gruyter Mouton.

Schackow, Diana. 2015. *A grammar of Yakka*. Berlin: Language Science Press.

Sharma, Bansi Ram. 1976. *Kinnar lok sahitya*. Bilaspur: Lalit prakashan.

Sharma, Devi Datta. 1984. Old Indo-Aryan element in Kinnauri. *International Journal of Dravidian Linguistics* 13(2): 354–359.

Sharma, Devi Datta. 1987. *The formation of Kumauni language. Part II: Morphology and syntax*. New Delhi: Bahri.

Sharma, Devi Datta. 1989a. *A descriptive grammar of Kinnauri*. Delhi: Mittal Publications.

Sharma, Devi Datta. 1989b. *Tibeto-Himalayan languages of Uttarakhand. Part one*. Delhi: Mittal Publications.

Sharma, Devi Datta. 1990. *Tibeto-Himalayan languages of Uttarakhand. Part two*. Delhi: Mittal Publications.

Sharma, Devi Datta. 1992. *Tribal languages of Himachal Pradesh. Part two*. Delhi: Mittal Publications.

Sharma, Devi Datta. 2003. *Munda sub-stratum of Tibeto-Himalayan languages*. Delhi: Mittal Publications.

Sharma, Suhnu Ram. 1987. Non-Tibeto-Burman features in PaTani. *Linguistics of the Tibeto-Burman Area* 10: 126–129.

Sharma, Suhnu Ram. 1991. *Questionnaire (Manchati)*. Unpublished.

Sharma, Suhnu Ram. 2001a. A sketch of Byangsi grammar / Byangsi-English, English-Byangsi glossary. In Yasuhiko Nagano & Randy J. LaPolla (eds.), *Bon studies 3: New research on Zhangzhung and related Himalayan languages* (Senri Ethnological Reports 19), 271–341. Osaka: National Museum of Ethnology.

Sharma, Suhnu Ram. 2001b. A sketch of Rongpo grammar / Rongpo-English, English-Rongpo glossary. In Yasuhiko Nagano & Randy J. LaPolla (eds.), *Bon studies 3: New research on Zhangzhung and related Himalayan languages* (Senri Ethnological Reports 19), 195–270. Osaka: National Museum of Ethnology.

Sharma, Suhnu Ram. 2001c. A study on the Tibeto-Burman languages of Uttar Pradesh. In Yasuhiko Nagano & Randy J. LaPolla (eds.), *Bon studies 3: New research on Zhangzhung and related Himalayan languages* (Senri Ethnological Reports 19), 187–194. Osaka: National Museum of Ethnology.

Southworth, Franklin C. 2005. *Linguistic archaeology of South Asia*. London: Routledge.

Thomas, Frederick W. 2011. Research notes on the Zhangzhung language by Frederick W. Thomas at the British Library. In Tsuguhito Takeuchi, Burkhard Kessel & Yasuhiko Nagano (eds.), *Senri ethnological reports 99*, 1–246. Osaka: National Museum of Ethnology.

Trail, Roland L. 1973. *Patterns in clause, sentence and discourse in selected languages of India and Nepal, Part IV. Word lists*. Norman: Summer Institute of Linguistics, Oklahoma University.

Turin, Mark. 2006. *A grammar of the Thangmi language with an ethnolinguistic introduction to the speakers and their culture*. Leiden: Leiden University. (PhD thesis).

Turner, Ralph L. 1966. *A comparative dictionary of the Indo-Aryan languages*. Available online: http://dsal.uchicago.edu/dictionaries/soas/. Oxford: Oxford University Press.

van Driem, George. 2001. *Languages of the Himalayas: An ethnolinguistic handbook of the Greater Himalayan region containing an introduction to the symbiotic theory of language, Vol 2*. Leiden: Brill.

Watters, David. 2006. Notes on Kusunda grammar: A language isolate of Nepal. *Himalayan Linguistics Archive* 3: 1–182.

Wichmann, Søren & Jan Wohlgemuth. 2008. Loan verbs in a typological perspective. In Thomas Stolz, Dik Bakker & Rosa Salas Palomo (eds.), *Aspects of language contact: New theoretical, methodological and empirical findings with special focus on Romancisation processes*, 89–121. Berlin: Mouton de Gruyter.

Widmer, Manuel. 2017. *A grammar of Bunan*. Berlin: De Gruyter Mouton.

Willis Oko, Christina. 2019. *A grammar of Darma*. Leiden: Brill.

Witzel, Michael. 1999. Substrate languages in Old Indo-Aryan. *Electronic Journal of Vedic Studies* 5: 1–67.

Yadava, Yogendra P. 2001. *A study of the Dhangar language. A preliminary report. Report submitted to the Endangered Language Fund*. Kathmandu: Tribhuvan University.

Zoller, Claus Peter. 1983. *Die Sprache von Rang Pas von Garhwal (Raṅ Pɔ Bhāsa): Grammatik, Texte, Wörterbuch*. Wiesbaden: Otto Harrassowitz.

A Similar corresponding nouns and adjectives with adaptive markers in Kanashi and Kinnauri

In this appendix we list nouns and adjectives in Kanashi and Kinnauri showing the adaptive markers *-(V)ŋ* and *-(V)s*. The main source of the data is our own fieldwork notes, but we have also used published descriptions of the two languages. In those cases when the gloss is different for Kanashi and Kinnauri, two glosses are shown in the "Gloss" column, separated by "/" (Kanashi gloss / Kinnauri gloss).

(POS: part of speech; A: adjective; N: noun; P: proper noun)

Kanashi (xns)	Kinnauri (kfk)	POS	Gloss
alesis	*lises*	A	lazy
aŋka:laŋ	*(an)ka:laŋ*	N	famine
aʃlaŋ	*a:ʃaraŋ*	P	a month name
adʒaŋ	*ãdʒaŋ*	N	intestines
badraŋ	*badraŋ*	P	a month name
bakras	*bəkʰaraŋ*	N	goat / she-goat
bandraŋ	*bandres*	N	monkey
baniŋ	*baniŋ, banes*	N	pot (utensil)
banɖa:raŋ	*banɖa:raŋ*	N	treasury, storage room
barʃaŋ	*boʃaŋ*	N	year
baɳaŋ	*boniŋ, bonaŋ*	N	forest
bijaŋ	*bajaŋ*	N	wedding
bijaɳ	*bijaŋ*	N	seed
bitiŋ	*bitiŋ*	N	wall
biʃaŋ	*biʃaŋ*	N	poison
boraŋ	*boraŋ*	N	sack, luggage
beʈiŋ	*bo:ʈʰaŋ*	N	tree
bumiŋ	*bubiŋ*	N	floor / storey
badraŋ	*badraŋ*	N	a month name
da:ɳaŋ	*ɖa:naŋ*	N	penalty
da:ɽaŋ, ɖa:raŋ	*da:raŋ*	N	cliff
deoraŋ	*deoraŋ, deoriŋ*	N	temple (Hindu)
deʃaŋ	*deʃaŋ*	N	village, country
dukʰis	*dukʰis*	A	sick, ill, sad
dumaŋ	*dumaŋ*	N	smoke, fog
dupaŋ	*dupaŋ*	N	incense
uʋaŋ	*eniŋ, aínaŋ*	N	udder
galaŋ	*galaŋ,*	N	talk
gallas	*golɖes*	N	eagle, vulture
ganʈʰaŋ	*ganʈʰaŋ*	N	bell
garkas	*garkas*	A	heavy
gaʈas	*gaʈes*	A	narrow
gaʈaŋ	*goʈaŋ*	N	watermill
ga:ɽiŋ	*ga:raŋ*	N	river
gitaŋ	*gitʰaŋ*	N	song
golaŋ	*golaŋ*	N	neck, throat
gaʈaŋ	*goʈaŋ*	N	water mill
gra:maŋ	*gra:maŋ*	N	village
halgaɖiŋ	*halgaŋ*	N	potato

Kanashi (xns)	Kinnauri (kfk)	POS	Gloss
talaŋ	*(həs)talaŋ*	N	palm of the hand
haɖɖaŋ	*haraŋ*	N	bone
heɽaŋ	*eraŋ*	N	hunting
indramaŋ	*indromaŋ*	P	a month name
nihares, jaras	*ãjares*	A	darkness
kaməŋ	*kamaŋ*	N	work
kaniʃʈʰas	*kanisʈʰas*	N	member of a social subclass
kaʧas	*kaʧas, kaʧes*	A	raw, unripe, uncooked
ka:saŋ	*ka:saŋ*	N	bronze
ka:ɳas	*ka:nes, ka:naŋ*	A	one-eyed, blind (person)
kesaraŋ	*ke:sraŋ*	N	yolk (egg)
kolaŋ	*kolaŋ*	N	memory
ku:ɽiŋ	*kuaŋ*	N	(water) well
kukaɽaŋ	*kukkras*	N	cock, rooster
kʰakaŋ	*kʰakaŋ*	N	mouth
kʰiraŋ	*kʰiraŋ*	N	milk
kʰolaŋ	*kʰolaŋ*	N	husk
kʰulas	*kʰulas*	A	wide
kʰuɖaŋ	*kʰuraŋ*	N	cellar, cattleshed, stable
laʈʰas	*laʈas*	A	dumb
la:laŋ	*la:laŋ*	N	drool
la:mas	*la:mes*	A	tall, long
lokas	*lokas*	N	(non-Kanashi) people / people
maɽʃaŋ	*morʧʰaŋ*	N	man
maʤaŋ	*maʤaŋ*	N	middle
matsis	*maʧʰes*	N	fish
mokʃiraŋ	*mokʃeraŋ*	N	a month name
mulaŋ	*molaŋ*	N	cow dung
monoŋ	*monaŋ*	N	temple / desire, heart
moʈas	*moʈʰes*	A	thick, fat (animate entities)
na:ges	*na:ges*	N	cobra / mythical, invisible snake
na:laŋ	*na:laŋ*	N	stream, brook
na:liŋ	*na:liŋ*	N	chimney, weaving shuttle
na:maŋ	*na:maŋ*	N	name
oʃaŋ	*oʃaŋ*	N	dew
pakres	*pakres*	N	people
pakʰiŋ	*pakʰaŋ*	N	wing, feather
pardeʃaŋ	*pardeʃaŋ*	N	foreign country
paʧaŋ	*patʰraŋ*	N	leaf
pa:laŋ	*pa:les*	N	herdsman
pitaŋ	*pitaŋ*	N	gate, door
piʃʈiŋ	*piʃʈiŋ*	N	back
piʈʰas	*piʈʰas*	N	flour
padras	*podres*	A	flat
poɳukes	*ponukes*	N	guest

Kanashi (xns)	Kinnauri (kfk)	POS	Gloss
poʃaŋ	*poʃaŋ*	P	a month name
poʈaŋ	*peʈiŋ, peʈaŋ*	N	stomach, belly
puʧʰaŋ	*putsuniŋ, paʧniŋ*	N	tail
pʰagɽaŋ	*pʰagnaŋ*	N	a month name
pʰolaŋ	*pʰolaŋ*	N	fruit
bijaŋ	*bajaŋ*	N	wedding
ra:tiŋ	*ra:tiŋ*	N	night
roʈʰas	*roʈʰas*	A	brave
samudraŋ	*somordaŋ*	N	sea, ocean, river
sargaŋ	*sorgaŋ*	N	sky
sastas	*sostas*	A	cheap, less expensive
saŋgis	*saŋgis*	N	friend
sa:mnas	*somaŋ*	A / N	flat, straight (e.g. path) / plain (land)
soraŋ	*soraŋ*	N	pond
suãraŋ	*sʊa:raŋ, suŋa:raŋ*	N	Monday
talaŋ	*talaŋ*	N	sole of foot
aʤaŋ	*ã:ʤaŋ*	N	intestines, guts
ɖaggis	*ɖagis*	N	male member of a specific social subgroup, blacksmith
ɖaliŋ	*ɖalaŋ*	N	plant
da:ɳaŋ	*ɖa:naŋ*	N	penalty, punishment
ɖibɽiŋ	*ɖibaliŋ*	N	pond; well (water) / swamp
ɖugas	*ɖuges*	A	deep
ʃakras	*ʃakras*	N	calf
ʃauɳaŋ	*ʃonaŋ*	P	a month name
ʃaɳaŋ	*ʈʰanaŋ*	N	ice
ʃokkuraŋ	*ʃokraŋ*	N	orphan
ʃauɳaŋ	*ʃonaŋ*	N	a month name
ʃores, ʃoras	*ʃores*	N	father-in-law
ʊeraŋ	*ʃupelaŋ*	N	evening
ʤeʃʈaŋ	*ʤeʃʈaŋ*	P	a month name
ʤeʃʈʰas	*ʤeʃʈʰas*	N	elder, senior
tsokʰas	*tsokʰes*	A	clean
ʧama:ras	*ʧama:res*	N	name of a social subgroup
ʧoras	*ʧoras, ʧores*	N	thief
ʧotraŋ	*tso:riŋ*	N	council platform / (ceremonial temple) platform

In some instances Kinnauri and Kanashi use two different IA nouns – but in both languages these items occur with an adaptive marker:

na:iŋ	*ga:raŋ*	N	river
re:tiŋ	*ba:liŋ, ba:laŋ*	N	sand
sa:laŋ, barʃaŋ	*boʃaŋ*	N	year

B Nouns and adjectives in Raji-Raute with (potential) adaptive markers

In this appendix we list nouns and adjectives in Raji (Section B.1) and Raute-Rawat (Section B.2) which potentially contain the adaptive marker *-(V)ŋ* (and its variations).

B.1 Adaptive markers in Raji

(A: adjective; N: noun)

abəŋ, ābaŋ	N	mango
aitsuŋ, aĩtʃuŋ, aitʃjaŋ	A	small
āitsuŋ	A	short
aḍaĩŋ	A	two and a half
bʰa:riŋ, purau	A	full
bʰokʰrəjaŋ	N	Adam's apple
bisəŋ	N	poison
bjaŋ, bijaŋ	N	seed, seedling
blaŋ	N	person from hills
breunaŋ	N	Tharu people
briŋ	N	name
bruŋ	N	honey
bəreŋ, ba:raŋ, barəŋ, bwaraŋ	A	big, strong
bərjaŋ	A	eldest (woman)
bəsejaŋ	A	stale
bəṭaŋ	N	rice
dudʰəŋ	N	milk
dumnjaŋ	A	rich, to be full
dʰjuŋ	N	day
dʰumaŋ	N	smoke
ʣatəŋ	N	caste
ʤuluŋ	N	cradle (of baby)
ʤəmpʰilaŋ	N	tide
galiŋ	N	abuse
garoŋ, garouŋ	N	girl
gʰiəŋ, gʰiŋ	N	clarified butter
gʰoṭenjaŋ	N	Badi ethnic group
gʰumaŋ	N	wheat
gʰuŋraŋ	N	curly (hair)
giroŋ	N	husband
goṭʰəŋ, toṭʰəŋ	N	ground floor
grenjaŋ	N	Magar (ethnic group)
griŋ	N	brother in law (elder sister's husband)
gudəŋ	N	belly
guləŋ, guraŋ	N	jaggery, molasses
guntʰaŋ	N	heel
gəlaŋ	N	echo
haḍəŋ	N	bone
hiṭənjaŋ	N	beggar
hokinjaŋ	N	snake
hələŋ, halaŋ	N	plough
həriəũ	A	green
kadʰaŋ	N	shoulders
kaṭʰaŋ	N	firewood
kʰokʰəŋ	N	a kind of fish
kʰolejaŋ	A	open, spacious
kʰopinjaŋ	A	overturned
kopriŋ	N	head
kwaŋ, kwoŋ	A	black
kəjã	N	body
kəlaṭjaŋ	N	seller
kərəŋ	N	rib
kətsuŋ	A	unripe
kətsəŋ	A	pure, untouched
kətsəŋ	N	money
mhalnjaŋ	A	warm
miʔtaŋ	N	wife
mohləŋ	N	pestle
moṭiŋ	N	pearl
mutuŋ	N	heart
məʣaŋ	A	healthy
məilejaŋ	A	dark
manəŋ, mənəŋ	N	forest
naniŋ	N	children
na:wəĩ, na:wə̃ĩ, noŋ	A	new
nihəŋ, mihaŋ	N	fingernail
nokna:ŋ	A	good
nəsjaŋ	N	nerve
pa:laŋ, plaŋ, p'laŋ, pəlaŋ	A	white, yellow
pa:tsʰjaũ, pətʃiaũ, putʃiũ	N	tail

p^{h}ulən	N	flower
p^{h}əiliŋ	N	plain land
pjaloŋ	N	cup
pokiaŋ	A	dry
preniŋ	N	big leaf plate
pənoŋ	N	bow
reunjaŋ	N	Tharu
rowhã	N	feather
rukaŋ, ruk^{h}ã	N	tree
rəpnjaŋ	N	ford
sioəŋ, sioaŋ	N	horn
sjaŋ	N	sickle
sujaŋ	A	rotten
sureikəŋ	N	sigh (in pain, tiredness)
sutsiŋ	N	needle
taliŋ	N	plate
tarniŋ	N	liquor
trẽijã	N	star
trijaŋ	N	money
ʧalok k^{h}ronnjaŋ	N	cobbler; ethnic Sarki
ʧanjaŋ	N	player
ʧarlaŋ	N	skin
ʧikainjaŋ	N	sneezing
ʧikinjaŋ glaŋ	N	to be suffered from a witch
ʧuiniŋ	A	red
ʦumnjaŋ	A	cold, wet
uhəŋ	N	dew
ɖarəŋ	N	stone
ʈot^{h}jaŋ	N	uvula
ʈuku reʈnjaŋ	N	Gaine people
ʈukəŋ	N	neck
ʈwaŋ	A	light
ʈənəŋ	N	forehead
xunəŋ	N	gold

B.2 Adaptive markers in Raute-Rawat

(A: adjective; N: noun; R: adverb)

abʌŋ	N	mango
baliŋ, b'liŋ, baləŋ	N	hill people, farmers
batliŋ	N	broom (v. sweep)
bisjaŋ	N	poison
daliŋ	N	leader ?
drimaŋ	A	first, eldest
dud^{h}ʌŋ	N	milk
d^{h}joŋkod^{h}joŋ	R	daily
galuŋ	N	center, hearth
gamaŋ	N	village
gamʌŋ	A	hot
gamʌŋ	N	sun
gaʈoŋ	N	girl
geŋ	N	ghee
gjuŋ	N	insect, worm
gliŋ	A	heavy
guduŋ, gudoŋ	N	stomach, belly
gumaŋ	N	children
gumʌŋ	N	wheat
gut^{h}aŋ	N	shed, stall, hut, pen
gəroŋ, giroŋ	N	husband
hadaŋ, haduŋ, harəŋ, hareŋ, haɖɖʌŋ, hařəm	N	bone
haddʌŋ	N	kingfisher
halʌŋ	N	plough
haraŋ	N	body
hmaŋ	N	face, mouth
ik^{h}uŋ	N	sugarcane
kabaŋ, kabɔŋ	N	post, pole
karijeŋ	N	niece
katuŋ, kaʈaŋ	N	wood, cutting
k^{h}araŋ	N	north
maŋ	N	song
mriŋ, miŋ	N	name
muk^{h}uŋ	N	face
mȟwɔm	N	tongue
mənəŋ, manəŋ, mənam, manən, manʌŋ, maŋ	N	forest
nihʌŋ, hnihaŋ, hnihəŋ, nihão	N	(finger)nail
nomaŋ	A	last, eldest
p^{h}jaŋ	N	granddaughter
p^{h}ul, p^{h}ulaŋ, p^{h}ulʌŋ	N	flower
rahoŋ	A	bright
sehaŋ	A	all
sigʌŋ, sikkəm, ʃiga:ŋ	N	horn
tunɪŋ	N	today
xroŋ	N	light, dawn
xrʊŋ	N	candle
ʃidaruŋ	N	net
ʔansaŋ	A	bad

Anju Saxena, Lars Borin, and Bernard Comrie

7 Clues to Kanashi prehistory 2: loanword adaptation in verbs

Abstract: In this chapter, we extend the investigation of common loanword adaptation patterns noted in Kanashi and Kinnauri to the verbal domain, where both languages use dedicated transitivity-signalling morphology exclusively on Indo-Aryan loan verbs. In the same way as with the nominal adaptive markers, we investigate the distribution of this adaptive mechanism in related and neighboring languages in the western Himalayas, and we also discuss possible sources for the verbal adaptive markers.

Keywords: Kanashi, Kinnauri, Sino-Tibetan, Indo-Aryan, language contact, comparative linguistics, verbal morphology

Chapter overview:

1 Introduction

Similarly to what we saw for the nominal domain in the previous chapter, Kanashi and Kinnauri also have a pair of adaptive markers used with borrowed Indo-Aryan (IA) verbs: the valency increasing marker *-ja:* and the intransitive marker *-e(d)*.[1] In

1 Notably and in contrast to the nominal adaptive markers, *-ja:* and *-e(d)* come with clear semantics: they are valency-indicating suffixes. Since they occur only on loanwords, we will still refer to them as "adaptive markers".

https://doi.org/10.1515/9783110703245-007

this chapter, we will describe these valency-indicating devices in Kanashi and Kinnauri in Section 2. In the same way as with the nominal adaptive markers, we will also examine (in Section 3) if the neighboring (ST and non-ST) languages show similarities to the Kanashi-Kinnauri patterns, and after an interim summary in Section 4, in Section 5 we turn to the question of the origin of these adaptive markers.

1.1 Background: transitivizing and intransitivizing strategies in Indo-Aryan and Sino-Tibetan

Many New Indo-Aryan[2] languages form transitive verbs from intransitive verbs using modern reflexes of OIA or MIA causative morphology. One line of development has led to a configuration where a set of transitive verbs only differ from their intransitive counterparts in having a different root vowel ("ablaut"), a situation similar to umlauting causatives in Germanic languages (e.g. English *fall* : *fell*). This pattern has often been analogically extended to other verb pairs not originally taking part in this formation. In all other cases, the transitivizing/causativizing derivational morphemes are suffixes. A number of NIA languages exhibit reflexes of the MIA causative suffix *-āvē*, surfacing in Hindi and many other NIA languages as *-ā* (primary causative), *-vā* (secondary causative < **-āv-āv*), but there are also other transitivizing suffixes found in NIA (e.g., *-āḍ*, *-āl*, *-ār*) (Masica 1991: 317ff).

Verbal transitivizing devices found across ST (in some cases postulated to go back to Proto-Sino-Tibetan) are at least (LaPolla 2017: 40ff; Matisoff 2003):

1. a causative prefix **s-*;
2. an initial-consonant voicing contrast (suggested to reflect an assimilatory sound change caused by a subsequently lost nasal prefix; Sagart 2006), where intransitive verbs begin with a voiced consonant and the transitive verb has the corresponding unvoiced initial consonant;
3. a middle/reciprocal suffix **-(n)si*;
4. a transitivizing suffix **-t*.

1–2 are not productive in ST. 3 has counterparts in many ST languages from different subbranches of the family (LaPolla 1996; DeLancey 2010). 4 occurs in Tibetan, Raji and some other ST languages. Many ST languages have also grammatical-

2 The three recognized distinct historical stages of IA are referred to in the literature as *Old Indo-Aryan* (OIA), *Middle Indo-Aryan* (MIA) and *New Indo-Aryan* (NIA).

ized light or serial verb constructions involving verbs such as 'do', 'give', 'send' (LaPolla 2017: 52).

Focusing specifically on Kanashi and Kinnauri, the attested valency changing mechanisms are:

1. a transitivizing prefix *s-*;
2. initial consonant voicing alternation;
3. a "middle marker" *-ʃi*;
4. a valency increasing marker *-ja:*;
5. an intransitive marker *-e(d)*.

1 and 2 (same as above) are not productive processes in Kanashi and Kinnauri. 3 (same as above) is productively used in both Kanashi and Kinnauri (see Chapter 3 and Saxena 2017; 2022). 4 and 5 in both Kanashi and Kinnauri occur only on IA loans and verbs of unknown etymologies, but not on ST verb stems.

2 *-e(d)* and *-ja:* in Kanashi and Kinnauri

To a subset of IA loans in Kinnauri, *-e(d)* is suffixed to form an intransitive verb and *-ja:* in the same slot is suffixed to increase valency, either to form the corresponding transitive (or causative) verb from an intransitive verb or to form a causative from a transitive verb. *-e(d)* is realized as *-en* in the examples shown in Table 1 (see more on this below).[3]

In some situations (for example, in the progressive aspect), the intransitive marker is realized in Kinnauri as *-ed* (instead of as *-en*) and the transitivizing marker *-ja:* is realized as *-j* (see Table 2).

The same general pattern can be seen in Kanashi too, as shown in Table 3, although the intransitive suffix appears as invariant *-e* in Kanashi.

2.1 Valency-increasing *-ja:*

No Kinnauri di- or polysyllabic verb stems with *-ja:* in the final syllable are intransitive (Table 4).

3 Note that in the pair *rukennu* : *rokja:mu* 'to stop (INTR : TR)' in Table 1 the transitive and intransitive verb forms here have different vowels, much like the "ablaut" in Hindi for transitivity. But even in this case we still see the regular valency increasing adaptive marker *-ja:* in Kinnauri.

Table 1: *-e(d)* and *-ja:* in Kinnauri

V(INTR)	Gloss	V(TR)	Gloss
polʈ-en-nu	'to turn around, to roll'	*polʈ-ja:-mu*	'to turn (sth) around, to roll (sth)'
ba:s-en-nu	'to smell'	*ba:s-ja:-mu*	'to smell (sth)'
pa:l-en-nu	'to grow'	*pa:l-ja:-mu*	'to grow (sth)'
ruk-en-nu	'to stop'	*rok-ja:-mu*	'to stop (sth)'
somʥ-en-nu	'to understand'	*somʥ-ja:-mu*	'to understand (sth)'
ʤonl-en-nu	'to swing'	*ʤonl-ja:-mu*	'to swing (sth)'

Table 2: *-e(d)* and *-ja:* in the Kinnauri structure [V-(TR/INTR)-PROG BE.PRS]

V(INTR)	Gloss (V-INTR-PROG BE.PRS)	V(TR)	Gloss (V-TR-PROG BE.PRS)
baʥ-ed-o du	'is playing'	*baʥ-j-o du*	'is making (sb) play'
hal-ed-o du	'is walking'	*hal-j-o du*	'is making (sb) walk'
bo:l-ed-o du	'is crazy'	*bo:l-j-o du*	'makes (sb) crazy'
sik-ed-o du	'is moving' (e.g leaving on their own)	*sik-j-o du*	'is moving (sth)'
biʃar-ed-o du	'is tense'	*biʃar-j-o du*	'is making (sb/sth) tense'
ba:t-ed-o du	'is talking to self'	*ba:t-j-o du*	'is making (sb) talk to self'
ʈʰur-ed-o du	'is running'	*ʈʰur-j-o du*	'is making (sb) run'
ʈokʰ-ed-o du	'is shouting'	*ʈokʰ-j-o du*	'is making (sb) shout'
pur-ed-o du	'is coming to an end'	*pur-j-o du*	'is finishing (sth)'

Once the valency increasing marker *-ja:* is affixed to the verb stem, it becomes part of the lexical item, which then undergoes the same processes as a regular lexical verb. In Kinnauri monosyllablic verb stems are reduplicated in the perfective aspect, if the verb stem does not end in *-ʧ* or *-ʃ*. If the verb stem is disyllabic, there is partial reduplication, where only the second syllable is reduplicated. In the perfective form of the verb stems with *-ja:*, the last consonant of the penultimate syllable together with the final syllable (*-ja:*) are reduplicated (Table 5).

As was the case with Kinnauri above, in Kanashi, the suffix *-ja:* attaches to stems of IA origin and to stems with unknown etymology. Transitive verbs with *-ja:* take the intransitive marker *-e* or the middle marker *-ʃi* in their corresponding decreased valency verb forms. See Table 6.

Notably, nasal stems do not drop their final consonant before *-ja:* (e.g. *gaŋ-ja:-m* 'to count'), which indicates that the *-j-* patterns as a vowel in the phonological system of Kanashi, for which additional support is provided by verbs such as *raŋgja:m* 'to dye, to color' and *saŋgja:m* 'to pile up', since *-ŋg-* is the expected intervocalic realization of *-ŋ-*.

Table 3: *-e* and *-ja:* in Kanashi

Gloss	V-INTR-INF	V-TR-INF
'to meet (INTR : TR)'	*mil-e-m*	*mil-ja:-m*
'to sleep (INTR : TR)'	*ʈul-e-m*	*ʈul-ja:-m*
'to press (INTR : TR)'	*ʥik-e-m*	*ʥik-ja:-m*
'to grow (INTR : TR)'	*roh-e-m*	*roj-ja:-m*
'to cook (INTR : TR)'	*siʈ-e-m*	*siʈi-ja:-m*
'to see (INTR : TR)'	*ba:l-e-m*	*ba:l-ja:-m*

Table 4: *-ja:* in Kinnauri

Etymology	Kinnauri	Gloss
T9822. mánas n. 'mind'	*mon-ja:-mu*	'to make sb agree'
T9092 phulla 'expanded, blown (of flowers)'	*pʰul-ja:-mu*	'to blow (sth)'
T1316 ārādhayati 'pleased, invited'	*ar-ja:-mu*	'to call (sb)'
T12959 saṁbudhyatē 'wakes up, understands'	*somʥ-ja:-mu*	'to explain (sth)'
T9106 *phēkk 'throw'	*pʰik-ja:-mu*	'to throw (sth)'
T7968 *pallaṭṭ 'turn, overturn'	*polʈ-ja:-mu*	'to turn over (e.g. chapati, quilt)'
T4998 chárdati chardáyati 'causes to flow over', 'vomits'	*tsʰuʈ-ja:-mu*	'to release (sth)'
T5979 tōlaka tōláyati 'lifts, weights, considers'	*tol-ja:-mu*	'to weigh (sth)'

Table 5: Perfective with verbs in *-j(a:)* in Kinnauri

Gloss	V-TR-INF	V(TR)~PFV
'to throw (sth)'	*pʰik-ja:-mu*	*pʰikja:~kja:*
'to cut (e.g. vegetables)'	*tsʰin-ja:-mu*	*tsʰinja:~nja:*
'to turn over (e.g. bread, quilt)'	*polʈ-ja:-mu*	*polʈja:~ʈja:*
'to increase (sth countable)'	*bod-ja:-mu*	*bodja:~dja:*
'to stop (sb)'	*rok-ja:-mu*	*rokja:~kja:*
'to gather (sth)'	*meʈ-ja:-mu*	*meʈja:~ʈja:*
'to wipe, to sweep (sth)'	*kuʃ-ja:-mu*	*kuʃja:~ʃja:*
'to swing (sth)'	*ʤonl-ja:-mu*	*ʤonlja:~lja:*
'to rub (e.g. clothes)'	*ʤekʰ-ja:-mu*	*ʤekʰja:~kʰja:*
'to leave (sth)'	*ʃoʈʰ-ja:-mu*	*ʃoʈʰja:~ʈʰja:*

Unlike Kinnauri, in Kanashi, there are some verbs which seem to contain both the transitive and the intransitive marker: *-ja:* and *-e* (Table 7). More data is needed to analyze this further.

Table 6: Transitive and intransitive IA loan verbs in Kanashi

Etymology	Kanashi	Gloss (V-TR-INF)	Kanashi	Gloss (V-INTR-INF)
T7968 *pallaṭṭ 'turn, overturn'	*palʈ-ja:-m*	'to turn (sth) over'	*palʈ-e-m*	'to turn over'
T2339 *ubbal 'rise, swell, boil'	*ubɽ-ja:-m*	'to boil (sth)'	*ubɽ-e-m*	'to boil'
T8037 pāṭhayati 'causes to read'	*paɽʰ-ja:-m*	'to teach (sth)'	*paɽ-e-m*	'to teach'
T13943 *haṭṭ 'move'	*hanɖ-ja:-m*	'to make (sb) walk'	*hanɖ-e-m*	'to walk'
T6173 *dabb 'press'	*ɖub-ja:-m*	'to sink, drown (sb/sth)'	*ɖubb-e-m*	'to sink, drown'
T11048 likháti 'scratches', 'writes'	*likʰ-ja:-m*	'to write (sth)'	*likʰ-e-m*	'to write'

As in Kinnauri, once the valency increasing marker *-ja:* is affixed to the verb stem, it becomes part of the lexical item, which then undergoes the same processes as a regular lexical verb. For example, the regular imperative marker is affixed to the verb stem, as shown in (1).

(1) *ba:l-ja:-u*
see-TR-IMP.M
'Look!'

Table 7: Kanashi loan verbs with *-ja:* and *-e*

Etymology	Kanashi	Gloss	Kanashi	Gloss
T1696 uḍḍayana n.'flying up'; T1697 uḍḍīyatē 'flies up'	*uɽ-ja:-m*	[fly-TR-INF]	*uɽ-j-e-m*	[fly-TR-INTR-INF]
T12429 śikṣaṇa n. 'act of learning'	*sikʰ-ja:-m*	[learn-TR-INF]	*sikʰ-j-e-m*	[learn-TR-INTR-INF]
T10560 raṅga[1] m. 'dye, colour'	*raŋg-ja:-m*	[color-TR-INF]	*raŋg-j-e-m*	[color-TR-INTR-INF]

2.2 Intransitive *-e(d)*

Di- and polysyllabic verb stems with *-e(d)* as the final syllable are intransitive verbs in Kinnauri. As was the case with the valency increasing marker *-ja:* above, *-e(d)* occurs only with IA loans or verbs of unknown etymologies, but never on ST verbs. *-e(d)* appears as *-e*, *-ed* or *-en* depending on its morphophonological context. The variant *-en* appears before infinitive *-mu*, which is then realized as *-nu*. See Table 8. The variant *-ed* is found e.g. before the progressive aspect marker *-o* (see Table 2), and *-e* appears before the past tense suffix *-kjo* and in the reduplicated perfective.

Table 8: Intransitive loan verbs in Kinnauri

Etymology	Kinnauri	Gloss
T7968 *pallaṭṭ 'turn, overturn'	*polʈ-en-nu*	[turn.over-INTR-INF] 'to turn over (INTR)'
T11592 vāsa³ m. 'perfume'. T11601 vāsayati³ 'perfumes'	*ba:s-en-nu*	[smell-INTR-INF] 'to smell (INTR)'
T8125 pālá m. 'protector', T8106 pāyáyati¹ 'brings over, rescues, brings to an end'	*pa:l-en-nu*	[grow-INTR-INF] 'to grow (INTR)'
T11453 vaha : váhati 'carries, bears along (of rivers), is carried along'	*boj-en-nu*	[flow-INTR-INF] 'to float, to blow (INTR)'
T10827 *rōkk 'stop'	*ruk-en-nu*	[stop-INTR-INF] 'to stop (INTR)'
T12959 saṁbudhyatē 'wakes up, understands'	*somʤ-en-nu*	[understand-INTR-INF] 'to understand (INTR)'
T5417 *jhōlayati 'causes to swing'	*ʤonl-en-nu*	[swing-INTR-INF] 'to swing (INTR)'

As the examples in Table 9 illustrate, the corresponding intransitive verb forms of the transitive verbs with *-ja:* can take either the intransitive marker *-e(d)*, or the middle marker *-ʃi*. In many cases both are possible, often with slightly different senses.

This holds true for the most part. However, a restricted set of verbs with the valency increasing marker *-ja:* do not permit the intransitive marker *-e(d)* (Table 10). It is unclear why this is the case. They only permit the middle marker.

In Kanashi, too, the intransitive marker *-e* occurs only with (IA) loan verbs (Table 11).

Apart from the intransitive marker *-e*, there are also some underived disyllabic transitive IA verb stems in Kanashi ending in *-e* (e.g., *ba:le-* 'look, see'; *kaʈe-* 'cut'). These are recognized by their occurrence in clear transitive clauses. In some cases there are also intransitive usages of these verbs in our Kanashi material, so that the

Table 9: Transitive-intransitive loan verb pairs in Kinnauri

Gloss (TR)	**V-TR-INF**	**V-TR-MDL-INF**	**V-INTR-INF**
'to smell'	*ba:s-ja:-mu*	*ba:s-ja:-ʃi-mu*	*ba:s-en-nu*
'to grow'	*pa:l-ja:-mu*	*pa:l-ja:-ʃi-mu*	*pa:l-en-nu*
'to drown'	*ɖub-ja:-mu*	*ɖub-ja:-ʃi-mu*	*ɖub-en-nu*
'to understand (X)'	*somʤ-ja:-mu*	*somʤ-ja:-ʃi-mu*	*somdz-en-nu*
'to move (X)'	*sik-ja:-mu*	*sik-ja:-ʃi-mu*	*sik-en-nu*
'to increase (X)'	*bod-ja:-mu*	*bod-ja:-ʃi-mu*	*bod-en-nu*
'to stop (X)'	*rok-ja:-mu*	*rok-ja:-ʃi-mu* [to be stopped, PL/collectively]	*ruk-en-nu* [on its own, SG]
'to swing (X)'	*ʤonl-ja:-mu*	*ʤonl-ja:-ʃi-mu* [to get swung, PL/collectively]'	*ʤonl-en-nu* [on its own, SG]
'to turn over'	*polʈ-ja:-mu*	*polʈ-ja:-ʃi-mu*	*polʈ-en-nu* [on its own, SG]

Table 10: Kinnauri loan verbs without *-e(d)*

Gloss (TR)	**V-TR-INF**	**V-TR-MDL-INF**	***V(INTR)**
'to squeeze'	*ʈru:tʰ-ja:-mu*	*ʈru:tʰ-ja:-ʃi-mu*	**ʈ(r)u:tʰennu*
'to leave (sb/sth)'	*ʃoʈʰ-ja:-mu*	*ʃoʈʰ-ja:-ʃi-mu*	**ʃoʈʰennu*
'to make sb agree'	*mon-ja:-mu*	*mon-ja:-ʃi-mu*	**monennu*
'to blow off (sth)'	*pʰul-ja:-mu*	*pʰul-ja:-ʃi-mu*	**pʰulxkennu*
'to call (sb)'	*ar-ja:-mu*	*ar-ja:-ʃi-mu*	**arennu*

Table 11: The intransitive marker *-e* in Kanashi

Etymology	**Kanashi**	**Gloss**	**Kanashi**	**Gloss**
T3945 *khōll 'to open'. 2. *khull 'to be open'	*kʰul-am*	[open-INF]	*kʰul-e-m*	[open-INTR-INF]
T11260 *vanvati 'to prepare, to make'	*baɳ-am*	[make-INF]	*baɳ-e-m*	[make-INTR-INF]

same verb stem may in principle receive two different analyses: *ba:le-m* [see-INF] 'to look, see' : *ba:l-e-m* [see-INTR-INF] 'to be visible'. This seems to lead to situations such as the ones shown in Table 12, where the same form has two different structural analyses.

Kanashi *-e* has a close correspondence in Kinnauri *-ed* (see above). As described above in Section 2.2, the Kinnauri suffix appears in the variants *-e*, *-ed* or *-en* depending on the (morphophonological) context. Unlike Kinnauri, the intransitive marker *-e* in Kanashi is invariant (2–3).

Table 12: Structurally ambiguous loan verbs in Kanashi

Etymology	Kanashi	Gloss	Kanashi	Gloss
T2854 kártati 'cuts'	*kaṭ-e-m* *kaṭe-ʃi-m*	'to get cut' [cut-INTR-INF] 'to get cut' [cut-MDL-INF]	*kaṭ-ja:-m*	'to cut (X)'
T9473 *bhāla2 'observation'	*ba:l-e-m* *ba:le-ʃi-m*	'to look' [see-INTR-INF] 'to look' [see-MDL-INF]	*ba:l-ja:-m*	'to look (at X)'
T10138 *miśrala 'mixed'	*mil-e-m* *mile-ʃi-m*	'to meet' [meet-INTR-INF] 'to meet' [meet-MDL-INF]	*mil-ja:-m*	'to meet, mix, stir (X)'

(2) *kaṭ-e-u-ta-ŋ*
cut-INTR-PROG-NPST-1/2PL
'(We) are cutting'

(3) *bidʑli-ga: tsamk-e-u to-ʃ*
lightning-PL shine-INTR-PROG be-3PL
'There is lightning'

We suggest that the Kanashi intransitive marker *-e* and the Kinnauri intransitive marker *-e(d)* are related. The most economical description is one where *-ed* is assumed to be the basic form of the suffix and the other two variants seen in Kinnauri are the results of assimilatory processes. Kanashi *-e* is invariable (except for normal phonetic variation involving the vowel /e/; see Chapter 2). It is reasonable to assume that Kinnauri presents the older situation, and that Kanashi has lost the final *-d* (or *-n*).[4] A supporting argument is that the cognates of original ST verb stems showing *-n* ~ *-d* variation in Kinnauri end in *-n* in Kanashi, e.g. *lonam* 'to tell'; *sanam* 'to kill').

3 The adaptive markers in neighboring languages

Next, we will examine if the valency increasing marker *-ja:* and/or the intransitive marker *-e(d)* are also attested in other ST and/or in IA languages of this region.

4 The original final segment could also be *-t*, since in Kinnauri voicing of stops is largely positionally determined. See below in Section 3.1.1 on Shumcho.

3.1 Sino-Tibetan languages

3.1.1 Sino-Tibetan languages of Himachal Pradesh

All ST languages of Himachal Pradesh have IA loans, but none of them show productive use of the suffixes discussed above or similar markers in borrowed verbs. There is no mention of either of these two markers in Tinani (D. D. Sharma 1989: 111–186), Navakat (Saxena 2022), Bunan (Widmer 2017); in Tibetan *-e* has a transitivizing function, not a detransitivizing function.

Chhitkuli does not seem to use these markers at all (D. D. Sharma 1992: 197–304; Martinez 2021), except for one possible example,[5] *gəltiŋ* 'to melt' : *gəl-ya-sə-ŋ* 'to cause to melt (TR)'), where we find a *-ja* ("-ya" in D. D. Sharma 1992: 197–304), which seems to correspond to Kinnauri/Kanashi *-jaː*. This *-ja* as a valency increasing marker is not a productive mechanism in Chhitkuli (Philippe Martinez p.c.). However, Chhitkuli regularly substitutes *-ea* for original (transitive/causative) *-aː* in Hindi loan verbs (Martinez 2021: 553).

On the other hand, the intransitive marker *-(ɐ)t* in Shumcho (Huber 2014; 2019) may plausibly be related to the Kanashi and Kinnauri intransitive marker *-e(d)*: "Transitive-intransitive pairs based on Indo-Aryan loans mostly have verb-final *-t* (or *-ɐt?*) as the intransitive marker, e.g. *hɐla-ma* [typo for *-mɐ*?] 'move (trans.)' vs. *hɐlɐt-mɐ* 'move (intrans.),' *hɪla-mɐ* 'shake (trans.)' vs. *hɪlɐt-mɐ* 'shake (intrans.),' [...] It remains to be investigated whether *-(ɐ)t* is also taken from an Indo-Aryan donor language in some way or other." (Huber 2014: 252f/fn. 33)

3.1.2 Sino-Tibetan languages of Uttarakhand and western Nepal

For the present investigation we have considered the following ST languages spoken in Uttarakhand and western Nepal:[6] Darma (Willis Oko 2019), Chaudangsi (Konow 1909), Byangsi (Konow 1909), Rongpo (S. R. Sharma 2001; Zoller 1983), Jad (D. D. Sharma 1990: 1–78), Raji (Nepal varieties: Khatri 2008) and Newar (Kathmandu Newar: Hargreaves 2017; Dolakha Newar: Genetti 2007). Darma, Chaudangsi, Byangsi and Rongpo are usually classified as WH languages (as are Kanashi and Kinnauri). Raji belongs to the Raji-Raute subgroup (Hammarström

5 Original transcription as in D. D. Sharma (1992: 197–304). Morpheme boundaries are our additions.

6 The selection of languages is constrained by the availability of the data.

et al. 2021),[7] Jad belongs to the Bodish sub-group (Hammarström et al. 2021), and the classification of Newar is unclear.

Jad, Darma and Kathmandu Newar show no traces of these markers in the sources that we have consulted.

According to S. R. Sharma (2001), IA transitivizing morphology is retained in IA loan verbs in Rongpo. Example, *haːrpəŋ* 'to be defeated' : *həraːpəŋ* 'to defeat'; *lekhpəŋ* 'to write' : *lekhaːpəŋ* 'to make someone write'. There are, however, some verb stems in Rongpo where *-ja* ("-ya" in S. R. Sharma 2001 and Zoller 1983) occurs in the second syllable of transitive verbs, many of which are IA loans.[8] For example, *bhəbəṛ-* 'to roast (IA.INTR)' : *bhəbəṛya-* 'to roast (IA.TR)'; *bhəṭyaː-* 'to call, to shout, to invite (TR)', *khəṛjaː-* 'to hunt, to rush', *rəṅya-* 'to color (TR)' (*rəṅ* 'color (N)'), *khoṛya* 'to bury'. But unlike Kanashi and Kinnauri, there also seem to be some intransitive verbs in Rongpo which have *-ja* in the second syllable (e.g. *dhəndyaː-* 'to walk (INTR)', *kuŋkyaː-* 'to bark (IA.INTR)'. More work is needed.

Distinct from this, Chaudangsi, Byangsi, Raji and possibly also Dolakha Newar seem to show some more solid traces of the markers under consideration. In Chaudangsi and Byangsi *-ai* seems to be a valency increasing marker, although appearing in ST items, as opposed to *-jaː*. Example, Chaudangsi *si* 'die' : *sai* 'kill', Chaudangsi *raa* 'come : *rai* 'bring'; Byangsi *raa* 'come' : *raai* 'bring'.

Raji has a periphrastic causative construction. Its schema is: V-*ɦja sla-* [V-INF CAUS-] (Khatri 2008: 25f). One possible hypothesis could be that the infinitive suffix *-ɦja* in Raji is related to the Kinnauri/Kanashi valency increasing marker *-jaː*, through a putative diachronic scenario where the infinitive marker is reanalyzed as a valency increasing marker *-ja*, and subsequently, *sla* [CAUS] becomes redundant and subsequently disappears.[9]

Further, the passive marker in Raji is *-i*, e.g.: *ramʌ-ɦatiŋ bʰwa sat-i-k-a* [ram-ABL bird kill-PASS-SAME.DAY-PST] 'The bird was killed by Ram' (Khatri 2008: 27). One possible hypothesis could be that the Raji passive marker *-i* is related to the Kanashi and Kinnauri intransitive marker *-e(d)*. Note that [e] ~ [i] variation is a regular feature of Kanashi pronunciation; hence the intransitive marker *-e* is also realized as *-i* (see Chapter 2).

---

7 Sometimes Raji-Raute is classified under WH in the literature.

8 We do not yet know if this transitivizing suffix is also found in ST items.

9 However, this begs the question of what happened to the infinitive marker in other verbs. There are known cases from other ST languages where nominalizers have developed into verbal morphology, e.g. in Tibetan where the perfective/evidential marker *-pa* has such an origin. It is easier to see how reanalysis of a nominalizer can result in a category which applies across the board, as it were, than in this case where the infinitive would become a valency increasing marker only in some verbs but not in others.

Dolakha Newar has a loan verb adaptation pattern which is reminiscent of the Kanashi and Kinnauri data provided above. Borrowed Nepali verbs are accommodated differently according to their transitivity as shown in Table 13 (Genetti 2007: 156f):

Table 13: IA loan verb accommodation in Dolakha Newar

INTR	Nepali	*phulnu* 'swell'	*khasnu* 'fall'	*janmanu* 'be born'
	Dolakha N.	*phul-ai jur-*	*khas-ai jur-*	*janm-ai jur-*
TR	Nepali	*mānu* 'obey'	*jitnu* 'win'	*ṭikranu* 'stand'
	Dolakha N.	*mānyet-*	*jityet-*	*ṭikret-*
TR/CAUS	Nepali	*patyāunu* 'believe'	*jalāunu* 'burn'	*tarkāunu* 'kindle'
	Dolakha N.	*patyāt-*	*jalyāt-*	*tarkyāt-*

jur- is the verb 'be, become, happen' and the *yet-/yāt-* element is the verb 'do'. Genetti (2007) glosses *-ai* as "BV" (borrowed verb), i.e. she analyzes it as a pure accommodating element added to borrowed intransitive verb stems, much like the adaptive markers in Kanashi and Kinnauri under discussion here. In Dolakha Newar the functional distribution of *-ai* and *yāt-* is reminiscent of the Kinnauri-Kanashi *-e(d)* and *-ja:*. But note that in Chaudangsi and Byangsi *-ai* seems to have a valency increasing function, and not the valency decreasing function.

To summarize thus far, among the ST languages considered here some possible correlates of the valency increasing marker *-ja:* and the intransitive marker *-e(d)* are found in Kinnauri, Kanashi and Shumcho in Himachal Pradesh and in some ST languages of Uttarakhand and Nepal (Chaudangsi, Byangsi, Raji and Dolakha Newar). Note that these languages cut across separate ST sub-groups.

3.2 Dravidian languages

Two Dravidian languages are spoken in this region: Brahui (Andronov 1980) and Kurukh (also Kurux, Dhangar; Hahn 1911; Mishra 1991). Both these Dravidian languages have many IA loans, but, they do not seem to show any trace of the transitive *-ja:* and/or the intransitive marker *-e(d)*.

3.3 Isolate: Kusunda

Many of the transitive verbs in Kusunda (including some identifiable IA loans) have the verb schema: V-*a*-*d*-, and their corresponding intransitive verbs have the verb schema: V-*e*-. If this observation is correct, there are some possible similarities between Kusunda transitive and intransitive markers and the Kinnauri/Kanashi valency increasing marker *-ja:* and/or intransitive marker *-e(d)*. However, Watters (2006: 61ff, 97) attributes the transitive/causative *-a* in Kusunda to language-internal development, originating in a support verb construction involving the verb *a-* 'do, make'.

3.4 Indo-Aryan: Western and Central Pahari languages

In this section we will examine if we find similar valency changing mechanisms in IA languages of this region (which are classified under the Western Pahari or Central Pahari sub-branches of IA). As with ST languages above, the selection of languages here is constrained by the data available. We have included the following IA languages for the present purposes: Kinnauri Pahari (Saxena 2022), Garhwali (Chandola 1966), Bajjika (Roy 2010), Saadri (Uranw & Yadaw 2009), Kotgarhi (Hendriksen 1986), Kumaoni (Apte & Pattanayak 1967), Chinali (D. D. Sharma 1991).

In Kinnauri Pahari (KP) some transitive verbs have corresponding intransitive verbs with *-i/-i:* suffixed to the transitive stem (which itself may contain the transitivizing *-a:* suffix).[10] For example, *ɖɔ:nɔ* 'to burn (TR)' : *ɖɔinɔ* 'to burn (INTR)'; *k^{h}ɔltsnɔ* 'to peel (TR)' : *k^{h}ɔlʧi:nɔ* 'to peel (INTR)' *hira:nɔ* 'to lose (TR)' : *hira:inɔ* 'to disappear (INTR)'. Further, as in Kinnauri (see above), in Kinnauri Pahari too, *-ja:* functions as a transitivizer (for example, KP: *p^{h}ikja:nɔ* 'to throw (X)', Hindi (H): *p^{h}ika:na:* 'to throw (X)'; KP: *bɔdlja:nɔ* 'to change (X)', H: *badla:na:* 'to change (X)'). It is very likely that its appearance in Kinnauri Pahari is the result of language contact, i.e., that the verbs containing it are loanwords from Kinnauri, despite their IA etymology. The same verb in other IA languages (e.g. Kotgarhi and Hindi) does not contain this *-ja:*. It is our suggestion that *-ja:* in Kinnauri Pahari is possibly due to its contact with ST Kinnauri.

In Chinali as in Chaudangsi and Byangsi *-ai* seems to have a valency increasing function. For example, *suṇ-ba* 'to listen', *suṇ-ai-ba* 'to tell, to narrate', *nəc-ba* 'to dance', *nəc-ai-ba* 'to make someone dance'. Apart from these two IA languages, none of the IA languages spoken in the the region and for which we have relevant

10 The Kinnauri Pahari verbs are cited in their infinitive form (suffix *-nɔ*, corresponding to Hindi *-na:*).

data (Kumaoni, Kotgarhi, Garhwali, Bajjika, Saadri) show any similarity with the Kinnauri-Kanashi valency changing markers *-ja:* and *-e(d)*.

4 Summary thus far: distribution of the verbal adaptive markers

To summarize, of the languages included in the present study at least the ones listed in Table 14 seem to show some traces of *-ja:* and *-e(d)* as transitive and intransitive markers. The ST languages in Table 14 cut across the prevailing ST genealogical classification, with the caveat that the really clear instances of these markers are found in Kanashi, Kinnauri and Shumcho (all Kinnauric Western WH).

Table 14: Transitive and intransitive markers

Family	**Language**	**Markers**	
		INTR	TR
ST	Kanashi	*-e*	*-ja:*
	Kinnauri	*-e(d)*	*-ja:*
	Shumcho	*-i*, *-(ɐ)t*	*-a*
	Chhitkuli		*-ea*
	Chaudangsi		*-ai*
	Byangsi		*-ai*
	Rongpo		*-ja*
	Raji	*-i/-e*	*-a/-wa*, *-ɦja ... sla*
	Dolakha Newar	*-ai*	*-yet/-yāt*
IA	Chinali		*-ai*
	Kinnauri Pahari	*-i*	*-ja:*
Isolate	Kusunda	*-e-*	*-a-d-*

5 Possible origins of the adaptive markers *-ja:* and *-e(d)*

Loan verbs are integrated into Kanashi and Kinnauri by at least two mechanisms. The first is the mechanism described in this chapter, which Wichmann & Wohlgemuth (2008) refer to as "indirect insertion" (see also Wohlgemuth 2009): "In many languages an affix is required to accommodate loan verbs. Once the affix is added the normal inflectional pattern may be applied." (Wichmann & Wohlgemuth 2008: 97). Both languages also additionally use the "light verb strategy" – i.e. turning the borrowed item into a kind of nominal object of a semantically light verb, such as 'do', 'be', or 'make' (e.g. Kinnauri *kəmaj lan-nu* [earn(N) do/make-INF] 'to earn'; also: *kəmaja:mu*, with *-ja:*) – a strategy which is extremely common among languages, both in the world and across South Asia, in all language families.

The loanword adaptation strategy described for nouns and adjectives in Chapter 6 is also an instance of indirect insertion, although in this case, we also find borrowings without the adaptive marker (which would constitute "direct insertion" in the terminology of Wichmann & Wohlgemuth 2008) or borrowings where the adaptive marker can optionally be replaced by inflectional suffixes. Neither happens in the verbal domain, making verb borrowing formally different from noun and adjective borrowing, something which has been noted in the literature also in other contexts (Wichmann & Wohlgemuth 2008: 110f).

From the data presented above, we are confronted with two questions:

1. What is the source of the intransitive marker *-e(d)* and the valency increasing marker *-j(a:)*?
2. How did it happen that Kanashi and Kinnauri show similar developments (including the choice of the form)? And that their plausible traces are also found in some ST languages of Uttarakhand and Nepal (see Table 14)? What does it say about the genealogical classification of these languages and of their prehistory?

Here we will present our preliminary thoughts about the first point, while the second point will be discussed in Chapter 8, although we note here that the set of languages showing the nominal adaptive markers discussed in Chapter 6 and the set of languages possessing the verbal adaptive morphology discussed in this chapter do not coincide fully.

5.1 Possible sources of the adaptive marker *-e(d)*

A relevant observation in relation to the question of the origin of the adaptive marker *-e(d)* is that there are a number of monosyllabic ST primary verbs in Kinnauri which behave morphophonologically in the same way as the intransitive marker *-e(d)*, i.e., they exhibit the variation CV ~ CV*d*-V ~ CV*n-nu*. This could point to an ST-internal origin of *-e(d)* in the form of an original (light) verb, i.e. that we are dealing with "grammaticalization of root-morphemes" (Matisoff 2003:

439), much like the transitivizing mechanism reported by Widmer (2017: 709–710) for Bunan.

Notable in this connection is that Shumcho has a number of ST verbs which in some morphological contexts show a final *-t*, which Huber (2014: 232f/fn. 17) refers to as a "root augmentation marker".[11] As mentioned above, in Shumcho we also find a intransitive marker *-(ɐ)t*, exclusive to IA loanwords. Given that a characteristic feature of Kinnauri is contextually determined voiced–unvoiced variation in stops, this means that the intransivizing adaptive marker in Kinnauri probably should be reconstructed as *-(V)t*.

If its origin is in a light or support verb, the most likely candidate would be a verb meaning 'do', although there are also other possibilities, such as 'be' or 'have'. Huber (2014: 239) notes the defective paradigm of the Shumcho verb stem *ɛ-* 'have' which occurs only in imperative forms, and Martinez (2021) lists a number of copulas in Chhitkuli, among which we find *a-*/*a:-* 'be, become' (Martinez 2021: 138f). Further, in Table 13 we have seen how the verb 'do' (*yet-*/*yāt-*) is used as a light verb accommodating IA loan verbs in Dolakha Newar. Under this assumption, it would still remain to be explained why a particular light verb is used only with (IA) loan verbs, and not used together with, e.g., ST-origin nominal stems.

5.2 Possible sources of the adaptive marker *-j(a:)*

Despite the apparent resemblance of the valency increasing marker *-ja:* to the *-ā* transitive/causative suffix found in several NIA languages, it is not immediately obvious how to posit this as the source of the Kanashi/Kinnauri *-j(a:)* (but see below). For one, the *-j-* of *-ja:* remains unexplained, not appearing in any IA language as far as we are aware,[12] and in addition, the *-a:* of *-ja:* is dropped before some endings (for example, in the perfective verb form), at least in Kinnauri, leaving only the *-j* as the marker of transitivity. For this reason, an ST-internal explanation would be more attractive.

On the other hand, it is a known fact that many ST languages have borrowed the IA transitive/causative suffix *-ā* directly. Consequently, we should not dismiss this as a possible source of *-j(a:)* in Kinnauri and Kanashi. The initial *-j* could then possibly be connected to *-e(d)*, via a morphophonological alternation independently established for Kinnauri, where in some *e*-final nouns, the *-e* appears as *-j*

11 These sets – *-(d/n)*-final ST-origin verbs in Kinnauri and Shumcho verbs with the root augmentation marker *-t* – show some (modest) overlap between the two languages, e.g. Shumcho *lɔ.t* 'say'; *lɐ.t* 'do' : Kinnauri *lonnu* 'tell'; *lannu* 'do, make'.

12 Except in Kinnauri Pahari, but there it is almost certainly borrowed from Kinnauri.

before some vowel-initial suffixes (e.g. *ate* 'brother' + *-u* [-POSS] > *atjo*; *banes* 'pot' + *-a:* [-PL] > *banja:*). Thus, the *-j* of *-j(a:)* could reflect the *-e-* of *-e(d)*, so that we are dealing with a sequence of morphs: a light verb **ed-* (or **et-*) and a borrowed IA valency-increasing suffix.

Also, as Wichmann & Wohlgemuth (2008: 97) note, in those cases when the origin is known of affixes used in a language exclusively to accommodate loan verbs, they are typically borrowed together with the verbs from a donor language, which however need not be the language of origin of the affix, in cases of "borrowing of borrowing patterns" (Wichmann & Wohlgemuth 2008: 105f). This would speak in favor of finding an external source of the adaptive marker *-j(a:)*, and the best candidate so far seems to be IA transitive/causative *-ā*.

6 Conclusion

Comparing the outcome of the investigations in this chapter (of verbal adaptive markers) and in Chapter 6 (of nominal and adjectival adaptive markers), we find that there are definitely more clear cases of corresponding morphs in other languages of this region for the latter than the former. Many of the correspondences listed in Table 14 are uncertain, while the data warranting that a language in Figure 4 of Chapter 6 is marked with a circle ("many clear instances") are quite unambiguous.

On the other hand, unlike the two nominal/adjectival adaptive markers *-(V)ŋ* and *-(V)s* described in the previous chapter, the two verbal adaptive markers *-e(d)* and *-j(a:)* seem to be closely connected, generally appearing as a pair, which may indicate that they have a common history, at least in Kanashi and Kinnauri.

References

Andronov, Mikhail Sergeevich. 1980. *The Brahui language*. Moscow: Nauka.
Apte, Mahadeo L. & D. P. Pattanayak. 1967. *An outline of Kumauni grammar*. Durham: Duke University.
Chandola, Anoop Chandra. 1966. *A syntactic sketch of Garhwali*. Chicago: The University of Chicago. (PhD thesis).
DeLancey, Scott. 2010. Towards a history of verb agreement in Tibeto-Burman. *Himalayan Linguistics* 9(1): 1–39.
Genetti, Carol. 2007. *A grammar of Dolakha Newar*. Berlin: Walter de Gruyter.
Hahn, Ferdinand. 1911. *Kurukh grammar*. Calcutta: Bengal Secretariat Press.

Hammarström, Harald, Robert Forkel, Martin Haspelmath & Sebastian Bank. 2021. *Glottolog 4.4*. Jena: Max Planck Institute for the Science of Human History. Available online at https://glottolog.org. DOI: 10.5281/zenodo.4761960.

Hargreaves, David. 2017. Kathmandu Newar (Nepāl Bhāśā). In Graham Thurgood & Randy J. LaPolla (eds.), *The Sino-Tibetan languages*, 2nd edn., 453–467. London: Routledge.

Hendriksen, Hans. 1986. *Himachali studies III: Grammar*. Copenhagen: Munksgaard.

Huber, Christian. 2014. Subject and object agreement in Shumcho. In Nathan Hill & Thomas Owen-Smith (eds.), *Trans-Himalayan linguistics*, 221–274. Berlin: Mouton de Gruyter.

Huber, Christian. 2019. Progressivity and habituality in Shumcho. *STUF – Language Typology and Universals* 72(1): 83–132.

Khatri, Ramesh. 2008. *The structure of verbs and sentences of Raji*. Kathmandu: Tribhuvan University Masters thesis.

Konow, Sten. 1909. *Linguistic survey of India, Vol 3: Tibeto-Burman family. Part I: General introduction, specimens of the Tibetan dialects, the Himalayan dialects, and the North Assam group*. (This and several other volumes of the LSI were edited by Sten Konow, although published as the work of George A. Grierson). Calcutta: Government of India, Central Publication Branch.

LaPolla, Randy J. 1996. Middle voice marking in Tibeto-Burman. In *Proceedings of the Fourth International Symposium on Languages and Linguistics: Pan-Asiatic Linguistics, volume 5*, 1940–1954. Bangkok: Mahidol University at Salaya.

LaPolla, Randy J. 2017. An overview of Sino-Tibetan morphosyntax. In Graham Thurgood & Randy J. LaPolla (eds.), *The Sino-Tibetan languages*, 2nd edn., 40–69. London: Routledge.

Martinez, Philippe Antoine. 2021. *A corpus-based account of morphosyntactic evidentiality in discourse in Chhitkul-Rākchham*. SOAS, University of London. (PhD thesis).

Masica, Colin P. 1991. *The Indo-Aryan languages*. Cambridge: Cambridge University Press.

Matisoff, James A. 2003. *Handbook of Proto-Tibeto-Burman: System and philosophy of Sino-Tibetan reconstruction*. Berkeley: University of California Press.

Mishra, Awadesh Kumar. 1991. *Word formation in Kurukh Oraon: A study of linguistic typology and language change*. New Delhi: Jawaharlal Nehru University. (PhD thesis).

Roy, Ram Rekha. 2010. *Verbal morphology in Bajjika*. Kathmandu: Tribhuvan University Masters thesis.

Sagart, Laurent. 2006. On intransitive nasal prefixation in Sino-Tibetan languages. *Cahiers de linguistique – Asie orientale* 35(1): 57–70. DOI: 10.3406/clao.2006.1747.

Saxena, Anju. 2017. Sangla Kinnauri. In Graham Thurgood & Randy J. LaPolla (eds.), *The Sino-Tibetan languages*, 2nd edn., 756–772. London: Routledge.

Saxena, Anju. 2022. *The linguistic landscape of the Indian Himalayas: Languages in Kinnaur*. Forthcoming 2022. Leiden: Brill.

Sharma, Devi Datta. 1989. *Tribal languages of Himachal Pradesh. Part one*. Delhi: Mittal Publications.

Sharma, Devi Datta. 1990. *Tibeto-Himalayan languages of Uttarakhand. Part two*. Delhi: Mittal Publications.

Sharma, Devi Datta. 1991. *A descriptive grammar and vocabulary of Chinali*. Shimla: Himachal Academy of Arts, Culture & Languages.

Sharma, Devi Datta. 1992. *Tribal languages of Himachal Pradesh. Part two*. Delhi: Mittal Publications.

Sharma, Suhnu Ram. 2001. A sketch of Rongpo grammar / Rongpo-English, English-Rongpo glossary. In Yasuhiko Nagano & Randy J. LaPolla (eds.), *Bon studies 3: New research on*

Zhangzhung and related Himalayan languages (Senri Ethnological Reports 19), 195–270. Osaka: National Museum of Ethnology.

Uranw, Ram Kisum & Dev Narayan Yadaw. 2009. Saadri (Kisaan) language: A brief introduction. *Nepalese Linguistics* 24: 379–390.

Watters, David. 2006. Notes on Kusunda grammar: A language isolate of Nepal. *Himalayan Linguistics Archive* 3: 1–182.

Wichmann, Søren & Jan Wohlgemuth. 2008. Loan verbs in a typological perspective. In Thomas Stolz, Dik Bakker & Rosa Salas Palomo (eds.), *Aspects of language contact: New theoretical, methodological and empirical findings with special focus on Romancisation processes*, 89–121. Berlin: Mouton de Gruyter.

Widmer, Manuel. 2017. *A grammar of Bunan*. Berlin: De Gruyter Mouton.

Willis Oko, Christina. 2019. *A grammar of Darma*. Leiden: Brill.

Wohlgemuth, Jan. 2009. *A typology of verbal borrowings*. Berlin: Mouton de Gruyter.

Zoller, Claus Peter. 1983. *Die Sprache von Rang Pas von Garhwal (Raṅ Pɔ Bhāsa): Grammatik, Texte, Wörterbuch*. Wiesbaden: Otto Harrassowitz.

Synthesis

Anju Saxena, Lars Borin, and Bernard Comrie

8 Kanashi and West Himalayish: genealogy, language contact, prehistoric migrations

Abstract: In this chapter, the findings from the loanword adaptation studies presented in previous chapters are combined with data on other linguistic features, socio-cultural phenomena, population genetics, and geography, in order to draw some conclusions about the genealogical and areal relationships of Kanashi to other languages of the region, about the internal classification of West Himalayish and Sino-Tibetan, and about the prehistoric migrations by which Kanashi and other West Himalayish languages arrived at their present locations.

Keywords: Kanashi, Kinnauri, Sino-Tibetan, West Himalayish, comparative linguistics, language contact

Chapter overview:

1 Introduction

The main purpose of this volume is to present some of the results of our work in an extensive Kanashi documentation project (Chapters 1–5 and 9). This documentation effort has been pursued in parallel with a broad investigation of (micro-) areality in South Asia in general and in the Himalayas in particular (Borin et al. 2021), and in this context our attention was drawn to some characteristic linguistic features of Kanashi: it shares specific loanword adaptation mechanisms – suffixes which we refer to as "adaptive markers" here – with its close relative Kinnauri, a language that Saxena has studied for decades (e.g. Saxena 1995; 2000; 2004; 2008; 2011; 2017; 2022). Looking for possible origins of these mechanisms, we found identical or very similar phenomena in several other Sino-Tibetan (ST) languages of the region, with a distribution among the languages which crosses ST subgroup boundaries. Thus, the investigation presented in Chapter 6 produced

https://doi.org/10.1515/9783110703245-008

the surprising result that within ST, at least one of the noun adaptation strategies is not confined to West Himalayish (WH) as standardly defined (e.g. by Widmer 2017) (see Figure 1). Identifying the origins of the adaptive markers has also turned out to be surprisingly difficult.

ST				
	West Himalayish	Western	Kinnauric	Chhitkuli Kinnauri Kanashi Shumcho
			Lahaulic	Pattani Tinani
		Eastern	Central	Bunan Sunnami Rongpo Zhangzhung(†)
			Pithauragarh	Chaudangsi Byangsi Darma Rangkas(†?)

Figure 1: The West Himalayish subgroup of Sino-Tibetan (internal subgrouping according to Widmer 2017)

As far as we can tell, the shared loanword adaptation strategies decribed in Chapters 6 and 7 have not been discussed as a crosslinguistic phenomenon in the literature on ST or WH.[1] They do serve to illustrate the complex linguistic ecology of the Himalayan region, which presents itself as a condensed version of the South Asian linguistic area, complete with the same major language families (although in different proportions), and some isolate languages in addition.

Our focus in this chapter is on throwing as much light as we can on the prehistory of Kanashi against this background: what is its position in the WH family tree and how did it end up in its present location, as a geographically isolated ST (WH) language completely surrounded by Indo-Aryan (IA) languages, and whose closest linguistic relatives are far away in Kinnaur?

The conclusions and hypotheses put forth in this chapter will by necessity be preliminary, even speculative and some conjectures made here may be mutually contradictory in their assumptions regarding e.g. phonological and semantic change. We hope that our planned further investigation will allow us to elimi-

1 The most widespread of the investigated adaptive markers (and preumably the oldest), *-(V)ŋ*, has been noted as such by authors of individual language descriptions (using terms such as "nativizing suffix", etc.); see Chapter 6.

nate these contradictions. The discussion draws on diverse kinds of information, treated in more detail in the subsections of Section 2 below:

- the loanword adaptation mechanisms described in Chapters 6 and 7 (Section 2.1);
- other linguistic (lexical and morphosyntactic) features (Section 2.2);
- some socio-cultural phenomena (Section 2.3);
- population genetics (Section 2.4);
- geography (Section 2.5).

2 Some pieces of the Kanashi puzzle

2.1 Loanword adaptation mechanisms

The loanword adaptation devices that have been described in Chapters 6 and 7 provide clues to the classification of Kanashi and Kinnauri, as well as to the internal structure of West Himalayish and its place in the Sino-Tibetan family tree. The similar or identical mechanisms used for adapting Indo-Aryan loanwords in some of these languages are arguably common traits that constitute innovations vis-à-vis the protolanguage (although they may be the result of contact in some cases), since they are used *only* for this purpose – as far as we can tell, the adaptive markers are not used with inherited vocabulary items – and since contact between ST and IA is assumed to be of considerably more recent date than the breakup of Proto-Sino-Tibetan. As mentioned in Chapter 6, the shape of the adapted IA loanwords reflects the New Indo-Aryan stage, indicating that they are at most approximately a millennium old.[2]

In Chapters 6 and 7 we investigated the distribution of four adaptive markers across the languages of the region:

1. *-(V)ŋ* – used on loan nouns and adjectives;
2. *-(V)s* – used on loan nouns and adjectives;
3. *-ja:* – used to form transitive or causative verbs from borrowed IA items;
4. *-e(d)* – used to form intransitive verbs from borrowed IA items.

Only three languages – all (Kinnauric Western) WH (see Figure 1) – exhibit all four features: Kanashi, Kinnauri and Shumcho. In fact, the wider distribution referred

2 A very clear demonstration that these items are New Indo-Aryan in origin is furnished by the Kinnauri verbs *ḍubja:mu* / *ḍubennu* 'to drown (TR / INTR)', etymology (Turner 1966): "5561 *ḍubb 'sink'. [...] [Metath. of MIA. buḍḍaï < *buḍyati."

to above primarily applies to one of the adaptive markers – *-(V)ŋ* – which is found in many languages from Kinnaur in the west, through Uttarakhand, into western Nepal. It is not confined to ST languages, and hence is at least partly an areal phenomenon. Apart from Kanashi, it is not found to the west or north of Kinnaur.

A small number of languages exhibit adaptive markers in the verbal domain which may be related to *-ja:*. Notably, in Chhitkuli, another WH language of Kinnaur for which we have relevant data, *-ea* is used to render (transitive/causative) *-a:* in Hindi loan verbs (Martinez 2021: 553). Relevant in this connection is that the Kinnauri suffix *-ja:* is written *-ĕā* in the Kinnauri vocabulary by Bailey (1911), where *ĕ* is described in the corresponding grammar sketch as "very short [...] rather like *e* in *pet*" (Bailey 1909: 662). Chhitkuli shows no trace of *-(V)s* or *-e(d)*. We are thus faced with a situation where Kinnauri and Shumcho are more similar to geographically distant Kanashi than they are to geographically close Chhitkuli. In our estimation, this is more likely to reflect a situation where the three languages Kanashi, Kinnauri and Shumcho should be classified together in a sub-group within Kinnauric, than one where Chhitkuli has lost two of the four features after split-up of a protolanguage common to all of Kinnauric Western WH.

Summing up, based on the distribution of the adaptive markers,

- Kanashi, Kinnauri and Shumcho may possibly form a separate subgroup within Kinnauric Western WH;
- Kinnauric Western WH shares unique linguistic features – through genealogy or contact or both – with languages now located to the east of it (in Uttarakhand and western Nepal).

2.2 Lexical and morphosyntactic features

The loanword adaptation mechanisms studied in Chapters 6 and 7 are only some of the linguistic features which must be investigated in order to be able to say more about the genealogy of Kanashi and Kinnauri within ST. Phonology, morphosyntax and basic vocabulary must all be considered in this connection, as well as sociocultural features and geography.

Currently suggested classifications of WH rely primarily on lexical comparison (Saxena & Borin 2011; 2013; Widmer 2017; 2018; 2021), where furthermore cognates and borrowed items are not distinguished, as a rule. Obviously, it is desirable to add other kinds of linguistic features to the data used for the comparison, e.g., specific sound changes and morphosyntactic features (such as characteristic affixes and irregular paradigms). The adaptive markers described in Chapters 6 and 7 are of this latter kind. They thus add important information allowing us to approach the question of classification of Kanashi and WH. Of course, we will also need to carry out a more thorough study involving a whole range of additional linguistic features, such as the reduplicated perfective found in some of these languages, verb indexing for affected SAP verb arguments, transitivity classes, case markers, and other features. Also, since almost all these languages are severely underdescribed, we do not necessarily have comparable data coverage for all of them even with respect to the loanword adaptation mechanisms forming the basis for our discussion here. Hence, a more thorough study of the genealogical and areal connections of WH has been initiated and will be reported on in future publications.

So far, we have relevant comparable data on three of the five recognized WH languages of Kinnaur, viz. Kinnauri, Chhitkuli and Shumcho, while we unfortunately lack data on the other two languages, Jangrami and Sunnami.[3]

2.3 Socio-cultural phenomena

The same general area in Uttarakhand where we find the adaptive markers discussed above is characterized by the presence of some socio-cultural traditions which are also found in Lower/Middle Kinnaur and along the migration routes between Lower Kinnaur and Kullu (Malana where Kanashi is spoken, is located in the Kullu region).

2.3.1 Local architecture

In the area of interest we find a traditional architectural style, in which the foundation platform of a building is made of stones and the structure on this platform is built with alternating layers of logs and masonry. This architectural style is known as *Kath-Kuni* in Himachal Pradesh and as *Koti Banal* in Uttarakhand. The map provided by Rautela & Joshi (2008)[4] shows that this construction style is found in southern Uttarakhand (Uttarkashi) and parts of Himachal Pradesh, including Kinnaur. This construction style is traditionally used to build family homes, temples and the structures commonly referred to as *kila* 'fort' in Kinnaur. These are compact, square, tall, multi-storeyed tower-like structures, standing alone, i.e., not sharing any walls with other buildings. Figure 2 shows a typical specimen, *Kamru kila* of Kinnaur.

3 There are also two Tibetic languages spoken in (Upper) Kinnaur.

4 Similar observations are also made by Kumar et al. (2016), according to which the Kath-Kuni construction style is predominantly found in the Kullu and Shimla regions in Himachal Pradesh.

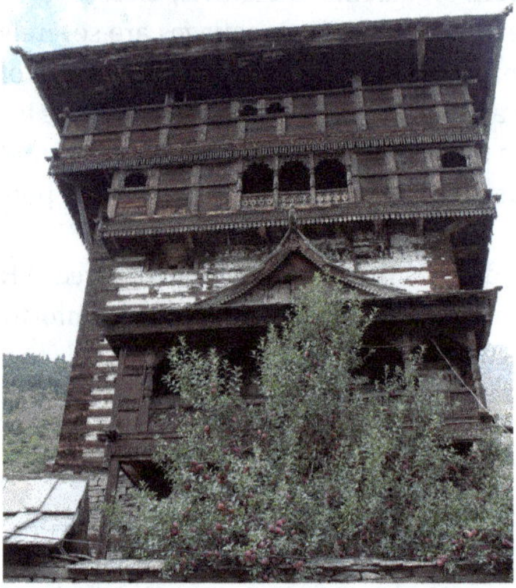

Figure 2: Kamru kila (Kamru village, Kinnaur): https://commons.wikimedia.org/wiki/File:Kamru_fort.jpg; copyright status: Attribution-Share Alike 4.0 International)

Both the exterior of these tower-like structures and their interior (e.g., organization of the various floors) seem to be similar in Uttarakhand and Kinnaur. In all the villages where they are found in Uttarakhand and Kinnaur, according to local oral tradition they were built to protect the villages from the enemy, and the enemy in each case, again according to the legends, are Gorkhas (people from Nepal). Further, each of these buildings is described against the contextual background of Hindu mythology. Nowadays some of these tower-like structures in Kinnaur (and elsewhere in Himachal Pradesh and Uttarakhand, see below) are Hindu temples or used as storage rooms of temples. In each of these instances the locals describe this structure as the oldest structure in the region.[5]

In Kinnaur there are five such structures (Labrang kila, Kamru kila, Sapni kila, Morang kila and *Chitkul ka kila* 'the fort of Chitkul'), while in the rest of Himachal Pradesh outside Kinnaur, we find only a few such tower-like structures, e.g. some temples in the Kullu district, and possibly the tower-like structure which

5 To describe the antiquity of the Kamru kila, locals say that this kila has been ruled by 122 kings.

now forms part of the temple in Sarahan (Pachhad tehsil, Sirmaur district), and the village temple in the Dodra village on the border with Uttarakhand.[6]

In Malana, too, traditional houses are made using the Kath-Kuni construction style. However, there is no tower-like structure in Malana today. Malana has had a number of large-scale fires, the latest in 2008 which destroyed a large part of the village, including the Kanashi community's most revered structure, the Jamlu temple.

In some parts of present-day Uttarakhand too, there are a few old tower-like structures whose architecture and original functionality are similar to the tower-like structures of Himachal Pradesh, as described above. The Panchpura bhawan in the Doni village is built in the Koti Banal style. It is said to be about 400 years old. Similarly, the old Shani dham temple in Kharsali village (Uttarkashi district), too, has a tower-like structure. The temple in Sewa town in Uttarakhand has a tower-like structure, very similar to that of the Kamru fort in Kinnaur. Interestingly, the Sewa temple is also known as the "Kinnauri temple". Radiocarbon dating of the samples of wood used in the Panchpura bhawan puts the age of the structure to about 900 years, i.e., it was erected in the 12th century CE (Rautela & Joshi 2008: 480).

To summarize, the tower-like structures built in the Kath-Kuni/Koti Banal style are found in the earlier Tehri region in Uttarakhand (present-day Uttarkashi and Tehri Garhwal districts, southern Uttarakhand) and in parts of Himachal Pradesh. They are found either along the route between present-day Lower and Middle Kinnaur (Labrang, Chitkul, Kamru) and Malana (Sarahan, Banjar, Sainj), or between southern Uttarakhand and Lower/Middle Kinnaur. This coincides with the region in Uttarakhand where we have observed in Chapters 6 and 7 some linguistic similarities with Kinnauri and Kanashi.

2.3.2 Diwali – one month later

Diwali is one of the most important festivals, celebrated by Hindus, Jains, Sikhs and Newar Buddhists. It falls on the 15th day of the Kartik month (following the Hindu calendar system) which is also a new moon (*ama:vasja:*). This festival is celebrated on this very date in large parts of India and Nepal, in both of which it is also celebrated as a national festival.

6 Villages like Kwar and Dodra are situated along the trail from Sangla village in Kinnaur via Rupin pass to Uttrakhand.

In Lower and Middle Kinnaur and in a few villages outside Kinnaur in Himachal Pradesh a Diwali-like festival is celebrated exactly one month after the national Diwali festival. As in the national Diwali festival, in this festival, too, fire is an important part of the celebration. The name of this festival in these villages is also similar to the name of the national festival. In the Sangla region in Kinnaur this festival is called *(teg) deva:l* [(big) diwali].[7] In the Kalpa sub-tehsil in Kinnaur it is known as *deya:li*.

Outside Kinnaur in Himachal Pradesh *budhi dewaal* is celebrated one month after the national festival Diwali in the following villages: Ani and Nirmand (Kullu district), Chopal (Shimla district), Transgiri (Sirmaur district), Karsog (Mandi district) and Rajgarh (Sirmaur district). In Rajgarh this festival is called *Diyali*. B. R. Sharma (1976: 185–187) describes some striking similarities between *deva:l* as celebrated in Sangla (Kinnaur) and the way it is celebrated in Nirmand (Kullu).

In Malana Diwali (either the national festival or the Budhi diwali) does not seem to play a role in the community.

As in Himachal Pradesh, in most of Uttarakhand and Nepal Diwali is celebrated on the same date as the national festival Diwali in India. In Nepal it is called *Tihar*. Among the non-Hindus, Diwali is celebrated among Newars, who call it *Swanti*, and among the Rautes (Fortier 2019).

However, one-month late Diwali is celebrated in the following villages in Uttarakhand: in the Jaunsar Bawar region,[8] in Chakrata, K(h)alsi and Damta in the Dehradun district, Jaunpur (Tehri Garhwal district), Dharasu, Barkot and Mugsayer village and some other parts of Uttarkashi. This festival is known as *(Budhi) Diyai*.

In short, broadly speaking the one-month late Diwali is attested in the same region in Uttarakhand and Himachal Pradesh where the Koti Banal/Kath-Kuni architectural style is found.

2.3.3 Communal dancing style

In both Himachal Pradesh and in Uttarakhand a form of communal ring dancing (called *nati* in Himachal Pradesh) is an integral part of local cultures. There are some slightly different regional varieties – known, for example, as *Kinnauri nati*, *Gaddi nati*, *Sirmauri nati*, *Kullu nati*. They differ both in the attire worn and in the dancing steps. However, the nati steps of the Uttarkashi region in Uttarkhand are

7 In Kinnauri the national Diwali festival is called *gaṭo deva:l* [small diwali].

8 Jaunsar-Bawar in Uttarakhand borders Himachal Pradesh.

very similar to those of Lower/Middle Kinnaur. For example, in both Uttarkhand and Lower/Middle Kinnaur people hold each other's hands in front (of the body), while in the Kullu nati, the steps are different and hands are held in the back, and not in the front. According to our Kinnauri consultants the Uttarkashi nati steps (and attire) are almost completely identical to those of the Sangla nati. Further, in Uttarkashi the traditional men's attire (including the cap) is exactly the same as that of Lower/Middle Kinnaur, which is different from that of the traditional men's attire (including the cap) in Himachal Pradesh outside Kinnaur.

2.3.4 Summary

To summarize, the socio-cultural phenomena discussed in this section are found in Lower/Middle Kinnaur, in a restricted area in Uttarakhand (Uttarkashi) and in some villages in Himachal Pradesh which either are situated close to the Uttarkashi region in Uttarakhand, or on the route between Lower Kinnaur and Malana. Note that it this also (approximately) the region in Uttarakhand where the ST languages show linguistic similarities with Kinnauri and Kanashi as seen in Chapters 6 and 7.

2.4 Population genetics

The results of an examination of a range of genetic variables among three groups of IA population, one group of ST population (from Uttarkashi, Chamoli district, Pithauragarh district), presented by Chahal et al. (2008), show that the ST groups in Uttarakhand show similarities with the ST population of Kinnaur[9] rather than with the IA populations of Uttarakhand or with other parts of Himachal Pradesh.[10]

Papiha et al. (1984) examined five sub-groups of the population of Kinnaur: Kalpa, Sangla, Nichar, Poo and the Indo-Aryan population ("koli" in Papiha et al. 1984), where the first four are ST speech communities. Kalpa, Sangla and Nichar represent the Lower and Middle Kinnaur regions while Poo represents the Upper Kinnaur region. They examined 23 variables in these five groups to examine how homogeneous or heterogeneous the population of Kinnaur is. Interestingly their results show that the ST community in Kinnaur shows heterogeneity, where the Poo group is very different from the remaining ST groups. Among the Kalpa,

9 Unfortunately the article does not mention the exact place in Kinnaur which was included in this study.

10 Twenty population groups of Himachal Pradesh were included in this examination.

Sangla and Nichar ST groups differences are relatively minor. The genetic make-up of the Poo population is more similar to the Tibetan population. This is consistent with the fact that the language of the latter belongs to the Tibetic sub-group of ST, while the former groups speak WH varieties.

P. Sharma & Bhalla (1987) examined 23 anthropometric variables (e.g. body dimensions) among members of four communities (all endogamous): 232 Kulluvis of the Parvati valley, 198 Lahaulis, 136 Malanese and 219 Kinnauris of the Kalpa tehsil (Lower/Middle Kinnaur). In total, 785 male individuals aged 20–50 years were examined. The results of their study suggest that Kanashi speakers show more similarities to Kulluvi and Kinnauri speakers/languages than to Lahuli speakers. According to them, probably the first group of Kanashi speakers were traders from Kinnaur and that the later groups arriving in Malana were from the more nearby Kullu region.

In summary, the WH-speaking groups of (Lower/Middle) Kinnaur are genetically linked both to ST communities of Uttarakhand and to the Kanashi community, and they are genetically distinct from the Tibetic-speaking communities of Upper Kinnaur.

2.5 Geography

The distribution and the spread of the linguistic features examined in Chapters 6 and 7 as well as the socio-cultural similarities described above seem to suggest a closer historical connection between ST languages and communities in southern Uttarakhand (the older Tehri/Terai region) and the Kinnauric Western WH languages and communities of Lower and Middle Kinnaur. LaPolla (2013) suggests that the present-day ST populations of the western Himalayas have arrived in their present locations from the postulated ST homeland in China via two different routes, either from the north, along the northern flank of the Himalayas, and through Tibet, or from the east, along the southern slopes of the Himalayas through present-day Nepal and Uttarakhand. We would suggest that the WH communities probably formed the vanguard of the latter migration, i.e. that their ancestral languages were at some point spoken somewhere around the Tehri/Tarai region (present-day Tehri Garhwal district and most of Uttarkashi district). This hypothesis is in line with some local legends. For example, according to one such folk legend (Verma 2002), ST-speaking Kinnauri people originally came from Garhwal. Similarly, according to Chatak (1966),[11] the indigenous communities

11 Govind Chatak is a leading scholar of Garhwali language and literature.

of Kinnaur are historically residents of Gahrwal (part of the older Tehri/Terai region).

There are several mountain passes which link present-day Himachal Pradesh to Uttarakhand and/or southern Nepal. Some of these mountain passes (e.g. Rupin Pass, Borasu Pass, Mana Pass) have been used actively for at least the past 500 years by traders, pilgrims and shepherds. Based on original documents from that time, Wessels (1992) describes the journey which the Jesuit priest Antonio de Andrade undertook in 1624 from Agra via Haridwar through the Mana Pass to the Tibet kingdom. The description also states that this was a much-frequented path which pilgrims and traders used going to/from Tibet (Wessels 1992).

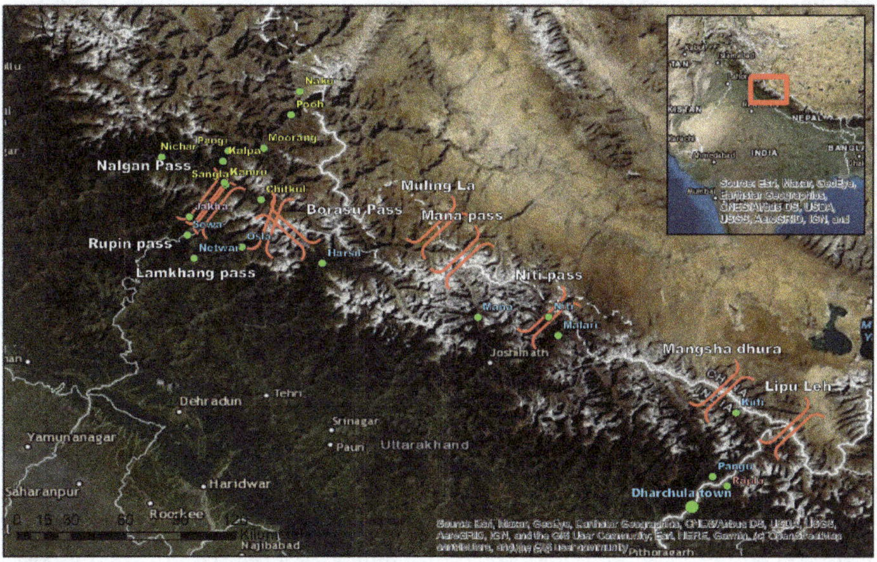

Figure 3: Mountain passes and key settlements in the region

Of these mountain passes, Borasu Pass, Lamkhang Pass, Rupin Pass and Nalgan Pass link southern Uttarakhand to the Sangla region in Kinnaur. When coming from Uttarakhand via Rupin Pass or Nalgan Pass the first region in Kinnaur is the Sangla village (before one reaches Chitkul).

The Borasu Pass connects Uttarakhand and Sangla valley, reaching Chitkul before one arrives in the Sangla village. The Lamkhang Pass, too, connects Chitkul in Kinnaur with Harsil in Uttarakhand. See Figure 3.

Present-day Kinnaur, too, has been a part of historic trade routes from the mountainous regions of Garhwal, Kashmir, Leh, Tibet to the plains of Bushahr (on the route between present-day Kinnaur and Malana). Cunningham (1854) reports that at least since the beginning of the 18th century Kinnaur formed part of a heavily used trade route with Tibet, Kashmir and Leh, where in November traders (and shepherds) from Leh/Tibet/Kinnaur used to come to Rampur (Bushahr) with wool, tea etc. Similarly traders from the plains (e.g. Bushahr) used to go to Tibet via Kinnaur.

Since the more northerly situated (Tibetic) ST languages (Jad, Navakat, Ladakhi, Spiti and Tibetan) do not exhibit the linguistic features discussed in Chapters 6 and 7, while the (WH) ST languages of Lower/Middle Kinnaur exhibit these features to varying degrees, it is plausible that the ancestors of the latter earlier resided somewhere in the Tehri region (southern Uttarakhand in India or southern Nepal), and that they entered Kinnaur, most likely, through Rupin Pass and/or Nalgan Pass.

Several of the WH communities practice, or have until recently practiced, *transhumance*, an annual migratory cycle where part of the community migrates to tend to livestock moved between higher-altitude pastures in the summer and grazing grounds in the Himalayan foothills during the winter season. Widmer (2021) notes that the Jangrami community of Kinnaur in earlier times would spend the summers in the Kullu valley, not far from Malana, the village of the Kanashi community. Even today Kanashi shepherds practice transhumance between high-altitude summer pastures and winter pastures in lower Himachal (e.g. Solan). Similarly, even today there is regular movement/contact (e.g. shepherds) between Uttarakhand and Kinnaur.

Widmer suggests that this seasonal migratory pattern may reflect an earlier stage where ST languages were spoken over a larger part of the Himalayas, including in the more fertile lowlands. Widmer (2021: 281f) explains the isolated location of Kanashi in basically the same way as his hypothesis about Central Eastern WH (Bunan, Sunnami, and Rongpo), namely as a remnant of such a postulated earlier wider distribution of WH languages, which have subsequently been pushed higher up into the Himalayas by encroaching populations speaking other languages (IA in the case of Kanashi and Western WH, and Tibetic in the case of Eastern WH). The case of Central Eastern WH is strengthened by historical evidence, placing Zhangzhung in the approximate right place and right time for it to be part of a postulated earlier wider distribution of Eastern WH languages, as well as by the unexpected presence of Eastern WH loanwords in the Western WH languages of Upper Kinnaur. This is basically the scenario posited to underlie what has been referred to in the literature as a "Burushaski distribution", where closely related linguistic varieties are scattered discontinuously over higher-altitude locations in mountainous regions, with other languages occupying the intervening lowland areas (see Urban 2020).

However, nothing similar is available to support the hypothesis about Kanashi in relation to the Western WH languages of Kinnaur. First, Malana is located at an altitude of approximately 3,000 meters, more or less the same as many of the WH-speaking villages in Lower Kinnaur. Second, there is an old methodological rule of thumb in historical linguistics, originally proposed by Sapir (1916) and elaborated by Dyen (1956), stating that the origin of past language migrations should preferably be sought in the location with greatest linguistic diversity in the present, since this requires the fewest assumed movements. In the case at hand this is Kinnaur, with its (at least) four Kinnauric Western WH languages against Malana, with only Kanashi.

However, there is some evidence to support an "intermediate" hypothesis, viz. that Common Kinnauric Western WH at some point in the past was spoken in lower Himachal Pradesh (e.g. in the Kullu Valley), and that Kanashi and the rest of Kinnauric Western WH were subsequently pushed uphill in different directions by IA-speaking groups.

Among the Kanashi speaking community some clan names seem to show their relation or connection to a village/region in lower Himachal Pradesh. This could also possibly provide clues as to where their ancestors came from and on the migratory pathway of the ancient and the "newer" Kanashi speakers. The names of the various clans of the Kanashi speakers are listed in Table 1.

Table 1: Malana clan names (Source: P. Sharma & Bhalla 1987: 338) and corresponding village names (Source: Ibbetson 1883; Maclagan 1892) (*Dhara/Sara Behr* 'upper/lower part of Malana')

Dhara Behr	Village name	*Sara Behr*	Village name
Dharaning	Dhara in Kais Kothi (Parvati and Kullu valley, Kullu district) (also mentioned by Rose 1914)	Nagwaning	Nagauni in Nagar Kothi (Kullu district) (also mentioned by Rose 1914; Tobdan 2011)
Puchaning	Pos in Kanawar Kothi (Parvati valley, Kullu district)	Tochbahru	Tosh, near Kasol (Parvati valley, Kullu district)
Shillu	Shilla in Kanawar Kothi (Parvati valley, Kullu district)		
Themaning	Thale in Baragarch Kothi (also mentioned by Rose 1914)		

Rose (1914) collected information from some Kanashi families about their ancestry. According to this information the "Nagwaning" family came originally from Nagauni in Nagar Kothi. The village god of Nagauni, too, has a kinship relationship with the Jamlu devta of Malana.

Similar stories of more recent waves of migration into Lower/Middle Kinnaur are also known from Kinnaur. In some cases the members of some clans are still known today by the names of villages in lower Himachal – possibly because they originally came from that village/area. For example, Ancestors of the *tsuarets-paŋ* in Sangla are claimed to have come from the Chhwara block in the Shimla district. Similarly, the *bungras-paŋ* claim that they originally came from the Bhangra village (Solan district) in the lower Himachal hills.

A close connection between Kanashi and Kinnauri has been noted in several older publications (Bailey 1909; Diack 1896; Hutchison & Vogel 1933; Jäschke 1865; Konow 1909; Ibbetson 1883; Maclagan 1892; Punjab district 1918; Tribe 1884; Gore 1895; Harcourt 1871). As we saw in Section 2.3, there are similarities in some socio-cultural aspects between some villages in the Kullu district and Lower/Middle Kinnaur (e.g. tower-like structures, one month "late" Diwali celebration). Howell (1918) discussed the relationship of the Kanashi people with those of Kullu, Kinnaur and Lahaul-Spiti in medieval periods, noting that:

> the whole of the Upper Parbati Valley is known to this day as Kothi Kanaur, while its inhabitants, though they have forgotten their language and are rapidly becoming assimilated to the Kulu people, are still regarded as "foreigners" and often show markedly Mongolian features. Probably they are Kanauris who gave up trade for farming generations before the road was abandoned. But they still know the road [...] from Phulga to Rampur. (Howell 1918: 70)

In the same vein, Hutchison & Vogel (1933) suggest that traders from Kinnaur, a long time ago, used to enter Parvati valley through the Pin Parvati ranges which lie to the east of this valley.

In this connection it is noteworthy that there are several villages ("kothis") in lower Himachal Pradesh outside Kinnaur which have the name Kanauri/Kanawari (all of them, however, without the adaptive marker *-(V)ŋ*) in their name. For example,

1. Kanauri village > Shimla rural tehsil, Shimla district, Himachal Pradesh
2. Kanauri village > Theog tehsil/block, Shimla district, Himachal Pradesh
3. Kanauri village > Kandaghat tehsil, Solan district, Himachal Pradesh
4. Kothi Kanawar > Bhuntar tehsil, Kullu district, Himachal Pradesh

All of these villages are in regions which, broadly speaking, lie geographically between Kinnaur and Malana. It is plausible that the shared place names may reflect the historic connection between Kinnaur and present-day Malana.

3 Summary and conclusion

The evidence – linguistic and extralinguistic – investigated so far points to a historical scenario like the following.

1. The future WH protolanguage enters the western Himalayas from the east via the southerly migration route (LaPolla 2013: 464).
2. Proto-WH spreads towards the west in several waves, with Central Eastern WH (predecessors of Zhangzhung, Bunan, Rongpo, and Sunnami) in the first wave.
3. The Kinnauric branch of Western WH enters Kinnaur, possibly via an intermediate location in lower Himachal Pradesh, and possibly also in several waves.
4. Future Kanashi speakers migrate further, to Kullu and Malana.

This sketchy account does not explain the distribution of the loan noun/adjective adaptive markers (see Chapter 6), where *-(V)ŋ* is found in Kinnauric Western WH and in some Eastern WH languages, but also in Raji-Raute and in unrelated Kusunda (isolate), while *-(V)s* appears in Kinnauric, in Jad (Bodish) and Newar (Himalayish), as well as possibly in unrelated Kurukh (Dravidian). In particular, the large number of loanwords in *-(V)ŋ* in Raji-Raute may indicate a closer genealogical relationship to WH or point to a long period in prehistory of very close contact. Further research is needed.

To conclude, if the preliminary observations made here hold true against a larger database and more in-depth studies, then one plausible conclusion could be that ancestors of common-Kinnauri-Kanashi moved to present-day Lower/Middle Kinnaur from the present-day southern Uttarakhand/Terai region in southern Nepal. Later on, some common-Kinnauri-Kanashi speakers moved towards the present-day Malana, where Kanashi continued developing – now in closer contact with geographically closer languages (ST and Kullu Pahari) and their socio-cultural traditions.

References

Bailey, Thomas Grahame. 1909. A brief grammar of the Kanauri language. *Zeitschrift der deutschen morgenländischen Gesellschaft* 63: 661–687.

Bailey, Thomas Grahame. 1911. Kanauri vocabulary in two parts: English-Kanauri and Kanauri-English. *Journal of the Royal Asiatic Society of Great Britain and Ireland* 43: Continued from 1910, p. 705, 315–364.

Borin, Lars, Anju Saxena, Shafqat Virk & Bernard Comrie. 2021. A bird's-eye view on South Asian languages through LSI: Areal or genetic relationships? *Journal of South Asian Languages and Linguistics* 7(2): 151–185.

Chahal, S. M. S., Parminder Singh, Harjit Singh & Rupinder Bansal. 2008. Genetic variation and structure of the people of Uttarakhand, central Himalayas, India. *Human Biology* 80(4): a5.

Chatak, Govind. 1966. *Madhya pahāṛībhāśāśāstrīyā addhyan* [Study of the linguistics of the Middle Pahari languages]. Delhi: Rādhākrīshṇa prakāsanā.

Cunningham, Alexander. 1854. *Ladák, physical, statistical, and historical; with notices of the surrounding countries*. London: Wm. H. Allen & Co.

Diack, Alexander Henderson. 1896. *The Kulu dialect of Hindi: some notes on its grammatical structure, with specimens of the songs and sayings current amongst the people, and a glossary*. Lahore: The Civil & Military Gazette.

Dyen, Isidore. 1956. Language distribution and migration theory. *Language* 32(4): 611–626.

Fortier, Jana. 2019. *A comparative dictionary of Raute and Rawat: Tibeto-Burman languages of the central Himalayas*. Boston: Harvard University Press.

Gore, F. St. J. 1895. *Lights and shades of hill life in the Afghan and Hindu highlands of the Punjab: A contrast*. London: John Murray.

Harcourt, Alfred Frederick Pollock. 1871. On the Himalayan valleys: Kooloo, Lahoul, and Spiti. *Journal of the Royal Geographical Society of London* 41: 245–257.

Howell, G. C. I. 1918. Some notes on ancient Kulu politics. *Journal of the Punjab Historical Society* 6(2): 69–81.

Hutchison, J. & J. Ph. Vogel. 1933. *History of the Panjab hill states*. Lahore: The Superintendent of Government Printing, Punjab.

Ibbetson, D. C. J. 1883. The races, castes and tribes of the people. In *Census of Punjab 1881*, 172–341. Calcutta: Superintendant government printing.

Jäschke, H. A. 1865. *A short practical grammar of the Tibetan language, with special reference to the spoken dialects*. Kyelang: Mission Press.

Konow, Sten. 1909. *Linguistic survey of India, Vol 3: Tibeto-Burman family. Part I: General introduction, specimens of the Tibetan dialects, the Himalayan dialects, and the North Assam group*. (This and several other volumes of the LSI were edited by Sten Konow, although published as the work of George A. Grierson). Calcutta: Government of India, Central Publication Branch.

Kumar, T. Akshya, Swtantra Kumar Singh & Arshad. 2016. An outline of vernacular architecture of Himachal Pradesh. In Anil Kumar Dubey, Kanhaiyalal Yadav & Sachin Kr Tiwari (eds.), *Studies of material remains in Indian prospective*. Delhi: Blackwell.

LaPolla, Randy J. 2013. Subgrouping in Tibeto-Burman: Can an individual-identifying standard be developed? How do we factor in the history of migrations and language contact? In Balthasar Bickel, Lenore A. Grenoble, David A. Peterson & Alan Timberlake (eds.), *Language typology and historical contingency: In honor of Johanna Nichols*, 463–474. Amsterdam: John Benjamins.

Maclagan, Sir Edward Douglas. 1892. *The Punjab and its feudatories*. Calcutta: Census of India 1891.

Martinez, Philippe Antoine. 2021. *A corpus-based account of morphosyntactic evidentiality in discourse in Chhitkul-Rākchham*. SOAS, University of London. (PhD thesis).

Papiha, S. S., S. M. S. Chahal, D. F. Roberts, K. J. R. Murty, R. L. Gupta & L. S. Sidhu. 1984. Genetic differentiation and population structure in Kinnaur district, Himachal Pradesh, India. *Human Biology* 56(2): 231–257.

Punjab district. 1918. *Punjab district gazetteer*. Lahore.
Rautela, Piyoosh & Girish Chandra Joshi. 2008. Earthquake-safe Koti Banal architecture of Uttarakhand, India. *Current Science* 95(4): 475–481.
Rose, Horace Arthur. 1914. *A glossary of the tribes and castes of the Punjab and North-West Frontier Province, Vol. III*. Lahore: Samuel T. Weston.
Sapir, Edward. 1916. *Time perspective in aboriginal American culture: A study in method*. Canada Department of Mines, Geological Survey, Memoir 90: N. 13, Anthropologial Series. Ottawa: Government Printing Bureau.
Saxena, Anju. 1995. Finite verb morphology in Kinnauri. *Cahiers de Linguistique, Asie Orientale* 24(2): 257–282.
Saxena, Anju. 2000. Diverging sources of new aspect morphology in Tibeto-Kinnauri: External motivation or internal development. In John Charles Smith & Delia Bentley (eds.), *Historical linguistics 1995. Volume 1: General issues and non-Germanic languages*, 361–375. Amsterdam: Benjamins.
Saxena, Anju. 2004. On discourse functions of the finite verb in Kinnauri narratives. In Anju Saxena (ed.), *Himalayan languages: Past and present*, 213–238. Berlin: Mouton de Gruyter.
Saxena, Anju. 2008. On *ñum* and *ɔm* in Kinnauri. In Birgitte Huber, Marianne Volkart & Paul Widmer (eds.), *Chomolangma, Demawend und Kasbek: Beiträge zur Zentralasienforschung*, 153–163. Bonn: IITBS.
Saxena, Anju. 2011. Towards empirical classification of Kinnauri varieties. In Peter K. Austin, Oliver Bond, David Nathan & Lutz Marten (eds.), *Proceedings of Conference on Language Documentation and Linguistic Theory 3*, 15–25. London: SOAS.
Saxena, Anju. 2017. Sangla Kinnauri. In Graham Thurgood & Randy J. LaPolla (eds.), *The Sino-Tibetan languages*, 2nd edn., 756–772. London: Routledge.
Saxena, Anju. 2022. *The linguistic landscape of the Indian Himalayas: Languages in Kinnaur*. Forthcoming 2022. Leiden: Brill.
Saxena, Anju & Lars Borin. 2011. Dialect classification in the Himalayas: A computational approach. In *Proceedings of Nodalida 2011*, 307–310. Riga: NEALT.
Saxena, Anju & Lars Borin. 2013. Carving Tibeto-Kanauri by its joints: Using basic vocabulary lists for genetic grouping of languages. In Lars Borin & Anju Saxena (eds.), *Approaches to measuring linguistic differences*, 175–198. Berlin: De Gruyter Mouton.
Sharma, Bansi Ram. 1976. *Kinnar lok sahitya*. Bilaspur: Lalit prakashan.
Sharma, P. & V. Bhalla. 1987. Malaneese of Malana glen: Analysis of morphometric data and ethnic relationship with some neighbouring populations of Himachal Pradesh, India. *Anthropologischer Anzeiger* 45(4): 337–350.
Tobdan. 2011. *Exploring Malana: An ancient culture hidden in the Himalayas*. New Delhi: Indus Publishing Company.
Tribe, W. H. 1884. The Kunawari language. *Panjab Notes and Queries* I: 104, 114, 127.
Turner, Ralph L. 1966. *A comparative dictionary of the Indo-Aryan languages*. Available online: http://dsal.uchicago.edu/dictionaries/soas/. Oxford: Oxford University Press.
Urban, Mathias. 2020. Mountain linguistics. *Language and Linguistics Compass* 14(9): e12393. DOI: 10.1111/lnc3.12393.
Verma, V. 2002. *Kanauras of Kinnaur: A scheduled tribe in Himachal Pradesh*. Delhi: B.R. Publishing Corp.
Wessels, C. 1992. *Early Jesuit travellers in Central Asia*. First published 1n 1924. The Hague: Nijhoff.

Widmer, Manuel. 2017. *A grammar of Bunan*. Berlin: De Gruyter Mouton.
Widmer, Manuel. 2018. Transitivity markers in West Himalayish. *Linguistics of the Tibeto-Burman Area* 41(1): 75–105.
Widmer, Manuel. 2021. Reconstructing the linguistic prehistory of the western Himalayas: Endangered minority languages as a window to the past. In Patience Epps, Danny Law & Na'ama Pat-El (eds.), *Historical linguistics and endangered languages: Exploring diversity in language change*, 263–293. London: Routledge.

Kanashi basic vocabulary

Anju Saxena, Padam Sagar, and Suari Devi

9 Kanashi basic vocabulary

Abstract: In this chapter we have compiled a (slightly extended) basic vocabulary of Kanashi, based on the IDS/LWT standard set of concepts.

Keywords: Kanashi, Kinnauri, Sino-Tibetan, vocabulary, Intercontinental Dictionary Series, Loanword Typology list

Chapter overview:

In this chapter we present a (slightly extended) basic vocabulary of Kanashi, compiled on the basis of linguistic fieldwork (conducted by Saxena and Sagar) and native-speaker knowledge of Kanashi (Devi).

The backbone of the vocabulary presented in this chapter is the Kanashi IDS/LWT list presented in Section A below. It has been compiled on the basis of the 1,310 items of the original Intercontinental Dictionary Series (IDS) concept list (Borin et al. 2013) plus the 150 items added to it in the Loanword Typology (LWT) project, for a total of 1,460 concepts (Haspelmath & Tadmor 2009). Further, we have also drawn on the additions made in the previously compiled IDS/LWT list for Kinnauri (Saxena 2022). In such added entries the minor part of their concept ID (the part after the point) begins with "999", e.g. "S08.99935 the onion". There are 29 such additions in the Kanashi list. Some IDS/LWT items have been left out from the list, as there were no equivalents in Kanashi or in our data. The resulting list as given in Appendix A contains 1,003 items (concepts), where often more than one Kanashi equivalent is provided. The list also includes loanwords.

For ease of comparison we have kept the original IDS/LWT glosses unchanged in all cases, and Kanashi senses which do not fit the IDS/LWT meaning completely are given more exact glosses in the Kanashi column. Sometimes there will be multiple (separately glossed) items in the Kanashi column when our Kanashi data exhibit differentiation of meaning or form within an IDS/LWT item. Pronunciation or form variants are separated by commas, and formally distinct items are separated by semicolons. Glosses and remarks belong with their enclosing "semicolon grouping".

For reference, the corresponding items from the Kinnauri IDS/LWT list (*Kinnauri basic vocabulary* by Anju Saxena and Santosh Negi, in Saxena 2022) are

https://doi.org/10.1515/9783110703245-009

given in the last column. In the Kinnauri column, "(B)", "(R)" and "(S)" indicate geographical varieties (the speech of Brua, Ropa and Sangla, respectively).

Since the IDS/LWT list is thematically organized and thus not easily searchable for items based on their form, in the other two appendices we also offer word lists alphabetically ordered by Kanashi (Appendix B) and English (Appendix C) headwords. In addition to cross-referencing the Kanashi IDS/LWT list, these word lists contain some 300 additional entries extracted from our data. This set does not include numerals, which are provided in a separate listing in Appendix A of Chapter 5.

References

Borin, Lars, Anju Saxena & Bernard Comrie. 2013. The Intercontinental Dictionary Series: A rich and principled database for language comparison. In Lars Borin & Anju Saxena (eds.), *Approaches to measuring linguistic differences*, 285–302. Berlin: De Gruyter Mouton.

Haspelmath, Martin & Uri Tadmor. 2009. The Loanword Typology project and the World Loanword Database. In Martin Haspelmath & Uri Tadmor (eds.), *Loanwords in the world's languages: A comparative handbook*, 1–34. Berlin: Mouton de Gruyter.

Saxena, Anju. 2022. *The linguistic landscape of the Indian Himalayas: Languages in Kinnaur.* Forthcoming 2022. Leiden: Brill.

A Kanashi IDS/LWT list

IDS	Gloss	Kanashi (xns)	Kinnauri (kfk)
S01.100	the world	*dart^{h}i* 'earth'; *deʃaŋ* 'country; village; world'; *dunija:*; *prit^{h}ʋi* 'earth; world'; *sansa:r*	*dunija:*; *sansa:r*, *sensa:r*
S01.212	the soil	*ʥi:mi:*; *ʤami:n*; *ka:m* 'soil; clay'	*maʈiŋ*
S01.213	the dust	*du:l*	*purʧuʈiŋ*
S01.214	the mud	*ʦikra*, *ʦikar*	*ʦikar*; *la:s*
S01.215	the sand	*bali*; *re:t*, *re:tiŋ*	*baliŋ*
S01.220	the mountain or hill	*ɖog*; *ka:ʈ^{h}iŋ*, *ka:ʈ^{h}i* 'mountain; mountain top; mountain pass'; *paha:ɽ* 'cliff; hill'; *ʧaŋ*	*ra:ŋ*; *ɖok^{h}aŋ* 'tall, big mountain'; *ʈ^{h}oll* 'small mountain'
S01.222	the cliff or precipice	*ɖag*, *ɖak^{h}* 'cliff'; *paha:ɽ* 'cliff; hill'	*da:r*; *k^{h}oro ɖok^{h}aŋ*
S01.230	the plain	*padras*, *padre*, *padraŋ*	*so:maŋ*
S01.240	the valley	*ga:ʈi*	*ga:ʈi*; *k^{h}ago*; *k^{h}unaŋ*
S01.250	the island	*ʈa:pu*	*ʈa:pu*
S01.260	the mainland	*so:* 'mainland; earth'	—
S01.270	the shore	*kina:ra*; *neɖaŋ*	*gara:ʈiŋ*
S01.280	the cave	*a:g*; *gup^{h}a*	*ag*
S01.310	the water	*ti(:)*	*ti*
S01.320	the sea	*samudra*, *samudraŋ* 'sea; ocean'	*somodraŋ* 'sea, ocean, river'
S01.322	calm	*ʃa:nt*	*sululuʧis*
S01.323	rough(2)	*kakʧos*	*bo:la:*

IDS	Gloss	Kanashi (xns)	Kinnauri (kfk)
S01.324	the foam	*ʃep*	*ʃub*
S01.329	the ocean	*najiŋ* 'river; ocean'; *samudra*, *samudraŋ* 'sea; ocean'	*somodraŋ* 'sea, ocean, river'
S01.330	the lake	*ɖibɽiŋ* 'pond; well'; *ʤil* 'lake; lagoon'; *tala:ʋ*	*soraŋ* 'natural pond'
S01.341	the lagoon	*ʤil* 'lake; lagoon'	–
S01.350	the wave	*lari*	*tsʰaʈeraŋ*
S01.360	the river or stream	*ʤairu* 'stream'; *ga:ɽiŋ* 'river'; *najiŋ* 'river; ocean'; *na:laŋ*, *na:la* 'stream; riverlet'	*ga:raŋ* 'river'; *na:laŋ* 'stream'; *somodraŋ* 'sea, ocean, river'
S01.370	the spring or well	*bai*; *ɖibɽiŋ* 'pond; well'; *ku:ɽiŋ*; *tsʰol* 'spring; waterfall'	*kuaŋ*, *koaŋ* 'well'
S01.390	the waterfall	*tsʰol* 'spring; waterfall'	*ʧʰodaŋ*
S01.410	the woods or forest	*baŋ*, *baɳaŋ*, *baɽaŋ*; *ʤad*; *ʤaŋgal* 'forest; barren land'	*boniŋ*; *baunaŋ*; *ʣaŋgal*
S01.430	the wood	*ʃiŋ* 'wood; firewood'; *tokta* 'wood used for making tables'	*ʃiŋ*
S01.440	the stone or rock	*gaʈʈi* 'pebble'; *kaŋ*; *paʈ* 'threshing stone'; *pa:n* 'threshing stone; threshing-floor'; *rudiŋ* 'rock'; *tog* 'stone (small, put under large rocks so that they don't tumble down the hill)'	*rag*; *pan* 'stone, slate'; *kʰaʈlaŋ* 'round red stones found in rivers'; *ʃaŋ* 'pebble'
S01.450	the earthquake	*bukamp*; *ʣaʣari*; *gururuga*	*bunʧilaŋ*
S01.510	the sky	*sargaŋ*	*sorgaŋ*
S01.520	the sun	*duppe*; *ʤa:ɽe*; *suraʤ*	*june*; *suraʤ*
S01.530	the moon	*ʤuʃʈʰa*, *ʤojʃʈʰaŋ*; *ʧand*	*golsaŋ*; *ʧand*
S01.540	the star	*kar*	*(s)kar*
S01.550	the lightning	*biʤeɽi* 'electricity; lightning; flashlight'	*biʣul* 'lightning (bolt)'
S01.560	the thunder	*guruɽuk*	*gurgur*
S01.570	the bolt of lightning	*ʧamak*	*biʣul* 'lightning (bolt)'
S01.580	the storm	*bijanna*	*ɖaro* 'rainstorm'
S01.590	the rainbow	*kʰuigopigol*; *pʰigolpigol*	*tila:nmets*
S01.610	the light	*tsʰag*	*tsʰatk*
S01.620	the darkness	*jaras*	*ãjares* (S), *aɲa:res* (B)
S01.630	the shade or shadow	*ʃilaŋ*	*la:*; *ʃilaŋ*; *ʧʰa:jaŋ*
S01.640	the dew	*oʃaŋ*; *pala* 'dew, frozen'	*oʃaŋ*
S01.720	the wind	*lipur* 'wind; air'	*la:n* 'air, wind'
S01.730	the cloud	*ʣuʃaŋ*	*ʣu*; *ʣuʃa* (R)
S01.740	the fog	*dumme*	*dumaŋ* 'fog; smoke'; *duma:saŋ*, *duma:so*
S01.750	the rain	*ʤab*; *nakʤab* 'drizzle'	*goeniŋ*; *ʧʰarʋa* (R)
S01.760	the snow	*pom*	*pom*; *titʰokolts* 'watery snow'
S01.770	the ice	*ʃaɳaŋ*	*ʈʰanaŋ*
S01.780	the weather	*mosam*; *sargã(ŋ)*; *tsarga:m*	*mosam*
S01.810	the fire	*mi:*	*me:*
S01.820	the flame	*g(ʰ)ana*	*melab*; *ləpəŋ*
S01.830	the smoke	*dumaŋ*	*dumaŋ* 'fog; smoke'
S01.840	the ash	*pod* 'ash; dandruff'	*bospa*
S01.841	the embers	*kojlag*	*ʈʰo*; *ʃuʈʰol*
S01.851	to burn(1)	*hiram ʃenam*	*pogmu* [TR]; *legmu* [TR]
S01.852	to burn(2)	*hiram*	*barmu* [INTR]; *bogmu* 'get burned'; *legʧimu* 'get burned'
S01.860	to light	*(mi:) sutam*; *mi: ʃaɳam*; *tsʰag baɽja:m*	*ʧonnu* [TR]; *parmu* [TR] 'set on fire'
S01.861	to extinguish	*mi: piɲam*	*pjugmu*
S01.870	the match	*tuɽi*	*meʃiŋ*, *me:ʃiŋ*
S01.880	the firewood	*ʃiŋ* 'wood; firewood'	*parʃiŋ*; *saŋ* 'a wood-type with natural oil, used as kindling'

IDS	Gloss	Kanashi (xns)	Kinnauri (kfk)
S01.890	the charcoal	*koile*; *tarkol*; *ʧopʈu*	*(ʃiŋ)ʈʰo*
S02.100	the person	*lok*, *lokas* 'person; non-Kanashi person'; *munuk* 'person; human'	*manuʃ*; *mi*
S02.210	the man	*madras*; *maɽʃaŋ*; *mi*; *munuk*	*morʧʰaŋ*; *mi*
S02.220	the woman	*beʈaɽi*, *bekaɽi*	*tsʰetses* 'adult woman (usually married)'; *tsʰesmi* 'woman, married; wife'
S02.250	the boy	*ʧʰak*, *ʧʰakts* 'boy; child'; *ʧʰaŋ* 'boy; child'; *ʧʰokra*	*ʧʰaŋ* 'boy (newborn to appr. 16–18 years of age); son (one's own or family's child)'; *kuʈu*; *tunaː*; *ɖekʰraːts*; *ʧʰak* 'boy, son'
S02.251	the young man	*ʥavaːn ʧʰakts*	*ɖekʰraːts* 'boy; young man appr. 18–30 years of age, usually unmarried'
S02.260	the girl	*ʧime(ts)*	*ʧimed* 'girl; daughter'; *tsʰetsats* 'girl, young woman (from birth to marrying age), daughter'; *ɖekʰorits* 'young girl (before she reaches marrying age)'
S02.261	the young woman	*ʤavaːn ʧimets*	*ɖekʰor*
S02.270	the child(1)	*ʧara* 'child; baby'; *ʧʰakts* 'boy; child''; *ʧʰaŋ* 'boy; child'; *ʧʰo* 'child; son'	–
S02.280	the baby	*alaːts*; *ʧara* 'child; baby'	*ãjanaŋts*; *ʥormets*
S02.310	the husband	*biɳis*, *biniʃ*	*ʧʰoŋ(mi)*; *daːts*
S02.320	the wife	*laɽi*; *ʧʰetsaŋ*, *ʧʰets*	*gone*; *tsʰesmi* 'wife; married woman'; *lari* 'bride, wife, daughter-in-law'; *sok* 'co-wife; sister-in-law'; *gunjale* 'bride'
S02.330	to marry	*bijaŋ ʃaɳam*	*ranekaŋ lannu*; *ʃadi lannu*; *bajaŋ lannu*
S02.340	the wedding	*bijaŋ*	*bajaŋ*; *ranekaŋ*; *ʃadi*
S02.341	the divorce	*burʃuk*; *uʃim*	–
S02.350	the father	*baː* 'father; uncle'	*bon*; *boa*, *boba* 'father; paternal uncle'; *bapu* 'father; father's younger brother'
S02.360	the mother	*jaː*	*ama*; *mən*; *mata*
S02.370	the parents	*jaːba*; *jaːʃbaː*	*mənbon*; *amaboa*
S02.380	the married man	*ʧʰets roʈas*	*ranekaŋ lants mi*
S02.390	the married woman	*basets beʈaɽi*, *basets bekaɽi*	*tsʰesmi* 'married woman, wife'; *tsʰetses* 'woman, adult (usually married)'; *ranekaŋ lants tsʰesmi*
S02.410	the son	*beʈa*; *ʃoru*; *ʧʰo*, *ʧʰok* 'child; son'	*ʧʰak*; *kuʈu*; *ʧʰaŋ(ts)* 'boy; son of the speaker or someone belonging to the speakers family'; *beʈa*
S02.420	the daughter	*ʧime*	*ʧimed* 'girl, daughter'; *beʈi*
S02.440	the brother	*bau*	*bai*; *juŋʥ*
S02.444	the older brother	*teg bau*	*ate*
S02.445	the younger brother	*pʰak bau*; *pʰakuʧ bats*	*beits* 'woman's younger brother'; *baja(ts)* 'man's younger brother'
S02.450	the sister	*daiju*; *riŋʥ*	*riŋʥ*; *ben* (B); *baits* (S)
S02.454	the older sister	*teg riŋʥ*	*(teg) dau(ts)*; *tege*; *teg riŋʥ*; *aputs (Ribba)*
S02.455	the younger sister	*hoʧi ba(h)u*; *pʰak(uʧ) riŋʥ*	*(tsʰetsats) beits* (B); *baja(ts)* (S)
S02.456	the sibling	*boi*; *riŋʥjuŋʥ*	*juŋriŋ*
S02.4562	the younger sibling	*boits*	*bai(ts)* (S); *beits* (B)
S02.458	the twins	*doɽag* 'twin; pair'	*ʥoːla*
S02.460	the grandfather	*daddu* 'paternal grandfather'; *daːda* 'paternal grandfather'; *naːnaː* 'maternal grandfather'	*tete*
S02.461	the old man	*buɽas*	*ruʥa(ts)* 'old and weak man'

IDS	Gloss	Kanashi (xns)	Kinnauri (kfk)
S02.470	the grandmother	*da:di* 'paternal grandmother'; *na:ni:* 'maternal grandmother'	*api*; *mapo api* 'maternal grandmother'
S02.471	the old woman	*buɽits*	*jaŋdze(ts)* 'old (human female, animate female)'
S02.4711	the grandparents	*da:dada:di* 'paternal grandparents'; *da:duse da:di* 'paternal grandparents'; *na:na:na:ni:* 'maternal grandparents'	*teteapi*
S02.5000	the grandchild	*pa:ts*	*(s)pa:ts*; *rimpa:ts* 'daughter's child'; *kimpa:ts* 'son's child'
S02.510	the uncle	*ba:* 'father; uncle'	—
S02.511	the mother§s brother	*ma:ma:* 'mother's brother; father-in-law'	*əpa* 'mother's brother; father-in-law'; *muma:*, *ma:ma:* 'mother's brother; father-in-law'
S02.512	the father§s brother	*ba: dʒeʈʰa* 'father's older brother'; *ba: pʰakutʃ* 'father's younger brother'	*bapu* 'father, father's brother'; *boa* 'father, father's brother'; *boba* 'father, father's brother'; *teg bua* 'father's older brother'
S02.521	the mother§s sister	*ja:dʒʈʰi*; *massi*	*amats*; *amri*
S02.522	the father§s sister	*bube* 'father's sister; mother-in-law'	*na:ne* 'aunt (mother's brother's wife; father's sister)'
S02.530	the nephew	*bʰaɳe*, *ba:ɳes* 'nephew; brother's son'	*bandʒo* 'man's sister's son'; *tʃʰaŋ(ts)* 'woman's sister's son'; *(ɖekʰra:ts)* *banuts* 'woman's brother's son'
S02.540	the niece	*ba:ɳek*	*(tsʰetsats) banuts* 'woman's brother's daughter'; *tʃimets* 'woman's sister's daughter'
S02.5410	the sibling§s child	*bau batʃa* 'brother's child'	*juŋriɳu tʃʰaŋ* 'sibling's son'
S02.610	the father-in-law (of a man)	*ma:ma:* 'mother's brother; father-in-law'; *ʃoras*, *ʃores*	*ʃores*; *əpa*; *muma:*, *ma:ma:* 'mother's brother; father-in-law'
S02.611	the father-in-law (of a woman)	*ma:ma:* 'mother's brother; father-in-law'; *ʃoras*, *ʃores*	*ʃores*; *əpa*; *muma:*, *ma:ma:* 'mother's brother; father-in-law'
S02.620	the mother-in-law (of a man)	*bube* 'father's sister; mother-in-law'; *juŋme*; *sauri*; *sa:su*	*jumed* 'mother-in-law; mother's brother's wife'
S02.621	the mother-in-law (of a woman)	*bube* 'father's sister; mother-in-law'; *juŋme*; *sauri*; *sa:su*	*jumed* 'mother-in-law; mother's brother's wife'
S02.6220	the parents-in-law	*sa:susa:uri:*	*jumedəpa*
S02.630	the son-in-law (of a man)	*dʒamais* 'son-in-law'	*tʃʰad*
S02.631	the son-in-law (of a woman)	*dʒamais* 'son-in-law'	*tʃʰad*
S02.640	the daughter-in-law (of a man)	*kuɽmani* 'daughter-in-law'; *tem* 'daughter-in-law; bride'; *ʋahu* 'daughter-in-law'	*tem*
S02.641	the daughter-in-law (of a woman)	*kuɽmani* 'daughter-in-law'; *tem* 'daughter-in-law; bride'; *ʋahu* 'daughter-in-law'	*tem*
S02.710	the stepfather	*ba: kan*	*bibon*; *biboba*
S02.720	the stepmother	*ja: kani*	*biama*; *bimən*
S02.730	the stepson	*raunɖa*	*soku tʃʰaŋ*
S02.740	the stepdaughter	*raunɖi*	*soku tʃimed*
S02.750	the orphan	*ana:tʰ*; *ʃokkuraŋ*, *ʃokkura*	*ʃokraŋ*
S02.760	the widow	*ranɖi*	*rãɖole*; *rantsʰesmi*
S02.770	the widower	*nuka tʃʰets ʃi:k*	*rãɖoles* 'widower (negative connotation)'
S02.810	the relatives	*na:ʈa*	*na:tarista*; *iʃpənek*; *peradʒora* 'closely related relatives'
S02.820	the family	*ʈabar*	*ʈobor* 'family (members)'; *pera(ŋ)* 'kinsman, clansman'
S02.910	I	*gu* [1SG]	*gə*
S02.920	you (singular)	*ka* [2SG]	*ki* [H]; *ka* [NH]

IDS	Gloss	Kanashi (xns)	Kinnauri (kfk)
S02.930	he/she/it	*du* [3SG.DIST]; *nu* [3SG.PROX]	*do* [3SG.DIST.NVIS]; *no* [3SG.DIST.VIS]; *ʤo* [3SG.PROX]; *an* [3SG.REFL]
S02.941	we (inclusive)	*ette* [1PLI]	*kiʃa* [1PLI]; *kiʃaŋ* [1DU]
S02.942	we (exclusive)	*ni* [1PLE]	*niŋo* [1PLE]; *kiʃaŋ* [1DU]
S02.950	you (plural)	*ki* [2PL]	*kino* [H]; *kano* [NH]; *kanego:* [NH]; *kiʃi, kisi* [2DU.H]; *kaniʃ* [2DU.NH]
S02.960	they	*duga:* [3PL.DIST]; *nuga:* [3PL.PROX]	*dogo:* [3PL.DIST.NVIS]; *nogo:* [3PL.DIST.VIS]; *ʤogo:* [3PL.PROX]; *anego:* [3PL.REFL]
S03.110	the animal	*ʤa:nʋar*; *ʥiu* 'living being; animal'	*ʤa:nʋar*, *ʤanvar*; *semʧen*
S03.130	female(2)	*mĩʧ*	*manʈ-*
S03.150	the livestock	*paʃu*	*noro*
S03.160	the pasture	*tʰaʧaŋ* 'pasture in lower regions'	*pabaŋ* 'pasture in the upper hills'; *panaŋ* 'pasture close to the village'
S03.180	the herdsman	*pʰoal*	*pa:les*
S03.200	the cattle	*laŋ kʰaga:*; *laŋokʰa: kʰas*	*norʧag*; *ʥed/ʥe:* 'sheep, goat [SG/PL]'
S03.210	the bull	*ra:d* 'bull; ox'	*tida:mes (noncastrated)*; *da:mes (castrated)*; *ʥo* 'mountain ox'
S03.220	the ox	*pag*; *ra:d* 'bull; ox'	—
S03.230	the cow	*hu(:)ʤ*; *laŋ*	*gau*; *laŋ*; *ʥomo* 'mountain cow'
S03.240	the calf	*ra:*; *ʃakras* 'calf [M]'; *ʃikran* 'calf [F]'	*rats*; *manʈrats* [F]; *ʃa:kurts* [F]; *ʃa:kuri:* [F]; *ʃa:kur* [M]
S03.250	the sheep	*kʰas* 'sheep; lamb'	*ʥed*
S03.260	the ram	*butkar*	*kar (castrated)*; *hules (non-castrated)*
S03.290	the lamb	*kʰas* 'sheep; lamb'; *kʰa:ts*	*kʰa:ts*; *ʃakras* [M]
S03.350	the pig	*su:ru*, *su:r* 'pig; swine'	*su:res* [M]; *su:ronig* [F]; *mansu:res* [F]
S03.360	the goat	*bakari* 'goat [F]'; *bakras*, *bakar*	*bəkʰaraŋ*
S03.380	the kid	*ma:ts* 'kid (of goat)'	*ma:ts*
S03.410	the horse	*goɽa* 'horse; stallion'; *raŋ*, *ra:ŋ*	*raŋ*
S03.420	the stallion	*goɽa* 'horse; stallion'	*(s)kjoraŋ*; *sʋa:rjarja raŋ* 'gelding'; *puʈkjakja raŋ* 'gelding'
S03.440	the mare	*goɽi*	*manʈraŋ*
S03.460	the donkey	*gadda*; *kaʧʰar* 'mule'	*pʰots*
S03.520	the cock/rooster	*kukaɽaŋ*; *murga:*	*(s)kjokukəri*
S03.540	the hen	*murgi:*	*manʈkukəri*
S03.550	the chicken	*kukaɽaŋ*; *kukuɽoka ʧʰaŋ*, *kukuɽoka ʧʰã*; *ʧikan*	*kukəri*; *ʧikan*
S03.570	the duck	*batak*	*tiares (domesticated)*
S03.580	the nest	*ʈukor*; *ʋa:*	*ʋa:(ts)*
S03.581	the bird	*gunɖu (ʧaɽig)* 'bird (a small species with a small crown on its head)'; *ʧaɽig*	*pja(ts)*
S03.582	the seagull	*tiuadz ʤju*	—
S03.583	the heron	*bagula*	—
S03.584	the eagle	*gallas* 'eagle; vulture'; *ilna:* 'eagle; vulture'	*la:npja*
S03.585	the hawk	*ʋa:ʥ*	*daŋʃu:res* 'hawk, falcon'
S03.586	the vulture	*gallas* 'eagle; vulture'; *ilna:* 'eagle; vulture'	*golɖes*
S03.591	the bat	*ʧamga:daɽ*	*turpjats*
S03.592	the parrot	*totta*	*tota:*
S03.593	the crow	*ka:g*	*ka:g*; *kaur*
S03.594	the dove	*gugut* 'pigeon'	*gugti:ts*
S03.596	the owl	*uɽug*	*ɖuɖu*
S03.610	the dog	*kui*; *kutta*; *kutti* 'dog, female'; *kuʧʧʰa*	*kui* [M/F]
S03.614	the rabbit	*kʰargoʃ* 'rabbit; hare'	*kʰargoʃ* 'rabbit; hare'
S03.620	the cat	*bura:ɽa* 'cat [M]'; *bura:ɽi* 'cat [F]'; *pũĩ*	*bila:ri*; *piʃi*

IDS	Gloss	Kanashi (xns)	Kinnauri (kfk)
S03.630	the mouse or rat	*muʃt̪ur* 'rat (in fields)'; *pʰuts* 'mouse; rat (in house)'	*pju(ts)* 'house rat'; *sakpju* 'outdoor rat'
S03.650	the fish	*matsis*; *matʃʰli*	*matʃʰes*, *matʃʰli*
S03.720	the lion	*tʰar*	*siŋ*
S03.730	the bear	*ho(ː)m*	*hom*; *rikʰaː* [M]; *bonjots*; *rikʰonig* [F]
S03.740	the fox	*ʃaːɽug*	*ʃalits*
S03.750	the deer	*hiran*	*pʰo*; *pʰomaːts* 'young deer'; *bena* '(musk) deer'
S03.760	the monkey	*bandraŋ*	*bandres*
S03.770	the elephant	*hattʰi*	*hatʰi*
S03.780	the camel	*ũʈ*	*ũʈ*
S03.810	the insect	*tʃʰatʃ kaʈãõ* 'insect; mosquito'	*tsʰatig*; *hoŋ*
S03.811	the head louse	*rig* 'head louse; body louse'	*ʃəmants* 'young louse (hair, body)'
S03.8112	the body louse	*rig* 'head louse; body louse'	*(gas)rig*
S03.812	the nit	*rikts*	*rukts*
S03.813	the flea	*jaŋ* 'flea; fly; bee; mosquito'; *puŋ*	—
S03.815	the scorpion	*bitʃu*	*sokʰo*
S03.817	the ant	*biːg*	*krog*
S03.818	the spider	*dzaːrs*, *dzaːts*; *ʈõʈidaːr*	*botokts*
S03.819	the spider web	*dzaɽi*	*botoktsu dʒaliŋ*; *botoktsu ʋaː*
S03.820	the bee	*jaŋ* 'flea; fly; bee; mosquito'; *raiŋ* 'bee (wild, large in size, and their honey is considered bad by the locals and not consumed by them)'; *ʋajaŋ*	*ʋasjaŋ*
S03.821	the beeswax	*muːm*; *pʰaluŋ*	*sitʰaŋ*
S03.822	the beehive	*ɖoɖre*; *muɖaːm*; *raitomʋe*; *tombe*	*jaŋɖoraŋ*; *jaŋkoʈ*
S03.830	the fly	*jaŋ* 'flea; fly; bee; mosquito'	*(kʰə)jaŋ*
S03.831	the sandfly or midge or gnat	*bigalits* 'midge'	*ɖãs* 'gnat'
S03.832	the mosquito	*jaŋ* 'flea; fly; bee; mosquito'; *tʃʰatʃ kaʈãõ* 'insect; mosquito'	*tsʰatig*
S03.840	the worm	*rinig* 'worm; snake'	*hoŋ*; *lashoŋ* 'mud worm'
S03.850	the snake	*naːges* 'cobra snake'; *rinig* 'worm; snake'; *sap*	*sapes*; *naːges* 'mythical snake'
S03.8630	the hare	*kʰargoʃ* 'rabbit; hare'	*kʰargoʃ* 'rabbit; hare'
S03.910	the firefly	*dʒugnu*; *mijaŋ*	*mehoŋ*
S03.9170	the buffalo	*baĩs*; *meʃi*	*bẽːs*
S03.920	the butterfly	*boɽits*	*ʃupjats*
S03.930	the grasshopper	*ʈiʈaɽa*	*bjonts*
S03.940	the snail	*huŋg*; *pʰil* 'snail without shell'; *pʰili gaɽe* 'snail with shell'	*goʈaŋhoŋ* 'snail with shell'; *tiʃam* 'snail without a shell'
S03.950	the frog	*meɖkas*	*tiʃpolokts*
S03.960	the lizard	*bɽitits*; *tʃʰabaːɽ*	*tsʰemar*
S03.970	the crocodile or alligator	*magarmatʃʰ*	*magarmatʃʰ*
S03.980	the turtle	*katʃʰua*	*ketʃʰua*
S03.99942	the tiger	*ʃer* 'tiger; leopard'	—
S04.110	the body	*ɖehi*	*ɖejaŋ*
S04.120	the skin or hide	*bod* 'skin (of animal); peel (of vegetable or fruit)'; *kʰolɖu*; *ʃa*	*ponaŋ* 'skin, hide, leather (of cows, oxen, buffaloes etc.)'; *kʰul* 'skin, hide (of sheep, goats, birds)'
S04.140	the hair	*kraː* 'head hair; body hair'	*kraː* 'head hair, pubic hair'
S04.144	the body hair	*kraː* 'head hair; body hair'	*(s)puː*
S04.146	the dandruff	*pod* 'ash; dandruff'	*kʰod*
S04.150	the blood	*kʰui*	*polaːts*; *ʃui*
S04.151	the vein or artery	*sirãõ*	*siːraŋ*
S04.160	the bone	*haɖɖaŋ*	*haraŋ*
S04.162	the rib	*praʃa*	*ribharaŋ* 'ribs, ribcage'; *riboː* 'ribs, ribcage'
S04.170	the horn	*ruːd*; *ʃiːŋ*	*ʃiːŋ*; *rud*

IDS	Gloss	Kanashi (xns)	Kinnauri (kfk)
S04.180	the tail	*puʧʰ*, *puʧʰaŋ*; *pʰainʤa*; *ʈʰuʈʰ(a)re*, *ʈʰuʈre*	*pəʧniŋ*
S04.190	the back	*ʧeka*	*piʃʈiŋ*
S04.200	the head	*bal*	*bal*; *ʃiraŋ*
S04.201	the temples	*piŋ* 'cheek'	—
S04.203	the brain	*kra:ɳ* 'brain (as food)'	*dima:g*
S04.204	the face	*ʃakal*; *toŋ*	*mukʰaŋ* 'mouth, face'; *(s)to*
S04.205	the forehead	*mattʰa*	*pʰja:konʈaŋ*; *pʰja:*
S04.207	the jaw	*ʧʰamga* 'chin; jaw'	*ʦo:nniŋ*
S04.209	the chin	*ʧʰamga* 'chin; jaw'	*ʧʰotkaŋ*, *ʧʰopkaŋ*
S04.210	the eye	*mig*	*mig*
S04.220	the ear	*ro:ɖ*	*ka:naŋ*
S04.221	the earlobe	*kri*	*(ka:naŋ)poʦ*
S04.230	the nose	*ta*; *takʰuʦ*	*takuʦ* 'nose; beak'
S04.231	the nostril	*kʰaʈaga:*; *taʋaʣa:*	*takʃuliŋ*
S04.240	the mouth	*kʰa(:)kaŋ*	*kʰakaŋ*; *kʰak*; *mukʰaŋ* 'mouth; face'
S04.241	the beak	*ʧuʤaŋ*	*ʃonaŋ*
S04.250	the lip	*tʰotoro*, *tʰotʰra*	*tunaŋ*
S04.260	the tongue	*le*	*le*
S04.270	the tooth	*ga:r*	*gar*
S04.272	the molar tooth	*ʤa:mgar*	*kongar*
S04.280	the neck	*golaŋ* 'neck; throat'; *kʰili*	*golaŋ*; *kakʦ*
S04.281	the nape of the neck	*kunaga*	*(ka:kʦ) mugro*
S04.290	the throat	*golaŋ* 'neck; throat'	*golaŋ* 'throat; neck'; *ʃaŋ* 'throat; narrow passage inside throat'; *ʈiŋ* 'windpipe, trachea'
S04.300	the shoulder	*pʰar*	*bid*; *raŋ* 'external part of shoulder'
S04.310	the arm	*guɖ* 'arm; hand'; *naʈa*	*gud* 'arm; hand'; *həst* 'arm; hand'; *kʰjuʦ* 'part of the arm between wrist and elbow'; *pʰarʦ* 'part of the arm from elbow to shoulder'
S04.312	the armpit	*keskʰaʈa*	*kjasaŋ*, *kjas*
S04.320	the elbow	*guska*	*krũ:ʦ*
S04.321	the wrist	*kʰurke*	—
S04.330	the hand	*guɖ* 'arm; hand'	*gud* 'arm; hand'; *həst* 'arm; hand'
S04.331	the palm of the hand	*talaŋ* 'palm of the hand; footsole'	*(həs)talaŋ*; *potilaŋ*; *ʃe(ʦ)* 'palm, hollowed palm to receive water/alchohol'
S04.340	the finger	*goʈʰi*; *káni góʈʰɪʦ*; *pra:d*, *pra:daŋ* 'finger; toe'	*praʦ* 'finger; toe'
S04.342	the thumb	*ʤeʃʈu(k) prá:d*	*bonpraʦ*
S04.344	the fingernail	*ʧi:nɖ* 'fingernail; toenail'	*(pratsu) ʧin* 'fingernail; toenail'
S04.350	the leg	*baole* 'leg; foot'; *goɖiŋ* 'leg; foot'; *ʈa:ŋg* 'leg; foot'; *ʈʰullaŋ*, *ʈʰulla* 'leg; foot'	*peraŋ*; *latʰaŋ*; *gompa*; *baŋ* 'leg; foot'
S04.351	the thigh	*baʣug*	*lum* 'thigh; hip'
S04.352	the calf of the leg	*pille*	*piliŋ(ʦ)*
S04.360	the knee	*ʧi:g*	*pəʃbaŋ*
S04.370	the foot	*baole* 'leg; foot'; *goɖiŋ* 'leg; foot'; *ʈa:ŋg* 'leg; foot'; *ʈʰullaŋ*, *ʈʰulla* 'leg; foot'	*baŋ* 'leg; foot'
S04.371	the ankle	*goʈa*	*pa:ʈ*
S04.372	the heel	*pʰine* 'heel; sole of foot'	*ʈʰoŋgol*
S04.374	the footprint	*kʰori*; *pʰine* 'heel; footsole'; *talaŋ* 'palm of the hand; footsole'	*baŋmod*
S04.380	the toe	*goɖinaʦ pra:d*; *pra:d*, *pra:daŋ* 'finger; toe'	*baŋpraʦ*
S04.392	the wing	*pakʰiŋ* 'wing; feather'	*pakʰaŋ* 'wing; feather'
S04.400	the chest	*hik* 'breast; chest'; *ʦʰa:ti*	*(s)ʈug* 'breast; chest'; *nunu:* 'breast; chest'

IDS	Gloss	Kanashi (xns)	Kinnauri (kfk)
S04.410	the breast	*hik* 'breast; chest'; *ma:mug*	*(s)ṭug* 'breast; chest'; *nunu:* 'breast; chest'
S04.412	the nipple or teat	*manu*	*nuni(bal)*
S04.420	the udder	*uʋaŋ*	*eniŋ*
S04.430	the navel	*naṛukʰ*	*naiŋts*
S04.4310	the belly	*poṭaŋ* 'stomach; belly'; *ʃon*	*peṭiŋ* 'stomach; belly'
S04.440	the heart	*buka* 'heart; liver'; *dil* 'heart; soul'; *kakaṛi*; *kardʑ* 'heart; mind'; *man* 'heart; soul; desire'	*ʃin* 'heart; liver'; *dil* 'heart; desire'; *monaŋ* 'heart; desire'; *dʑiʋa* 'heart; soul; spirit'
S04.441	the lung	*baʃ* 'lung'	*tʰab*
S04.450	the liver	*buka* 'heart; liver'	*kaledʒi*; *ʃin* 'heart; liver'
S04.460	the stomach	*poṭaŋ* 'stomach; belly'	*peṭiŋ* 'stomach; belly'
S04.461	the intestines or guts	*adʒaŋ*	*ãdʒaŋ*
S04.462	the waist	*kʰo:*	*kʰo:*; *gatʃko*
S04.463	the hip	*kʰutaṇi* 'hip (of domesticated animal)'	*lum* 'thigh; hip'
S04.492	the penis	*kʰutu*	*pjats (when talking to children)*
S04.510	to breathe	*ʃã: ḍuṇam*	*sa:saŋ unnu*
S04.520	to yawn	*dʒama:em*	*haʃ kamʃimu*; *tsonʃimu* 'stretch; yawn by stretching (one's arms)'
S04.530	to cough	*kʰaŋem*	*tsu:mu*; *tsu: lannu*
S04.540	to sneeze	*gisam*	*gismu*
S04.550	to perspire	*parsed dʋanam*	*dusti: donnu*
S04.560	to spit	*letu buṛam*	*tʰukaŋ pʰikja:mu*
S04.570	to vomit	*pʰasam*	*pʰasmu*
S04.580	to bite	*ga:rts raṭam*	*tʃigmu*
S04.590	to lick	*lemam*	*lemmu*
S04.610	to sleep	*ṭulem*, *ṭuljem*	*jagmu*
S04.612	to snore	*garaṛiga: raṇam*	*kʰrõgennu*; *kʰorennu* 'to limp; to snore'
S04.620	to dream	*supna: baram*	*maŋmu*
S04.630	to wake up	*atʃʰim* 'wake up; arise'; *sarʃim*	*sərmu* [TR] 'to raise up, to wake up'; *sərʃimu (human subject)*; *jantʃimu* 'to experience first moment of waking up'
S04.680	to shiver	*kʰanam*	*kriŋmu*
S04.690	to bathe	*sum* [TR]; *suʃim* [MDL]	*suʃimu* [MDL]; *sumu* [TR]
S04.730	pregnant	*a:n ma:ts*	*garbʋati* (human); *ɲumtsu* (human); *magore* (human); *ga:bin* (animals)
S04.732	to conceive	*tʃʰaulem*	*tʰobmu*
S04.7410	the life	*dʑan*; *dʑindagi*	*dʑan*; *malḍogaŋ*
S04.750	to die	*ʃi:m*	*ʃimu*
S04.7501	dead	*ʃi:k* 'dead; corpse'	*ʃiʃi*
S04.751	to drown	*ḍub(b)em* 'to sink; to drown'	*ḍubennu* 'to drown, to sink'
S04.760	to kill	*sanam*	*sannu*
S04.770	the corpse	*ʃi:dʑ maṛʃaŋ*; *ʃi:k* 'dead; corpse'	*moro*; *ʃimi*; *ʃiʃi*
S04.780	to bury	*dabja:m* 'to press; to squeeze; to bury'; *potʰja:m*	*kʰaro ʃennu*
S04.810	strong	*naṛija*; *polak*; *dʑarka:ris*	*dʑob*; *dʑobonsja:*; *takra:*
S04.820	weak	*dʒaŋtʃ* 'thin; weak'; *kumdʑor*	*bila:jets*; *ṭorts* 'weak (healthwise)'; *ko:rko:r* 'weak; very thin'; *ka:ṭʰes* 'weak, malnourished or dehydrated'; *dʒunṭʰa* 'weak (healthwise, humans or animals)'
S04.840	sick/ill	*dukʰis* 'sad; sick/ill'	*dukʰis* 'sick (person); sad (person)'
S04.841	the fever	*dʑo:r*	*tao*; *bukʰa:r*
S04.842	the goitre/goiter	*ganam*	*ga:nuŋ*
S04.8440	the disease	*buma:ri*; *dukʰ(e)*, *dukʰis* 'disease; grief; misery'	*ṭod*; *dukʰaŋ* 'disease; grief'
S04.850	the wound or sore	*raʃug* 'wound; sore'	*akʰa* 'wound, sore; pain'

IDS	Gloss	Kanashi (xns)	Kinnauri (kfk)
S04.852	the bruise	*kʰulʃig*	*ʃukʰreb*
S04.853	the swelling	*ʧug*; *ʧurʤ*	*ʈuʈu*
S04.854	the itch	*luk*	*hərʧo*
S04.8541	to scratch	*ʋaʈʃum*	*hərmu*; *bal ʧikʧimu* 'to scratch head (hair)'
S04.857	the pus	*ta:g*	*tag*
S04.858	the scar	*nusa:li*	*pa:raŋ*
S04.860	to cure	*ʃe:l ʃaɳam*	*ʃelman lannu*
S04.870	the physician	*ɖakʈar*	*ɖakʈar* 'physician (modern medicine)'; *bed* 'traditional healer'
S04.880	the medicine	*ʃe(:)l*	*ʃel*
S04.890	the poison	*biʃaŋ*; *ʤeher*	*biʃaŋ*
S04.910	tired	*tʰak*	*jaljal* 'physically tired'; *kaniŋ* 'mentally tired'
S04.912	to rest	*naʃim* 'to rest; to sit; to stay'	*ara:m lannu*; *rana ʃennu*; *naʃimu* 'to sit; to stay; to rest'
S04.920	lazy	*alesis*; *matslis*; *sust*	*a:lsi*
S04.930	bald	*tsattsaʈʈa*	*(pi)toŋlo*; *pitogtog* '(completely) bald'
S04.950	deaf	*ʈauɲa*	*ʈonja:* [M, impolite], *ʈone* [F]; *ʤaro*
S04.960	mute	*laʈʰas*; *maɖa*	*laʈa:* [M.SG], *laʈe:* [F.SG] 'dumb, mute'
S04.970	blind	*ka:ɳas*, *ka:ɳo* 'one-eyed; blind'	*ka:nes* [M], *ka:ne* [F]; *ãdoliŋ*
S04.980	drunk	*tuŋtuŋ*	*pʰasurija:*
S04.990	naked	*naŋʈa*	*salgi*
S05.110	to eat	*ʤa:m*	*ʤa:mu*; *pasmu* 'to eat (something dry, flour-like)'
S05.120	the food	*ʤa:m*; *kʰa:na*	*kʰou* 'food, meal'
S05.121	cooked	*pakets* 'ripe; cooked'; *paʃiʤ*	*papa*; *baba*
S05.122	raw	*kaʧas* 'raw; unripe; uncooked'	*kaʧas*; *maʃoʃo* 'uncooked'; *mababa* 'uncooked'; *mapapa* 'uncooked (raw, e.g; carrots which can be eaten raw)'
S05.123	ripe	*pakets* 'ripe; cooked'	*pakits*; *ʃoʃo*
S05.124	unripe	*kaʧas* 'raw; unripe; uncooked'	*tsispru*
S05.125	rotten	*ʧokets*	*tsis*; *namnam (kʰou)* 'stale (food, rotten as well as non-rotten)'
S05.130	to drink	*tuɳam*, *tu:ŋem*, *tu:gem* 'drink; smoke'	*tuŋmu* 'to drink; to smoke'
S05.140	to be hungry	*ʋaɳam*	*onnu*
S05.141	the famine	*aŋka:laŋ*	*(aŋ)ka:laŋ*
S05.150	to be thirsty	*ʃokkʰem*	*tiskarmu*
S05.160	to suck	*ʧusja:m*	*ʈubmu*; *ʈəbmu* 'to suck (mother's milk)'
S05.180	to chew	*tsapem*	*bragmu*
S05.181	to swallow	*miŋgam*	*mjuŋmu*
S05.210	to cook	*ʤa:miʤ ʃaɳam*; *kʰaɳaga: haʃim* [INTR]; *kʰaɳaga: ʃaɳam*; *siʈem* [INTR]; *siʈja:m* [TR]	*pannu*; *kʰou lannu*; *bannu* [INTR] 'to get cooked'
S05.220	to boil	*ubʈem*; *ubʈja:m*	*kʋasmu*; *kʰʋaʧimu* [INTR]
S05.230	to roast or fry	*ra:ʈ gaɳam*	*pogmu* 'to roast'; *dammu* 'to roast (wheat, oats)'; *bulɖja:mu* 'to deep-fry'; *polʈennu* 'to turn over egg (in the frying pan)'
S05.250	the oven	*geʈʈʰaŋ* 'oven; fireplace; stove'; *tundur*	*meliŋ*; *pʰa:liŋ* 'oven, fireplace'
S05.260	the pot	*baniŋ*; *ɖiksa*, *ɖigtsa:*; *kod* 'pot to measure cereal, flour etc'; *kunɖi*; *pata:l*	*pətila*; *banes*; *ɖig* 'pot with narrow neck'; *baniŋ* 'kitchen utensils (e.g., pots, cups)'
S05.270	the kettle	*ketali*	*ketəli*
S05.280	the pan	*pʰrajbin* 'frying pan; pan'	*bogunts*

IDS	Gloss	Kanashi (xns)	Kinnauri (kfk)
S05.320	the plate	*puleʈ*	*tʰa:l*; *pəleʈ*; *prat*; *kʰon*; *naŋ* 'a kind of bronze plate'; *tenle tʰa:l* 'flat plate'; *ɖuga tʰa:l* 'deep plate'
S05.330	the bowl	*kaʈora*	*ɖuna:ʦ*; *baʈiʦ* 'brass bowl'
S05.340	the jug/pitcher	*ʤag*	*suraji(ʦ)*
S05.350	the cup	*kap*	*baʈiʦ* 'brass cup with a foot'
S05.370	the spoon	*kʰarʦul* 'ladle; spoon'; *ʧamʧiŋ*, *ʧamʧi*, *ʧammaʧ*	*kʰeɳʈ*
S05.380	the knife(1)	*ʦʰure* 'knife'	*ʦəku* 'knife (instrument to cut e.g., vegetables)'; *gumʦ* 'knife (occurs only in folktales)'
S05.391	the tongs	*ʦumʈak* 'tongs (cooking utensil)'	*ʃoneʃaŋ*; *ʦimʈo* 'tongs (cooking utensil)'
S05.410	the meal	*bja:le* 'meal; dinner'	–
S05.420	the breakfast	*kula:r*, *som kula:r*	*ʧajudo*
S05.430	the lunch	*dupa:ri*; *laje* 'day; daytime; midday; lunch'	*ʃil*
S05.440	the dinner	*bja:le* 'meal; dinner'	*ra:tiŋ kʰou*
S05.460	to peel	*kʰulam* 'to open; to peel'	*ʦʰinja:mu*
S05.480	to scrape	*goarʃim* [MDL]; *ʧʰeɽa raɳam*	*kʰjulmu* [TR]; *gjulmu* [INTR], *gjulʃimu* [MDL]
S05.490	to stir or to mix	*millem* 'to stir; to find; to get'	*kəsmu*
S05.510	the bread	*hoɖ*; *kodra* 'roti made with kathu flour'; *roʈʰe* 'bread; chapati'	*hod* 'barley bread'; *ʦapʈi* 'chapati'; *roʈ* 'chapati'; *pol* 'puri'; *tʰispol* 'fried bread made of watery dough'
S05.530	the dough	*a:ri*	*ʦisaŋ pinʈu*
S05.540	to knead	*pʰram*	*tremu*
S05.550	the flour	*a:r*; *medda* 'flour (refined)'; *piʈʰas*; *ʦʰali piʈʰas* 'flour (of corn)'; *ʧisaŋ* 'flour (of buckwheat)'	*ʦisaŋ*; *meda*; *piʈʰas*; *ga:ʃa:ŋ* 'buckwheat (ogla) flour'; *konika:ŋ* 'wheat flour'; *ʦʰəlija piʈʰas* 'corn flour'; *jud* 'roasted barley flour'
S05.560	to crush or to grind	*ʈʰokja:m* 'to crush; to grind'	*rabmu* 'crush edibles in mortar'; *junnu* 'grind cereal to flour'; *pʰramu* 'to crush (potatoes)'
S05.610	the meat	*ʃabɽi*	*ʃa* 'meat; flesh'
S05.630	the sausage	*ʤuma*	*gʰima:*
S05.650	the vegetables	*barnog* 'vegetable (a wild species, used in cooking)'; *ba:ʥi*; *poʈo* 'vegetable; fruit'	*kan*; *ba:ʥi* 'cooked vegetable'
S05.700	the potato	*halg*	*halgaŋ*
S05.710	the fruit	*poʈo* 'vegetable; fruit'; *pʰolaŋ*; *pʰruʈ*	*pʰolaŋ*; *pʰruʈ*
S05.712	the bunch	*ʧʰu:nɖ*	*ʧʰonʈaŋ*
S05.760	the grape	*aŋgu:r*	*aŋgu:r (cultivated)*; *da:kʰaŋ (wild indigenous)*
S05.790	the oil	*tela*	*telaŋ*
S05.810	the salt	*ʦʰa*	*ʦʰa*
S05.820	the pepper	*pipli*, *pipɽi* 'pepper; chilli (red)'	–
S05.821	the chili pepper	*pipli*, *pipɽi* 'pepper; chilli (red)'	*pipli*
S05.840	the honey	*ʋa:s*	*ʋas*
S05.850	the sugar	*kʰanɖ*	*ʦi:ni*; *kʰanɖ*
S05.860	the milk	*kʰiraŋ*	*kʰiraŋ*
S05.870	to milk	*ʦuram*	*(kʰiraŋ) ʦurmu*
S05.880	the cheese	*punir* 'panir'	*kokpol (a traditional food item which has a similar preparation method as cheese)*; *panir*
S05.890	the butter	*bu:r* 'butter (local)'; *makkʰaɳ* 'butter; ghee'; *ma(:)r* 'ghee (local)'	*makʰan*; *gi* 'ghee (clarified butter)'; *mar* 'butter; ghee'
S05.900	the drink	*meʋasi*	–
S05.930	the beer	*gliŋ* 'barley beer'; *lugɽi* 'rice beer'	–

IDS	Gloss	Kanashi (xns)	Kinnauri (kfk)
S05.940	the fermented drink	*sura:b* 'alcohol; fermented drink'	*rak* 'a local alcoholic beverage'; *pʰa:sur, ti pʰa:sur* 'a local alcoholic beverage'; *ɖaŋle* 'a local alcoholic beverage'; *bijər* 'beer (modern)'
S05.970	the egg	*anɖa; li:ʧ*	*anɖa; li:ʈ; ʃaraŋ*
S05.971	the yolk	*kesaraŋ*	*golɖuŋ*
S05.99906	the biscuit	*biskuʈ*	*biskuʈ*
S05.99908	the cabbage	*bandgobi*	*(band)gobi*
S06.110	to put on	*garʃim* [MDL]	*ligmu* [TR] 'to put on (clothes, jewelry)'; *likʃimu* [MDL] 'to put on (clothes, jewelry)'; *lanʧimu* [MDL] 'to put on (clothes, jewelry)'; *ga:ʤimu, ga:ʧimu* [MDL] 'to put on clothes, also in group'
S06.120	the clothing or clothes	*lapta* 'garment'; *laʈpaʈ(a)* 'garment'	*gasa:* [PL]
S06.130	the tailor	*darʥi; laʈpaʈa poʧ*	*sujī* 'tailor making traditional coat and cap (also a subcategory of the IA Chamang group)'
S06.210	the cloth	*gas; kapra*	*gas; kapʰra:* 'cloth, fabric'; *ʧuʥ* 'kitchen cloth'
S06.220	the wool	*tsa:m* 'wool (of sheep)'	*tsam*
S06.290	the leather	*kʰults* 'leather (of goat)'; *ʧamɽa*	*tsəmra; ponaŋ* 'skin, hide, leather (of cows, oxen, buffaloes etc.)'
S06.310	to spin	*tsa:m katja:m*	*pannu* 'spin wool'
S06.320	the spindle	*tsanɖuk*	*paŋʈ*
S06.330	to weave	*gundja:m* 'to weave; to knit'	*tagmu* 'weave, knit'
S06.350	to sew	*poɳam*	*ponnu* 'to sew (with a sewing machine)'
S06.360	the needle(1)	*keb; sui*	*kepts; keb* 'needle, awl'; *sua* 'large needle; injection needle'
S06.380	the thread	*dauga*	*rid*
S06.390	to dye	*raŋgja:m* 'to dye; to paint'	*raŋgja:mu*
S06.420	the (woman§s) dress	*gasa* 'dress (traditional for women)'	*gasa:; tsʰesmju gas*
S06.430	the coat	*ʤakʈ* 'jacket'; *ko:ʈ*	*ko:ʈ; tsamuko:ʈ* 'men's traditional long (woolen) coat'; *ʧʰuba* 'long woollen cloak/coat worn by bridegroom'; *ʧo:li* 'traditional (green) women's jacket'
S06.440	the shirt	*kurti*	*kurta (traditional); kamiʥ (modern)*
S06.450	the collar	*kanɖe*	*bran*
S06.480	the trousers	*penʈ; sutʰon*	*sutʰon* 'traditional men's woolen trousers'; *penʈ (modern)*
S06.490	the sock or stocking	*ʥura:b*	*gusab; baŋsab* 'woolen socks or shoes which cover feet, but not ankles, worn indoors'
S06.510	the shoe	*bu:ʈ* 'boot; shoe'; *ʥoɽ, ʥoɽa; ekʃana bu:ʈ* 'shoe (modern sneaker)'; *kʰoʃori bu:ʈ* 'shoe (rubber, worn by women)'; *poɳ* 'straw shoe'	*pon*
S06.520	the boot	*bu:ʈ* 'boot; shoe'	*gambu:ʈ*
S06.540	the shoemaker	*ʧama:ras* 'a particular community'	*mutsi:* 'cobbler'; *ʧama:res; ʧamaŋ* 'male member of a particular community'
S06.550	the hat or cap	*pagriŋ* 'turban'; *ʈope*	*ʈop* 'hat, cap, helmet'; *ʈʰepaŋ* 'traditional cap'; *peʈʈʰepaŋ* 'black cap worn by bride'; *pa:guri* 'turban'; *pa:g* 'turban worn by bridegroom'
S06.570	the belt	*kʰo* 'belt (traditional)'; *peʈi*	*gaʧʰiŋ, gaʧʰaŋ* 'traditional woven belt worn by women'; *ɖori* 'belt, rope'

IDS	Gloss	Kanashi (xns)	Kinnauri (kfk)
S06.580	the glove	*guḍpa ʥura:bba:*	*gud baŋgusab; gusab*
S06.610	the pocket	*kʰissa, kʰisaŋ*	*kʰisog*
S06.620	the button	*piple*	*boṭon*
S06.630	the pin	*pitsuga* 'pin (traditional for women)'	*kobʥa (traditional pin worn by women)*
S06.710	the ornament or adornment	*ʥa:ŋ* 'gold; ornament'	*ṭa:naŋ*
S06.730	the ring	*mundaṛi*	*mundi*
S06.740	the bracelet	*baŋga* 'bracelet (modern)'; *paṭṭʰa* 'bracelet (traditional)'	*paṭaŋ* 'traditional broad gold bracelet'; *ṭo:ru* 'traditional broad silver bracelet'
S06.750	the necklace	*ha:r; tsandraha:r*	*trəmol* 'traditional necklace'; *tsandraha:r* 'traditional necklace'; *ma:laŋ, ma:liŋ* 'necklace, garland of dried fruit'; *u:ma:laŋ* 'necklace, garland of flowers'
S06.770	the earring	*ka:nṭa*	*ka:nṭʰe* 'traditional earring'
S06.820	the towel	*taoli*	*tolija*
S06.910	the comb	*buruʃ; kant*	*kotʰaŋ; kuʃ; ʃor* 'wool carding tool'
S06.920	the brush	*burʃ*	*bruʃ*
S06.921	the plait/braid	*linḍis* 'plait; braid'	*kjar:ʃid kra:* 'plaited/braided hair'
S06.930	the razor	*paṭṭi*	*kʰurts* 'large knife; large razor'
S06.950	the soap	*subu:n*	*samon*
S06.960	the mirror	*arʃug, arʃuk*	*arʃuk; siso:, ʃiʃa:* 'mirror; glass'
S06.9800	the snowshoe	*kʰobba*	—
S06.99901	the bag	*beg; boṭuaŋ* 'purse'	*tʰela:; ʥola:; beg; kʰul* 'leather bag for storing food items'; *boṭua* 'purse'
S06.99907	the sandal	*ʧapli* 'sandal (for women)'	*senḍal*
S06.99911	to wear	*gaʃam*	*ga:ʤimu* 'put on (clothes)'
S07.110	to live	*naʃim* 'to rest; to sit; to stay'	*nimu; naʃimu* 'sit, stay, rest'
S07.120	the house	*kim* 'house (traditional); home'; *lenṭern* 'house (modern)'	*kim* 'house, home'; *arsisi kim* 'modern house, built with bricks and cement'; *gora* 'stone house'
S07.130	the hut	*kʰuṭaŋ* 'cattleshed'; *ʃeṇi* 'house in the fields'; *tʰakuʧaṭi; ṭainta*	*ḍog* 'small house'; *ʃennaŋ* 'small house in mountain or fields'
S07.140	the tent	*tambu*	*ṭenṭ* 'tent for ceremonies'; *tombua* 'tarpaulin'
S07.150	the yard or court	*kʰo(l)*	*kʰataŋ*
S07.170	the cookhouse	*kʰotar* 'kitchen'	*panṭʰaŋ* 'room with stove in traditional house'; *kuṭiŋ* 'outside kitchen for preparing large amount of food for celebrations etc'
S07.180	the meeting house	*ʧotraŋ* 'council platform'	*dumsa kim; tso:riŋ* 'raised platform in the center of the temple complex for placing devta on, where people gather'
S07.210	the room	*kamra, kamraŋ; pa:ṭi* 'room; floor'	*panṭʰaŋ* 'room with stove in traditional house, floor, the main residential room/area in a house'
S07.220	the door or gate	*pitaŋ* 'door; doorpost'	*dʋaraŋ; pitaŋ* 'gate, door'; *kajaŋ 'door with doorframe'*
S07.221	the doorpost	*pitaŋ* 'door; doorpost'	—
S07.230	the lock	*ʃaiŋ; ta:ṛi* 'lock; padlock'	*ʃa:naŋ, ʃa:niŋ* 'traditional large iron lock on the main door'
S07.231	the latch or door-bolt	*baṛʋa; ʧiṭkani*	*ʋanṭʰaŋ*
S07.2320	the padlock	*ta:ṛi* 'lock; padlock'	—
S07.240	the key	*kunʥi*	*talaŋ(ts), ta:lits*
S07.250	the window	*ṭaki*	*bodiŋ*
S07.260	the floor	*bumiŋ; dʰart; pa:ṭi* 'room; floor'; *pʰarʃ*	*pʰor* 'floor; ground'; *panṭʰaŋ* 'floor (inside a traditional house); room'

IDS	Gloss	Kanashi (xns)	Kinnauri (kfk)
S07.270	the wall	*bitiŋ*	*bitiŋ*
S07.310	the fireplace	*geʈʈʰaŋ* 'oven; fireplace; stove'	*meliŋ; pʰa:liŋ* 'oven, fireplace'
S07.320	the stove	*geʈʈʰaŋ* 'oven; fireplace; stove'; *sʈop*	*ge:s* 'modern (gas) stove'
S07.330	the chimney	*na:liŋ; tandura:ʥ pajp*	*dusraŋ*
S07.370	the ladder	*uŋgeɽa* 'staircase; ladder'	*tʰem(ts); tsʰam* 'ladder; bridge'
S07.420	the bed	*palaŋg, palag; pʰog*	*palaŋg* 'modern bed'; *tsa:rpa:j* 'cot with wooden frame; matress part of a bed made of woven ropes'; *poʃ* 'bedding (traditionally people sleep on bedding on the floor)'
S07.421	the pillow	*kum*	*kum*
S07.422	the blanket	*kambaɽ, kamɽ; ruʤai* 'quilt'	*kambal; ruʤai; kʰjar* 'blanket made of goat's hair'
S07.430	the chair	*kursi*	*k(ʰ)ursi*
S07.440	the table	*ʈebal, ʈeble*	*meʥ*
S07.450	the lamp or torch	*biʤeɽi* 'electricity; lightning; flashlight'; *tsimani* 'lamp (kerosene)'	*beʈri* 'flashlight'; *lalʈen* 'kerosene lamp'; *lomp* 'small kerosene lamp'; *divaŋ* 'earthen lamp'
S07.460	the candle	*mombatti*	*mumbati*
S07.510	the roof	*kaʈʰa* 'shade against rain; roof (wooden)'; *pa:ʈ* 'roof (stone/slate)'; *rokʈʰa, rokʈʰaŋ; tsadri:* 'roof (tin)'	*tsʰapraŋ* 'A-shaped roof of a traditional house or a temple'; *ʃoll* 'flat stone roof'; *lenʈer* 'modern brick-tile roof'; *məltʰaŋ* 'thatched roof'
S07.550	the beam	*ʥa:ɖe; ʥa:kʰ*	*ba:ʃaŋ; ʤalda:raŋ* 'roof beam'
S07.560	the post or pole	*kʰamba* 'pillar'; *tʰamba* 'pillar; pole'	*tʰamgaŋ* 'pole (in traditional Kinnauri homes there used to be a pole adorned with decorative intricate carving in the middle of a house)'
S07.610	the mason	*mistrits*	*mistri*
S07.620	the brick	*ĩ:ʈʰ, iʈ*	*ĩ:ʈ*
S07.6500	the camp	*ɖera* 'home, camping'	*tsatʰaŋ*
S07.6700	to tan	*kʰulʃim*	*ʧʰomu*
S08.110	the farmer	*ʥimida:(r)*	*ʥimda:r*
S08.120	the field	*ʃo* 'field; orchard'	*rim; ropaŋ* 'large farming field'; *se:riŋ* 'large farming field'; *ɲol* 'farm below village'; *kanɖa* 'farm just below mountain top'; *ɖabəraŋ* 'farm with many rocks/stones'; *paʈaŋ* 'terraced farm'
S08.1210	the paddy	*ʥatka sila:ŋ*	*da:n*
S08.150	to cultivate	*sanam*	*pəʃmu* 'to sow; to cultivate'
S08.160	the fence	*ɖe:k*	*ba:ʈaŋ*
S08.170	the ditch	*gaɳ*	*kʰa:ruŋ*
S08.210	to plough/plow	*ra:lam*	*halaŋ hemu; stal hemu*
S08.212	the furrow	*ʥoɖega:*	*si:tʰaŋ*
S08.220	to dig	*kotja:m*	*ko:rmu*
S08.240	the shovel	*belʧa; kuda:ɽi* 'spade'	*biltsa* 'shovel with a wooden handle and aluminium base, used in farming'; *korpanaŋ* 'wooden shovel for snow shuffling'
S08.250	the hoe	*tsʰarʥ ʃiŋ*	*ʃor; kudali; pʰorua* 'spade, hoe'
S08.310	to sow	*puʃam*	*pəʃmu* 'sow, cultivate'
S08.311	the seed	*bedʥa; bijaɳ; mog* 'birdseed'	*poʈo; bijaŋ; boʈaŋ* 'soybean-like seed'; *re:mo:* 'apricot seeds'; *mog* 'bird seed'; *pug* 'roasted seeds'

IDS	Gloss	Kanashi (xns)	Kinnauri (kfk)
S08.320	to mow	*tʃi kaʈem*	*labmu*
S08.340	to thresh	*tsʰaʈa kja:ʈam*	*pʰammu* 'to thresh manually using a stick'; *tsʰaʈja:mu* 'to thresh manually while holding the sheaf in hand and beating it against a hard surface'
S08.350	the threshing-floor	*kʰo*; *pa:n* 'threshing stone; threshing-floor'	*kʰolaŋ*
S08.410	the harvest	*pʰasal*	*pʰosol*
S08.430	the wheat	*ʥa:(d)*	*ʥod*
S08.440	the barley	*ʥubaŋ*	*ʈag*
S08.460	the oats	*tʃa:g*	—
S08.470	the maize/corn	*tsʰali piʈʰas* 'flour, corn'	*tsʰəli*, *tsʰəlija*
S08.480	the rice	*la:r* 'rice (uncooked)'; *pʰul* 'rice (cooked)'	*ral* 'modern rice (cooked or uncooked)'; *koni* 'a local rice variety (cooked or uncooked)'
S08.530	the plant	*beʈiŋ* 'tree; plant; tree trunk'; *pʰakuts ɖaliŋ*	*ɖa:laŋ*; *ba:laŋ* 'seedling'
S08.531	to plant	*roʋam*	*pəʃmu*; *ʈuŋmu* 'to plant; to make stand'
S08.540	the root	*ʤa:ŋ*	*ʤi:laŋ*
S08.550	the branch	*paŋ*; *ʃaŋ*; *ʃiŋ ɖa(:)liŋ* 'tree branch'	*ɖalaŋ*, *ɖaliŋ*; *bar*
S08.560	the leaf	*patti*; *patʃaŋ*	*patʰraŋ*
S08.570	the flower	*boddi* 'flower (a species planted as decoration)'; *goguŋ* 'flower (a wild species, blue-white; people put this flower on their caps)'; *kamal u:* 'lotus flower'; *kaʈa:ŋ* 'flower (a wild species, red-white; people put this flower on their caps)'; *pʰoʃʈare* 'flower (a wild species, blue-white)'; *pʰul*; *sartʰas* 'flower (a species cultivated in flowerpots, yellow-orange)'; *u:*	*pʰul*; *u:*
S08.600	the tree	*beʈiŋ* 'tree; plant; tree trunk'	*bo:ʈʰaŋ*
S08.640	the pine	*deodar* 'cedrus deodara (tree)'; *li:m*	*li:m*; *kjalmaŋ* 'Deodar cedar'
S08.650	the fir	*kʰrok*	*pan*
S08.660	the acorn	*tita:n*, *titã:(n)* 'acorn; cone (of pine tree)'	—
S08.680	the tobacco	*tamba:ku*	*toma:ku*
S08.690	to smoke	*surgiʈ tuŋam*	*tuŋmu* 'to drink; to smoke'; *sigriʈ tuŋmu* 'to smoke a cigarette'
S08.691	the pipe	*hukka*; *pajp*	*nodi*; *ʃotʰes*; *hukka*
S08.730	the tree trunk	*polak*	*goniŋ* 'tree stump; tree trunk'; *ɖoŋa* 'tree stump; tree trunk'; *bo:ʈʰaŋu ɖuza*
S08.750	the bark	*lebʈa* 'bark; eggshell'	*bod* '(human) skin , bark, peel'; *pəd* 'bark of the Himalayan birch'
S08.840	the banana	*keʈa*	*kela*
S08.910	the sweet potato	*ʤetʃialga* 'sweet potato, red'; *katʃas halga* 'sweet potato, white'	—
S08.931	the pumpkin or squash	*kaddu* 'pumpkin'	*reʈʰo* 'pumpkin with hard peel, inedible'; *kondu* 'pumpkin with soft peel, edible'; *kaddu* 'pumpkin'
S08.980	the mushroom	*kʰiri tʃʰatʃe* 'mushroom (a wild species)'; *muʈuʃa* 'mushroom (a wild species)'; *tsʰutsurug* 'mushroom (a wild species)'; *tʃʰatʃe* 'mushroom (a wild species)'	*ʤaŋmuts*
S08.9960	the cone	*tita:n*, *titã:(n)* 'acorn; cone (of pine tree)'	*toŋlo*; *pʰrus*; *ʈʰa:ŋga:le*
S08.99901	the almond	*bada:m*	*bədam*

IDS	Gloss	Kanashi (xns)	Kinnauri (kfk)
S08.99905	the apple	*seʋ, seb, seo*	*sjo, seo (modern); pal (indigenous, traditional)*
S08.99910	the carrot	*ga:dʒar*	*ga:dʒar*
S08.99911	the cashew	*ka:dʒu*	*kadʒu*
S08.99918	the dung	*kod* 'cow dung'; *molaŋ* 'cow dung'	*molaŋ*
S08.99930	the mango	*a:m*	*a:m*
S08.99935	the onion	*pja:dz*	*pja:dz*
S08.99936	the orange	*santra*	*sontra*
S08.99937	the pea	*maʈar*	*maʈar*
S08.99941	the plum	*ʧul* 'plum (edible)'	*lutsa* 'wild plum'
S08.99952	the turnip	*salgam*	*ʃakar*
S08.99962	to raise or grow	*roja:m*	*jogmu* [TR] *(animals, humans)*; *pa:lja:mu* [TR] *(animate)*; *podzja:mu* [TR] *(inanimate)*
S09.110	to do	*lanam* 'to do; to make'; *ʃa:ɳam* 'to do; to make'	*lannu* 'to do, to make'
S09.1110	to make	*baɳem* 'to make; to build'; *lanam* 'to do; to make'; *ʃa:ɳam* 'to do; to make'	*lannu* 'to do, to make'; *ʈuja:mu* 'to prepare, to make ready (with 3 person object)'; *ʈuja:ʃimu* [MDL] 'to get oneself prepared'
S09.120	the work	*ka:m, ka:maŋ*	*kamaŋ*; *nukuri* 'service, job'
S09.140	to bend	*moroʈja:m*; *ʈumrigja:m*	*kʰoŋmu* [TR]; *kʰoŋʃimu* [MDL] 'to bend, to bow slightly (e.g., for greeting)'
S09.150	to fold	*pʰuɽigija:m*; *tolam*	*kulugmu*
S09.160	to tie	*ts(ʰ)unam*	*tsʰunnu*
S09.161	to untie	*ʈaʈam*	*ʈʰormu*
S09.180	the chain	*ʃaŋgle*	*ʃaŋliŋ*
S09.190	the rope	*buʃ*	*bəʃ*; *ɖori*; *ʃakʰro*; *ʧʰo:nliŋ* 'clothesline'
S09.192	the knot	*gurʃu*	*ganʈʰaŋ*
S09.210	to strike or hit or beat	*kulam* 'to beat; to thrash'; *raʈam* 'to strike; to hit; to beat'; *togam* 'to beat'; *toŋam* 'to beat'	*kulmu*; *pʰoʈno: rannu*; *tugmu*
S09.220	to cut	*kaʈem*; *kaʈja:m*	*kaʈja:mu*; *məlmu*; *pʰralmu* 'to cut down'; *pʰolmu* 'to cut/chop wood'
S09.223	to stab	*raɳam* 'to stab (=give)'	*ʧʰuris rannu*
S09.240	the scissors or shears	*kanʧi*	*kətu* 'modern scissors'; *ʧʰəmpa* 'traditional scissors'
S09.250	the axe/ax	*ka:r*	*lasta*; *ostorsostor* 'battle axe'
S09.260	to break	*dʒuɳam* [INTR] 'to break; to split; to tear'; *ʧuɳam* [TR] 'to break; to split; to tear'	*ʈəgmu* [TR]; *dʒəgmu* [INTR]; *ʈəgʃimu* [MDL]; *baʃmu* [INTR]
S09.270	to split	*dʒuɳam* [INTR] 'to break; to split; to tear'; *paʈakja:m*; *ʧuɳam* 'to break; to split; to tear'	*pʰərmu* 'to split; to tear'
S09.290	to skin	*lebɽa kʰulam*	*kʰo:mu* 'to remove skin, bark, etc.'
S09.3110	to wipe	*ʈuʃja:m*	*kuʃja:mu* [TR]; *kuʃja:ʃimu* [MDL]
S09.320	to stretch	*dzu:r la:tam*	*tsonnu* [TR]; *tsonʃimu* [MDL] 'to stretch (oneself), to yawn by stretching (one's arms)'
S09.330	to pull	*kʰitsja:m*	*ɖabmu* [TR]; *ɖabʃimu* [MDL]
S09.340	to spread out	*pʰelʈam*	*pramu* [TR] *(cereals etc)*; *bramu* [INTR]; *praʃimu* [MDL]; *sunnu* [TR] *(batter)*
S09.341	to hang up	*laʈam*	*dʒontaŋ ʃennu*
S09.342	to press	*dabja:m* 'to press; to squeeze; to bury'; *dzikem* [INTR]; *dzikja:m* [TR]	*dobja:mu*; *letʰja:mu* 'to press edibles or cow dung'; *setʰja:mu* 'to press to straighten something'
S09.343	to squeeze	*dabja:m* 'to press; to squeeze; to bury'; *moroʈja:m*	*ʈrumu* [TR]; *ʈrutʰja:mu* [TR]
S09.350	to pour	*gaɳam*	*osmu*

IDS	Gloss	Kanashi (xns)	Kinnauri (kfk)
S09.360	to wash	*dʒim* [INTR]; *ʧim* [TR]	*ʧimu* [TR] *(non-living objects)*; *ʧiʃimu* [MDL]; *dʒiʃimu* [MDL] 'wash one's hands'
S09.370	to sweep	*kʰutam*	*kuʧaŋ lannu* 'to sweep with a broom'; *ʃoja:mu* 'to sweep/clean (in general)'
S09.380	the broom	*peg, pek*	*kuʧaŋ*; *kuʧots* 'small broom for clearing ash around traditional stove in the middle of living room'
S09.430	the carpenter	*mistri:* 'carpenter; sculptor'; *tʰauʊis*	*ores* 'male member of the ores community (a social sub-group which traditionally were carpenters)'; *oronig* 'female member of the ores community'
S09.440	to build	*baɳem* 'to make; to build'; *gaɳam*; *g(ʰ)oɳam* 'build structure from foundation'; *kim ʃaɳam*	*paɳmu*
S09.460	to bore	*kʰaʈa gaɳam* 'to bore (a hole)'	*dʊənnu*; *ɖogiŋ lannu*; *ɖogiŋ tonnu* 'to bore, to take out something'
S09.480	the saw	*a:ra*	*a:ra*
S09.490	the hammer	*g(ʰ)aɽam*; *tabru*; *ʈʰolu* 'hammer; chisel'	*hatʰoɽa*
S09.500	the nail	*preg*	*kilaŋ*
S09.560	the glue	*gud, gu:nd*	*ʧʰiti*
S09.600	the blacksmith	*ɖaggis* 'blacksmith (male member of traditional community)'; *ɖagi* 'blacksmith (traditional community)'	*ɖomaŋ* 'traditional blacksmith community'; *ɖomes* 'male member of this community'
S09.640	the gold	*ʥa(:)ŋ*	*ʥaŋ*
S09.650	the silver	*mu(:)l*	*mul*
S09.660	the copper	*tramba*; *ʧamo*	*ʈromaŋ*
S09.670	the iron	*roɳ*	*ron*
S09.730	the clay	*ka:m* 'soil; clay'	*ma(:)ʈiŋ* 'land, soil, clay'
S09.740	the glass	*gula(:)s, kantsu gula(:)s* 'glass; tumbler'	*ʃiʃa*; *siso* 'glass; drinking glass; mirror'
S09.750	to weave or plait/braid	*gundja:m* 'weave'; *linɖis ʃaɳ-am* 'to plait; to braid'	*tagmu* 'weave'; *kjarmu* 'braid (someone's hair)'; *kjarʃimu* [MDL] 'braid (one's own hair)'
S09.760	the basket	*kilʈi* 'basket carried on the back'; *ʈokri* 'basket (small, to put wood etc. in)'	*ʈokri*; *koʈiŋ* 'basket carried on the back'; *ʧaŋger* 'woven basket without handle or lid'; *tsʰaʈots* 'basket with handle'; *ɖanli* 'large bamboo basket used for storing large quantities of cooked food at gatherings (not used these days)'
S09.770	the mat	*dari* 'mat; rug'; *poʃmukʰ* 'bedspread; mat (to sit on)'; *sela*	*kʰjar* 'blanket made of goat's hair; mat (rough, to sit on)'
S09.771	the rug	*dari* 'mat; rug'; *guli:ʧa* 'carpet'	—
S09.810	to carve	*guleʥ ʃaɳam*	*mərap tonnu*
S09.820	the sculptor	*mistri:* 'carpenter; sculptor'	*kunɖa dʒaɳtsja:* 'sculptor of clay statues'
S09.840	the chisel	*ʈʰolu* 'hammer; chisel'	*tsʰeniŋ*
S09.880	the paint	*raŋg* 'color; paint'	*raŋg* 'paint, color'
S09.890	to paint	*raŋgja:m* 'to dye; to paint'	*raŋgja:mu*; *raŋgʃennu*; *si: tonnu* 'to paint (a special kind of Buddhist painting on silk or cotton, created by lamas)'; *ʧemu* 'to write; to draw; to paint'
S09.9000	to draw water	*ti: ɖuʈam*	*ti ʈimu*
S09.99915	the pencil	*prisin*	*pensil*
S09.99917	the sack	*boraŋ* 'sack; luggage'	*boraŋ, bori*
S09.99931	to dwell or stay	*naʃim* 'to rest; to sit; to stay'	*nimu*

IDS	Gloss	Kanashi (xns)	Kinnauri (kfk)
S09.99936	to smear	*ʃatarja:m*	*ʃelmu* [TR]; *ʃelʃimu* [MDL]
S10.110	to move	*talja:m* [TR]; *taljem*	*sikja:mu* [TR]; *sikja:ʃimu* [MDL] 'to get moved, shaken'
S10.120	to turn	*palʈem* [INTR] 'to turn (around)'; *palʈja:m* [TR] 'to turn (around)'	*ʃurja:mu*; *kʰoŋmu* 'to turn, to bend, to mold'; *polʈja:ʃimu* [MDL] 'to turn around, to roll [PL] (collectively)'; *polʈja:mu* 'to flip over (e.g., chapati, quilt)'
S10.130	to turn around	*palʈem* [INTR] 'to turn (around)'; *palʈja:m* [TR] 'to turn (around)'	*polʈennu* [INTR] 'to turn around, to return, to come back'; *ʃurja:ʃimu* [MDL] 'to circle back'; *kʰoŋʃimu* [MDL] 'to get turned, bent, molded'
S10.140	to wrap	*laʈpaʈja:m* 'to wrap (in cloth)'	*meʃnja:mu* [TR]; *brinlja:mu* [TR]; *brinlja:ʃimu* [MDL]
S10.160	to drop	*danam* [INTR] 'to drop; to fall'; *pʰunam* [INTR] 'to drop; to fall'; *tʰanam* [TR] 'to drop; to fell'	*tʰannu*; *ʧogmu*; *pʰralmu* 'fell, drop, topple'; *gərmu* [TR] '(unintentionally) drop, topple'
S10.210	to rise	*baram* 'to rise (of sun)'; *dʋanam* 'to come out; to rise (of sun)'	*tʰoʃimu* [MDL]; *donnu*, *dʋənnu* 'to come out [INTR], to rise (sun)'; *ʥərmu (sun, moon)*; *sarʃimu* [MDL] (human); *janʧimu* 'to wake up [MDL]'
S10.230	to fall	*danam* [INTR] 'to drop; to fall'; *pʰunam* [INTR] 'to drop; to fall'	*bralmu*; *dannu* 'to get dropped, by natural force'; *tʰaʃimu* [MDL] 'to get dropped (on its own or unintentionally)'
S10.240	to drip	*ti: dʋanam* 'to drip (of water)'	*ʧogmu* [TR]; *ʤogmu* [INTR]
S10.250	to throw	*buɽam* 'to throw; to leave'; *pʰikja:m*	*paja:mu*; *pʰikja:mu* 'to throw out, to discard '; *bərʃja:mu* 'to throw, to leave behind (a devta) somewhere and return to the village'; *ʃoʈʰja:mu* 'to throw, to leave (forever)'
S10.252	to catch	*ts(ʰ)u(:)mam* 'to catch; to hold'	*ʦummu* 'to grasp, to catch'
S10.260	to shake	*milam*; *ʧʰal balja:m*	*ʥuɳlja:mu* [TR] *(animate)*; *ʧʰoklja:mu* [TR] *(liquid)*; *ʈʰoŋʃimu* [MDL] 'to shake dust off clothes'
S10.320	to flow	*ti: boŋam* 'to flow (of water)'	*bojennu* [INTR] 'to blow; to flow'; *boja:ʃimu* [MDL] 'to blow; to float [PL] (collectively)'
S10.330	to sink	*ɖub(b)em* [INTR] 'to sink; to drown'; *ɖubja:m* [TR] 'to sink; to drown'	*ɖubja:mu* [TR]; *ɖubennu* [INTR]
S10.350	to swim	*bara raɳam*	*trabʃimu* [MDL] 'to swim or to cross the river on a rope'
S10.370	to fly	*uɽja:m* [TR]; *uɽjem* [INTR]	*jabmu* [TR]
S10.380	to blow	*pʰu lanam*	*pʰulja:mu* [TR]
S10.410	to crawl	*leʈpeʈjem*	*ɖabʃimu* [MDL]
S10.430	to jump	*tsʰapuk raɳam*	*gʋaʃimu* [MDL]; *gʋamu* [TR]; *la:ŋ tsʰerja:mu* [TR]; *(s)kʋamu* 'to make jump' (causative)'
S10.431	to kick	*latas raɳam*	*latʰos rannu*
S10.440	to dance	*ʧa:m*	*ʧa:mu*
S10.450	to walk	*hanɖem*; *hanɖja:m*	*junnu* [INTR]; *halennu* [INTR] 'to take a walk, to roam'; *junnu ʃennu* [TR]; *halja:mu* [TR] 'to walk, to roam'
S10.451	to limp	*benɖerem*	*kʰorennu* 'to limp; to snore'
S10.460	to run	*ʈʰoroga: raɳam*	*ʈʰurennu*; *ʈʰurja:mu* [TR]
S10.470	to go	*bonam*	*bjomu* (S), *bimu* (B)
S10.471	to go up	*riŋ bonam*	*tʰug bjomu*
S10.472	to climb	*ʈaŋam*	*(tʰug) bjomu*
S10.473	to go down	*ʃoŋnu bonam*	*(jug) ʤabmu*
S10.474	to go out	*ba:ro boŋʈam*	*ba:riŋ donnu*
S10.480	to come	*baram*	*bənnu*
S10.481	to come back	*lo baram*	*polʈennu* [INTR]; *polʈja:mu* [TR]

IDS	Gloss	Kanashi (xns)	Kinnauri (kfk)
S10.490	to leave	*buɽam* 'to throw; to leave'	*ʃoʈʰja:mu* 'to throw, to leave (for ever)'; *bərʃja:mu* 'to throw, to leave behind (a devta) somewhere and return to the village'
S10.491	to disappear	*bi:m*	*ʃo bjomu*
S10.510	to flee	*pʰoʧim*	*bjomu* 'to leave, to go away, to run away'; *ʃoʈʰja:mu* 'to throw, to leave (for ever)'
S10.520	to follow	*ʈʰurja:m*	*ɲumʧ junnu*
S10.550	to arrive	*ʈapem*	*pənnu* 'arrive, approach'
S10.570	to enter	*kuba:r piʃim*	*komo bjomu*; *saŋʃimu* [MDL] (forcefully, e.g., thief)
S10.610	to carry	*anam*	*tʰomu*; *kjubmu* 'carry on one's back'
S10.612	to carry in hand	*guɖpa anam*	*gudo tʰomu*
S10.614	to carry on head	*bala anam*	*bale tʰomu*
S10.620	to bring	*kanam*	*karmu*
S10.630	to send	*ʃenam*	*ʃennu*
S10.670	to push	*ʤakka raɳam*	*(s)tugmu* 'push, strike, hit'; *pʰutugmu* 'push (to hurt the other person)'
S10.710	the road	*ʃaɽak*	*solok*
S10.720	the path	*om* 'path; way; mountain pass'	*om* 'mountain path'
S10.740	the bridge	*tsʰam*	*tsʰam*
S10.760	the wheel	*guʈnu:ga:*	*paija*
S10.810	the ship	*samudri ʤahaʤ*	*paniʤaʥ*
S10.830	the boat	*kiʃti*	*kiʃti*
S11.110	to have	*tam*; *tonam*	*haʧimu* 'to have, to become'
S11.130	to take	*u:nam*	*unnu* 'to take, to seize'
S11.160	to get	*millem* 'to stir; to find; to get'	*tʰobmu* [TR]; *porennu* [INTR] 'to get, to find'
S11.170	to keep	*piʧim* 'to keep; to put'; *tam*	*ta:mu* 'to keep; to put'
S11.180	the thing	*suma:n*; *ʧiʥ*	*bastuŋ*; *tsi:ʥ*
S11.210	to give	*dem*; *kenam* [1/2O]; *raɳam* [NON-1/2O]	*rannu* [NON-1/2O]; *kemu* [1/2O]
S11.220	to give back	*bapas raɳam*	*polʧa:ʈja: rannu*
S11.240	to preserve	*batsja:s piʧim*	*mapipi ta:mu*
S11.250	to rescue	*batsja:m*	*botsja:mu*
S11.270	to destroy	*suaʃim*	*tsʰaka lannu*
S11.280	to injure	*raʃim*	*akʰa bjomu*
S11.320	to find	*la:m*; *la:mʃim* [MDL]; *millem* 'to stir; to find; to get'	*porennu* [INTR]; *paja:mu* [TR]
S11.330	to lose	*pi:m*	*pi:ʃimu* [MDL]
S11.430	the money	*ɖabua* 'currency'; *loʈ* 'banknote'; *ʈaka*	*ʃugu*
S11.440	the coin	*nagadi*	*pesaʦ*
S11.510	rich	*seʈ*	*soukar*
S11.520	poor	*gari:b*; *nagaɽija*	*ɖa:lɖis*; *biʧa:res*, *biʧa:rikas* 'helpless, poor'; *ala:tsar* 'poor (man)'
S11.530	the beggar	*bikʰari*, *bikʰa:rija*	*untsja:*
S11.540	stingy	*kanʤus*; *kubeka*	*bra:ʈ*
S11.620	to borrow	*riɳ uɳam*	*rin rannu*
S11.640	the debt	*riɳ* 'loan'	*rin*
S11.690	the tax	*ba:r* 'revenue; tax; rent; ticket'; *koraŋ*, *kora*; *ʈeks*; *tʰeka* 'revenue'	*ʈeks*; *kar*, *kər*
S11.770	to hire	*kura:ʋas raɳam*	—
S11.790	to earn	*ʈaka kuma:m*	*kəmaj lannu*; *kəmaja:mu*
S11.810	to buy	*kʰaɳam*	*ʥogmu*
S11.820	to sell	*renam*	*rennu*
S11.840	the merchant	*lala*	*dukanda:r*; *bepari*
S11.850	the market	*baʥa:(r)*	*baʥa:r*
S11.860	the shop/store	*biʥanes* 'business; shop'; *ha:ʈi*	*ha:ʈi*; *duka:n*

IDS	Gloss	Kanashi (xns)	Kinnauri (kfk)
S11.870	the price	*mulaŋ* 'cost; price'	*molaŋ*; *kimot*
S11.880	expensive	*ma:gas*	*me(h)eŋga*, *mẽga*; *tjoŋ molaŋ*
S11.890	cheap	*sastas*	*sostas*, *sosta*
S11.910	to share	*banḍija:m*; *benḍerem*	*kagmu* 'to distribute'; *kagʧimu* [MDL] 'to distribute'
S11.920	to weigh	*tolija:m*	*tolja:mu*
S11.99904	the property	*ma:la*	*ma:ja*; *gorbon*; *ma:l*
S12.0100	after	*ba:d*; *hipiʧ* 'after; last'	*ɲum*; *nipi*
S12.0110	behind	*ipiʤ*, *ipiʧ* 'behind (spatial); backwards'	*ɲumsko*; *ɲums*; *piʃṭiŋ*
S12.0120	in	*kuba:r* 'in; inside'	*dor* 'in, near'; *komo* 'inside'
S12.0200	beside	*soŋgus* 'beside; near'	*dəŋ* 'near, beside, next'
S12.0300	down	*ʤo* 'down; bottom'; *ʃoŋ*	*joʧriŋ* 'below', *jeṭʰaŋ* 'under; inside; down'; *jug* 'down; below'
S12.0400	before	*nandris*; *pela* 'first; earlier'	*oms*
S12.0410	in front of	*agraŋ* 'ahead; beyond'; *no:ʧas* 'front(side)'; *sa:mana*	*omsko*
S12.0600	outside	*ba:ro*, *ba:ru*	*ba:raŋ*; *ba:riŋ* (B); *be:riŋ* (S)
S12.0700	under	*nje:n*	*jeṭʰaŋ* 'under; inside; down'
S12.0800	up	*riŋ* 'top; up'; *tʰo*	*tʰug* 'at; up; above'; *den* 'on; above; over'
S12.0810	above	*rigi:n* 'above; upper'	*den* 'on; above; over'
S12.110	the place	*ʣa:ga*; *sõts*	*ʣa:ga*
S12.120	to put	*gaṉam*	*ta:mu* 'to keep; to put'
S12.130	to sit	*naʃim* 'to rest; to sit; to stay'	*toʃimu* [MDL] 'sit'; *naʃimu* 'to sit; to stay; to rest'
S12.140	to lie down	*pʰeṭa paem*	*dinnu*
S12.150	to stand	*kʰaṛa aʧim*	*ḍen nimu*
S12.210	to gather	*kaṭʰe ʃaṉam*	*meṭja:mu* [TR]; *meṭja:ʃimu* [MDL]; *ʣabmu* [TR] (small-size objects)
S12.212	to pick up	*ḍuṭam* 'to take out'	*tʰomu*
S12.220	to join	*ʧiŋam* 'to join; to shut'	*ṭigmu*
S12.230	to separate	*aŋgi ʃaṉam*	*kʰetsi lannu* [TR]; *ṭomu* 'to take apart a man-made object'
S12.232	to divide	*ṭukra ʃaṉam*	*kʰa:mu* [TR] 'to distribute'; *kagmu* [TR] 'to distribute'
S12.240	to open	*kʰulam* [TR]; *kʰulem* [INTR]; *kʰulʃim* [MDL]; *tʰʋaṉam* [TR]	*toŋmu* [TR]
S12.250	to shut	*ʧiŋam* 'to join; to shut'	*pinnu* [TR]; *piʃimu* [MDL]; *binnu* [INTR]
S12.260	to cover	*pʰuktam*	*pʰogmu* [TR] (animate objects); *lubmu* [TR] (inanimate objects, e.g., large pots, but not grass); *gorja:mu* [TR] (inanimate objects such as grass)
S12.270	to hide	*ta(:)tam*	*məŋmu*
S12.310	high	*uṭʰras*	*raŋk* 'high, tall (human, animate, inanimate)'
S12.320	low	*niʃṭʰas*	*melk*
S12.330	the top	*ka:ṭʰiŋ* 'mountain top; summit'; *raŋ* 'mountain top; summit'; *riŋ* 'top; up'	*bəll* 'head, top'
S12.340	the bottom	*ḍug*, *ḍugas* 'deep; bottom'; *ʤo* 'down; bottom'; *kʰuteni*	*tol*; *tʰa:saŋ*
S12.353	the edge	*koṉe* 'corner; edge'; *rask*	*da:r*
S12.360	the side	*kinare*	*paʃ*
S12.370	the middle	*maʤaŋ*, *moʤoŋ* 'between; middle'	*maʤaŋ*
S12.410	right(1)	*ʣa(:)b*; *loʤoŋ*	*ʣakʰaŋ* 'right, south'
S12.420	left	*buṛ*; *ḍeb*; *pʰeṭṭo*	*kʰoʤaŋ* 'left, north'
S12.430	near	*di*; *neṛaŋ*; *ʧʰuŋ*	*dor*; *dəŋ* 'nearby (visible), beside'; *neraŋ* 'near, close'
S12.440	far	*du:(r)*, *durane*	*ʋarko*

IDS	Gloss	Kanashi (xns)	Kinnauri (kfk)
S12.530	to grow	*rohem*	*pa:lennu* [INTR]
S12.540	to measure	*ɖa:lem*	*pəgmu* (edible objects); *rinnu* (non-edibles); *napja:mu* (non-edibles)
S12.550	big	*ʤiŋ*; *teg* 'big; older'	*teg*
S12.560	small	*pʰak*, *pʰakuʧ* 'small; short; young'	*gaʈo(ʦ)* (S); *ʥigiʦ* (B) 'small; young'
S12.570	long	*la:mas* 'tall; long'	–
S12.580	tall	*la:mas* 'tall; long'	*la:mes* 'long; tall'; *raŋk* 'high; tall (human, animate, inanimate)'
S12.590	short	*pʰak*, *pʰakuʧ* 'small; short; young'	*ʧʰoʈaʦ* (human)
S12.610	wide	*bellis*; *kʰulas*	*kʰulas* 'wide; open (e.g., landscape or a large house with more open space)'; *kunʧ* 'wide (inanimate objects, e.g., clothes, facial features, road)'
S12.620	narrow	*gaʈas*	*gaʈes*
S12.630	thick	*moʈas* 'fat; thick'	*moʈʰes* 'thick, fat (e.g., dog, tree, man)'; *bakʰles* (non-human)
S12.650	thin	*bag*; *ʤaŋʧ* 'thin; physically weak'	*bagiʦ*; *nakiʦ* (e.g., tree, man, child but not domestic animals)
S12.670	deep	*ɖug*, *ɖugas* 'deep; bottom'	*ɖuges* (e.g., river, well); *ɖuga* (e.g., plate)
S12.680	shallow	*ɖugas ma:j*	–
S12.710	flat	*sa:mnas* 'flat; straight'	*somaŋ*; *podres*; *maʃʈi:ʦ* 'smooth, flat (cloth)'; *pentenle* (e.g., plate)
S12.730	straight	*sa:mnas* 'flat; straight'; *sidda*	*solɖes* 'straight, simple-natured (person)'; *solɖi* 'straight, humble, non-crooked (person)'
S12.740	crooked	*ɖiŋga*, *ɖiŋgas*	*koŋʈa* [M], *koŋʈi* [F] 'crooked, humpbacked'
S12.760	the corner	*koɳe* 'corner; edge'	*ʥər*
S12.810	round	*gol*; *raɳ goʈunas*	*ba:ʈles* (inanimate objects); *gola* 'round; circle'
S12.830	the ball	*gindi*	*gīdu*; *pinʈu*
S12.850	the hole	*kʰaʈ* 'hole; injury'	*ɖogiŋ*; *ʥabra:*
S13.0100	one	*ek*; *i:d*	*id*; *ek*
S13.0200	two	*niʃ*	*niʃ*
S13.0300	three	*ʃu(:)m*	*ʃum*, *sum*
S13.0400	four	*pu*	*pə*
S13.0500	five	*ŋa*, *na*; *pãʧ*	*ŋa*
S13.0600	six	*ʧʰa*	*ʈug*
S13.0700	seven	*sat*	*(s)ʈiʃ*
S13.0800	eight	*aʈʰ*	*re*
S13.0900	nine	*nao*	*(s)gui*; *id mats se*
S13.100	ten	*das*	*se:*
S13.101	eleven	*gjara*	*sigid*
S13.102	twelve	*bara*	*soniʃ*
S13.103	fifteen	*pandra*	*soŋa*
S13.104	twenty	*bi*; *niʥa*	*niʥa*
S13.105	a hundred	*ʃo*, *i:d ʃo*	*ra:*
S13.106	a thousand	*haʥa:r*, *huʤa:r*, *i:d haʥa:r*, *i:d huʤa:r*	*haʥa:r*
S13.107	to count	*gaɲja:m*	*narmu*
S13.140	all	*sab*; *sa:re*	*ʦeik* 'all; whole'; *saləm* 'all; whole (objects)'; *pura* 'whole (e.g., city, village, country)'; *gui* 'all; whole (duration)'; *sares* 'all; whole'

IDS	Gloss	Kanashi (xns)	Kinnauri (kfk)
S13.150	many	*barits* 'much; many; more; full'; *dʒinḍ* 'a lot'; *nonda* 'so many'	*banbant*; *kus* 'much, many (countable objects)'; *ʋal* 'much, many (non-countable objects)'; *botabot* (this is used only in connection with beating or fighting with solid round objects)
S13.160	more	*barits* 'much; many; more; full'	*tjoŋ* (non-countable objects); *bodi* (countable objects)
S13.170	few	*dalak*	*san*; *sants*
S13.181	some	*koi*; *tʃʰugu*	*tʃʰəd* 'what; some'; *domri*; *san*; *sants*
S13.190	the crowd	*barits munuk*	*dzomgoṭ*
S13.210	full	*barits* 'much; many; more; full'	*bəŋgi*
S13.220	empty	*ʃag*	*ʃagi*
S13.230	the part	*bãḍa* 'share; portion'; *hisa* 'share; portion'	*hisa*
S13.240	the half	*adʰa*; *saɽe* 'plus half (in numerals)'	*kʰa:naŋ* (non-liquids); *a:daŋ* (liquids)
S13.330	only	*tsʰuɽe*	*eko*
S13.3310	alone	*ketsi:*	*ertsʰi*
S13.340	first	*pela* 'first; earlier'; *ʃuruŋats*	*dzo oms*; *pele*
S13.350	last	*hipitʃ* 'after; last'	*dzo ɲums*
S13.360	second	*dudʒa*	*dzo omskotʃ ɲums*
S13.370	the pair	*dzõũɽi*, *dzoɽi*	*dʒoɽi*
S13.380	twice/two times	*niʃ pʰeraga:*	*niʃ beraŋ* 'two times'; *dugna* 'twice'
S13.420	third	*tisraŋ*, *tisraŋadz*	*ʃumu densja:*; *ʃum ba:g*; *ʃum hisa:* 'one third'
S13.440	three times	*ʃum pʰeriga:*	*ʃum beraŋ*
S13.99901	a little	*tʰi:d*; *tʰoɽa*	*tʰoɽa*; *sa:nts*
S13.99907	to fill	*barem* [INTR] 'to fill'; *barja:m* [TR] 'to fill'	*bəŋmu* [INTR]; *pəŋmu* [TR]
S14.110	the time	*ʋakt*	*ṭʰonaŋ*; *la:mdes* 'duration, time period'; *rəŋ* 'times' (e.g., pə rəŋ 'four times)'
S14.120	the age	*umra*	*umor* (human); *adʒokʰa*; *tsʰe* (in buddhism)
S14.130	new	*jug* 'fresh; new'	*ɲu:g* 'young; new'
S14.140	young	*dʒaʋa:n*; *jaŋagats*; *pʰak*, *pʰakutʃ* 'small; short; young'	*ɲu:g* 'young; new'; *gaṭots* 'young; small'; *dzigits* 'young; small'; *ḍekʰor* (human); *dzuan* [M] (human); *konsaŋ* 'young(er in kinship relation'
S14.150	old	*juʃk*	*uʃk* (non-human); *sjano* (human); *jaŋdze(ts)* (animate [F])
S14.160	early	*tsʰika* 'early; soon; fast; quickly'	—
S14.170	late	*kubaleke*	*kʰrakʰra*
S14.180	now	*dza:b*; *tʃʰabaja*	*hun*
S14.190	immediately	*ardzi*; *tsʰikatsʰika*	*hunei*
S14.210	fast	*tsʰika* 'early; soon; fast; quickly'	*hasəl* 'soon; fast (speed)'; *dele* 'quickly'; *pʰaṭak* 'quickly'
S14.220	slow	*sulus*	—
S14.230	to hurry	*tsʰika ʃaŋam*	*ʃumu* [INTR]
S14.240	to be late	*sulus ʃaŋam*	*kʰramu*
S14.250	to begin	*ʃuru ʃaŋam*	*duʃimu* [MDL]
S14.2510	the beginning	*ʃuru*, *ʃuruŋ*	*ʃuru*; *dzode beraŋ*
S14.260	the end(2)	*ʋeʃiŋ* 'end; finish'	—
S14.270	to finish	*nibja:m* [TR]; *ʋesam*	*(ʃuŋmu) tsʰekja:mu* [TR]; *purja:mu* [TR] 'to finish; to complete'; *ʃuŋmu* [INTR]

IDS	Gloss	Kanashi (xns)	Kinnauri (kfk)
S14.280	to cease	*gunaʃim* [MDL] 'to stop'; *rokja:m* [TR] 'to stop; to cease'; *rukem* [INTR] 'to stop; to cease'; *ʈʰaprja:m* [TR] 'to stop; to cease'	*rokja:mu* [TR] 'to stop; to cease'; *rukennu* [INTR] 'to stop; to cease'; *rokja:ʃimu* [MDL] 'to stop; to cease'
S14.310	always	*roʣ* 'always; every day; daily'; *sada*	*dja:ro* 'always; every day, daily'
S14.320	often	*kebbikebbi* 'often; sometimes'	*ipaipa*
S14.330	sometimes	*kebbikebbi* 'often; sometimes'; *kebigas*	*ipa*; *isən*
S14.331	soon	*ʦʰika* 'early; soon; fast; quickly'	*hasəl* 'soon; fast (speed)'
S14.350	again	*hed*	*he*; *dema* (S), *tema* (B) 'then; again'
S14.410	the day(1)	*laje* 'day; daytime; midday; lunch'; *un*	*mja*; *laje*, *le*
S14.4110	the day(2)	*ʤaɽe*; *un*	*dja:r*; *djusaŋ*; *tʰa:ro*
S14.420	the night	*ra:tiŋ*, *ra:t*	*ra:tiŋ*
S14.430	the dawn	*som ʤiʃa*	*somsi*
S14.440	the morning	*som*	*som*
S14.450	the midday	*laje* 'day; daytime; midday; lunch'	*maʤaŋ laje*, *maʤaŋ le*
S14.460	the evening	*ʋeraŋ*	*ʃupa*; *ʃupelaŋ*
S14.470	today	*dalaʦ*; *tʰi:d*	*toro*
S14.480	tomorrow	*na:b*	*na:b*
S14.481	the day after tomorrow	*romi*	*romi*
S14.490	yesterday	*hid*; *muɖ*	*me:*
S14.491	the day before yesterday	*njuʦ*; *ri:d*	*ri:*
S14.510	the hour	*ganʈa*	*ganʈa(:)*
S14.530	the clock	*gaɽi* 'clock; watch'	*gəɽi*, *gaɽi:*
S14.610	the week	*hapta*	*həpta*
S14.620	Sunday	*tʋa:r*	*tʋa:r*, *tʋa:raŋ*
S14.630	Monday	*soar*, *suãraŋ*	*suãraŋ*
S14.640	Tuesday	*maŋgal*	*maŋgla:raŋ*
S14.650	Wednesday	*bud(d)*	*buda:raŋ*
S14.660	Thursday	*b(ʰ)rest*	*brespot*
S14.670	Friday	*ʃukkar*	*ʃukaraŋ*
S14.680	Saturday	*ʃuɳiʧare*	*ʃonʃeres*
S14.710	the month	*bina*; *mahina*	*gol*
S14.730	the year	*barʃ*, *barʃaŋ*; *sa:l*, *sa:laŋ*	*boʃaŋ*
S14.740	the winter	*gu(:)n*; *sardaŋ*; *ʈʰanɖas* 'cold; winter'	*gun*
S14.760	the summer	*garmi* 'summer; warm (weather)'; *ʃa:l*	*ʃol*
S14.770	the autumn/fall	*sadraŋ*	*ʦʰarmi*
S15.210	to smell(1)	*ba:s baram*; *ba:s punʃim*	*ba:sennu* [INTR] (one entity); *ba:sja:ʃimu* [MDL] (collectively); *tamʃimu* [MDL]; *basennu* [INTR]
S15.212	to sniff	*ba:s pʰum*; *ba:s suŋam*	*ba:sja:mu* [TR]; *(ba:s) tammu* [TR]
S15.310	to taste	*prekʰja:m* [TR]	—
S15.350	sweet	*tʰig*	*tʰi:g*; *em*
S15.360	salty	*kruk*; *ʦʰa ʣada*	*ʦʰakore*; *surk* 'salty; sour'
S15.380	sour	*surg*	*surk* 'salty; sour'
S15.410	to hear	*ʦʰa:m* 'hear; listen'	*tʰəsmu*
S15.420	to listen	*ʦʰa:m* 'hear; listen'	*ronʧimu*
S15.440	the sound or noise	*deg* 'sound'; *kaɽi* 'sound; noise; voice'	*(s)kad*
S15.450	loud	*zori*	*ʣores*
S15.510	to see	*ba:lem* [INTR]; *ba:lja:m* [TR]	*kʰja:mu* (S), *kʰima* (B)
S15.520	to look	*taŋam* 'to look; to watch'; *taŋʃim* [MDL] 'to look; to watch'	*taŋmu* 'observe'
S15.560	to shine	*tsamkem*	*ʣəlmələnnu* [INTR]; *ʣəkməkennu* [INTR]
S15.610	the colour/color	*raŋg* 'color; paint'	*raŋg* 'paint; color'
S15.630	dark	*turaŋ*; *ʧʰras*	*ajã:raŋ*; *tur*

IDS	Gloss	Kanashi (xns)	Kinnauri (kfk)
S15.640	white	*tʃʰog*	*ʈʰog*
S15.650	black	*rok* 'black; dark-skinned'	*rok*
S15.660	red	*la:l*	*ʃʋi:g*
S15.670	blue	*arak*; *hara* 'blue; green'; *ra:g* 'blue; green'	*əsmani*; *ra:g* 'blue; green'
S15.680	green	*hara* 'blue; green'; *ra:g* 'blue; green'	*ra:g* 'blue; green'
S15.690	yellow	*pi:g* 'yellow; orange'	*pi:g* 'yellow'; *pigulgulo* 'orange'
S15.710	to touch	*bi:nam*	*ʈʰəŋmu*
S15.712	to pinch	*tʃis raɳam*	*tʃũɖus rannu*
S15.810	heavy	*garkas*	*li:g*
S15.820	light(1)	*haʈka:ts*	*lamgits*
S15.830	wet	*tʃits* 'wet; washed'	*tʃits*; *pintʃ*
S15.840	dry	*ʃukaʃ* 'dry; thirsty'; *tsʰardʑ*; *tʃika*; *tʃʰamjurts*	*tsʰarts* (e.g., plant leaves, stems); *kʰuʃk* (inanimate objects)
S15.851	warm	*dʒog*; *garmi* 'summer; warm (weather)'	*dʒogits*; *dʒ(r)ãŋk* 'very warm (weather)'
S15.860	cold	*sardi*; *ʈʰaɳɖas* 'cold; winter'	*lis(k)*
S15.870	clean	*tsokʰas*	*sapʰ*; *tsokʰes*; *ʃuʃes*, *ʃuʃkes* 'clean (human)'; *nira:nes* 'clean; pure (liquids)'
S15.880	dirty	*ganda*; *mand*	*kri:* 'dirty (internally generated dirt in humans)'; *ʋaʃ* 'dirty, impure'; *ma:ri* 'filthy (human)'
S16.250	to laugh	*ʋanam*	*ʋannu*
S16.251	to smile	*kʰuʃiga: dem*	—
S16.260	to play	*odʑim*	*jotʃimu*; *badʑja:mu* [TR]; *badʑennu* [INTR]
S16.290	to kiss	*peim*	*pʰapu rannu*
S16.310	the pain	*bedna*; *binɖra*	*əkʰa* (physical); *piraŋ* (mental)
S16.320	the grief	*dukʰe*; *dukʰis* 'disease; grief'	*dukʰaŋ* 'disease; grief'
S16.370	to cry	*krabam*	*krabmu*
S16.380	the tear	*piti*	*misti*
S16.420	the anger	*dʑikke*	*roʃaŋ*
S16.520	brave	*roʈʰ*, *roʈʰas*	*roʈʰas*; *ba:dur*
S16.530	the fear	*baŋ*	*bjaŋ*, *bjaŋməg*
S16.540	the danger	*batr*	*kʰətərnak*
S16.660	true	*sahi*; *sutʃai*, *suttsai* 'truth'	*sotskolaŋ*
S16.670	to lie(2)	*tʃora golop lonam*	*alkoləŋ batennu*
S16.690	to forgive	*ma:p ʃunim*	*ma:pʰ lannu*
S16.710	good	*daʈʰis* 'good (nature); correct; sweet'; *ʃobil*, *ʃobilas* 'good; delicious; lovely'	*dam*
S16.720	bad	*bura*; *ma:ɽa* 'bad; wrong'; *nark* 'hell; sorrow; evil; bad'; *ʃʋaʃi*	*ma:ri* 'bad, filthy (human)'; *narək* 'bad; sorrow; hell; evil'; *pa:paŋ* 'evil [N]'
S16.730	right(2)	*daʈʰis* 'good (nature); correct; sweet'; *ʈʰi:k*	*dimaŋ*
S16.740	wrong	*ma:ɽa* 'bad; wrong'	*ʋamaŋ*
S16.780	the blame	*kusur*	*bodi*
S16.810	beautiful	*ʃobil*, *ʃobilas* 'good; delicious; lovely'	*ʃaro* [M], *ʃare* [F]
S16.820	ugly	*ʃobi:l ma:j*	*maʃare* [F]
S16.830	greedy	*laltʃi*; *lartʃis muruk*	*laltsi*
S16.99903	thank you!	*kanka bala meradi*; *tegje ɖaʈʰis*	*ho:lase*
S16.99914	wild	*dʒaŋgali*	*bonsak* 'wild entities (animal, plant) [N]'
S17.130	to think(1)	*sotʃem*	*suntsennu* [INTR]; *tsalmu* 'to think; to feel'
S17.140	to think(2)	*buʃa ʃaɳam* 'to believe'	*suntsja:mu* [TR]
S17.160	to understand	*samdʑem* [INTR]; *samdʑja:m* [TR]	*somdʑennu* [INTR]; *gomu* [INTR]; *somdʑja:mu* [TR] 'to understand; to explain'

IDS	Gloss	Kanashi (xns)	Kinnauri (kfk)
S17.170	to know	*sesam* 'to know; to recognize'	*nemu*
S17.210	wise	*akli*	*okolsja:* 'wise [N]'
S17.230	mad	*ba:jlits*; *bekup^h* 'foolish'; *pagal* 'idiot; eccentric'	*bo:la:* 'mad (person)'; *pagal* 'mad, idiot'
S17.240	to learn	*sik^{h}ja:m* [TR]; *sik^{h}jem* [INTR]	*huʃimu* [MDL] 'to learn; to read'
S17.242	to study	*paɽem* [INTR] 'to study; to teach; to read'; *paɽ^{h}ja:m* [TR] 'to study; to teach; to read'	*bəntsja:mu*
S17.250	to teach	*paɽem* [INTR] 'to study; to teach; to read'; *paɽ^{h}ja:m* [TR] 'to study; to teach; to read'	*hunnu*
S17.260	the pupil	*paɽets ts^{h}akts*	*huʃid ʧ^{h}aŋ*
S17.270	the teacher	*guru* 'guru; teacher'; *ma:sʈar*	*maʃʈor*
S17.280	the school	*sukul*	*səkul*
S17.310	to remember	*ja:d baram*	*ja:d lannu* [VOL]; *kolaŋ lannu* [VOL]; *kolaŋ bənnu* [NVOL]; *ja:d bənnu* [NVOL]
S17.320	to forget	*boʃ(u)ʈam*	*boʃimu* [MDL]
S17.430	the doubt	*ʃakk*	*ʃok*; *bem*
S17.440	to suspect	*ʃak ʃaɳam*	*ʃok lannu*
S17.450	the need or necessity	*ʥaruri*	*gjaməg*
S17.470	difficult	*ʥuniɳas*; *muʃkil*	*kotsaŋ*; *muʃkil*
S17.480	to try	*koʃiʃ ʃaɳam*	*koʃiʃ lannu*
S17.510	and	*aj*; *haid*	*raŋ*; *aj*
S17.530	if	*netat*	—
S17.550	yes	*hoi*	*ã*
S17.560	no	*ma:j*	*mani*; *nei*; *ma:ts*
S17.610	how?	*hale*	*hales*; *hala*
S17.630	how much?	*tada* 'how many'	*te*; *tetra*; *teta* 'how many, how much'
S17.640	what?	*ʧ^{h}u*, *ʧ^{h}ugge*	*ʧ^{h}əd* 'what; some'
S17.650	when?	*ʧ^{h}ub*	*teraŋ*
S17.660	where?	*ham*	*ham*
S17.670	which?	*hatte*	*hat*; *hatsja:*
S17.680	who?	*hat*	*hat*
S17.690	why?	*k^{h}ue*	*ʧ^{h}u*, *t^{h}u*
S18.110	the voice	*kaɽi* 'sound; noise; voice'	*(s)kad*; *avaʥ*
S18.120	to sing	*gitaŋ lanam*	*git^{h}a: lannu*
S18.130	to shout	*kaɽa ʃaɳam*	*ʈok^{h}ennu* [INTR] 'to shout; to shriek; to call out loud'; *ʈok^{h}ja:mu* [TR] 'to shout; to shriek; to call out loud'
S18.150	to whisper	*sulus lonam*	*k^{h}uʃ puʃja:mu* [TR]; *ʃutputja:mu* [TR]
S18.170	to whistle	*ʃuĩ ʃaɳam*	*ʃuĩgja:mu*
S18.210	to speak or talk	*lonam* 'to say; to tell; to speak; to talk'	*lonnu* [NON-1/2O] 'to tell; to speak; to talk'; *riŋmu* [B], *rəŋmu* [S] [1/2O] 'to tell; to speak; to talk'
S18.220	to say	*lonam* 'to say; to tell; to speak; to talk'	*ba:tja:mu* [TR]; *ba:tennu* [INTR]
S18.221	to tell	*lonam* 'to say; to tell; to speak; to talk'	*ba:tja:mu* [TR]; *ba:tennu* [INTR]; *lonnu* [NON-1/2O] 'to tell; to speak; to talk'; *riŋmu* [B], *rəŋmu* [S] [1/2O] 'to tell; to speak; to talk'
S18.222	the speech	*bat*; *galaŋ*	*baʃən*; *ba:t*, *ba:taŋ*, *ba:tiŋ*; *galaŋ*
S18.240	the language	*ba:ʃa*; *boli*	*boli*; *b(^{h})a:ʃa*; *(s)kad*
S18.280	the name	*na:maŋ*, *na:m*	*na:maŋ*
S18.310	to ask(1)	*riʧim*	*imu*; *unnu* 'to take; to ask for'
S18.340	to deny	*mukrem*	*hurʃimu* [MDL]
S18.370	to refuse	*ma:j mullam*	*məna lannu*
S18.380	to forbid	*ma:j lonam*	*malannu*
S18.390	to scold	*ʃapoga: lonam*	*dopkja:mu*; *galja: rannu* 'to abuse'
S18.410	to call(1)	*a:ɽem*; *ʤaru lonam*	*ʈok^{h}ja:mu*; *arja:mu* 'to call; to invite'
S18.440	to threaten	*boŋam ʃeɳam*	*pjaŋmu*

IDS	Gloss	Kanashi (xns)	Kinnauri (kfk)
S18.510	to write	*likʰja:m* [TR]	*ʧemu* 'to write; to draw'
S18.520	to read	*paɽem* [INTR] 'to study; to teach; to read'; *paɽʰja:m* [TR] 'to study; to teach; to read'	*huʃimu* [MDL]
S18.560	the paper	*kagad*	*kagli*
S18.570	the pen	*pen*	*pen*; *kolom*
S18.610	the book	*kita:b*, *kuta:b*, *katab*	*kətab*; *kotʰi* 'Buddhist scriptures'
S18.710	the flute	*bẽʃur*, *bẽʃuri*	*banʃuri*; *murli*; *ba:ʃaŋ*
S18.720	the drum	*ɖolki*; *naga:ra*	*ɖol* 'drum with a leather membrane on both ends'
S18.730	the horn or trumpet	*ka:ɽi*	*raŋsiŋ* 'trumpet'
S19.110	the country	*deʃaŋ* 'country; village; world'	*deʃaŋ*; *muluk* 'country; village'
S19.150	the town	*ʃeher*	*ʃer*
S19.160	the village	*deʃaŋ* 'country; village; world'; *gra:m*, *gra:maŋ*	*gra:maŋ*; *nogriŋ*; *muluk* 'country; village'
S19.210	the people	*lok*, *lokas*; *mo*; *pakres*; *taŋʥa*	*lokas*
S19.240	the chieftain	*prada:n*	*gobats*; *karda:r*
S19.250	the walking stick	*loɽiʈom*; *loɽiʈua*	*ʧʰumma:*
S19.320	the king	*ba:dʃa*; *ra:ʤa*	*ra:ʤa*
S19.330	the queen	*ra:ni*	*ra:ni*
S19.430	the servant	*nokar*; *ʈʰinɖ*	*ʧʰunpa* [F]; *lantsja:* [M] 'slave, worker'; *nukur* [M/F]
S19.510	the friend	*dost*; *mitar(a)*, *mita:r*; *saŋgis*	*dost*; *saŋgis*; *gurba:i*; *kones* 'male friend of a man'; *konets* 'female friend of a woman'
S19.520	the enemy	*duʃman*	*dusmon*
S19.550	the stranger	*jug marʃaŋ*	*na:maŋ mi*
S19.560	the guest	*paɳaŋa*; *pa:una*; *ponukes*, *poɳukes*	*ponukes*
S19.5650	to invite	*paɳaŋa ʤaram*	*arja:mu* [TR] (formal); *kunnu* [TR] (informal); *arja:ʃimu* [MDL]
S19.580	to help	*mat ʃaɳam*	*seta rannu*
S19.610	the custom	*riʋa:ʥ* 'tradition; custom'; *sara*	*riʋa:ʥ* 'tradition; custom'
S19.650	to meet	*milem*, *millem* 'to meet; to intermingle; to join'; *mileʃim* [MDL]; *milja:m* [TR] 'to meet; to mix'	*ʧʰukmu* [TR]; *ʧʰukʃimu* [MDL]
S20.110	to fight	*ʥagɽiʃim ʃenam*; *toʃim* [MDL]	*kulʃimu* [MDL]; *da:ʃimu* [MDL] 'to fight verbally; to quarrel'
S20.140	the peace	*sukʰ* 'peace; happiness'	*ʃa:nti* 'peace; happiness'
S20.170	the soldier	*sipahi*, *sipahis*	*pʰoʤi*
S20.240	the bow	*danuʃ*; *ga:rts*	*danuʃ*
S20.250	the arrow	*ti:r*	*ba:n*; *ti:r*
S20.270	the sword	*tarʋa:r*, *talʋa:r*	*trəʋal*
S20.280	the gun	*tupka*, *tupkʰ*	*tupuk*
S20.360	the tower	*ʈʰomba*	*kʰãba*
S20.610	to hunt	*heraŋa boŋtam*	*eraŋ lannu*
S20.620	to shoot	*tupkas raɳam*	*tupuk baʥja:mu*
S20.640	the trap	*pinʤra* 'cage; trap'	*pinʥor*; *koŋ*
S21.110	the law	*ka:nun*	*ka:nun*
S21.230	the witness	*gaʋais*	*gʋa*
S21.240	to swear	*kaʃmi raɳam*	*ren ʥa:mu*
S21.360	innocent	*naɖa*; *ʃantida:r*	*sa:daŋ* 'innocent; simple (character-wise)'; *beksur*
S21.370	the penalty or punishment	*da:ɳaŋ*, *ɖa:ɳaŋ*	*ɖa:naŋ*
S21.380	the fine	*loʃito*	*səʥa*, *saʥa*
S21.390	the prison	*ʈʰaɳa*	*ked*; *obor* 'dungeon'
S21.510	to steal	*ʧorikega: ʃaɳam*	*kʰuʧimu*; *ʧorjaŋ lannu*
S21.520	the thief	*ʧoras*	*ʧoras*, *ʧores*
S22.110	the religion	*daram*	*dorom*, *daram*

IDS	Gloss	Kanashi (xns)	Kinnauri (kfk)
S22.120	the god	*bagʋaːn*; *ʤaŋ*	*bogan* 'Hindu god'; *deʋi* 'Hindu godess'; *deʋtaː* 'Hindu god'; *pormeʃeres* [M]; *ʃu* 'village god,'; *ʤ^{h}oŋraːʤas* [M] 'death god'
S22.130	the temple	*deog^{h}ar*; *deoraŋ*; *ʤaka kima*; *ʤaka piːbu*; *mandir*; *monoŋ*	*deoriŋ*; *koʈ^{h}i*; *koʈ^{h}iʃelaŋ*; *gonpa* 'Buddhist temple'; *sant^{h}aŋ* 'temple compound'
S22.170	to pray	*ʥap ʃaɳam*	*donʈrennu* 'pray (in one's heart)'; *orʥ lannu* 'pray (orally)'
S22.180	the priest	*gur* 'mouthpiece of the god'; *puʥʥaːra*, *puʤari*	*piʤares*; *ʤomo* [F] 'lama'; *sod* [M], *sodonig*, *sodnig* [F]; *bramən* 'priest/brahmin'
S22.260	to fast	*ʋaʃe naʃim*	*kadaʃ lannu*
S22.310	the heaven	*sʋarg*	*sorg*; *soroglok*
S22.320	the hell	*nark* 'hell; sorrow; evil; bad'	*norok*, *narək*
S22.420	the magic	*ʥaddu*	*ʥaːdu*
S22.430	the sorcerer or witch	*ʧuɽel* 'witch'	*ɖagin* 'sorcerer, witch'; *ʧuɽel* [F]
S22.450	the ghost	*b(^{h})utaŋ*; *raks*	*rakʃas*; *ʃuna*
S22.99909	the muslim	*musalman*	*musəlman*
S23.1000	the radio	*roɖije*	*reɽu*
S23.1100	the television	*biɖio*, *ʋiɖiɔ*; *ʈiʋi*	*ʈibi*
S23.1200	the telephone	*mobajl*, *mobajlaŋ* 'mobile telephone'; *p^{h}on*; *ʈelip^{h}on*	*mobajl*; *(teli)p^{h}on*
S23.1400	the car	*gaːɽiŋ*, *gaːɽi* 'car; bus'; *kaːr*	*gaːɽi*; *kaːr*
S23.1500	the bus	*bas*; *gaːɽiŋ*, *gaːɽi* 'car; bus'	*bos*, *bas*
S23.1550	the train	*rel*; *ʈren*	*rel*; *ʈren*
S23.1600	the airplane	*ʋai ʤahaʤ*	*(haʋai)ʤaʥ*
S23.1700	the electricity	*biʤeɽi* 'electricity; lightning; flashlight'	*biʥəli*
S23.1750	the battery	*baʈari*	*sel(l)*
S23.1900	the machine	*muʃiːn*	*maʃin*
S23.2000	the hospital	*aspataːl*, *haspataːl*	*aspətal*
S23.2300	the injection	*sua*	*sua*
S23.2400	the spectacles/glasses	*enak*; *ʧaʃma*	*enək*; *ʧaʃma*
S23.3000	the government	*sirkar*	*gormenʈ*
S23.3200	the minister	*ʤeʃʈ^{h}as* 'elected member of Kanashi village council; elder; senior'	*mantri*; *elkar*; *ʤeʃʈ^{h}as*, *gobaʦ*; *ʤeʃʈ^{h}aŋ* 'elder [N]'
S23.3300	the police	*purʦ*	*pulis*
S23.3950	the street	*gali* 'street (narrow)'	*goːliŋ*
S23.4200	the letter	*ʧiʈʈ^{h}i*	*ʦiʈ^{h}i*, *ʧiʈ^{h}i*
S23.5200	the toilet	*ʈaʈʈik^{h}ana*	*k^{h}əsuriŋ*
S23.5600	the bottle	*bottal*	*botol*
S23.5650	the candy/sweets	*miʈ^{h}a*; *sauda*	*emeʦ*; *miʈ^{h}ai*
S23.5900	the cigarette	*surgiʈ*	*sigriʈ*
S23.6200	the film/movie	*p^{h}ilam*	*p^{h}ilam*
S23.6400	the song	*gaɳa*; *gitaŋ*	*gana*; *gitaŋ*
S23.9000	the tea	*ʧa(ː)*	*ʧaː*
S23.9100	the coffee	*kop^{h}i*	*kop^{h}i*
S24.0100	to be	*maːje-* [NEG.BE/EXIST]; *nem* 'to exist; to be'; *to* 'be-'	*to*; *du*; *nimu* 'exist, stay'
S24.0400	with	*saŋ*	*(-)rəŋ* [(-)COM]
S24.0600	not	*maːj*	*ma-*
S24.0700	this	*ʤo*; *nu*	*hojo*, *ʤo* [DEM.PROX]
S24.0800	that	*du*; *tes*	*hodo*; *no*, *hono* [DEM.DIST.VIS]
S24.0900	here	*lo*; *nid*	*həʤəŋ*
S24.1000	there	*didd*; *njo*	*dəŋ* [THERE.VIS]; *nəŋ* [THERE.NVIS]
S24.1100	other	*hedde* 'other; next'	*aid*
S24.1200	next	*hedde* 'other; next'	*daŋ* 'near; next; beside'
S24.1400	nothing	*ʧ^{h}igi maːʃ*	*ʧ^{h}ətsi*, *mani*

IDS	Gloss	Kanashi (xns)	Kinnauri (kfk)
S24.99912	then	*da; dabadʑp^{h}eʈa; dabode; dabre; dok; ɖaba; tabo*	*dok* 'then; after'; *dema* (S), *tema* (B) 'then; again'

B Kanashi–English word list

The Kanashi headwords in this list are ordered according to the following sorting order. Symbols in parentheses are treated as equal for sorting purposes, i.e. differences in length and nasality are ignored when sorting vowel symbols. Sorting is word-by-word, i.e., *ʧis raɳam* 'to pinch' is sorted before *ʧisaŋ* 'flour (of buckwheat)'.

Sorting order for the Kanashi headwords
(a, a:, ã, ã:), b, b^{h}, d, d^{h}, ɖ, ɖ^{h}, ʥ, ʤ, (e, e:, ẽ, ẽ:), f, g, g^{h}, h, (i, i:, ĩ, ĩ:), j, k, k^{h}, l, m, n, ɳ, ŋ, (o, o:, õ, õ:), p, p^{h}, r, ɽ, ɽ^{h}, s, ʃ, t, t^{h}, ʈ, ʈ^{h}', 'ts, ts^{h}, ʧ, ʧ^{h}, (u, u:, ũ, ũ:), ʋ, z

adrak N : ginger (—)
ad^{h}a N : half (S13.240)
aʤaŋ N : guts; intestines (S04.461)
aʤaɽ N : apricot (—)
a:g N : cave (S01.280)
agraŋ : ahead; beyond (S12.0410)
aj : and (S17.510)
aja:m V : agree (—)
akli : wise (S17.210)
aksa : probably (—)
a:l N : lentils (—)
alag N : separation (—)
ala:ts N : baby (S02.280)
alesis : lazy (S04.920)
alo : since (—)
a:m N : mango (S08.99930)
a:n ma:ts : pregnant (S04.730)
anam V : carry (S10.610)
ana:t^{h} N : orphan (S02.750)
anɖa N : egg (S05.970)
aŋganʋa:ɽiŋ N : child care center (—)
aŋgi ʃaɳam V : separate (S12.230)
aŋgu:r N : grape (S05.760)
aŋka:laŋ N : famine (S05.141)
a:r N : flour (S05.550)
a:r p^{h}ram V : make dough (—)
a:ra N : saw (S09.480)
arak : blue (S15.670)
ara:m N : relaxation (—)
arʥ N : entreaty (—)
arʥi : immediately (S14.190)
a:ri N : dough (S05.530)
arʃug N : mirror (S06.960)
arʃuk N : mirror (S06.960)
a:ɽem V : call(1) (S18.410)
asli : in reality; original (—)
aspata:l N : hospital (S23.2000)
a:ʃa:ŋ : barren (land) (—)
aʈ^{h} : eight (S13.0800)
aʧa:r N : pickle (—)
aʧ^{h}im V : arise; wake up (S04.630)
agost : August (—)
ba: N : father; uncle (S02.350, S02.510)
ba: ʤeʈ^{h}a N : father's older brother (S02.512)
ba: kan N : stepfather (S02.710)
ba: p^{h}akuʧ N : father's younger brother (S02.512)
ba:d : after (S12.0100)
bada N : order (—)
bada:m N : almond (S08.99901)
ba:dʃa N : king (S19.320)
bãɖa N : portion; share (S13.230)
baʥa:(r) N : market (S11.850)
ba:ʥi N : vegetables (S05.650)
baʥug N : thigh (S04.351)
bag : thin (S12.650)
bagula N : heron (S03.583)
bagʋa:n N : god (S22.120)

baːhudʒi N : full sleeve (—)
bai N : spring; well (S01.370)
baĩs N : buffalo (S03.9170)
baːjlits : mad (S17.230)
bakar N : goat (S03.360)
bakari N : goat [F] (S03.360)
bakras N : goat (S03.360)
baks N : box (—)
bal N : head (S04.200)
bala anam V : carry on head (S10.614)
baːlem [INTR] V : see (S15.510)
bali N : sand (S01.215)
baːljaːm [TR] V : see (S15.510)
balʈiŋ N : bucket (—)
bandgobi N : cabbage (S05.99908)
bandraŋ N : monkey (S03.760)
banɖaːraŋ N : storage room; treasury (—)
banɖijaːm V : share (S11.910)
baniŋ N : pot (S05.260)
baɳ N : forest; woods (S01.410)
baɳaŋ N : forest; woods (S01.410)
baːɳek N : niece (S02.540)
baɳem V : build; make (S09.1110, S09.440)
baːɳes N : brother's son; nephew (S02.530)
baŋ N : fear (S16.530)
baŋga N : bracelet (modern) (S06.740)
baole N : foot; leg (S04.350, S04.370)
bapas N : return (—)
bapas raɳam V : give back (S11.220)
baːr N : rent; revenue; tax; ticket (S11.690)
bara : twelve (S13.102)
bara raɳam V : swim (S10.350)
baram V : come; rise (of sun) (S10.210, S10.480)
barem [INTR] V : fill (S13.99907)
barits : full; many; more; much (S13.150, S13.160, S13.210)
barits munuk N : crowd (S13.190)
barjaːm [TR] V : fill (S13.99907)
barnog N : vegetable (a wild species, used in cooking) (S05.650)
baːro : outside (S12.0600)
baːro boŋʈam V : go out (S10.474)
barʃ N : year (S14.730)
barʃaŋ N : year (S14.730)
barʈ N : prophet (—)
baːru : outside (S12.0600)
baɽaŋ N : forest; woods (S01.410)
baɽʋa N : door-bolt; latch (S07.231)
bas N : bus (S23.1500)
baːs N : odor; scent; smell (—)
baːs baram V : smell(1) (S15.210)
baːs puŋʃim V : smell(1) (S15.210)
baːs pʰum V : sniff (S15.212)
baːs suŋam V : sniff (S15.212)
basets bekaɽi N : married woman (S02.390)
basets beʈaɽi N : married woman (S02.390)
baʃ N : lung (S04.441)
baːʃa N : language (S18.240)
bat N : speech (S18.222)
batak N : duck (S03.570)
batr N : danger (S16.540)
baʈari N : battery (S23.1750)
batsjaːm V : rescue (S11.250)
batsjaːs piʧim V : preserve (S11.240)
bau N : brother (S02.440)
bau baʧa N : brother's child (S02.5410)
beddza N : seed (S08.311)
bedna N : pain (S16.310)
beg N : bag (S06.99901)
beiman : dishonest (—)
bekaɽi N : woman (S02.220)
bekupʰ : foolish (S17.230)
bellis : wide (S12.610)
belʧa N : shovel (S08.240)
benɖerem V : limp; share (S10.451, S11.910)
besaɳe N : chickpea flour (—)
bẽʃur N : flute (S18.710)
bẽʃuri N : flute (S18.710)
beʈa N : son (S02.410)
beʈaɽi N : woman (S02.220)
beʈaɽi mord N : eunuch (—)
beʈiŋ N : plant; tree; tree trunk (S08.530, S08.600)
bi : twenty (S13.104)
biɖio N : television (S23.1100)
bidzanes N : business; shop (S11.860)
bidʒeɽi N : electricity; flashlight; lightning (S01.550, S07.450, S23.1700)
biːg N : ant (S03.817)
bigalits N : midge (S03.831)
bijanna N : storm (S01.580)
bijaɳ N : seed (S08.311)
bijaŋ N : wedding (S02.340)
bijaŋ ʃaɳam V : marry (S02.330)
bikʃuar N : turmeric (—)
bikʰari N : beggar (S11.530)
bikʰaːrija N : beggar (S11.530)
bilkul : absolutely; totally (—)
biːm V : disappear (S10.491)
bina N : month (S14.710)
biːnam V : touch (S15.710)
binɖi N : okra (vegetable) (—)
binɖra N : pain (S16.310)
biniʃ N : husband (S02.310)
biɳis N : husband (S02.310)
biskuʈ N : biscuit (S05.99906)
biʃaŋ N : poison (S04.890)
bitiŋ N : wall (S07.270)
biʧu N : scorpion (S03.815)
biːʧʰa N : alms (—)
bjaːle N : dinner; meal (S05.410, S05.440)
bod N : peel (of vegetable or fruit); skin (of animal) (S04.120)
bodam V : spare (—)

boddi N : flower (a species planted as decoration) (S08.570)

boi N : sibling (S02.456)

boits N : younger sibling (S02.4562)

boli N : language (S18.240)

bonam V : go (S10.470)

boŋam ʃeɳam V : threaten (S18.440)

boraŋ N : luggage; sack (S09.99917)

bori : much (—)

boɽits N : butterfly (S03.920)

boʃ(u)ʈam V : forget (S17.320)

bottal N : bottle (S23.5600)

boʈuaŋ N : purse (S06.99901)

bout^h : very (—)

b(r)es N : kaʈ^{h}u (a wheat-like cereal) (—)

bɽitits N : lizard (S03.960)

bube N : father's sister; mother-in-law (S02.522, S02.620, S02.621)

bud(d) : Wednesday (S14.650)

buka N : heart; liver (S04.440, S04.450)

bukamp N : earthquake (S01.450)

buma:ri N : disease (S04.8440)

bumiŋ N : floor (S07.260)

bumle N : strawberry (wild) (—)

bunen N : sweater (—)

bu:r N : butter (local) (S05.890)

bura : bad (S16.720)

bura:ɽa N : cat [M] (S03.620)

bura:ɽi N : cat [F] (S03.620)

burʃ N : brush (S06.920)

burʃuk N : divorce (S02.341)

buruʃ N : comb (S06.910)

buɽ : left (S12.420)

buɽam V : leave; throw (S10.250, S10.490)

buɽas N : old man (S02.461)

buɽits N : old woman (S02.471)

buʃ N : rope (S09.190)

buʃa ʃaɳam V : believe (S17.140)

butkar N : ram (S03.260)

bu:ʈ N : boot; shoe (S06.510, S06.520)

b^{h}aɳe N : brother's son; nephew (S02.530)

b(^{h})rest : Thursday (S14.660)

b(^{h})utaŋ N : ghost (S22.450)

da : then (S24.99912)

da:ba : perhaps (—)

dabaʥe : anyhow (—)

dabaʥp^{h}eʈa : then (S24.99912)

dabja:m V : bury; press; squeeze (S04.780, S09.342, S09.343)

dabode : then (S24.99912)

dabre : then (S24.99912)

da:da N : paternal grandfather (S02.460)

da:dada:di N : paternal grandparents (S02.4711)

daddu N : paternal grandfather (S02.460)

dade : that much (—)

da:di N : paternal grandmother (S02.470)

da:duse da:di N : paternal grandparents (S02.4711)

daʥi N : threshhold (—)

daftra N : office (—)

dahi N : yoghurt (—)

daiju N : sister (S02.450)

da:l N : lentils (—)

dalak : few (S13.170)

dalats : less; today (—, S14.470)

da:n N : donation; temper (—)

danam [INTR] V : drop; fall (S10.160, S10.230)

danuʃ N : bow (S20.240)

da:ɳaŋ N : penalty; punishment (S21.370)

daram N : religion (S22.110)

darʥi N : tailor (S06.130)

dari N : mat; rug (S09.770, S09.771)

dart^{h}i N : earth (S01.100)

das : ten (S13.100)

daʈ^{h}is : correct; good (nature); sweet (S16.710, S16.730)

dauga N : thread (S06.380)

de : thus (—)

deg N : sound (S15.440)

dem V : give (S11.210)

deodar N : cedrus deodara (tree) (S08.640)

deog^{h}ar N : temple (S22.130)

deoraŋ N : temple (S22.130)

deɽ : one and a half (—)

deʃaŋ N : country; village; world (S19.110, S19.160, S01.100)

di : near (S12.430)

didd : there (S24.1000)

dil N : heart; soul (S04.440)

dili : Delhi (—)

diliŋ : Delhi (—)

dimaki : intelligent (—)

disambar : December (—)

dok : then (S24.99912)

doɽag N : pair; twin (S02.458)

dost N : friend (S19.510)

du : [3SG.DIST]; that (S02.930, S24.0800)

duʣ : whatever (—)

duʤa : second (S13.360)

duga: : [3PL.DIST] (S02.960)

duk^h(e) N : disease; grief; misery (S04.8440)

duk^{h}e N : grief (S16.320)

duk^{h}is : sad; sick/ill (S04.840)

duk^{h}is N : disease; grief; misery (S04.8440, S16.320)

du:l N : dust (S01.213)

dumaŋ N : smoke (S01.830)

dumme N : fog (S01.740)

dumsa N : gathering (large) (—)

dunija: N : world (S01.100)

dupaŋ N : incense (—)

dupa:ri N : lunch (S05.430)

duppe N : sun (S01.520)

du:(r) : far (S12.440)

durane : far (S12.440)
duʃman N : enemy (S19.520)
dutso : whatever (—)
dʊanam V : come out; rise (of sun) (S10.210)
dʊa:re N : balcony (—)
dʊaregan N : room for firewood (—)
dʰalak : less (—)
dʰara behad N : upper part of Malana (—)
dʰaraŋ N : upper part of Malana (—)
dʰart N : floor (S07.260)
ɖaba : then (S24.99912)
ɖabaŋ N : box; container; jar (—)
ɖabua N : currency (S11.430)
ɖag N : cliff (S01.222)
ɖaggis N : blacksmith (male member of traditional community) (S09.600)
ɖagi N : blacksmith (traditional community) (S09.600)
ɖakʈar N : physician (S04.870)
ɖakʰ N : cliff (S01.222)
ɖa:lem V : measure (S12.540)
ɖa:ɳaŋ N : penalty; punishment (S21.370)
ɖeb : left (S12.420)
ɖehi N : body (S04.110)
ɖe:k N : fence (S08.160)
ɖera N : home, camping (S07.6500)
ɖibɽiŋ N : pond; well (S01.330, S01.370)
ɖigtsa: N : pot (S05.260)
ɖiksa N : pot (S05.260)
ɖiŋga : crooked (S12.740)
ɖiŋgas : crooked (S12.740)
ɖoɖre N : beehive (S03.822)
ɖog N : hill; mountain (S01.220)
ɖolki N : drum (S18.720)
ɖu N : ground (e.g. football ground) (—)
ɖub(b)em [INTR] V : drown; sink (S04.751, S10.330)
ɖubja:m [TR] V : drown; sink (S10.330)
ɖug N : bottom; deep (S12.340)
ɖug : bottom; deep (S12.670)
ɖugas N : bottom; deep (S12.340)
ɖugas : bottom; deep (S12.670)
ɖugas ma:j : shallow (S12.680)
ɖuɽam V : come out (—)
ɖuʈam V : take out (S12.212)
ʣa(:)b : right(1) (S12.410)
ʥa:b : now (S14.180)
ʥa:(d) N : wheat (S08.430)
ʥad(d)a : much (—)
ʥaddu N : magic (S22.420)
ʥa:ɖe N : beam (S07.550)
ʥaʥari N : earthquake (S01.450)
ʥa:ga N : place (S12.110)
ʥagɽiʃim ʃenam V : fight (S20.110)
ʥahaʥ N : plane (—)
ʥa:kʰ N : beam (S07.550)
ʥala:ʊ N : diarrhoea (—)
ʥa:m V : eat (S05.110)
ʥa:m N : food (S05.120)
ʥa:miʥ ʃaɳam V : cook (S05.210)
ʥan N : life (S04.7410)
ʥa(:)ŋ N : gold (S09.640)
ʥa:ŋ N : gold; ornament (S06.710)
ʥa:ŋmamula: N : necklace (golden) (—)
ʥap ʃaɳam V : pray (S22.170)
ʥarka:ris : strong (S04.810)
ʥa:rs N : spider (S03.818)
ʥaruri N : necessity; need (S17.450)
ʥaruri : necessary (—)
ʥaɽi N : spider web (S03.819)
ʥatka sila:ŋ N : paddy (S08.1210)
ʥats : fair (—)
ʥa:ts N : spider (S03.818)
ʥaʊa:n ʧʰakts N : young man (S02.251)
ʥeher N : poison (S04.890)
ʥibaɳ : please (—)
ʥikem [INTR] V : press (S09.342)
ʥikja:m [TR] V : press (S09.342)
ʥikke N : anger (S16.420)
ʥi:mi: N : soil (S01.212)
ʥimida:(r) N : farmer (S08.110)
ʥindagi N : life (S04.7410)
ʥiu N : animal; living being (S03.110)
ʥoɖega: N : furrow (S08.212)
ʥo:r N : fever (S04.841)
ʥoɽ N : dish (with lassi and wheat flour); shoe (—, S06.510)
ʥoɽa N : shoe (S06.510)
ʥoɽam [INTR] V : get stuck (—)
ʥoɽi N : pair (S13.370)
ʥoɽja:m [TR] V : stick (—)
ʥõũɽi N : pair (S13.370)
ʥubaŋ N : barley (S08.440)
ʥuniŋas : difficult (S17.470)
ʥu:r la:tam V : stretch (S09.320)
ʥura:b N : sock; stocking (S06.490)
ʥururi : essential (—)
ʥʰa: : much (—)
ʤab N : rain (S01.750)
ʤad N : forest; woods (S01.410)
ʤag N : jug; pitcher (S05.340)
ʤagɽa ʃim V : dispute (—)
ʤairu N : stream (S01.360)
ʤaka kima N : temple (S22.130)
ʤaka pi:bu N : temple (S22.130)
ʤakka raɳam V : push (S10.670)
ʤakʈ N : jacket (S06.430)
ʤalamdin N : birthday (—)
ʤama:em V : yawn (S04.520)
ʤamais N : son-in-law (S02.630, S02.631)
ʤa:mgar N : molar tooth (S04.272)
ʤami:n N : soil (S01.212)
ʤanaŋ N : community hall (—)
ʤa:nʊar N : animal (S03.110)
ʤaŋ N : god (S22.120)
ʤa:ŋ N : root (S08.540)

dʒaŋgal N : barren land; forest (S01.410)
dʒaŋgali : wild (S16.99914)
dʒaŋʧ : physically weak; thin; weak (S04.820, S12.650)
dʒaru lonam V : call(1) (S18.410)
dʒaɽe N : day(2) (S14.4110)
dʒa:ɽe N : sun (S01.520)
dʒaʋa:n : young (S14.140)
dʒaʋa:n ʧimets N : young woman (S02.261)
dʒeʃtʰaŋ N : upper house in traditional Malana parliament (—)
dʒeʃtu(k) prá:d N : thumb (S04.342)
dʒeʃtʰas N : elder; elected member of Kanashi village council; senior (S23.3200)
dʒeʈʰ : senior (—)
dʒeʧialga N : sweet potato, red (S08.910)
dʒil N : lagoon; lake (S01.330, S01.341)
dʒim [INTR] V : wash (S09.360)
dʒiɖ : a lot (S13.150)
dʒiɖije : much (—)
dʒiŋ : big (S12.550)
dʒo : bottom; down; down south; this (—, S12.0300, S24.0700)
dʒo N : bottom; down (S12.340)
dʒog : warm (S15.851)
dʒohaŋ N : deity (—)
dʒojʃtʰaŋ N : moon (S01.530)
dʒugnu N : firefly (S03.910)
dʒula:ha N : weaver of nets (—)
dʒuma N : sausage (S05.630)
dʒuɳam [INTR] V : break; split; tear (S09.260, S09.270)
dʒuriŋ N : glacier (—)
dʒuʃaŋ N : cloud (S01.730)
dʒuʃtʰa N : moon (S01.530)
ei : four days after today (—)
ek : one (S13.0100)
ekʃana bu:ʈ N : shoe (modern sneaker) (S06.510)
enak N : glasses; spectacles (S23.2400)
ette : [1PLI] (S02.941)
eʧei : four days after tomorrow (—)
fikri N : matter (—)
gadda N : donkey (S03.460)
ga:dʒar N : carrot (S08.99910)
ga:jek N : singer (—)
galaŋ N : speech (S18.222)
galband N : muffler (—)
gali N : street (narrow) (S23.3950)
gallas N : eagle; vulture (S03.584, S03.586)
ganam N : goiter; goitre (S04.842)
ganda : dirty (S15.880)
ganʈa N : hour (S14.510)
ganʈʰaŋ N : bell (—)
gaɳ N : ditch (S08.170)
gaɳa N : song (S23.6400)
gaɳam V : build; pour; put (S09.350, S09.440, S12.120)
ganja:m V : count (S13.107)
ga:r N : tooth (S04.270)
garaɽiga: N : snores(PL) (—)
garaɽiga: raɳam V : snore (S04.612)
gari:b : poor (S11.520)
garkas : heavy (S15.810)
garmi N : summer; warm (weather) (S14.760)
garmi : summer; warm (weather) (S15.851)
garʃim [MDL] V : put on (S06.110)
ga:rts N : bow (S20.240)
ga:rts raʈam V : bite (S04.580)
gaɽi N : clock; watch (S14.530)
ga:ɽi N : bus; car (S23.1400, S23.1500)
ga:ɽiŋ N : bus; car; river (S01.360, S23.1400, S23.1500)
gas N : cloth (S06.210)
gasa N : dress (traditional for women) (S06.420)
gaʃam V : wear (S06.99911)
gata : loss (—)
gaʈa:ŋ N : watermill (—)
gaʈas : narrow (S12.620)
ga:ʈi N : valley (S01.240)
gaʈʈi N : pebble (S01.440)
gaʋais N : witness (S21.230)
geʈʈʰaŋ N : fireplace; oven; stove (S05.250, S07.310, S07.320)
gidaɽ N : jackal (—)
gindi N : ball (S12.830)
gisam V : sneeze (S04.540)
gitaŋ N : song (S23.6400)
gitaŋ lanam V : sing (S18.120)
gjara : eleven (S13.101)
gliŋ N : barley beer (S05.930)
goarʃim [MDL] V : scrape (S05.480)
gobi N : cauliflower (—)
goɖinats pra:d N : toe (S04.380)
goɖiŋ N : foot; leg (S04.350, S04.370)
godʒ N : grazing (—)
goguŋ N : flower (a wild species, blue-white; people put this flower on their caps) (S08.570)
gol : round (S12.810)
golaŋ N : neck; throat; way in (—, S04.280, S04.290)
goɽa N : ankle; horse; stallion (S03.410, S03.420, S04.371)
goɽi N : mare (S03.440)
goʈʰ N : grinding stone (—)
goʈʰi N : finger (S04.340)
gra:m N : village (S19.160)
gra:maŋ N : village (S19.160)
gro:ɳ N : eclipse (—)
gu : [1SG] (S02.910)
gud N : glue (S09.560)
guɖ N : arm; hand (S04.310, S04.330)
guɖpa anam V : carry in hand (S10.612)
guɖpa ʤura:bba: N : glove (S06.580)

gugut N : pigeon (S03.594)
gula:b u: N : rose (flower) (—)
gula(:)s N : glass; tumbler (S09.740)
gule N : apricot seed (dried) (—)
guledʑ ʃaɳam V : carve (S09.810)
guli:ʧa N : carpet (S09.771)
gu(:)n N : winter (S14.740)
gunaʃim [MDL] V : stop (S14.280)
gu:nd N : glue (S09.560)
gundja:m V : knit; weave (S06.330, S09.750)
gunɖu (ʧaɽig) N : bird (a small species with a small crown on its head) (S03.581)
guŋge N : bark (of a dog) (—)
gup^{h}a N : cave (S01.280)
gur N : mouthpiece of the god (S22.180)
gurʃu N : knot (S09.192)
guru N : guru; teacher (S17.270)
gururuga N : earthquake (S01.450)
guruɽuk N : thunder (S01.560)
guska N : elbow (S04.320)
guʈnu:ga: N : wheel (S10.760)
g(^{h})ana N : flame (S01.820)
g(^{h})aɽam N : hammer (S09.490)
g(^{h})oɳam V : build structure from foundation (S09.440)
g^{h}unɖi N : bell (—)
haɖɖaŋ N : bone (S04.160)
hadʑa:r : thousand (S13.106)
haid : and (S17.510)
hakima N : traditional Malana parliament (—)
hakkma N : traditional Malana parliament (—)
hale : how? (S17.610)
halg N : potato (S05.700)
ham : where? (S17.660)
hanɖem V : walk (S10.450)
hanɖja:m V : walk (S10.450)
hapta N : week (S14.610)
ha:r N : necklace (S06.750)
hara : blue; green (S15.670, S15.680)
haɽka:ʦ : light(1) (S15.820)
haspata:l N : hospital (S23.2000)
hat : who? (S17.680)
ha:ti N : shop; store (S11.860)
hatte : which? (S17.670)
hatt^{h}i N : elephant (S03.770)
hed : again (S14.350)
hedde : next; other (S24.1100, S24.1200)
help^{h} N : help (—)
heraɳa boŋtam V : hunt (S20.610)
heɽaŋ N : hunting (—)
hid : yesterday (S14.490)
hik N : breast; chest (S04.400, S04.410)
him(a)t N : courage (—)
him(a)t : courageous (—)
himd N : courage (—)
himd : courageous (—)
hi:p N : foreigner (—)
hipiʧ : after; last (S12.0100, S13.350)
hiram V : burn(2) (S01.852)
hiram ʃenam V : burn(1) (S01.851)
hiran N : deer (S03.750)
hisa N : portion; share (S13.230)
hoɖ N : bread (S05.510)
hoi : yes (S17.550)
ho(:)m N : bear (S03.730)
honɖes : back (—)
hoʃ N : consciousness; sense (—)
hoʧi ba(h)u N : younger sister (S02.455)
hu(:)ʤ N : cow (S03.230)
huʤa:r : thousand (S13.106)
hukka N : pipe (S08.691)
huŋg N : snail (S03.940)
i:d : one (S13.0100)
i:d hadʑa:r : thousand (S13.106)
i:d huʤa:r : thousand (S13.106)
i:d ʃo : hundred (S13.105)
idʑat N : honor (—)
ilna: N : eagle; vulture (S03.584, S03.586)
ipiʤ : backwards; behind (spatial) (S12.0110)
ipiʧ : backwards; behind (spatial) (S12.0110)
iʈ N : brick (S07.620)
ĩ:ʈ^{h} N : brick (S07.620)
ja: N : mother (S02.360)
ja: kani N : stepmother (S02.720)
ja:ba N : parents (S02.370)
ja:d N : remembrance (—)
ja:d baram V : remember (S17.310)
ja:ʤʈ^{h}i N : mother's sister (S02.521)
ja:k N : yak (—)
jaɳagats : young (S14.140)
jaŋ N : bee; flea; fly; mosquito (S03.813, S03.820, S03.830, S03.832)
jaras N : darkness (S01.620)
ja:ʃba: N : parents (S02.370)
jug : fresh; new (S14.130)
jug marʃaŋ N : stranger (S19.550)
juŋme N : mother-in-law (of a man); mother-in-law (of a woman) (S02.620, S02.621)
juʃk : old (S14.150)
ka : [2SG] (S02.920)
kadam N : step (—)
kaddu N : pumpkin (S08.931)
ka:ʤu N : cashew (S08.99911)
ka:g N : crow (S03.593)
kagad N : paper (S18.560)
kakaɽi N : heart (S04.440)
kakɽi N : cucumber (—)
kakʧos : rough(2) (S01.323)
kam : less (—)
kam N : shortage (—)
ka:m N : clay; soil; work (S01.212, S09.120, S09.730)
kamal u: N : lotus flower (S08.570)

ka:maŋ N : work (S09.120)
kambaɽ N : blanket (S07.422)
kamra N : room (S07.210)
kamraŋ N : room (S07.210)
kamɽ N : blanket (S07.422)
kan : bastard; step- (—)
kan N : curry sabzi (—)
ka:n N : mustard leaves (green) (—)
kanam V : bring (S10.620)
kana:ʃi : Kanashi (—)
kanɖe N : collar (S06.450)
kandʒus : stingy (S11.540)
kani N : canister (—)
kaniʃʈʰaŋ N : lower house in traditional Malana parliament (—)
kaniʃʈʰas : younger (—)
kaniʃʈʰas N : member of a lower class (—)
kanka bala meradi : thank you! (S16.99903)
kant N : comb (S06.910)
ka:nʈa N : earring (S06.770)
kanʦu gula(:)s N : glass; tumbler (S09.740)
kanʧi N : scissors; shears (S09.240)
ka:nun N : law (S21.110)
ka:ɳas : blind; one-eyed (S04.970)
ka:ɳo : blind; one-eyed (S04.970)
kaŋ N : rock; stone (S01.440)
kap N : cup (S05.350)
kapra N : cloth (S06.210)
kar N : star (S01.540)
ka:r N : ax; axe; car (S09.250, S23.1400)
karda:r N : temple treasurer (—)
karʥ N : heart; mind (S04.440)
karela N : bitter gourd (—)
kaɽa ʃaɳam V : shout (S18.130)
kaɽi N : noise; sound; voice (S15.440, S18.110)
ka:ɽi N : horn; trumpet (S18.730)
kaɽʦʰi N : spatula (—)
kasu:r N : sin (—)
kaʃmi raɳam V : swear (S21.240)
kat : together (—)
katab N : book (S18.610)
katʰa: N : story (—)
kaʈa:ɳ N : flower (a wild species, red-white; people put this flower on their caps) (S08.570)
kaʈem V : cut (S09.220)
kaʈja:m V : cut (S09.220)
kaʈora N : bowl (S05.330)
kaʈʰa N : roof (wooden); shade against rain (S07.510)
kaʈʰe ʃaɳam V : gather (S12.210)
ka:ʈʰi N : mountain; mountain pass; mountain top (S01.220)
ka:ʈʰiŋ N : mountain; mountain pass; mountain top; summit (S01.220, S12.330)
katʰu N : katʰu (a wheat-like cereal) (—)
kaʧas : raw; uncooked; unripe (S05.122, S05.124)
kaʧas halga N : sweet potato, white (S08.910)
kaʧʰ N : underwear (—)
kaʧʰar N : mule (S03.460)
kaʧʰua N : turtle (S03.980)
keb N : needle(1) (S06.360)
kebbikebbi : often; sometimes (S14.320, S14.330)
kebigas : sometimes (S14.330)
kenam [1/2o] V : give (S11.210)
keɽa N : banana (S08.840)
kesaraŋ N : yolk (S05.971)
keskʰaʈa N : armpit (S04.312)
ketali N : kettle (S05.270)
keʦi: : alone (S13.3310)
ki : [2PL] (S02.950)
kilo N : kilogram (—)
kilomiʈar N : kilometer (—)
kilʈi N : basket carried on the back (S09.760)
kim N : home; house (traditional) (S07.120)
kim ʃaɳam V : build (S09.440)
kina:ra N : shore (S01.270)
kinare N : side (S12.360)
kirjakaram N : death ceremony (—)
kiʃiʥ : domesticated (—)
kiʃti N : boat (S10.830)
kita:b N : book (S18.610)
kiʧan N : kitchen (—)
kobel N : cable (—)
kod N : cow dung; pot to measure cereal, flour etc (S05.260, S08.99918)
kodra N : roti made with kathu flour (S05.510)
koi : some (S13.181)
koile N : charcoal (S01.890)
kojlag N : embers (S01.841)
koɳe N : corner; edge (S12.353, S12.760)
kopʰi N : coffee (S23.9100)
kora N : tax (S11.690)
koraije : right away (—)
koraŋ N : tax (S11.690)
koʃiʃ ʃaɳam V : try (S17.480)
kotja:m V : dig (S08.220)
ko:ʈ N : coat (S06.430)
koʈaŋ N : room for storing god Jamlu's musical instruments which are played by SCs (e.g drums) (—)
kra: N : body hair; head hair (S04.140, S04.144)
krabam V : cry (S16.370)
kra:ɳ N : brain (as food) (S04.203)
kri N : earlobe (S04.221)
kruk : salty (S15.360)
kubaleke : late (S14.170)
kuba:r : in; inside (S12.0120)
kuba:r piʃim V : enter (S10.570)

kubeka : stingy (S11.540)
kubo:r : inside (—)
kuda:ɽi N : spade (S08.240)
kui N : dog (S03.610)
kukar N : pressure cooker (—)
kukaɽaŋ N : chicken; cock; rooster (S03.520, S03.550)
kukuɽoka ʧʰã N : chicken (S03.550)
kukuɽoka ʧʰaŋ N : chicken (S03.550)
kulam V : beat; thrash (S09.210)
kula:r N : breakfast (S05.420)
kultaŋʥa N : people of Kullu (—)
kum N : pillow (S07.421)
kumʥor : weak (S04.820)
kunaga N : nape of the neck (S04.281)
kuna:ʃi : Kanashi (—)
kunɖi N : pot (S05.260)
kunʥi N : key (S07.240)
kura:ʋas raɳam V : hire (S11.770)
kursi N : chair (S07.430)
kurti N : shirt (S06.440)
ku:ɽiŋ N : spring; well (S01.370)
kuɽmani N : daughter-in-law (S02.640, S02.641)
kusur N : blame (S16.780)
kusur ʃaɳam V : blame (—)
kuta:b N : book (S18.610)
kutta N : dog (S03.610)
kutti N : dog, female (S03.610)
kuʧʧʰa N : dog (S03.610)
káni góʈʰɪts N : finger (S04.340)
kʰa(:)kaŋ N : mouth (S04.240)
kʰamba N : pillar (S07.560)
kʰa:na N : food (S05.120)
kʰanam V : shiver (S04.680)
kʰanɖ N : sugar (S05.850)
kʰaɳaga: haʃim [INTR] V : cook (S05.210)
kʰaɳaga: ʃaɳam V : cook (S05.210)
kʰaŋam V : buy (S11.810)
kʰaŋem V : cough (S04.530)
kʰaram V : spend (—)
kʰare : very (—)
kʰargoʃ N : hare; rabbit (S03.614, S03.8630)
kʰartsul N : ladle; spoon (S05.370)
kʰaɽa aʧʃim V : stand (S12.150)
kʰas N : lamb; sheep (S03.250, S03.290)
kʰasats : honest (—)
kʰaʈ N : hole; injury (S12.850)
kʰaʈa gaɳam V : bore (a hole) (S09.460)
kʰaʈaga: N : nostril (S04.231)
kʰa:ts N : lamb (S03.290)
kʰila:m V : feed (—)
kʰili N : neck (S04.280)
kʰiraŋ N : milk (S05.860)
kʰiri ʧʰaʧʃe N : mushroom (a wild species) (S08.980)
kʰisaŋ N : pocket (S06.610)
kʰissa N : pocket (S06.610)
kʰitsja:m V : pull (S09.330)
kʰo N : belt (traditional); threshing-floor (S06.570, S08.350)
kʰo: N : waist (S04.462)
kʰobba N : snowshoe (S06.9800)
kʰo(l) N : court; yard (S07.150)
kʰolɖu N : hide; skin (S04.120)
kʰori N : footprint (S04.374)
kʰoɽa aʧʃim V : be flooded (—)
kʰoɽam V : snatch (—)
kʰoʃori bu:ʈ N : shoe (rubber, worn by women) (S06.510)
kʰotar N : kitchen (S07.170)
kʰrok N : fir (S08.650)
kʰuɖ N : animal shelter; cellar (—)
kʰuɖaŋ N : animal shelter; cellar (—)
kʰue : why? (S17.690)
kʰui N : blood (S04.150)
kʰuigopigol N : rainbow (S01.590)
kʰukʰuʈi N : dagger (—)
kʰulam V : open; peel (S05.460)
kʰulam [TR] V : open (S12.240)
kʰulas : wide (S12.610)
kʰulaʧ N : hall (—)
kʰulem [INTR] V : open (S12.240)
kʰulʃig N : bruise (S04.852)
kʰulʃim V : tan (S07.6700)
kʰulʃim [MDL] V : open (S12.240)
kʰults N : leather (of goat) (S06.290)
kʰu:nis N : murderer (—)
kʰurke N : wrist (S04.321)
kʰuɽaŋ N : cattleshed (S07.130)
kʰuʃi : happy; merry (—)
kʰuʃi N : celebration; happiness (—)
kʰuʃiga: dem V : smile (S16.251)
kʰutam V : sweep (S09.370)
kʰutaɳi N : hip (of domesticated animal) (S04.463)
kʰuteni N : bottom (S12.340)
kʰutu N : penis (S04.492)
lage : for (—)
laje N : day; daytime; lunch; midday (S05.430, S14.410, S14.450)
la:l : red (S15.660)
lala N : merchant (S11.840)
la:laŋ N : drool (—)
lalʧi : greedy (S16.830)
la:m V : find (S11.320)
la:mas : long; tall (S12.570, S12.580)
la:mʃim [MDL] V : find; pitch (—, S11.320)
lanam V : do; make (S09.110, S09.1110)
laŋ N : cow (S03.230)
laŋ kʰaga: N : cattle (S03.200)
laŋgija:m V : cross (—)
laŋokʰa: kʰas N : cattle (S03.200)
lapta N : garment (S06.120)
la:r N : rice (uncooked) (S08.480)
lari N : wave (S01.350)

lartʃis muruk : greedy (S16.830)
laɽi N : wife (S02.320)
lasaɳ N : garlic (—)
latas raɳam V : kick (S10.431)
laʈam V : hang up (S09.341)
laʈpaʈ(a) N : garment (S06.120)
laʈpaʈa potʃ N : tailor (S06.130)
laʈpaʈja:m V : wrap (in cloth) (S10.140)
la:ʈu N : bulb (of a lamp) (—)
latʰas : mute (S04.960)
le N : tongue (S04.260)
lebɽa N : bark; eggshell (S08.750)
lebɽa kʰulam V : skin (S09.290)
lemam V : lick (S04.590)
lenʈern N : house (modern) (S07.120)
leptupʰ N : spit (—)
letu N : spit (—)
letu buɽam V : spit (S04.560)
leʈpeʈjem V : crawl (S10.410)
likʰja:m [TR] V : write (S18.510)
li:m N : pine (S08.640)
linɖis N : braid; plait (S06.921)
linɖis ʃaɳ-am V : braid; plait (S09.750)
lipur N : air; wind (S01.720)
li:tʃ N : egg (S05.970)
lo : here (S24.0900)
lo N : zodiac sign (—)
lo baram V : come back (S10.481)
lodʒoŋ : right(1) (S12.410)
lok N : non-Kanashi person; people; person (S02.100, S19.210)
lokas N : non-Kanashi person; people; person (S02.100, S19.210)
lonam V : say; speak; talk; tell (S18.210, S18.220, S18.221)
loɽiʈom N : walking stick (S19.250)
loɽiʈua N : walking stick (S19.250)
loʃito N : fine (S21.380)
loʈ N : banknote (S11.430)
louk N : jump (—)
lugɽi N : rice beer (S05.930)
luk N : itch (S04.854)
lupʰa N : dish (with rice and seljara) (—)
luʈ N : loot (—)
madras N : man (S02.210)
maɖa : mute (S04.960)
madza N : pleasure (—)
madza:r N : tenant (—)
madʒaŋ N : between; middle (S12.370)
magarmatʃʰ N : alligator; crocodile (S03.970)
ma:gas : expensive (S11.880)
mahina N : month (S14.710)
ma:j : no; not (S17.560, S24.0600)
ma:j lonam V : forbid (S18.380)
ma:j mullam V : refuse (S18.370)
maja:m V : celebrate (—)
ma:je- V : [NEG.BE/EXIST] (S24.0100)
makkʰaɳ N : butter; ghee (S05.890)
ma:la N : property (S11.99904)
ma:ma: N : father-in-law; mother's brother (S02.511, S02.610, S02.611)
ma:mi: N : maternal uncle's wife (—)
ma:mug N : breast (S04.410)
man N : desire; heart; soul (S04.440)
mand : dirty (S15.880)
mandir N : temple (S22.130)
manu N : nipple; teat (S04.412)
ma:ŋ N : demand; request (—)
maŋgal : Tuesday (S14.640)
ma:p ʃunim V : forgive (S16.690)
ma:pʰi N : apology (—)
ma(:)r N : ghee (local) (S05.890)
marhaŋ N : guesthouse (traditional) (—)
ma:ɽa : bad; wrong (S16.720, S16.740)
maɽʃaŋ N : man (S02.210)
masa:la N : spices (—)
massi N : mother's sister (S02.521)
ma:sʈar N : teacher (S17.270)
masuri da:ɽ N : lentils (Indian brown) (—)
mat ʃaɳam V : help (S19.580)
mattʰa N : forehead (S04.205)
maʈar N : pea (S08.99937)
ma:ts N : kid (of goat) (S03.380)
matsis N : fish (S03.650)
matslis : lazy (S04.920)
matʃʰli N : fish (S03.650)
medda N : flour (refined) (S05.550)
meɖkas N : frog (S03.950)
mehendi N : henna (—)
meʃi N : buffalo (S03.9170)
meʋasi N : drink (S05.900)
mi N : man (S02.210)
mi: N : fire (S01.810)
mi: piŋam V : extinguish (S01.861)
(mi:) sutam V : light (S01.860)
mi: ʃaɳam V : light (S01.860)
mig N : eye (S04.210)
mijak N : yak(F) (—)
mijaŋ N : firefly (S03.910)
milam V : shake (S10.260)
milem V : intermingle; join; meet (S19.650)
mileʃim [MDL] V : meet (S19.650)
milja:m [TR] V : meet; mix (S19.650)
millem V : find; get; intermingle; join; meet; stir (S05.490, S11.160, S11.320, S19.650)
miŋgam V : swallow (S05.181)
mistri: N : carpenter; sculptor (S09.430, S09.820)
mistrits N : mason (S07.610)
mita:r N : friend (S19.510)
mitar(a) N : friend (S19.510)
miʈʈika tel N : kerosene (—)
miʈʰa N : candy; sweets (S23.5650)
mĩtʃ : female(2) (S03.130)
mo N : people (S19.210)
mobajl N : mobile telephone (S23.1200)

mobajlaŋ N : mobile telephone (S23.1200)
moʤoŋ N : between; middle (S12.370)
mog N : birdseed (S08.311)
moit : otherwise (—)
molaŋ N : cow dung (S08.99918)
mombatti N : candle (S07.460)
monoŋ N : temple (S22.130)
mord N : gentleman (—)
moroʈja:m V : bend; squeeze (S09.140, S09.343)
mosam N : weather (S01.780)
moʈas : fat; thick (S12.630)
muɖ : yesterday (S14.490)
muɖa:m N : beehive (S03.822)
muɖe N : head of goat; sheep meat (—)
mujaŋ ri:d : two days before yesterday (—)
mukadma N : court case (—)
mukrem V : deny (S18.340)
mu(:)l N : silver (S09.650)
mulaŋ N : cost; price (S11.870)
muli N : radish (—)
mu:m N : beeswax (S03.821)
mundaʈi N : ring (S06.730)
munuk N : human; man; person (S02.100, S02.210)
muŋgpʰali N : peanut (—)
murga: N : cock; rooster (S03.520)
murgi: N : hen (S03.540)
musalman N : muslim (S22.99909)
muʃi:n N : machine (S23.1900)
muʃkil : difficult (S17.470)
muʃʈur N : rat (in fields) (S03.630)
muʈuʃa N : mushroom (a wild species) (S08.980)
mutsʰ N : mustache (—)
na : five (S13.0500)
na:b : tomorrow (S14.480)
naɖa : innocent (S21.360)
nafa N : profit (—)
nagadi N : coin (S11.440)
naga:ra N : drum (S18.720)
nagaʈija : poor (S11.520)
na:ges N : cobra snake (S03.850)
na:hĩ : four days after tomorrow (—)
najiŋ N : ocean; river (S01.329, S01.360)
nakʤab N : drizzle (S01.750)
nakʃa N : map (—)
na:la N : riverlet; stream (S01.360)
na:laŋ N : riverlet; stream (S01.360)
naliŋ : last year (—)
na:liŋ N : chimney (S07.330)
nalka N : water faucet (—)
na:m N : name (S18.280)
na:maŋ N : name (S18.280)
na:mi : even; ever (—)
na:na: N : maternal grandfather (S02.460)
na:na:na:ni: N : maternal grandparents (S02.4711)
nandris : before (S12.0400)
na:ni: N : maternal grandmother (S02.470)
naŋʈa : naked (S04.990)
nao : nine (S13.0900)
nark : bad; evil; hell; sorrow (S16.720)
nark N : bad; evil; hell; sorrow (S22.320)
naʈa N : arm (S04.310)
naʈija : strong (S04.810)
naʈukʰ N : navel (S04.430)
naʃim V : rest; sit; stay (S04.912, S07.110, S09.99931, S12.130)
na:ʈa N : relative; relatives (—, S02.810)
neɖaŋ N : shore (S01.270)
neije : like that (—)
nem V : be; exist (S24.0100)
neneije : there also (—)
nenk : thus (—)
neʈaŋ : near (S12.430)
nesiki : whatever (—)
neskaŋ N : good weather (—)
netat : if (S17.530)
ni : [1PLE] (S02.942)
nibja:m [TR] V : finish (S14.270)
nid : here (S24.0900)
niʣa : twenty (S13.104)
ni:m N : neem tree (Azadirachta indica) (—)
nimbu N : lime (—)
niʃ : two (S13.0200)
niʃ pʰeraga: : twice; two times (S13.380)
niʃʈʰas : low (S12.320)
nje:n : under (S12.0700)
njo : there (S24.1000)
njuts N : day before yesterday (S14.491)
nokar N : servant (S19.430)
nokri N : service (—)
nonda : so many (S13.150)
no:ʧas : front(side) (S12.0410)
noʋal N : mongoose (—)
nu : [3SG.PROX]; this (S02.930, S24.0700)
nu: : oh (—)
nubari N : cloth-stand (—)
nuga: : [3PL.PROX] (S02.960)
nuka ʧʰets ʃi:k N : widower (S02.770)
nusa:li N : scar (S04.858)
ɳija N : chopper (traditional) (—)
ŋa : five (S13.0500)
ŋaʣ : from (—)
oʤim V : play (S16.260)
om N : mountain pass; path; way (S10.720)
oʃaŋ N : dew (S01.640)
pa: : on (—)
padraŋ N : plain (S01.230)
padras N : plain (S01.230)
padre N : plain (S01.230)
pag N : ox (S03.220)
pagal : eccentric; idiot (S17.230)
pagriŋ N : turban (S06.550)
paha:ʈ N : cliff; hill (S01.220, S01.222)

pa:ji : two days after tomorrow (—)
pajp N : pipe (S08.691)
pakeʦ : cooked; ripe (S05.121, S05.123)
pakres N : people (S19.210)
pak^{h}iŋ N : feather; wing (S04.392)
pala N : dew, frozen (S01.640)
palag N : bed (S07.420)
palaŋ : hollow (—)
palaŋg N : bed (S07.420)
palʈem [INTR] V : turn (around) (S10.120, S10.130)
palʈja:m [TR] V : turn (around) (S10.120, S10.130)
pa:n N : threshing stone; threshing-floor (S01.440, S08.350)
pandra : fifteen (S13.103)
paɳaŋa N : guest (S19.560)
paɳaŋa ʤaram V : invite (S19.5650)
paŋ N : branch (S08.550)
parda N : curtain (—)
pardeʃaŋ N : foreign country (—)
parijar N : transhumance; winter migration (—)
parsed N : perspiration; sweat (—)
parsed dʊanam V : perspire (S04.550)
paɽa:j N : frost (—)
paɽem [INTR] V : read; study; teach (S17.242, S17.250, S18.520)
paɽeʦ ʦ^{h}akʦ N : pupil (S17.260)
paɽ^{h}ja:m [TR] V : read; study; teach (S17.242, S17.250, S18.520)
pasand N : liking (—)
paʃiʥ : cooked (S05.121)
paʃu N : livestock (S03.150)
pata N : knowledge (—)
pata:l N : pot (S05.260)
patti N : leaf (S08.560)
paʈ N : threshing stone (S01.440)
pa:ʈ N : roof (stone/slate) (S07.510)
paʈakja:m V : split (S09.270)
pa:ʈi N : floor; room (S07.210, S07.260)
paʈʈi N : razor (S06.930)
paʈʈu N : shawl (—)
paʈʈ^{h}a N : bracelet (traditional) (S06.740)
pa:ʦ N : grandchild (S02.5000)
pãʧ : five (S13.0500)
paʧaka ba:dzi N : dish (with dried kaʈ^{h}u leaves) (—)
paʧaŋ N : leaf (S08.560)
paʧeja:m [TR] V : digest (—)
paʧ^{h}iŋ N : assembly (—)
pa:una N : guest (S19.560)
pedal : on foot (—)
peg N : broom (S09.380)
peim V : kiss (S16.290)
pek N : broom (S09.380)
pela : earlier; first (S12.0400, S13.340)
pen N : pen (S18.570)
penʈ N : trousers (S06.480)
peʈi N : belt (S06.570)
pi : also (—)
pi:g : orange; yellow (S15.690)
pilija N : jaundice (—)
pille N : calf of the leg (S04.352)
pi:m V : lose (S11.330)
pinʤra N : cage; trap (S20.640)
piŋ N : cheek (S04.201)
piple N : button (S06.620)
pipli N : chilli (red); pepper (S05.820, S05.821)
pipɽi N : chilli (red); pepper (S05.820, S05.821)
pital N : brass (—)
pitaŋ N : door; doorpost (S07.220, S07.221)
piti N : tear (S16.380)
pit^{h}as N : flour (S05.550)
piʦ N : starch (—)
piʦuga N : pin (traditional for women) (S06.630)
piʧim V : keep; put (S11.170)
pja:ʥ N : onion (S08.99935)
plen : fill (—)
pod N : ash; dandruff (S01.840, S04.146)
polak : strong (S04.810)
polak N : tree trunk (S08.730)
polɖaɽ N : rajma (dish with red kidney beans) (—)
pom N : snow (S01.760)
pompiɽiŋ N : snowball (—)
ponukes N : guest (S19.560)
poɳ N : straw shoe (S06.510)
poɳam V : sew (S06.350)
poɳukes N : guest (S19.560)
poʃ(e) N : bedding (—)
poʃmuk^h N : bedspread; mat (to sit on) (S09.770)
pot^{h}ja:m V : bury (S04.780)
poʈaŋ N : belly; stomach (S04.4310, S04.460)
poʈo N : fruit; vegetable (S05.650, S05.710)
pra:d N : finger; toe (S04.340, S04.380)
prada:n N : chieftain (S19.240)
pra:daŋ N : finger; toe (S04.340, S04.380)
pragu N : rhododendron (—)
praʃa N : rib (S04.162)
preg N : nail (S09.500)
prek^{h}ja:m [TR] V : taste (S15.310)
prisin N : pencil (S09.99915)
prit^{h}ʊi N : earth; world (S01.100)
pu : four (S13.0400)
puʥʥa:ra N : priest (S22.180)
puʤa N : prayer; worship (—)
puʤari N : priest (S22.180)
pũĩ N : cat (S03.620)
puleʈ N : plate (S05.320)
punir N : panir (S05.880)

puŋ N : flea (S03.813)
purts N : police (S23.3300)
puʃam V : sow (S08.310)
puʧ^{h} N : tail (S04.180)
puʧ^{h}aŋ N : tail (S04.180)
p^{h}a:g baʤu N : half sleeve (—)
p^{h}ainʤa N : tail (S04.180)
p^{h}ak : short; small; young (S12.560, S12.590, S14.140)
p^{h}ak bau N : younger brother (S02.445)
p^{h}akuts ɖaliŋ N : plant (S08.530)
p^{h}akuʧ : short; small; young (S12.560, S12.590, S14.140)
p^{h}akuʧ bats N : younger brother (S02.445)
p^{h}ak(uʧ) riŋʤ N : younger sister (S02.455)
p^{h}aluŋ N : beeswax (S03.821)
p^{h}ar N : shoulder (S04.300)
p^{h}arʃ N : floor (S07.260)
p^{h}asal N : harvest (S08.410)
p^{h}asam V : vomit (S04.570)
p^{h}asʈiŋ N : vomit (—)
p^{h}elʈam V : spread out (S09.340)
p^{h}eʈa paem V : lie down (S12.140)
p^{h}eʈʈo : left (S12.420)
p^{h}igolpigol N : rainbow (S01.590)
p^{h}ikja:m V : throw (S10.250)
p^{h}il N : snail without shell (S03.940)
p^{h}ilam N : film; movie (S23.6200)
p^{h}ili gaɽe N : snail with shell (S03.940)
p^{h}ine N : footsole; heel; sole of foot (S04.372, S04.374)
p^{h}oal N : herdsman (S03.180)
p^{h}og N : bed (S07.420)
p^{h}olaŋ N : fruit (S05.710)
p^{h}on N : telephone (S23.1200)
p^{h}oʃʈare N : flower (a wild species, blue-white) (S08.570)
p^{h}oʧim V : flee (S10.510)
p^{h}rajbin N : frying pan; pan (S05.280)
p^{h}ram V : knead (S05.540)
p^{h}ruʈ N : fruit (S05.710)
p^{h}u lanam V : blow (S10.380)
p^{h}uktam V : cover (S12.260)
p^{h}ul N : flower; rice (cooked) (S08.480, S08.570)
p^{h}ulgobbi N : cauliflower (—)
p^{h}unam [INTR] V : drop; fall (S10.160, S10.230)
p^{h}uraŋgi N : foreigner (—)
p^{h}uɽigija:m V : fold (S09.150)
p^{h}uts N : mouse; rat (in house) (S03.630)
ra: N : calf (S03.240)
ra deo N : Kanashi community (—)
ra:d N : bull; ox (S03.210, S03.220)
ra:ʤa N : king (S19.320)
ra:g : blue; green (S15.670, S15.680)

raiŋ N : bee (wild, large in size, and their honey is considered bad by the locals and not consumed by them) (S03.820)
raitomʊe N : beehive (S03.822)
raks N : ghost (S22.450)
ra:lam V : plough; plow (S08.210)
ranɖi N : widow (S02.760)
ra:ni N : queen (S19.330)
raɳ goʈunas : round (S12.810)
raɳam V : stab (=give) (S09.223)
raɳam [NON-1/2O] V : give (S11.210)
raŋ N : horse; mountain top; summit (S03.410, S12.330)
ra:ŋ N : horse (S03.410)
raŋg N : color; paint (S09.880, S15.610)
raŋgja:m V : dye; paint (S06.390, S09.890)
ra:ɽ gaɳam V : fry; roast (S05.230)
rask N : edge (S12.353)
raʃim V : injure (S11.280)
raʃug N : sore; wound (S04.850)
ra:t N : night (S14.420)
ra:tiŋ N : night (S14.420)
raʈam V : beat; hit; strike (S09.210)
ra:ʈ^{h}i : delicious (—)
raunɖa N : stepson (S02.730)
raunɖi N : stepdaughter (S02.740)
rel N : train (S23.1550)
renam V : sell (S11.820)
re:t N : sand (S01.215)
re:tiŋ N : sand (S01.215)
ri:d N : day before yesterday (S14.491)
rig N : body louse; head louse (S03.811, S03.8112)
ri:(g) N : glacier (—)
rigi:n : above; on; upper (—, S12.0810)
rikts N : nit (S03.812)
rinig N : snake; worm (S03.840, S03.850)
riɳ N : loan (S11.640)
riɳ uɳam V : borrow (S11.620)
riŋ : top; up (S12.0800)
riŋ N : top; up (S12.330)
riŋ bonam V : go up (S10.471)
riŋʤ N : sister (S02.450)
riŋʤjuŋʤ N : sibling (S02.456)
riʧim V : ask(1) (S18.310)
riʊa:ʤ N : custom; tradition (S19.610)
ro:ɖ N : ear (S04.220)
roɖije N : radio (S23.1000)
roʤ : always; daily; every day (S14.310)
rohem V : grow (S12.530)
roja:m V : grow; raise (S08.99962)
rok : black; dark-skinned (S15.650)
rokda:l N : black lentil (—)
rokja:m [TR] V : cease; stop (S14.280)
rokʈ^{h}a N : roof (S07.510)
rokʈ^{h}aŋ N : roof (S07.510)
romi N : day after tomorrow (S14.481)
roɳ N : iron (S09.670)

roʃni N : brightness; light (arctic) (—)
roʃutʃ N : injury (—)
rotʰ : brave (S16.520)
rotʰas : brave (S16.520)
rotʰe N : bread; chapati (S05.510)
roʊam V : plant (S08.531)
ru:d N : horn (S04.170)
rudiŋ N : rock (S01.440)
rudʒai N : quilt (S07.422)
rudʒult N : result (—)
rukem [INTR] V : cease; stop (S14.280)
ɽigi:nnaʃiŋ N : upper house (—)
sab : all (S13.140)
sada : always (S14.310)
sadraŋ N : autumn; fall (S14.770)
sadzara : fresh (—)
sahi : true (S16.660)
sa:l N : year (S14.730)
sa:laŋ N : year (S14.730)
salgam N : turnip (S08.99952)
sa:mana : in front of (S12.0410)
samdʑem [INTR] V : understand (S17.160)
samdʑja:m [TR] V : understand (S17.160)
sa:mna : in front (—)
sa:mnas : flat; straight (S12.710, S12.730)
samudra N : ocean; sea (S01.320, S01.329)
samudraŋ N : ocean; sea (S01.320, S01.329)
samudri dʒahadʒ N : ship (S10.810)
sanam V : cultivate; kill (S04.760, S08.150)
sanper N : snake man (—)
sansa:r N : world (S01.100)
santra N : orange (S08.99936)
saŋ : with (S24.0400)
saŋgis N : friend (S19.510)
sap N : snake (S03.850)
sar : awake (—)
sara N : custom (S19.610)
saraŋ N : lower part of Malana (—)
sardaŋ N : winter (S14.740)
sardi : cold (S15.860)
sa:re : all (S13.140)
sargaŋ N : sky (S01.510)
sargã(ŋ) N : weather (S01.780)
sarʃim V : wake up (S04.630)
sartʰas N : flower (a species cultivated in flowerpots, yellow-orange) (S08.570)
saɽe N : plus half (in numerals) (S13.240)
sastas : cheap (S11.890)
sa:su N : mother-in-law (of a man); mother-in-law (of a woman) (S02.620, S02.621)
sa:susa:uri: N : parents-in-law (S02.6220)
sat : seven (S13.0700)
saʈi:l N : steel (—)
sauda N : candy; sweets (S23.5650)
saura behad N : lower part of Malana (—)
sauri N : mother-in-law (of a man); mother-in-law (of a woman) (S02.620, S02.621)
seb N : apple (S08.99905)
sejle N : goat hair (—)
sela N : mat (S09.770)
seljara N : sesame seeds (—)
seo N : apple (S08.99905)
sesam V : know; recognize (S17.170)
seʈ : rich (S11.510)
seʊ N : apple (S08.99905)
sidda : straight (S12.730)
sikʰja:m [TR] V : learn (S17.240)
sikʰjem [INTR] V : learn (S17.240)
sima N : border (—)
simiʈ N : cement (—)
sipahi N : soldier (S20.170)
sipahis N : soldier (S20.170)
sirãõ N : artery; vein (S04.151)
sirkar N : government (S23.3000)
siʈem [INTR] V : cook (S05.210)
siʈja:m [TR] V : cook (S05.210)
so: N : earth; mainland (S01.260)
soar : Monday (S14.630)
som N : morning (S14.440)
som dʒiʃa N : dawn (S14.430)
som kula:r N : breakfast (S05.420)
soŋgus : beside; near (S12.0200)
sõʦ N : place (S12.110)
soʧem V : think(1) (S17.130)
sʈop N : stove (S07.320)
sua N : injection (S23.2300)
suãraŋ : Monday (S14.630)
suaʃim V : destroy (S11.270)
subu:n N : soap (S06.950)
sudʑi N : semolina (—)
sui N : needle(1) (S06.360)
sukul N : school (S17.280)
sukʰ N : happiness; peace (S20.140)
sulus : slow (S14.220)
sulus lonam V : whisper (S18.150)
sulus ʃaɳam V : be late (S14.240)
sum [TR] V : bathe (S04.690)
suma:n N : thing (S11.180)
supen N : suspension bridge (—)
supna N : dream (—)
supna: baram V : dream (S04.620)
su:r N : pig; swine (S03.350)
sura:b N : alcohol; fermented drink (S05.940)
suradʒ N : sun (S01.520)
surg : sour (S15.380)
surgiʈ N : cigarette (S23.5900)
surgiʈ tuŋam V : smoke (S08.690)
su:ru N : pig; swine (S03.350)
sust : lazy (S04.920)
suʃim [MDL] V : bathe (S04.690)
suttsai : truth (S16.660)
sutʰon N : trousers (S06.480)

sutʃai : truth (S16.660)
sʊarg N : heaven (S22.310)
ʃa N : hide; skin (S04.120)
ʃã: ɖuɳam V : breathe (S04.510)
ʃabɽi N : meat (S05.610)
ʃag : empty (S13.220)
ʃaiɳ N : lock (S07.230)
ʃak ʃaɳam V : suspect (S17.440)
ʃakal N : face (S04.204)
ʃakk N : doubt (S17.430)
ʃakras N : calf [M] (S03.240)
ʃa:l N : summer (S14.760)
ʃa:nt : calm (S01.322)
ʃantida:r : innocent (S21.360)
ʃa:ɳam V : do; make (S09.110, S09.1110)
ʃaɳaŋ N : ice (S01.770)
ʃaŋ N : branch (S08.550)
ʃaŋgle N : chain (S09.180)
ʃapo N : abuse (—)
ʃapoga: lonam V : scold (S18.390)
ʃaru N : hail (—)
ʃaɽak N : road (S10.710)
ʃa:ɽug N : fox (S03.740)
ʃatarja:m V : smear (S09.99936)
ʃaʈan tsa:hib N : assistant commissioner (—)
ʃeher N : town (S19.150)
ʃe(:)l N : medicine (S04.880)
ʃe:l ʃaɳam V : cure (S04.860)
ʃenam V : send (S10.630)
ʃeɳi N : house in the fields (S07.130)
ʃep N : foam (S01.324)
ʃer N : leopard; tiger (S03.99942)
ʃi:ʤ marʃaŋ N : corpse (S04.770)
ʃi:k : corpse; dead (S04.7501)
ʃi:k N : corpse; dead (S04.770)
ʃika:r N : hunting (—)
ʃikran N : calf [F] (S03.240)
ʃilaŋ N : shade; shadow (S01.630)
ʃi:m V : die (S04.750)
ʃiŋ N : firewood; wood (S01.430, S01.880)
ʃi:ŋ N : horn (S04.170)
ʃiŋ ɖa(:)liŋ N : tree branch (S08.550)
ʃo N : field; orchard (S08.120)
ʃo : hundred (S13.105)
ʃobil : delicious; good; lovely (S16.710, S16.810)
ʃobi:l ma:j : ugly (S16.820)
ʃobilas : delicious; good; lovely (S16.710, S16.810)
ʃokkura N : orphan (S02.750)
ʃokkuraŋ N : orphan (S02.750)
ʃokkʰem V : be thirsty (S05.150)
ʃon N : belly (S04.4310)
ʃoŋ : down (S12.0300)
ʃoŋnu bonam V : go down (S10.473)
ʃoras N : father-in-law (of a man); father-in-law (of a woman) (S02.610, S02.611)
ʃores N : father-in-law (of a man); father-in-law (of a woman) (S02.610, S02.611)
ʃoru N : son (S02.410)
ʃukaʃ : dry; thirsty (S15.840)
ʃukkar : Friday (S14.670)
ʃulakutoŋ N : stomach ache (—)
ʃu(:)m : three (S13.0300)
ʃum pʰeriga: : three times (S13.440)
ʃumin kuin ba:d : three days after (—)
ʃu:min poien ba:d : four days after (—)
ʃuɳitʃare : Saturday (S14.680)
ʃupa N : flail; threshing stick (—)
ʃuru N : beginning (S14.2510)
ʃuru ʃaɳam V : begin (S14.250)
ʃuruŋ N : beginning (S14.2510)
ʃuruŋats : first (S13.340)
ʃʊaʃi : bad (S16.720)
ʃʊĩ ʃaɳam V : whistle (S18.170)
ta N : nose (S04.230)
tabo : then (S24.99912)
tabru N : hammer (S09.490)
tada : how many (S17.630)
taʤa : fresh (—)
ta:g N : pus (S04.857)
tain N : purpose (—)
tak : until (—)
takʰuts N : nose (S04.230)
talaŋ N : footsole; palm of the hand (S04.331, S04.374)
tala:ʊ N : lake (S01.330)
talja:m [TR] V : move (S10.110)
taljem V : move (S10.110)
talʊa:r N : sword (S20.270)
tam V : have; keep (S11.110, S11.170)
tama:ʃa N : festival (—)
tamba:ku N : tobacco (S08.680)
tambu N : tent (S07.140)
tamti N : snot (—)
tandura:ʤ pajp N : chimney (S07.330)
taŋ N : bother (—)
taɳam V : look; watch (S15.520)
taŋʤa N : people (S19.210)
taŋs : from (—)
taŋʃim [MDL] V : look; watch (S15.520)
taoli N : towel (S06.820)
ta:r N : wire (—)
ta:rik N : date (calendar) (—)
tarkol N : charcoal (S01.890)
tarʊa:r N : sword (S20.270)
ta:ɽi N : lock; padlock (S07.230, S07.2320)
tasma N : shoelace (—)
ta(:)tam V : hide (S12.270)
taʊaʤa: N : nostril (S04.231)
teg : big; older (S12.550)
teg bau N : older brother (S02.444)
teg riŋʤ N : older sister (S02.454)
tegje : very (—)

tegje ɖaʈʰis : thank you! (S16.99903)
tela N : oil (S05.790)
tem N : bride; daughter-in-law (S02.640, S02.641)
tes : that (S24.0800)
ti(:) N : water (S01.310)
ti: boŋam V : flow (of water) (S10.320)
ti: dʊanam V : drip (of water) (S10.240)
ti: ɖuʈam V : draw water (S09.9000)
tiha:r N : festival (—)
ti:r N : arrow (S20.250)
tisraŋ : third (S13.420)
tisraŋaʤ : third (S13.420)
tita:n N : acorn; cone (of pine tree) (S08.660, S08.9960)
titã:(n) N : acorn; cone (of pine tree) (S08.660, S08.9960)
tiuadz ʤju N : seagull (S03.582)
to V : be- (S24.0100)
tog N : stone (small, put under large rocks so that they don't tumble down the hill) (S01.440)
togam V : beat (S09.210)
tokta N : wood used for making tables (S01.430)
tolam V : fold (S09.150)
tolem [INTR] V : swing (—)
tolija:m V : weigh (S11.920)
tolja:m [TR] V : swing (—)
tombe N : beehive (S03.822)
tonam V : have (S11.110)
toŋ N : bother; face (—, S04.204)
toŋam V : beat (S09.210)
toɽe : necessary (—)
toʃim [MDL] V : fight (S20.110)
totta N : parrot (S03.592)
tramba N : copper (S09.660)
tu:gem V : drink; smoke (S05.130)
tundur N : oven (S05.250)
tuŋam V : drink; smoke (S05.130)
tu:ŋem V : drink; smoke (S05.130)
tuŋtuŋ : drunk (S04.980)
tupka N : gun (S20.280)
tupkas raŋam V : shoot (S20.620)
tupkʰ N : gun (S20.280)
turaŋ : dark (S15.630)
tuɽi N : match (S01.870)
tʊanam V : take out (—)
tʊa:r : Sunday (S14.620)
tʰak : tired (S04.910)
tʰakem V : get tired (—)
tʰakuʧaʈi N : hut (S07.130)
tʰalo : while ago (—)
tʰamba N : pillar; pole (S07.560)
tʰanam [TR] V : drop; fell (S10.160)
tʰaŋa N : prison (S21.390)
tʰar N : lion (S03.720)
tʰaʧaŋ N : pasture in lower regions (S03.160)
tʰauʊis N : carpenter (S09.430)
tʰep(a)r N : slap (—)
tʰi:d : little; today (S13.99901, S14.470)
tʰig : sweet (S15.350)
tʰo : up (S12.0800)
tʰomba N : tower (S20.360)
tʰoɽa : little (S13.99901)
tʰotoro N : lip (S04.250)
tʰotʰra N : lip (S04.250)
tʰʊaŋam [TR] V : open (S12.240)
ʈabar N : family (S02.820)
ʈainta N : hut (S07.130)
ʈaka N : money (S11.430)
ʈaka kuma:m V : earn (S11.790)
ʈaki N : window (S07.250)
ʈaŋam V : climb (S10.472)
ʈa:ŋg N : foot; leg (S04.350, S04.370)
ʈapem V : arrive (S10.550)
ʈa:pu N : island (S01.250)
ʈaʈam V : untie (S09.161)
ʈaʈʈikʰana N : toilet (S23.5200)
ʈauɲa : deaf (S04.950)
ʈebal N : table (S07.440)
ʈeble N : table (S07.440)
ʈeks N : tax (S11.690)
ʈelipʰon N : telephone (S23.1200)
ʈhak N : tire (—)
ʈiʈaɽa N : grasshopper (S03.930)
ʈiʊi N : television (S23.1100)
ʈokri N : basket (small, to put wood etc. in) (S09.760)
ʈope N : cap; hat (S06.550)
ʈõʈida:r N : spider (S03.818)
ʈren N : train (S23.1550)
ʈruk N : truck (—)
ʈukor N : nest (S03.580)
ʈukra ʃaŋam V : divide (S12.232)
ʈulem V : sleep (S04.610)
ʈuljem V : sleep (S04.610)
ʈumaʈar N : tomato (—)
ʈumrigja:m V : bend (S09.140)
ʈuʃja:m V : wipe (S09.3110)
ʈʰanɖas N : cold; winter (S14.740)
ʈʰanɖas : cold; winter (S15.860)
ʈʰaprja:m [TR] V : cease; stop (S14.280)
ʈʰeka N : revenue (S11.690)
ʈʰi:k : right(2) (S16.730)
ʈʰinɖ N : servant (S19.430)
ʈʰokja:m V : crush; grind (S05.560)
ʈʰolu N : chisel; hammer (S09.490, S09.840)
ʈʰor(o) N : running (—)
ʈʰoroga: raŋam V : run (S10.460)
ʈʰulla N : foot; leg (S04.350, S04.370)
ʈʰullaŋ N : foot; leg (S04.350, S04.370)
ʈʰumre N : bush (—)
ʈʰurja:m V : follow (S10.520)
ʈʰuʈre N : tail (S04.180)
ʈʰuʈʰ(a)re N : tail (S04.180)

tsadri: N : roof (tin) (S07.510)
tsa:m N : wool (of sheep) (S06.220)
tsa:m katja:m V : spin (S06.310)
tsamkem V : shine (S15.560)
tsandraha:r N : necklace (S06.750)
tsanɖuk N : spindle (S06.320)
tsapem V : chew (S05.180)
tsaraŋ N : glacier (—)
tsarga:m N : weather (S01.780)
tsattsaʈʈa : bald (S04.930)
tsikar N : mud (S01.214)
tsikra N : mud (S01.214)
tsimani N : lamp (kerosene) (S07.450)
tso N : thorn (—)
tsok^{h}as : clean (S15.870)
tsumʈak N : tongs (cooking utensil) (S05.391)
tsuŋmat : whatever (—)
tsuram V : milk (S05.870)
ts^{h}a N : salt (S05.810)
ts^{h}a ʥada : salty (S15.360)
ts^{h}ag N : light (S01.610)
ts^{h}ag baʈja:m V : light (S01.860)
ts^{h}ali N : corn kernel (—)
ts^{h}ali piʈ^{h}as N : flour (of corn); flour, corn (S05.550, S08.470)
ts^{h}am N : bridge (S10.740)
ts^{h}a:m V : hear; listen (S15.410, S15.420)
ts^{h}am ʃetam V : recite (—)
ts^{h}apuk raɳam V : jump (S10.430)
ts^{h}arʥ : dry (S15.840)
ts^{h}arʥ ʃiŋ N : hoe (S08.250)
ts^{h}a:ti N : chest (S04.400)
ts^{h}aʈa kja:ʈam V : thresh (S08.340)
ts^{h}ika : early; fast; quickly; soon (S14.160, S14.210, S14.331)
ts^{h}ika ʃaɳam V : hurry (S14.230)
ts^{h}ikats^{h}ika : immediately (S14.190)
ts^{h}ol N : spring; waterfall (S01.370, S01.390)
ts^{h}os N : fat (of goat); fat (of sheep) (—)
ts(^{h})u(:)mam V : catch; hold (S10.252)
ts(^{h})unam V : tie (S09.160)
ts^{h}ure N : knife (S05.380)
ts^{h}urnu N : ice drop (—)
ts^{h}uʈe : only (S13.330)
ts^{h}utsurug N : mushroom (a wild species) (S08.980)
ʧa(:) N : tea (S23.9000)
ʧadar N : bedsheet (—)
ʧa:g N : oats (S08.460)
ʧa:m V : dance (S10.440)
ʧamak N : bolt of lightning (S01.570)
ʧama:ras N : particular community (S06.540)
ʧamga:daʈ N : bat (S03.591)
ʧammaʧ N : spoon (S05.370)
ʧamo N : copper (S09.660)
ʧamʈa N : leather (S06.290)
ʧamʧi N : spoon (S05.370)
ʧamʧiŋ N : spoon (S05.370)
ʧana N : chickpea (—)
ʧand N : moon (S01.530)
ʧaŋ N : hill; mountain (S01.220)
ʧapli N : sandal (for women) (S06.99907)
ʧara N : baby; child (S02.270, S02.280)
ʧa:ri N : attic; attic room (—)
ʧaʈig N : bird (S03.581)
ʧaʃma N : glasses; spectacles (S23.2400)
ʧaʈpapʈi N : snacks (—)
ʧa:ʧi N : paternal uncle’s wife (—)
ʧeka N : back (S04.190)
ʧi kaʈem V : mow (S08.320)
ʧiʥ N : thing (S11.180)
ʧi:g N : knee (S04.360)
ʧika : dry (S15.840)
ʧikan N : chicken (S03.550)
ʧiktela N : mustard oil (—)
ʧim [TR] V : wash (S09.360)
ʧime N : daughter (S02.420)
ʧime(ts) N : girl (S02.260)
ʧi:nɖ N : fingernail; toenail (S04.344)
ʧinin N : glue (from chil tree) (—)
ʧiŋam V : get stuck; join; shut (—, S12.220, S12.250)
ʧis raɳam V : pinch (S15.712)
ʧisaŋ N : flour (of buckwheat) (S05.550)
ʧiʈkani N : door-bolt; latch (S07.231)
ʧiʈʈ^{h}i N : letter (S23.4200)
ʧits : washed; wet (S15.830)
ʧokets : rotten (S05.125)
ʧopʈu N : charcoal (S01.890)
ʧora golop lonam V : lie(2) (S16.670)
ʧoras N : thief (S21.520)
ʧori(g) N : theft (—)
ʧorikega: ʃaɳam V : steal (S21.510)
ʧotraŋ N : council platform (S07.180)
ʧoʈi N : urine (—)
ʧuʤaŋ N : beak (S04.241)
ʧug N : swelling (S04.853)
ʧul N : plum (edible) (S08.99941)
ʧum N : kiss (—)
ʧuŋam V : break; split; tear (S09.270)
ʧuŋam [TR] V : break; split; tear (S09.260)
ʧurʥ N : swelling (S04.853)
ʧuʈel N : witch (S22.430)
ʧusja:m V : suck (S05.160)
ʧ^{h}a : six (S13.0600)
ʧ^{h}abaja : now (S14.180)
ʧ^{h}aba:ʈ N : lizard (S03.960)
ʧ^{h}ak N : boy; child (S02.250)
ʧ^{h}akts N : boy; child (S02.250, S02.270)
ʧ^{h}al balja:m V : shake (S10.260)
ʧ^{h}amga N : chin; jaw (S04.207, S04.209)
ʧ^{h}amjurts : dry (S15.840)
ʧ^{h}aŋ N : boy; child (S02.250, S02.270)
ʧ^{h}aʧ kaʈãõ N : insect; mosquito (S03.810, S03.832)

tʃʰatʃe N : mushroom (a wild species) (S08.980)
tʃʰaulem V : conceive (S04.732)
tʃʰeɽa raɳam V : scrape (S05.480)
tʃʰets N : wife (S02.320)
tʃʰets roʈas N : married man (S02.380)
tʃʰetsaŋ N : wife (S02.320)
tʃʰige : anything; what; whatever else (—)
tʃʰigi maːʃ : nothing (S24.1400)
tʃʰo N : child; son (S02.270, S02.410)
tʃʰog : white (S15.640)
tʃʰok N : child; son (S02.410)
tʃʰokra N : boy (S02.250)
tʃʰras : dark (S15.630)
tʃʰu : what? (S17.640)
tʃʰub : when? (S17.650)
tʃʰugge : what? (S17.640)
tʃʰugu : some (S13.181)
tʃʰulam V : chop; cut (—)
tʃʰuːnɖ N : bunch (S05.712)
tʃʰuŋ : near (S12.430)
uː N : flower (S08.570)
ubɽem V : boil (S05.220)
ubɽjaːm V : boil (S05.220)
umle : contrary (—)
umra N : age (S14.120)
un N : day(1); day(2) (S14.410, S14.4110)
uːnam V : take (S11.130)
uŋgeɽa N : ladder; staircase (S07.370)
uŋma N : demand; request (—)
uɽjaːm [TR] V : fly (S10.370)
uɽjem [INTR] V : fly (S10.370)
uɽug N : owl (S03.596)
uʃim N : divorce (S02.341)
uta : foolish (—)
ũʈ N : camel (S03.780)
uʈʰras : high (S12.310)
uʋaŋ N : udder (S04.420)
ʋaː N : nest (S03.580)
ʋaːʥ N : hawk (S03.585)
ʋahu N : daughter-in-law (S02.640, S02.641)
ʋai ʤahaʤ N : airplane (S23.1600)
ʋajaŋ N : bee (S03.820)
ʋakiːl N : advocate (—)
ʋakt N : time (S14.110)
ʋaluŋ N : grass bundle (—)
ʋanam V : laugh (S16.250)
ʋaɳam V : be hungry (S05.140)
ʋaɽʃum V : scratch (S04.8541)
ʋaːs N : honey (S05.840)
ʋaʃe naʃim V : fast (S22.260)
ʋeraŋ N : evening (S14.460)
ʋesam V : finish (S14.270)
ʋeʃiŋ N : end; finish (S14.260)
ʋiɖiɔ N : television (S23.1100)
ʋoʃ N : hunger (—)
zori : loud (S15.450)

C English–Kanashi word list

[1PLE] : ni (S02.942)
[1PLI] : ette (S02.941)
[1SG] : gu (S02.910)
[2PL] : ki (S02.950)
[2SG] : ka (S02.920)
[3PL.DIST] : duga: (S02.960)
[3PL.PROX] : nuga: (S02.960)
[3SG.DIST] : du (S02.930)
[3SG.PROX] : nu (S02.930)
a lot : ʤinɖ (S13.150)
above : rigiːn (—, S12.0810)
absolutely : bilkul (—)
abuse N : ʃapo (—)
acorn N : titaːn; titãː(n) (S08.660, S08.9960)
advocate N : ʋakiːl (—)
after : baːd; hipitʃ (S12.0100, S13.350)
again : hed (S14.350)
age N : umra (S14.120)
agree V : ajaːm (—)
ahead : agraŋ (S12.0410)
air N : lipur (S01.720)
airplane N : ʋai ʤahaʤ (S23.1600)
alcohol N : suraːb (S05.940)
all : sab; saːre (S13.140)
alligator N : magarmatʃʰ (S03.970)
almond N : badaːm (S08.99901)
alms N : biːtʃʰa (—)
alone : ketsiː (S13.3310)
also : pi (—)
always : roʥ; sada (S14.310)
and : aj; haid (S17.510)
anger N : ʥikke (S16.420)
animal N : ʤaːnʋar; dziu (S03.110)
animal shelter N : kʰuɖ; kʰuɖaŋ (—)
ankle N : goɽa (S04.371)
ant N : biːg (S03.817)
anyhow : dabaʥe (—)
anything : tʃʰige (—)
apology N : maːpʰi (—)
apple N : seb; seo; seʋ (S08.99905)
apricot N : aʤaɽ (—)
apricot seed (dried) N : gule (—)

arise V : aʧ^{h}im (S04.630)

arm N : guɖ; naɽa (S04.310, S04.330)

armpit N : kesk^{h}aʈa (S04.312)

arrive V : ʈapem (S10.550)

arrow N : ti:r (S20.250)

artery N : sirãõ (S04.151)

ash N : pod (S01.840, S04.146)

ask(1) V : riʧim (S18.310)

assembly N : paʧ^{h}iŋ (—)

assistant commissioner N : ʃaʈan tsa:hib (—)

attic N : ʧa:ri (—)

attic room N : ʧa:ri (—)

August : agost (—)

autumn N : sadraŋ (S14.770)

awake : sar (—)

ax N : ka:r (S09.250)

axe N : ka:r (S09.250)

baby N : ala:ʦ; ʧara (S02.270, S02.280)

back : honɖes (—)

back N : ʧeka (S04.190)

backwards : ipiʤ; ipiʧ (S12.0110)

bad : bura; ma:ɽa; nark; ʃʊaʃi (S16.720, S16.740)

bad N : nark (S22.320)

bag N : beg (S06.99901)

balcony N : dʊa:re (—)

bald : ʦatʦaʈʈa (S04.930)

ball N : gindi (S12.830)

banana N : keɽa (S08.840)

banknote N : loʈ (S11.430)

bark N : lebɽa (S08.750)

bark (of a dog) N : guŋge (—)

barley N : ʣubaŋ (S08.440)

barley beer N : gliŋ (S05.930)

barren (land) : a:ʃa:ŋ (—)

barren land N : ʤaŋgal (S01.410)

basket (small, to put wood etc. in) N : ʈokri (S09.760)

basket carried on the back N : kilʈi (S09.760)

bastard : kan (—)

bat N : ʧamga:daɽ (S03.591)

bathe V : sum [TR]; suʃim [MDL] (S04.690)

battery N : baʈari (S23.1750)

be V : nem (S24.0100)

be V : to (S24.0100)

be flooded V : k^{h}oɽa aʧim (—)

be hungry V : ʊaɳam (S05.140)

be late V : sulus ʃaɳam (S14.240)

be thirsty V : ʃokk^{h}em (S05.150)

beak N : ʧuʤaŋ (S04.241)

beam N : ʣa:ɖe; ʣa:k^{h} (S07.550)

bear N : ho(:)m (S03.730)

beat V : kulam; raʈam; togam; toŋam (S09.210)

bed N : palag; palaŋ; p^{h}og (S07.420)

bedding N : poʃ(e) (—)

bedsheet N : ʧadar (—)

bedspread N : poʃmuk^{h} (S09.770)

bee N : jaŋ; ʊajaŋ (S03.813, S03.820, S03.830, S03.832)

bee (wild, large in size, and their honey is considered bad by the locals and not consumed by them) N : raiŋ (S03.820)

beehive N : ɖoɖre; muɖa:m; raitomʊe; tombe (S03.822)

beeswax N : mu:m; p^{h}aluŋ (S03.821)

before : nandris (S12.0400)

beggar N : bik^{h}ari; bik^{h}a:rija (S11.530)

begin V : ʃuru ʃaɳam (S14.250)

beginning N : ʃuru; ʃuruŋ (S14.2510)

behind (spatial) : ipiʤ; ipiʧ (S12.0110)

believe V : buʃa ʃaɳam (S17.140)

bell N : ganʈ^{h}aŋ; g^{h}unɖi (—)

belly N : poʈaŋ; ʃon (S04.4310, S04.460)

belt N : peʈi (S06.570)

belt (traditional) N : k^{h}o (S06.570)

bend V : moroɽja:m; ʈumrigja:m (S09.140)

beside : soŋgus (S12.0200)

between N : maʤaŋ; moʤoŋ (S12.370)

beyond : agraŋ (S12.0410)

big : ʤiŋ; teg (S12.550)

bird N : ʧaɽig (S03.581)

bird (a small species with a small crown on its head) N : gunɖu (ʧaɽig) (S03.581)

birdseed N : mog (S08.311)

birthday N : ʤalamdin (—)

biscuit N : biskuʈ (S05.99906)

bite V : ga:rʦ raʈam (S04.580)

bitter gourd N : karela (—)

black : rok (S15.650)

black lentil N : rokda:l (—)

blacksmith (male member of traditional community) N : ɖaggis (S09.600)

blacksmith (traditional community) N : ɖagi (S09.600)

blame N : kusur (S16.780)

blame V : kusur ʃaɳam (—)

blanket N : kambaɽ; kamɽ (S07.422)

blind : ka:ɳas; ka:ɳo (S04.970)

blood N : k^{h}ui (S04.150)

blow V : p^{h}u lanam (S10.380)

blue : arak; hara; ra:g (S15.670, S15.680)

boat N : kiʃti (S10.830)

body N : ɖehi (S04.110)

body hair N : kra: (S04.140, S04.144)

body louse N : rig (S03.811, S03.8112)

boil V : ubɽem; ubɽja:m (S05.220)

bolt of lightning N : ʧamak (S01.570)

bone N : haɖɖaŋ (S04.160)

book N : katab; kita:b; kuta:b (S18.610)

boot N : bu:ʈ (S06.510, S06.520)

border N : sima (—)

bore (a hole) V : k^{h}aʈa gaɳam (S09.460)

borrow V : riɳ uɳam (S11.620)

bother N : taŋ; toŋ (—)

bottle N : bottal (S23.5600)

bottom : ɖug; ɖugas; ʤo (S12.0300, S12.670)
bottom N : ɖug; ɖugas; ʤo; kʰuteni (S12.340)
bow N : danuʃ; ga:rʦ (S20.240)
bowl N : kaʈora (S05.330)
box N : baks; ɖabaŋ (—)
boy N : ʧʰak; ʧʰakʦ; ʧʰaŋ; ʧʰokra (S02.250, S02.270)
bracelet (modern) N : baŋga (S06.740)
bracelet (traditional) N : paʈʈʰa (S06.740)
braid N : linɖis (S06.921)
braid V : linɖis ʃaɳ-am (S09.750)
brain (as food) N : kra:ɳ (S04.203)
branch N : paŋ; ʃaŋ (S08.550)
brass N : pital (—)
brave : roʈʰ; roʈʰas (S16.520)
bread N : hoɖ; roʈʰe (S05.510)
break V : ʤuɳam [INTR]; ʧuɳam; ʧuŋam [TR] (S09.260, S09.270)
breakfast N : kula:r; som kula:r (S05.420)
breast N : hik; ma:mug (S04.400, S04.410)
breathe V : ʃã: ɖuɳam (S04.510)
brick N : iʈ; ĩ:ʈʰ (S07.620)
bride N : tem (S02.640, S02.641)
bridge N : ʦʰam (S10.740)
brightness N : roʃni (—)
bring V : kanam (S10.620)
broom N : peg; pek (S09.380)
brother N : bau (S02.440)
brother's child N : bau baʧa (S02.5410)
brother's son N : ba:ɳes; bʰaɳe (S02.530)
bruise N : kʰulʃig (S04.852)
brush N : burʃ (S06.920)
bucket N : balʈiŋ (—)
buffalo N : baĩs; meʃi (S03.9170)
build V : baɳem; gaɳam; kim ʃaɳam (S09.1110, S09.440)
build structure from foundation V : g(ʰ)oɳam (S09.440)
bulb (of a lamp) N : la:ʈu (—)
bull N : ra:d (S03.210, S03.220)
bunch N : ʧʰu:nɖ (S05.712)
burn(1) V : hiram ʃenam (S01.851)
burn(2) V : hiram (S01.852)
bury V : dabja:m; potʰja:m (S04.780, S09.342, S09.343)
bus N : bas; ga:ɽi; ga:ɽiŋ (S23.1400, S23.1500)
bush N : ʈʰumre (—)
business N : biʣanes (S11.860)
butter N : makkʰaɳ (S05.890)
butter (local) N : bu:r (S05.890)
butterfly N : boɽiʦ (S03.920)
button N : piple (S06.620)
buy V : kʰaɳam (S11.810)
cabbage N : bandgobi (S05.99908)
cable N : kobel (—)
cage N : pinʤra (S20.640)
calf N : ra: (S03.240)
calf [F] N : ʃikran (S03.240)
calf [M] N : ʃakras (S03.240)
calf of the leg N : pille (S04.352)
call(1) V : a:ɽem; ʤaru lonam (S18.410)
calm : ʃa:nt (S01.322)
camel N : ũʈ (S03.780)
candle N : mombatti (S07.460)
candy N : miʈʰa; sauda (S23.5650)
canister N : kani (—)
cap N : ʈope (S06.550)
car N : ga:ɽi; ga:ɽiŋ; ka:r (S23.1400, S23.1500)
carpenter N : mistri:; tʰauʋis (S09.430, S09.820)
carpet N : guli:ʧa (S09.771)
carrot N : ga:ʤar (S08.99910)
carry V : anam (S10.610)
carry in hand V : guɖpa anam (S10.612)
carry on head V : bala anam (S10.614)
carve V : guleʣ ʃaɳam (S09.810)
cashew N : ka:ʤu (S08.99911)
cat N : pũĩ (S03.620)
cat [F] N : bura:ɽi (S03.620)
cat [M] N : bura:ɽa (S03.620)
catch V : ʦ(ʰ)u(:)mam (S10.252)
cattle N : laŋ kʰaga:; laŋokʰa: kʰas (S03.200)
cattleshed N : kʰuɽaŋ (S07.130)
cauliflower N : gobi; pʰulgobbi (—)
cave N : a:g; gupʰa (S01.280)
cease V : rokja:m [TR]; rukem [INTR]; ʈʰaprja:m [TR] (S14.280)
cedrus deodara (tree) N : deodar (S08.640)
celebrate V : maja:m (—)
celebration N : kʰuʃi (—)
cellar N : kʰuɖ; kʰuɖaŋ (—)
cement N : simiʈ (—)
chain N : ʃaŋgle (S09.180)
chair N : kursi (S07.430)
chapati N : roʈʰe (S05.510)
charcoal N : koile; tarkol; ʧopʈu (S01.890)
cheap : sastas (S11.890)
cheek N : piŋ (S04.201)
chest N : hik; ʦʰa:ʈi (S04.400, S04.410)
chew V : tsapem (S05.180)
chicken N : kukaɽaŋ; kukuɽoka ʧʰaŋ; kukuɽoka ʧʰã; ʧikan (S03.550)
chickpea N : ʧana (—)
chickpea flour N : besaɳe (—)
chieftain N : prada:n (S19.240)
child N : ʧara; ʧʰak; ʧʰakʦ; ʧʰaŋ; ʧʰo; ʧʰok (S02.250, S02.270, S02.280, S02.410)
child care center N : aŋganʋa:ɽiŋ (—)
chilli (red) N : pipli; pipɽi (S05.820, S05.821)
chimney N : na:liŋ; tandura:ʣ pajp (S07.330)
chin N : ʧʰamga (S04.207, S04.209)

chisel N : ʈʰolu (S09.490, S09.840)
chop V : ʧʰulam (—)
chopper (traditional) N : ɳija (—)
cigarette N : surgiʈ (S23.5900)
clay N : ka:m (S01.212, S09.730)
clean : ʦokʰas (S15.870)
cliff N : ɖag; ɖakʰ; paha:ɽ (S01.220, S01.222)
climb V : ʈaɳam (S10.472)
clock N : gaɽi (S14.530)
cloth N : gas; kapra (S06.210)
cloth-stand N : nubari (—)
cloud N : dʒuʃaŋ (S01.730)
coat N : ko:ʈ (S06.430)
cobra snake N : na:ges (S03.850)
cock N : kukaɽaŋ; murga: (S03.520)
coffee N : kopʰi (S23.9100)
coin N : nagadi (S11.440)
cold : sardi; ʈʰanɖas (S15.860)
cold N : ʈʰanɖas (S14.740)
collar N : kanɖe (S06.450)
color N : raŋg (S09.880, S15.610)
comb N : buruʃ; kant (S06.910)
come V : baram (S10.480)
come back V : lo baram (S10.481)
come out V : dʊanam; ɖuɽam (—, S10.210)
community hall N : ʤanaŋ (—)
conceive V : ʧʰaulem (S04.732)
cone (of pine tree) N : tita:n; titã:(n) (S08.660, S08.9960)
consciousness N : hoʃ (—)
container N : ɖabaŋ (—)
contrary : umle (—)
cook V : ʣa:miʣ ʃaɳam; kʰaɳaga: haʃim [INTR]; kʰaɳaga: ʃaɳam; siʈem [INTR]; siʈja:m [TR] (S05.210)
cooked : pakeʦ; paʃiʣ (S05.121, S05.123)
copper N : tramba; ʧamo (S09.660)
corn kernel N : ʦʰali (—)
corner N : koɳe (S12.353, S12.760)
corpse : ʃi:k (S04.7501)
corpse N : ʃi:ʣ maɽʃaŋ; ʃi:k (S04.770)
correct : daʈʰis (S16.710, S16.730)
cost N : mulaŋ (S11.870)
cough V : kʰaɳem (S04.530)
council platform N : ʧotraŋ (S07.180)
count V : gaɳja:m (S13.107)
country N : deʃaŋ (S19.110, S19.160, S01.100)
courage N : him(a)t; himd (—)
courageous : him(a)t; himd (—)
court N : kʰo(l) (S07.150)
court case N : mukadma (—)
cover V : pʰuktam (S12.260)
cow N : hu(:)ʤ; laŋ (S03.230)
cow dung N : kod; molaŋ (S08.99918)
crawl V : leʈpeʈjem (S10.410)
crocodile N : magarmaʧʰ (S03.970)
crooked : ɖiŋga; ɖiŋgas (S12.740)
cross V : laŋgija:m (—)
crow N : ka:g (S03.593)
crowd N : bariʦ munuk (S13.190)
crush V : ʈʰokja:m (S05.560)
cry V : krabam (S16.370)
cucumber N : kakɽi (—)
cultivate V : sanam (S08.150)
cup N : kap (S05.350)
cure V : ʃe:l ʃaɳam (S04.860)
currency N : ɖabua (S11.430)
curry sabzi N : kan (—)
curtain N : parda (—)
custom N : riʊa:ʣ; sara (S19.610)
cut V : kaʈem; kaʈja:m; ʧʰulam (—, S09.220)
dagger N : kʰukʰuʈi (—)
daily : roʣ (S14.310)
dance V : ʧa:m (S10.440)
dandruff N : pod (S01.840, S04.146)
danger N : batr (S16.540)
dark : turaŋ; ʧʰras (S15.630)
dark-skinned : rok (S15.650)
darkness N : jaras (S01.620)
date (calendar) N : ta:rik (—)
daughter N : ʧime (S02.420)
daughter-in-law N : kuɽmani; tem; ʊahu (S02.640, S02.641)
dawn N : som ʤiʃa (S14.430)
day N : laje (S05.430, S14.410, S14.450)
day(1) N : un (S14.410)
day(2) N : ʤaɽe; un (S14.4110)
day after tomorrow N : romi (S14.481)
day before yesterday N : njuʦ; ri:d (S14.491)
daytime N : laje (S05.430, S14.410, S14.450)
dead : ʃi:k (S04.7501)
dead N : ʃi:k (S04.770)
deaf : ʈauɳa (S04.950)
death ceremony N : kirjakaram (—)
December : disambar (—)
deep : ɖug; ɖugas (S12.670)
deep N : ɖug; ɖugas (S12.340)
deer N : hiran (S03.750)
deity N : ʤohaŋ (—)
Delhi : dili; diliŋ (—)
delicious : ra:ʈʰi; ʃobil; ʃobilas (—, S16.710, S16.810)
demand N : ma:ŋ; uŋma (—)
deny V : mukrem (S18.340)
desire N : man (S04.440)
destroy V : suaʃim (S11.270)
dew N : oʃaŋ (S01.640)
dew, frozen N : pala (S01.640)
diarrhoea N : ʣala:ʊ (—)
die V : ʃi:m (S04.750)
difficult : ʣuniŋas; muʃkil (S17.470)
dig V : kotja:m (S08.220)
digest V : paʧeja:m [TR] (—)
dinner N : bja:le (S05.410, S05.440)
dirty : ganda; mand (S15.880)
disappear V : bi:m (S10.491)

disease N : buma:ri; duk^h(e); duk^{h}is (S04.8440, S16.320)
dish (with dried kaṭ^{h}u leaves) N : paʧaka ba:dzi (—)
dish (with lassi and wheat flour) N : ʣoɽ (—)
dish (with rice and seljara) N : lup^{h}a (—)
dishonest : beiman (—)
dispute V : ʤagɽa ʃim (—)
ditch N : gaɳ (S08.170)
divide V : ṭukra ʃaɳam (S12.232)
divorce N : burʃuk; uʃim (S02.341)
do V : lanam; ʃa:ŋam (S09.110, S09.1110)
dog N : kui; kutta; kuʧʧ^{h}a (S03.610)
dog, female N : kutti (S03.610)
domesticated : kiʃiʣ (—)
donation N : da:n (—)
donkey N : gadda (S03.460)
door N : pitaŋ (S07.220, S07.221)
door-bolt N : baɽɒa; ʧiṭkani (S07.231)
doorpost N : pitaŋ (S07.220, S07.221)
doubt N : ʃakk (S17.430)
dough N : a:ri (S05.530)
down : ʤo; ʃoŋ (S12.0300)
down N : ʤo (S12.340)
down south : ʤo (—)
draw water V : ti: ḍuṭam (S09.9000)
dream N : supna (—)
dream V : supna: baram (S04.620)
dress (traditional for women) N : gasa (S06.420)
drink N : meɒasi (S05.900)
drink V : tuŋam; tu:gem; tu:ŋem (S05.130)
drip (of water) V : ti: dɒanam (S10.240)
drizzle N : nakʤab (S01.750)
drool N : la:laŋ (—)
drop V : danam [INTR]; p^{h}unam [INTR]; t^{h}anam [TR] (S10.160, S10.230)
drown V : ḍub(b)em [INTR]; ḍubja:m [TR] (S04.751, S10.330)
drum N : ḍolki; naga:ra (S18.720)
drunk : tuŋtuŋ (S04.980)
dry : ʃukaʃ; ts^{h}arʣ; ʧika; ʧ^{h}amjurts (S15.840)
duck N : batak (S03.570)
dust N : du:l (S01.213)
dye V : raŋgja:m (S06.390, S09.890)
eagle N : gallas; ilna: (S03.584, S03.586)
ear N : ro:ḍ (S04.220)
earlier : pela (S12.0400, S13.340)
earlobe N : kri (S04.221)
early : ts^{h}ika (S14.160, S14.210, S14.331)
earn V : ṭaka kuma:m (S11.790)
earring N : ka:nṭa (S06.770)
earth N : dart^{h}i; prit^{h}ɒi; so: (S01.260, S01.100)
earthquake N : bukamp; ʣaʣari; gururuga (S01.450)
eat V : ʣa:m (S05.110)
eccentric : pagal (S17.230)
eclipse N : gro:ɳ (—)
edge N : koɳe; rask (S12.353, S12.760)
egg N : anḍa; li:ʧ (S05.970)
eggshell N : lebɽa (S08.750)
eight : aṭ^h (S13.0800)
elbow N : guska (S04.320)
elder N : ʤeʃṭ^{h}as (S23.3200)
elected member of Kanashi village council N : ʤeʃṭ^{h}as (S23.3200)
electricity N : biʤeɽi (S01.550, S07.450, S23.1700)
elephant N : hatt^{h}i (S03.770)
eleven : gjara (S13.101)
embers N : kojlag (S01.841)
empty : ʃag (S13.220)
end N : ɒeʃiŋ (S14.260)
enemy N : duʃman (S19.520)
enter V : kuba:r piʃim (S10.570)
entreaty N : arʣ (—)
essential : ʣururi (—)
eunuch N : beṭaɽi mord (—)
even : na:mi (—)
evening N : ɒeraŋ (S14.460)
ever : na:mi (—)
every day : roʣ (S14.310)
evil : nark (S16.720)
evil N : nark (S22.320)
exist V : nem (S24.0100)
expensive : ma:gas (S11.880)
extinguish V : mi: piŋam (S01.861)
eye N : mig (S04.210)
face N : ʃakal; toŋ (S04.204)
fair : ʣats (—)
fall N : sadraŋ (S14.770)
fall V : danam [INTR]; p^{h}unam [INTR] (S10.160, S10.230)
family N : ṭabar (S02.820)
famine N : aŋka:laŋ (S05.141)
far : durane; du:(r) (S12.440)
farmer N : ʣimida:(r) (S08.110)
fast : ts^{h}ika (S14.160, S14.210, S14.331)
fast V : ɒaʃe naʃim (S22.260)
fat : moṭas (S12.630)
fat (of goat) N : ts^{h}os (—)
fat (of sheep) N : ts^{h}os (—)
father N : ba: (S02.350, S02.510)
father-in-law (of a man) N : ʃoras; ʃores (S02.610)
father-in-law (of a woman) N : ʃoras; ʃores (S02.611)
father-in-law N : ma:ma: (S02.511, S02.610, S02.611)
father's older brother N : ba: ʤeṭ^{h}a (S02.512)
father's sister N : bube (S02.522, S02.620, S02.621)
father's younger brother N : ba: p^{h}akuʧ (S02.512)

fear N : baŋ (S16.530)
feather N : pakʰiŋ (S04.392)
feed V : kʰila:m (—)
fell V : tʰanam [TR] (S10.160)
female(2) : mĩʧ (S03.130)
fence N : ɖe:k (S08.160)
fermented drink N : sura:b (S05.940)
festival N : tama:ʃa; tiha:r (—)
fever N : ʥo:r (S04.841)
few : dalak (S13.170)
field N : ʃo (S08.120)
fifteen : pandra (S13.103)
fight V : ʥagɽiʃim ʃenam; toʃim [MDL] (S20.110)
fill : plen (—)
fill V : barem [INTR]; barja:m [TR] (S13.99907)
film N : pʰilam (S23.6200)
find V : la:m; la:mʃim [MDL]; millem (S05.490, S11.160, S11.320)
fine N : loʃito (S21.380)
finger N : goʈʰi; káni góʈʰɪʦ; pra:d; pra:daŋ (S04.340, S04.380)
fingernail N : ʧi:nɖ (S04.344)
finish N : ʋeʃiŋ (S14.260)
finish V : nibja:m [TR]; ʋesam (S14.270)
fir N : kʰrok (S08.650)
fire N : mi: (S01.810)
firefly N : ʤugnu; mijaŋ (S03.910)
fireplace N : geʈʈʰaŋ (S05.250, S07.310, S07.320)
firewood N : ʃiŋ (S01.430, S01.880)
first : pela; ʃuruɳats (S12.0400, S13.340)
fish N : matsis; maʧʰli (S03.650)
five : na; ŋa; pãʧ (S13.0500)
flail N : ʃupa (—)
flame N : g(ʰ)ana (S01.820)
flashlight N : biʤeɽi (S01.550, S07.450, S23.1700)
flat : sa:mnas (S12.710, S12.730)
flea N : jaŋ; puŋ (S03.813, S03.820, S03.830, S03.832)
flee V : pʰoʧim (S10.510)
floor N : bumiŋ; dʰart; pa:ʈi; pʰarʃ (S07.210, S07.260)
flour N : a:r; piʈʰas (S05.550)
flour (of buckwheat) N : ʧisaŋ (S05.550)
flour (of corn) N : tsʰali piʈʰas (S05.550)
flour (refined) N : medda (S05.550)
flour, corn N : tsʰali piʈʰas (S08.470)
flow (of water) V : ti: boɳam (S10.320)
flower N : pʰul; u: (S08.570)
flower (a species cultivated in flowerpots, yellow-orange) N : sartʰas (S08.570)
flower (a species planted as decoration) N : boddi (S08.570)
flower (a wild species, blue-white N : goguŋ (S08.570)
flower (a wild species, blue-white) N : pʰoʃʈare (S08.570)
flower (a wild species, red-white N : kaʈa:ɳ (S08.570)
flute N : bẽʃur; bẽʃuri (S18.710)
fly N : jaŋ (S03.813, S03.820, S03.830, S03.832)
fly V : uɽja:m [TR]; uɽjem [INTR] (S10.370)
foam N : ʃep (S01.324)
fog N : dumme (S01.740)
fold V : pʰuɽigija:m; tolam (S09.150)
follow V : ʈʰurja:m (S10.520)
food N : ʥa:m; kʰa:na (S05.120)
foolish : bekupʰ; uta (—, S17.230)
foot N : baole; goɖiŋ; ʈa:ŋg; ʈʰulla; ʈʰullaŋ (S04.350, S04.370)
footprint N : kʰori (S04.374)
footsole N : pʰine; talaŋ (S04.331, S04.374)
for : lage (—)
forbid V : ma:j lonam (S18.380)
forehead N : mattʰa (S04.205)
foreign country N : pardeʃaŋ (—)
foreigner N : hi:p; pʰuraŋgi (—)
forest N : baŋ; baɳaŋ; baɽaŋ; ʤad; ʤaŋgal (S01.410)
forget V : boʃ(u)ʈam (S17.320)
forgive V : ma:p ʃunim (S16.690)
four : pu (S13.0400)
four days after : ʃu:min poien ba:d (—)
four days after today : ei (—)
four days after tomorrow : eʧei; na:hĩ (—)
fox N : ʃa:ɽug (S03.740)
fresh : jug; sadzara; taʥa (—, S14.130)
Friday : ʃukkar (S14.670)
friend N : dost; mitar(a); mita:r; saŋgis (S19.510)
frog N : meɖkas (S03.950)
from : ŋaʥ; taŋs (—)
front(side) : no:ʧas (S12.0410)
frost N : paɽa:j (—)
fruit N : poʈo; pʰolaŋ; pʰruʈ (S05.650, S05.710)
fry V : ra:ɽ gaɳam (S05.230)
frying pan N : pʰrajbin (S05.280)
full : barits (S13.150, S13.160, S13.210)
full sleeve N : ba:huʤi (—)
furrow N : ʥoɖega: (S08.212)
garlic N : lasaɳ (—)
garment N : lapta; laʈpaʈ(a) (S06.120)
gather V : kaʈʰe ʃaɳam (S12.210)
gathering (large) N : dumsa (—)
gentleman N : mord (—)
get V : millem (S05.490, S11.160, S11.320)
get stuck V : ʥoɽam [INTR]; ʧiɳam (—)
get tired V : tʰakem (—)
ghee N : makkʰaɳ (S05.890)
ghee (local) N : ma(:)r (S05.890)
ghost N : b(ʰ)utaŋ; raks (S22.450)

ginger N : adrak (—)
girl N : ʧime(ʦ) (S02.260)
give V : dem; kenam [1/2o]; raɳam [NON-1/2o] (S11.210)
give back V : bapas raɳam (S11.220)
glacier N : ʤuriŋ; ri:(g); ʦaraŋ (—)
glass N : gula(:)s; kanʦu gula(:)s (S09.740)
glasses N : enak; ʧaʃma (S23.2400)
glove N : guɖpa ʥura:bba: (S06.580)
glue N : gud; gu:nd (S09.560)
glue (from chil tree) N : ʧinin (—)
go V : bonam (S10.470)
go down V : ʃoŋnu bonam (S10.473)
go out V : ba:ro boŋʈam (S10.474)
go up V : riŋ bonam (S10.471)
goat [F] N : bakari (S03.360)
goat hair N : sejle (—)
goat N : bakar; bakras (S03.360)
god N : bagʋa:n; ʤaŋ (S22.120)
goiter N : ganam (S04.842)
goitre N : ganam (S04.842)
gold N : ʥa(:)ŋ; ʥa:ŋ (S06.710, S09.640)
good : ʃobil; ʃobilas (S16.710, S16.810)
good (nature) : daʈ^{h}is (S16.710, S16.730)
good weather N : neskaŋ (—)
government N : sirkar (S23.3000)
grandchild N : pa:ʦ (S02.5000)
grape N : aŋgu:r (S05.760)
grass bundle N : ʋaluŋ (—)
grasshopper N : ʈiʈaɽa (S03.930)
grazing N : goʤ (—)
greedy : lalʧi; larʧis muruk (S16.830)
green : hara; ra:g (S15.670, S15.680)
grief N : duk^{h}(e); duk^{h}e; duk^{h}is (S04.8440, S16.320)
grind V : ʈ^{h}okja:m (S05.560)
grinding stone N : goʈ^{h} (—)
ground (e.g. football ground) N : ɖu (—)
grow V : rohem; roja:m (S08.99962, S12.530)
guest N : paɳaɳa; pa:una; ponukes; poɳukes (S19.560)
guesthouse (traditional) N : marhaŋ (—)
gun N : tupka; tupk^{h} (S20.280)
guru N : guru (S17.270)
guts N : aʤaŋ (S04.461)
hail N : ʃaru (—)
half N : ad^{h}a (S13.240)
half sleeve N : p^{h}a:g baʤu (—)
hall N : k^{h}ulaʧ (—)
hammer N : g(^{h})aɽam; tabru; ʈ^{h}olu (S09.490, S09.840)
hand N : guɖ (S04.310, S04.330)
hang up V : laʈam (S09.341)
happiness N : k^{h}uʃi; suk^{h} (—, S20.140)
happy : k^{h}uʃi (—)
hare N : k^{h}argoʃ (S03.614, S03.8630)
harvest N : p^{h}asal (S08.410)
hat N : ʈope (S06.550)
have V : tam; tonam (S11.110)
hawk N : ʋa:ʥ (S03.585)
head N : bal (S04.200)
head hair N : kra: (S04.140, S04.144)
head louse N : rig (S03.811, S03.8112)
head of goat N : muɖe (—)
hear V : ʦ^{h}a:m (S15.410, S15.420)
heart N : buka; dil; kakaɽi; karʥ; man (S04.440, S04.450)
heaven N : sʋarg (S22.310)
heavy : garkas (S15.810)
heel N : p^{h}ine (S04.372, S04.374)
hell : nark (S16.720)
hell N : nark (S22.320)
help N : help^{h} (—)
help V : mat ʃaɳam (S19.580)
hen N : murgi: (S03.540)
henna N : mehendi (—)
herdsman N : p^{h}oal (S03.180)
here : lo; nid (S24.0900)
heron N : bagula (S03.583)
hide N : k^{h}olɖu; ʃa (S04.120)
hide V : ta(:)tam (S12.270)
high : uʈ^{h}ras (S12.310)
hill N : ɖog; paha:ɽ; ʧaŋ (S01.220, S01.222)
hip (of domesticated animal) N : k^{h}utaɳi (S04.463)
hire V : kura:ʋas raɳam (S11.770)
hit V : raʈam (S09.210)
hoe N : ʦ^{h}arʥ ʃiŋ (S08.250)
hold V : ʦ(^{h})u(:)mam (S10.252)
hole N : k^{h}aʈ (S12.850)
hollow : palaŋ (—)
home N : kim (S07.120)
home, camping N : ɖera (S07.6500)
honest : k^{h}asaʦ (—)
honey N : ʋa:s (S05.840)
honor N : iʥat (—)
horn N : ka:ɽi; ru:d; ʃi:ŋ (S04.170, S18.730)
horse N : goɽa; raŋ; ra:ŋ (S03.410, S03.420)
hospital N : aspata:l; haspata:l (S23.2000)
hour N : ganʈa (S14.510)
house (modern) N : lenʈern (S07.120)
house (traditional) N : kim (S07.120)
house in the fields N : ʃeɳi (S07.130)
how many : tada (S17.630)
how? : hale (S17.610)
human N : munuk (S02.100)
hundred : i:d ʃo; ʃo (S13.105)
hunger N : ʋoʃ (—)
hunt V : heraɳa boŋʈam (S20.610)
hunting N : heɽaŋ; ʃika:r (—)
hurry V : ʦ^{h}ika ʃaɳam (S14.230)
husband N : biniʃ; biɳis (S02.310)
hut N : ʈ^{h}akuʧaʈi; ʈainta (S07.130)
ice N : ʃaɳaŋ (S01.770)
ice drop N : ʦ^{h}urnu (—)
idiot : pagal (S17.230)

if : netat (S17.530)
immediately : arʤi; tsʰikatsʰika (S14.190)
in : kuba:r (S12.0120)
in front : sa:mna (—)
in front of : sa:mana (S12.0410)
in reality : asli (—)
incense N : dupaŋ (—)
injection N : sua (S23.2300)
injure V : raʃim (S11.280)
injury N : kʰaʈ; roʃuʧ (—, S12.850)
innocent : naɖa; ʃantida:r (S21.360)
insect N : ʧʰaʧ kaʈãõ (S03.810, S03.832)
inside : kuba:r; kubo:r (—, S12.0120)
intelligent : dimaki (—)
intermingle V : milem; millem (S19.650)
intestines N : aʤaŋ (S04.461)
invite V : paɳaɳa ʤaram (S19.5650)
iron N : roɳ (S09.670)
island N : ʈa:pu (S01.250)
itch N : luk (S04.854)
jackal N : gidaɽ (—)
jacket N : ʤakʈ (S06.430)
jar N : ɖabaŋ (—)
jaundice N : pilija (—)
jaw N : ʧʰamga (S04.207, S04.209)
join V : milem; millem; ʧiŋam (S12.220, S12.250, S19.650)
jug N : ʤag (S05.340)
jump N : louk (—)
jump V : tsʰapuk raɳam (S10.430)
Kanashi : kana:ʃi; kuna:ʃi (—)
Kanashi community N : ra deo (—)
kaʈʰu (a wheat-like cereal) N : b(r)es; kaʈʰu (—)
keep V : piʧim; tam (S11.170)
kerosene N : miʈʈika tel (—)
kettle N : ketali (S05.270)
key N : kunʤi (S07.240)
kick V : latas raɳam (S10.431)
kid (of goat) N : ma:ts (S03.380)
kill V : sanam (S04.760)
kilogram N : kilo (—)
kilometer N : kilomiʈar (—)
king N : ba:dʃa; ra:ʤa (S19.320)
kiss N : ʧum (—)
kiss V : peim (S16.290)
kitchen N : kiʧan; kʰotar (—, S07.170)
knead V : pʰram (S05.540)
knee N : ʧi:g (S04.360)
knife N : tsʰure (S05.380)
knit V : gundja:m (S06.330)
knot N : gurʃu (S09.192)
know V : sesam (S17.170)
knowledge N : pata (—)
ladder N : uŋgeɽa (S07.370)
ladle N : kʰartsul (S05.370)
lagoon N : ʤil (S01.330, S01.341)
lake N : ʤil; tala:ɒ (S01.330, S01.341)
lamb N : kʰas; kʰa:ts (S03.250, S03.290)
lamp (kerosene) N : tsimani (S07.450)
language N : ba:ʃa; boli (S18.240)
last : hipiʧ (S12.0100, S13.350)
last year : naliŋ (—)
latch N : baɽɒa; ʧiʈkani (S07.231)
late : kubaleke (S14.170)
laugh V : ɒanam (S16.250)
law N : ka:nun (S21.110)
lazy : alesis; matslis; sust (S04.920)
leaf N : patti; paʧaŋ (S08.560)
learn V : sikʰja:m [TR]; sikʰjem [INTR] (S17.240)
leather N : ʧamɽa (S06.290)
leather (of goat) N : kʰults (S06.290)
leave V : buɽam (S10.250, S10.490)
left : buɽ; ɖeb; pʰeʈʈo (S12.420)
leg N : baole; goɖiŋ; ʈa:ŋg; ʈʰulla; ʈʰullaŋ (S04.350, S04.370)
lentils N : a:l; da:l (—)
lentils (Indian brown) N : masuri da:ɽ (—)
leopard N : ʃer (S03.99942)
less : dalats; dʰalak; kam (—)
letter N : ʧiʈʈʰi (S23.4200)
lick V : lemam (S04.590)
lie(2) V : ʧora golop lonam (S16.670)
lie down V : pʰeʈa paem (S12.140)
life N : ʣan; ʣindagi (S04.7410)
light N : tsʰag (S01.610)
light V : (mi:) sutam; mi: ʃaɳam; tsʰag baɽja:m (S01.860)
light(1) : haɽka:ts (S15.820)
light (arctic) N : roʃni (—)
lightning N : biʤeɽi (S01.550, S07.450, S23.1700)
like that : neije (—)
liking N : pasand (—)
lime N : nimbu (—)
limp V : benɖerem (S10.451)
lion N : tʰar (S03.720)
lip N : tʰotoro; tʰotʰra (S04.250)
listen V : tsʰa:m (S15.410, S15.420)
little : tʰi:d; tʰoɽa (S13.99901)
liver N : buka (S04.440, S04.450)
livestock N : paʃu (S03.150)
living being N : ʣiu (S03.110)
lizard N : bɽitits; ʧʰaba:ɽ (S03.960)
loan N : riɳ (S11.640)
lock N : ʃaiŋ; ta:ɽi (S07.230, S07.2320)
long : la:mas (S12.570, S12.580)
look V : taɳam; taɳʃim [MDL] (S15.520)
loot N : luʈ (—)
lose V : pi:m (S11.330)
loss : gata (—)
lotus flower N : kamal u: (S08.570)
loud : zori (S15.450)
lovely : ʃobil; ʃobilas (S16.710, S16.810)
low : niʃʈʰas (S12.320)

lower house in traditional Malana parliament N : kaniʃʈʰaŋ (–)
lower part of Malana N : saraŋ; saura behad (–)
luggage N : boraŋ (S09.99917)
lunch N : dupa:ri; laje (S05.430, S14.410, S14.450)
lung N : baʃ (S04.441)
machine N : muʃi:n (S23.1900)
mad : ba:jliʦ (S17.230)
magic N : ʥaddu (S22.420)
mainland N : so: (S01.260)
make V : baɳem; lanam; ʃa:ɳam (S09.110, S09.1110, S09.440)
make dough V : a:r pʰram (–)
man N : madras; maɽʃaŋ; mi; munuk (S02.210)
mango N : a:m (S08.99930)
many : bariʦ (S13.150, S13.160, S13.210)
map N : nakʃa (–)
mare N : goɽi (S03.440)
market N : baʥa:(r) (S11.850)
married man N : ʧʰeʦ roʈas (S02.380)
married woman N : baseʦ bekaɽi; baseʦ beʈaɽi (S02.390)
marry V : bijaŋ ʃaɳam (S02.330)
mason N : mistriʦ (S07.610)
mat N : dari; sela (S09.770, S09.771)
mat (to sit on) N : poʃmukʰ (S09.770)
match N : tuɽi (S01.870)
maternal grandfather N : na:na: (S02.460)
maternal grandmother N : na:ni: (S02.470)
maternal grandparents N : na:na:na:ni: (S02.4711)
maternal uncle's wife N : ma:mi: (–)
matter N : fikri (–)
meal N : bja:le (S05.410, S05.440)
measure V : ɖa:lem (S12.540)
meat N : ʃabɽi (S05.610)
medicine N : ʃe(:)l (S04.880)
meet V : milem; mileʃim [MDL]; milja:m [TR]; millem (S19.650)
member of a lower class N : kaniʃʈʰas (–)
merchant N : lala (S11.840)
merry : kʰuʃi (–)
midday N : laje (S05.430, S14.410, S14.450)
middle N : maʤaŋ; moʤoŋ (S12.370)
midge N : bigaliʦ (S03.831)
milk N : kʰiraŋ (S05.860)
milk V : ʦuram (S05.870)
mind N : karʥ (S04.440)
mirror N : arʃug; arʃuk (S06.960)
misery N : dukʰ(e); dukʰis (S04.8440)
mix V : milja:m [TR] (S19.650)
mobile telephone N : mobajl; mobajlaŋ (S23.1200)
molar tooth N : ʤa:mgar (S04.272)
Monday : soar; suãraŋ (S14.630)
money N : ʈaka (S11.430)
mongoose N : noɒal (–)
monkey N : bandraŋ (S03.760)
month N : bina; mahina (S14.710)
moon N : ʤojʃʈʰaŋ; ʤuʃʈʰa; ʧand (S01.530)
more : bariʦ (S13.150, S13.160, S13.210)
morning N : som (S14.440)
mosquito N : jaŋ; ʧʰaʧ kaʈãõ (S03.810, S03.813, S03.820, S03.830, S03.832)
mother N : ja: (S02.360)
mother-in-law (of a man) N : juŋme; sauri; sa:su (S02.620)
mother-in-law (of a woman) N : juŋme; sauri; sa:su (S02.621)
mother-in-law N : bube (S02.522, S02.620, S02.621)
mother's brother N : ma:ma: (S02.511, S02.610, S02.611)
mother's sister N : ja:ʤʈʰi; massi (S02.521)
mountain N : ɖog; ka:ʈʰi; ka:ʈʰiŋ; ʧaŋ (S01.220)
mountain pass N : ka:ʈʰi; ka:ʈʰiŋ; om (S01.220, S10.720)
mountain top N : ka:ʈʰi; ka:ʈʰiŋ; raŋ (S01.220, S12.330)
mouse N : pʰuʦ (S03.630)
mouth N : kʰa(:)kaŋ (S04.240)
mouthpiece of the god N : gur (S22.180)
move V : talja:m [TR]; taljem (S10.110)
movie N : pʰilam (S23.6200)
mow V : ʧi kaʈem (S08.320)
much : bariʦ; bori; ʥad(d)a; ʥʰa:; ʤinɖije (–, S13.150, S13.160, S13.210)
mud N : ʦikar; ʦikra (S01.214)
muffler N : galband (–)
mule N : kaʧʰar (S03.460)
murderer N : kʰu:nis (–)
mushroom (a wild species) N : kʰiri ʧʰaʧe; muʈuʃa; ʦʰuʦurug; ʧʰaʧe (S08.980)
muslim N : musalman (S22.99909)
mustache N : muʦʰ (–)
mustard leaves (green) N : ka:n (–)
mustard oil N : ʧiktela (–)
mute : laʈʰas; maɖa (S04.960)
nail N : preg (S09.500)
naked : naŋʈa (S04.990)
name N : na:m; na:maŋ (S18.280)
nape of the neck N : kunaga (S04.281)
narrow : gaʈas (S12.620)
navel N : naɽukʰ (S04.430)
near : di; neɽaŋ; soŋgus; ʧʰuŋ (S12.0200, S12.430)
necessary : ʥaruri; toɽe (–)
necessity N : ʥaruri (S17.450)
neck N : golaŋ; kʰili (S04.280, S04.290)
necklace N : ha:r; ʦandraha:r (S06.750)

necklace (golden) N : dʑa:ŋmamula: (—)
need N : dʑaruri (S17.450)
needle(1) N : keb; sui (S06.360)
neem tree (Azadirachta indica) N : ni:m (—)
[NEG.BE/EXIST] V : ma:je- (S24.0100)
nephew N : ba:ɳes; b^{h}aɳe (S02.530)
nest N : ʈukor; ʋa: (S03.580)
new : jug (S14.130)
next : hedde (S24.1100, S24.1200)
niece N : ba:ɳek (S02.540)
night N : ra:t; ra:tiŋ (S14.420)
nine : nao (S13.0900)
nipple N : manu (S04.412)
nit N : rikʦ (S03.812)
no : ma:j (S17.560)
noise N : kaɽi (S15.440, S18.110)
non-Kanashi person N : lok; lokas (S02.100)
nose N : ta; tak^{h}uʦ (S04.230)
nostril N : k^{h}aʈaga:; taʋadʑa: (S04.231)
not : ma:j (S24.0600)
nothing : ʧ^{h}igi ma:ʃ (S24.1400)
now : dʑa:b; ʧ^{h}abaja (S14.180)
oats N : ʧa:g (S08.460)
ocean N : najiŋ; samudra; samudraŋ (S01.320, S01.329, S01.360)
odor N : ba:s (—)
office N : daftra (—)
often : kebbikebbi (S14.320, S14.330)
oh : nu: (—)
oil N : tela (S05.790)
okra (vegetable) N : binɖi (—)
old : juʃk (S14.150)
old man N : buɽas (S02.461)
old woman N : buɽiʦ (S02.471)
older : teg (S12.550)
older brother N : teg bau (S02.444)
older sister N : teg riŋdʑ (S02.454)
on : pa:; rigi:n (—)
on foot : pedal (—)
one : ek; i:d (S13.0100)
one and a half : deɽ (—)
one-eyed : ka:ɳas; ka:ɳo (S04.970)
onion N : pja:dʑ (S08.99935)
only : ʦ^{h}uɽe (S13.330)
open V : k^{h}ulam; k^{h}ulam [TR]; k^{h}ulem [INTR]; k^{h}ulʃim [MDL]; t^{h}ʋaɳam [TR] (S05.460, S12.240)
orange : pi:g (S15.690)
orange N : santra (S08.99936)
orchard N : ʃo (S08.120)
order N : bada (—)
original : asli (—)
ornament N : dʑa:ŋ (S06.710)
orphan N : ana:t^h; ʃokkura; ʃokkuraŋ (S02.750)
other : hedde (S24.1100, S24.1200)
otherwise : moit (—)
outside : ba:ro; ba:ru (S12.0600)
oven N : geʈʈ^{h}aŋ; tundur (S05.250, S07.310, S07.320)
owl N : uɽug (S03.596)
ox N : pag; ra:d (S03.210, S03.220)
paddy N : dʑatka sila:ŋ (S08.1210)
padlock N : ta:ɽi (S07.230, S07.2320)
pain N : bedna; binɖra (S16.310)
paint N : raŋg (S09.880, S15.610)
paint V : raŋgja:m (S06.390, S09.890)
pair N : doɽag; dʑõũɽi; dʑoɽi (S02.458, S13.370)
palm of the hand N : talaŋ (S04.331, S04.374)
pan N : p^{h}rajbin (S05.280)
panir N : punir (S05.880)
paper N : kagad (S18.560)
parents N : ja:ba; ja:ʃba: (S02.370)
parents-in-law N : sa:susa:uri: (S02.6220)
parrot N : totta (S03.592)
particular community N : ʧama:ras (S06.540)
pasture in lower regions N : t^{h}aʧaŋ (S03.160)
paternal grandfather N : daddu; da:da (S02.460)
paternal grandmother N : da:di (S02.470)
paternal grandparents N : da:dada:di; da:duse da:di (S02.4711)
paternal uncle's wife N : ʧa:ʧi (—)
path N : om (S10.720)
pea N : maʈar (S08.99937)
peace N : suk^h (S20.140)
peanut N : muŋgp^{h}ali (—)
pebble N : gaʈʈi (S01.440)
peel V : k^{h}ulam (S05.460)
peel (of vegetable or fruit) N : bod (S04.120)
pen N : pen (S18.570)
penalty N : da:ɳaŋ; ɖa:ɳaŋ (S21.370)
pencil N : prisin (S09.99915)
penis N : k^{h}utu (S04.492)
people N : lok; lokas; mo; pakres; taŋdʑa (S19.210)
people of Kullu N : kultaŋdʑa (—)
pepper N : pipli; pipɽi (S05.820, S05.821)
perhaps : da:ba (—)
person N : lok; lokas; munuk (S02.100)
perspiration N : parsed; parset (—)
perspire V : parsed dʋanam (S04.550)
physically weak : dʒaŋʧ (S12.650)
physician N : ɖakʈar (S04.870)
pickle N : aʧa:r (—)
pig N : su:r; su:ru (S03.350)
pigeon N : gugut (S03.594)
pillar N : k^{h}amba; t^{h}amba (S07.560)
pillow N : kum (S07.421)
pin (traditional for women) N : pitsuga (S06.630)
pinch V : ʧis raɳam (S15.712)
pine N : li:m (S08.640)
pipe N : hukka; pajp (S08.691)

pitch V : laːmʃim [MDL] (—)
pitcher N : ʤag (S05.340)
place N : ʥaːga; sõts (S12.110)
plain N : padraŋ; padras; padre (S01.230)
plait N : linɖis (S06.921)
plait V : linɖis ʃaɳ-am (S09.750)
plane N : ʥahaʥ (—)
plant N : beʈiŋ; pʰakuts ɖaliŋ (S08.530, S08.600)
plant V : roʊam (S08.531)
plate N : puleʈ (S05.320)
play V : oʤim (S16.260)
please : ʥibaɳ (—)
pleasure N : maʥa (—)
plough V : raːlam (S08.210)
plow V : raːlam (S08.210)
plum (edible) N : ʧul (S08.99941)
plus half (in numerals) N : saɽe (S13.240)
pocket N : kʰisaŋ; kʰissa (S06.610)
poison N : biʃaŋ; ʥeher (S04.890)
pole N : tʰamba (S07.560)
police N : purts (S23.3300)
pond N : ɖibɽiŋ (S01.330, S01.370)
poor : gariːb; nagaɽija (S11.520)
portion N : bãɖa; hisa (S13.230)
pot N : baniŋ; ɖigtsaː; ɖiksa; kunɖi; pataːl (S05.260)
pot to measure cereal, flour etc N : kod (S05.260)
potato N : halg (S05.700)
pour V : gaɳam (S09.350)
pray V : ʥap ʃaɳam (S22.170)
prayer N : puʤa (—)
pregnant : aːn maːts (S04.730)
preserve V : batsjaːs piʧim (S11.240)
press V : dabjaːm; ʥikem [INTR]; ʥikjaːm [TR] (S04.780, S09.342, S09.343)
pressure cooker N : kukar (—)
price N : mulaŋ (S11.870)
priest N : puʥʥaːra; puʤari (S22.180)
prison N : tʰaɳa (S21.390)
probably : aksa (—)
profit N : nafa (—)
property N : maːla (S11.99904)
prophet N : barʈ (—)
pull V : kʰitsjaːm (S09.330)
pumpkin N : kaddu (S08.931)
punishment N : daːɳaŋ; ɖaːɳaŋ (S21.370)
pupil N : paɽets tsʰakts (S17.260)
purpose N : tain (—)
purse N : boʈuaŋ (S06.99901)
pus N : taːg (S04.857)
push V : ʤakka raɳam (S10.670)
put V : gaɳam; piʧim (S11.170, S12.120)
put on V : garʃim [MDL] (S06.110)
queen N : raːni (S19.330)
quickly : tsʰika (S14.160, S14.210, S14.331)
quilt N : ruʤai (S07.422)
rabbit N : kʰargoʃ (S03.614, S03.8630)
radio N : roɖije (S23.1000)
radish N : muli (—)
rain N : ʤab (S01.750)
rainbow N : kʰuigopigol; pʰigolpigol (S01.590)
raise V : rojaːm (S08.99962)
rajma (dish with red kidney beans) N : polɖaɽ (—)
ram N : butkar (S03.260)
rat (in fields) N : muʃʈur (S03.630)
rat (in house) N : pʰuts (S03.630)
raw : kaʧas (S05.122, S05.124)
razor N : paʈʈi (S06.930)
read V : paɽem [INTR]; paɽʰjaːm [TR] (S17.242, S17.250, S18.520)
recite V : tsʰam ʃetam (—)
recognize V : sesam (S17.170)
red : laːl (S15.660)
refuse V : maːj mullam (S18.370)
relative N : naːʈa (—)
relatives N : naːʈa (S02.810)
relaxation N : araːm (—)
religion N : daram (S22.110)
remember V : jaːd baram (S17.310)
remembrance N : jaːd (—)
rent N : baːr (S11.690)
request N : maːŋ; uŋma (—)
rescue V : batsjaːm (S11.250)
rest V : naʃim (S04.912, S07.110, S09.99931, S12.130)
result N : ruʤulʈ (—)
return N : bapas (—)
revenue N : baːr; ʈʰeka (S11.690)
rhododendron N : pragu (—)
rib N : praʃa (S04.162)
rice (cooked) N : pʰul (S08.480)
rice (uncooked) N : laːr (S08.480)
rice beer N : lugɽi (S05.930)
rich : seʈ (S11.510)
right(1) : ʥa(ː)b; loʤoŋ (S12.410)
right(2) : ʈʰiːk (S16.730)
right away : koraije (—)
ring N : mundaɽi (S06.730)
ripe : pakets (S05.121, S05.123)
rise (of sun) V : baram; dʊanam (S10.210)
river N : gaːɽiŋ; najiŋ (S01.329, S01.360)
riverlet N : naːla; naːlaŋ (S01.360)
road N : ʃaɽak (S10.710)
roast V : raːɽ gaɳam (S05.230)
rock N : kaŋ; rudiŋ (S01.440)
roof N : rokʈʰa; rokʈʰaŋ (S07.510)
roof (stone/slate) N : paːʈ (S07.510)
roof (tin) N : tsadriː (S07.510)
roof (wooden) N : kaʈʰa (S07.510)
room N : kamra; kamraŋ; paːʈi (S07.210, S07.260)
room for firewood N : dʊaregan (—)

room for storing god Jamlu's musical instruments which are played by SCs (e.g drums) N : koʈaŋ (—)
rooster N : kukaɽaŋ; murga: (S03.520)
root N : ʤa:ŋ (S08.540)
rope N : buʃ (S09.190)
rose (flower) N : gula:b u: (—)
roti made with kathu flour N : kodra (S05.510)
rotten : ʧokets (S05.125)
rough(2) : kakʧos (S01.323)
round : gol; raɳ goʈunas (S12.810)
rug N : dari (S09.770, S09.771)
run V : ʈʰoroga: raɳam (S10.460)
running N : ʈʰor(o) (—)
sack N : boraŋ (S09.99917)
sad : dukʰis (S04.840)
salt N : tsʰa (S05.810)
salty : kruk; tsʰa ʥada (S15.360)
sand N : bali; re:t; re:tiŋ (S01.215)
sandal (for women) N : ʧapli (S06.99907)
Saturday : ʃuɳiʧare (S14.680)
sausage N : ʤuma (S05.630)
saw N : a:ra (S09.480)
say V : lonam (S18.210, S18.220, S18.221)
scar N : nusa:li (S04.858)
scent N : ba:s (—)
school N : sukul (S17.280)
scissors N : kanʧi (S09.240)
scold V : ʃapoga: lonam (S18.390)
scorpion N : biʧu (S03.815)
scrape V : goarʃim [MDL]; ʧʰeɽa raɳam (S05.480)
scratch V : ɒaɽʃum (S04.8541)
sculptor N : mistri: (S09.430, S09.820)
sea N : samudra; samudraŋ (S01.320, S01.329)
seagull N : tiuadz ʤju (S03.582)
second : duʤa (S13.360)
see V : ba:lem [INTR]; ba:lja:m [TR] (S15.510)
seed N : bedʥa; bijaɳ (S08.311)
sell V : renam (S11.820)
semolina N : suʥi (—)
send V : ʃenam (S10.630)
senior : ʤetʰ (—)
senior N : ʤeʃtʰas (S23.3200)
sense N : hoʃ (—)
separate V : aŋgi ʃaɳam (S12.230)
separation N : alag (—)
servant N : nokar; ʈʰinɖ (S19.430)
service N : nokri (—)
sesame seeds N : seljara (—)
seven : sat (S13.0700)
sew V : poɳam (S06.350)
shade N : ʃilaŋ (S01.630)
shade against rain N : kaʈʰa (S07.510)
shadow N : ʃilaŋ (S01.630)
shake V : milam; ʧʰal balja:m (S10.260)
shallow : ɖugas ma:j (S12.680)
share N : bãɖa; hisa (S13.230)
share V : banɖija:m; benɖerem (S11.910)
shawl N : paʈʈu (—)
shears N : kanʧi (S09.240)
sheep N : kʰas (S03.250, S03.290)
sheep meat N : muɖe (—)
shine V : tsamkem (S15.560)
ship N : samudri ʤahaʤ (S10.810)
shirt N : kurti (S06.440)
shiver V : kʰanam (S04.680)
shoe N : bu:ʈ; ʥoɽ; ʥoɽa (S06.510, S06.520)
shoe (modern sneaker) N : ekʃana bu:ʈ (S06.510)
shoe (rubber, worn by women) N : kʰoʃori bu:ʈ (S06.510)
shoelace N : tasma (—)
shoot V : tupkas raɳam (S20.620)
shop N : biʥanes; ha:ti (S11.860)
shore N : kina:ra; neɖaŋ (S01.270)
short : pʰak; pʰakuʧ (S12.560, S12.590, S14.140)
shortage N : kam (—)
shoulder N : pʰar (S04.300)
shout V : kaɽa ʃaɳam (S18.130)
shovel N : belʧa (S08.240)
shut V : ʧiŋam (S12.220, S12.250)
sibling N : boi; riŋʥjuŋʥ (S02.456)
sick/ill : dukʰis (S04.840)
side N : kinare (S12.360)
silver N : mu(:)l (S09.650)
sin N : kasu:r (—)
since : alo (—)
sing V : gitaŋ lanam (S18.120)
singer N : ga:jek (—)
sink V : ɖub(b)em; ɖubja:m [TR] (S04.751, S10.330)
sister N : daiju; riŋʥ (S02.450)
sit V : naʃim (S04.912, S07.110, S09.99931, S12.130)
six : ʧʰa (S13.0600)
skin N : kʰolɖu; ʃa (S04.120)
skin (of animal) N : bod (S04.120)
skin V : lebɽa kʰulam (S09.290)
sky N : sargaŋ (S01.510)
slap N : tʰep(a)r (—)
sleep V : ʈulem; ʈuljem (S04.610)
slow : sulus (S14.220)
small : pʰak; pʰakuʧ (S12.560, S12.590, S14.140)
smear V : ʃatarja:m (S09.99936)
smell N : ba:s (—)
smell(1) V : ba:s baram; ba:s puŋʃim (S15.210)
smile V : kʰuʃiga: dem (S16.251)
smoke N : dumaŋ (S01.830)
smoke V : surgiʈ tuɳam; tuɳam; tu:gem; tu:ŋem (S05.130, S08.690)
snacks N : ʧaʈpapɽi (—)

snail N : huŋg (S03.940)
snail with shell N : p^{h}ili gaɽe (S03.940)
snail without shell N : p^{h}il (S03.940)
snake N : rinig; sap (S03.840, S03.850)
snake man N : sanper (—)
snatch V : k^{h}oɽam (—)
sneeze V : gisam (S04.540)
sniff V : ba:s p^{h}um; ba:s suɳam (S15.212)
snore V : garaɽiga: raɳam (S04.612)
snores(PL) N : garaɽiga: (—)
snot N : tamti (—)
snow N : pom (S01.760)
snowball N : pompiɽiŋ (—)
snowshoe N : k^{h}obba (S06.9800)
so many : nonda (S13.150)
soap N : subu:n (S06.950)
sock N : ʣura:b (S06.490)
soil N : ʣi:mi:; ʤami:n; ka:m (S01.212, S09.730)
soldier N : sipahi; sipahis (S20.170)
sole of foot N : p^{h}ine (S04.372)
some : koi; ʧ^{h}ugu (S13.181)
sometimes : kebbikebbi; kebigas (S14.320, S14.330)
son N : beʈa; ʃoru; ʧ^{h}o; ʧ^{h}ok (S02.270, S02.410)
son-in-law N : ʤamais (S02.630, S02.631)
song N : gaɳa; gitaŋ (S23.6400)
soon : ʦ^{h}ika (S14.160, S14.210, S14.331)
sore N : raʃug (S04.850)
sorrow : nark (S16.720)
sorrow N : nark (S22.320)
soul N : dil; man (S04.440)
sound N : deg; kaɽi (S15.440, S18.110)
sour : surg (S15.380)
sow V : puʃam (S08.310)
spade N : kuda:ɽi (S08.240)
spare V : bodam (—)
spatula N : kaɽʦ^{h}i (—)
speak V : lonam (S18.210, S18.220, S18.221)
spectacles N : enak; ʧaʃma (S23.2400)
speech N : bat; galaŋ (S18.222)
spend V : k^{h}aram (—)
spices N : masa:la (—)
spider N : ʣa:rs; ʣa:ʦ; ʈõʈida:r (S03.818)
spider web N : ʣaɽi (S03.819)
spin V : ʦa:m katja:m (S06.310)
spindle N : ʦanɖuk (S06.320)
spit N : leptup^h; letu (—)
spit V : letu buɽam (S04.560)
split V : ʤuɳam [INTR]; paʈakja:m; ʧuɳam; ʧuɳam [TR] (S09.260, S09.270)
spoon N : k^{h}artsul; ʧammaʧ; ʧamʧi; ʧamʧiŋ (S05.370)
spread out V : p^{h}elʈam (S09.340)
spring N : bai; ku:ɽiŋ; ʦ^{h}ol (S01.370, S01.390)
squeeze V : dabja:m; moroɽja:m (S04.780, S09.342, S09.343)
stab (=give) V : raɳam (S09.223)
staircase N : uŋgeɽa (S07.370)
stallion N : goɽa (S03.410, S03.420)
stand V : k^{h}aɽa aʧim (S12.150)
star N : kar (S01.540)
starch N : piʦ (—)
stay V : naʃim (S04.912, S07.110, S09.99931, S12.130)
steal V : ʧorikega: ʃaɳam (S21.510)
steel N : saʈi:l (—)
step N : kadam (—)
step- : kan (—)
stepdaughter N : raunɖi (S02.740)
stepfather N : ba: kan (S02.710)
stepmother N : ja: kani (S02.720)
stepson N : raunɖa (S02.730)
stick V : ʣoɽja:m [TR] (—)
stingy : kanʤus; kubeka (S11.540)
stir V : millem (S05.490, S11.160, S11.320)
stocking N : ʣura:b (S06.490)
stomach N : poʈaŋ (S04.4310, S04.460)
stomach ache N : ʃulakutoŋ (—)
stone (small, put under large rocks so that they don't tumble down the hill) N : tog (S01.440)
stone N : kaŋ (S01.440)
stop V : gunaʃim [MDL]; rokja:m [TR]; rukem [INTR]; ʈ^{h}aprja:m [TR] (S14.280)
storage room N : banɖa:raŋ (—)
store N : ha:ti (S11.860)
storm N : bijanna (S01.580)
story N : kat^{h}a: (—)
stove N : geʈʈ^{h}aŋ; sʈop (S05.250, S07.310, S07.320)
straight : sa:mnas; sidda (S12.710, S12.730)
stranger N : jug marʃaŋ (S19.550)
straw shoe N : poɳ (S06.510)
strawberry (wild) N : bumle (—)
stream N : ʤairu; na:la; na:laŋ (S01.360)
street (narrow) N : gali (S23.3950)
stretch V : ʣu:r la:tam (S09.320)
strike V : raʈam (S09.210)
strong : naɽija; polak; ʣarka:ris (S04.810)
study V : paɽem [INTR]; paɽ^{h}ja:m [TR] (S17.242, S17.250, S18.520)
suck V : ʧusja:m (S05.160)
sugar N : k^{h}anɖ (S05.850)
summer : garmi (S15.851)
summer N : garmi; ʃa:l (S14.760)
summit N : ka:ʈ^{h}iŋ; raŋ (S12.330)
sun N : duppe; ʤa:ɽe; suraʤ (S01.520)
Sunday : tʊa:r (S14.620)
suspect V : ʃak ʃaɳam (S17.440)
suspension bridge N : supen (—)
swallow V : miŋgam (S05.181)
swear V : kaʃmi raɳam (S21.240)

sweat N : parsed (—)
sweater N : bunen (—)
sweep V : kʰutam (S09.370)
sweet : daʈʰis; tʰig (S15.350, S16.710, S16.730)
sweet potato, red N : ʤeʧialga (S08.910)
sweet potato, white N : kaʧas halga (S08.910)
sweets N : miʈʰa; sauda (S23.5650)
swelling N : ʧug; ʧurʣ (S04.853)
swim V : bara raɳam (S10.350)
swine N : su:r; su:ru (S03.350)
swing V : tolem [INTR]; tolja:m [TR] (—)
sword N : talʋa:r; tarʋa:r (S20.270)
table N : ʈebal; ʈeble (S07.440)
tail N : puʧʰ; puʧʰaŋ; pʰainʤa; ʈʰuʈre; ʈʰuʈʰ(a)re (S04.180)
tailor N : darʣi; laʈpaʈa poʧ (S06.130)
take V : u:nam (S11.130)
take out V : ɖuʈam; tʋanam (—, S12.212)
talk V : lonam (S18.210, S18.220, S18.221)
tall : la:mas (S12.570, S12.580)
tan V : kʰulʃim (S07.6700)
taste V : prekʰja:m [TR] (S15.310)
tax N : ba:r; kora; koraŋ; ʈeks (S11.690)
tea N : ʧa(:) (S23.9000)
teach V : paɽem [INTR]; paɽʰja:m [TR] (S17.242, S17.250, S18.520)
teacher N : guru; ma:sʈar (S17.270)
tear N : piti (S16.380)
tear V : ʤuŋam [INTR]; ʧuŋam; ʧuŋam [TR] (S09.260, S09.270)
teat N : manu (S04.412)
telephone N : pʰon; ʈelipʰon (S23.1200)
television N : biɖio; ʈiʋi; ʋiɖiɔ (S23.1100)
tell V : lonam (S18.210, S18.220, S18.221)
temper N : da:n (—)
temple N : deogʰar; deoraŋ; ʤaka kima; ʤaka pi:bu; mandir; monoŋ (S22.130)
temple treasurer N : karda:r (—)
ten : das (S13.100)
tenant N : maʣa:r (—)
tent N : tambu (S07.140)
thank you! : kanka bala meradi; tegje ɖaʈʰis (S16.99903)
that : du; tes (S24.0800)
that much : dade (—)
theft N : ʧori(g) (—)
then : da; dabaʣpʰeʈa; dabode; dabre; dok; ɖaba; tabo (S24.99912)
there : didd; njo (S24.1000)
there also : neneije (—)
thick : moʈas (S12.630)
thief N : ʧoras (S21.520)
thigh N : baʣug (S04.351)
thin : bag; ʤaŋʧ (S04.820, S12.650)
thing N : suma:n; ʧiʣ (S11.180)
think(1) V : soʧem (S17.130)
third : tisraŋ; tisraŋaʣ (S13.420)
thirsty : ʃukaʃ (S15.840)
this : ʤo; nu (S24.0700)
thorn N : ʦo (—)
thousand : haʣa:r; huʤa:r; i:d haʣa:r; i:d huʤa:r (S13.106)
thrash V : kulam (S09.210)
thread N : dauga (S06.380)
threaten V : boŋam ʃeɳam (S18.440)
three : ʃu(:)m (S13.0300)
three days after : ʃumin kuin ba:d (—)
three times : ʃum pʰeriga: (S13.440)
thresh V : ʦʰaʈa kja:ʈam (S08.340)
threshhold N : daʣi (—)
threshing stick N : ʃupa (—)
threshing stone N : paʈ; pa:n (S01.440, S08.350)
threshing-floor N : kʰo; pa:n (S01.440, S08.350)
throat N : golaŋ (S04.280, S04.290)
throw V : buɽam; pʰikja:m (S10.250, S10.490)
thumb N : ʤeʃʈu(k) prá:d (S04.342)
thunder N : guruɽuk (S01.560)
Thursday : b(ʰ)rest (S14.660)
thus : de; nenk (—)
ticket N : ba:r (S11.690)
tie V : ʦ(ʰ)unam (S09.160)
tiger N : ʃer (S03.99942)
time N : ʋakt (S14.110)
tire N : ʈhak (—)
tired : tʰak (S04.910)
tobacco N : tamba:ku (S08.680)
today : dalaʦ; tʰi:d (S14.470)
toe N : goɖinaʦ pra:d; pra:d; pra:daŋ (S04.340, S04.380)
toenail N : ʧi:nɖ (S04.344)
together : kat (—)
toilet N : ʈaʈʈikʰana (S23.5200)
tomato N : ʈumaʈar (—)
tomorrow : na:b (S14.480)
tongs (cooking utensil) N : ʦumʈak (S05.391)
tongue N : le (S04.260)
tooth N : ga:r (S04.270)
top : riŋ (S12.0800)
top N : riŋ (S12.330)
totally : bilkul (—)
touch V : bi:nam (S15.710)
towel N : taoli (S06.820)
tower N : tʰomba (S20.360)
town N : ʃeher (S19.150)
tradition N : riʋa:ʣ (S19.610)
traditional Malana parliament N : hakima; hakkma (—)
train N : rel; ʈren (S23.1550)
transhumance N : parijar (—)
trap N : pinʤra (S20.640)
treasury N : banɖa:raŋ (—)

tree N : beʈiŋ (S08.530, S08.600)
tree branch N : ʃiŋ ɖa(:)liŋ (S08.550)
tree trunk N : beʈiŋ; polak (S08.530, S08.600, S08.730)
trousers N : penʈ; sut^{h}on (S06.480)
truck N : ʈruk (—)
true : sahi (S16.660)
trumpet N : ka:ɽi (S18.730)
truth : suttsai; suʧai (S16.660)
try V : koʃiʃ ʃaɳam (S17.480)
Tuesday : maŋgal (S14.640)
tumbler N : gula(:)s; kantsu gula(:)s (S09.740)
turban N : pagriŋ (S06.550)
turmeric N : bikʃuar (—)
turn (around) V : palʈem [INTR]; palʈja:m [TR] (S10.120, S10.130)
turnip N : salgam (S08.99952)
turtle N : kaʧ^{h}ua (S03.980)
twelve : bara (S13.102)
twenty : bi; niʤa (S13.104)
twice : niʃ p^{h}eraga: (S13.380)
twin N : doɽag (S02.458)
two : niʃ (S13.0200)
two days after tomorrow : pa:ji (—)
two days before yesterday : mujaŋ ri:d (—)
two times : niʃ p^{h}eraga: (S13.380)
udder N : uʊaŋ (S04.420)
ugly : ʃobi:l ma:j (S16.820)
uncle N : ba: (S02.350, S02.510)
uncooked : kaʧas (S05.122, S05.124)
under : nje:n (S12.0700)
understand V : samʤem [INTR]; samʤja:m [TR] (S17.160)
underwear N : kaʧ^{h} (—)
unripe : kaʧas (S05.122, S05.124)
untie V : ʈaʈam (S09.161)
until : tak (—)
up : riŋ; t^{h}o (S12.0800)
up N : riŋ (S12.330)
upper : rigi:n (S12.0810)
upper house N : ɽigi:nnaʃiŋ (—)
upper house in traditional Malana parliament N : ʤeʃt^{h}aŋ (—)
upper part of Malana N : d^{h}ara behad; d^{h}araŋ (—)
urine N : ʧoʈi (—)
valley N : ga:ʈi (S01.240)
vegetable N : poʈo (S05.650, S05.710)
vegetable (a wild species, used in cooking) N : barnog (S05.650)
vegetables N : ba:ʤi (S05.650)
vein N : sirãõ (S04.151)
very : bout^{h}; k^{h}are; tegje (—)
village N : deʃaŋ; gra:m; gra:maŋ (S19.110, S19.160, S01.100)
voice N : kaɽi (S15.440, S18.110)
vomit N : p^{h}asʈiŋ (—)
vomit V : p^{h}asam (S04.570)
vulture N : gallas; ilna: (S03.584, S03.586)
waist N : k^{h}o: (S04.462)
wake up V : aʧ^{h}im; sarʃim (S04.630)
walk V : hanɖem; hanɖja:m (S10.450)
walking stick N : loɽiʈom; loɽiʈua (S19.250)
wall N : bitiŋ (S07.270)
warm : ʤog (S15.851)
warm (weather) : garmi (S15.851)
warm (weather) N : garmi (S14.760)
wash V : ʤim [INTR]; ʧim [TR] (S09.360)
washed : ʧits (S15.830)
watch N : gaɽi (S14.530)
watch V : taɳam; taɳʃim [MDL] (S15.520)
water N : ti(:) (S01.310)
water faucet N : nalka (—)
waterfall N : ts^{h}ol (S01.370, S01.390)
watermill N : gaʈa:ŋ (—)
wave N : lari (S01.350)
way N : om (S10.720)
way in N : golaŋ (—)
weak : ʤaŋʧ; kumʤor (S04.820)
wear V : gaʃam (S06.99911)
weather N : mosam; sargã(ŋ); tsarga:m (S01.780)
weave V : gundja:m (S06.330, S09.750)
weaver of nets N : ʤula:ha (—)
wedding N : bijaŋ (S02.340)
Wednesday : bud(d) (S14.650)
week N : hapta (S14.610)
weigh V : tolija:m (S11.920)
well N : bai; ɖibɽiŋ; ku:ɽiŋ (S01.330, S01.370)
wet : ʧits (S15.830)
what : ʧ^{h}ige (—)
what? : ʧ^{h}u; ʧ^{h}ugge (S17.640)
whatever : duʤ; dutso; nesiki; tsuŋmat (—)
whatever else : ʧ^{h}ige (—)
wheat N : ʤa:(d) (S08.430)
wheel N : guʈnu:ga: (S10.760)
when? : ʧ^{h}ub (S17.650)
where? : ham (S17.660)
which? : hatte (S17.670)
while ago : t^{h}alo (—)
whisper V : sulus lonam (S18.150)
whistle V : ʃʊĩ ʃaɳam (S18.170)
white : ʧ^{h}og (S15.640)
who? : hat (S17.680)
why? : k^{h}ue (S17.690)
wide : bellis; k^{h}ulas (S12.610)
widow N : ranɖi (S02.760)
widower N : nuka ʧ^{h}ets ʃi:k (S02.770)
wife N : laɽi; ʧ^{h}ets; ʧ^{h}etsaŋ (S02.320)
wild : ʤaŋgali (S16.99914)
wind N : lipur (S01.720)
window N : ʈaki (S07.250)
wing N : pak^{h}iŋ (S04.392)
winter : ʈ^{h}anɖas (S15.860)
winter N : gu(:)n; sardaŋ; ʈ^{h}anɖas (S14.740)

winter migration N : parijar (—)
wipe V : ʈuʃja:m (S09.3110)
wire N : ta:r (—)
wise : akli (S17.210)
witch N : ʧuɽel (S22.430)
with : saŋ (S24.0400)
witness N : gaʊais (S21.230)
woman N : bekaɽi; beʈaɽi (S02.220)
wood N : ʃiŋ (S01.430, S01.880)
wood used for making tables N : tokta (S01.430)
woods N : baŋ; baɳaŋ; baɽaŋ; ʤad (S01.410)
wool (of sheep) N : ʦa:m (S06.220)
work N : ka:m; ka:maŋ (S09.120)
world N : deʃaŋ; dunija:; prit^{h}ʊi; sansa:r (S19.110, S19.160, S01.100)
worm N : rinig (S03.840, S03.850)
worship N : puʤa (—)
wound N : raʃug (S04.850)
wrap (in cloth) V : laʈpaʈja:m (S10.140)
wrist N : k^{h}urke (S04.321)
write V : lik^{h}ja:m [TR] (S18.510)
wrong : ma:ɽa (S16.720, S16.740)
yak N : ja:k (—)
yak(F) N : mijak (—)
yard N : k^{h}o(l) (S07.150)
yawn V : ʤama:em (S04.520)
year N : barʃ; barʃaŋ; sa:l; sa:laŋ (S14.730)
yellow : pi:g (S15.690)
yes : hoi (S17.550)
yesterday : hid; muɖ (S14.490)
yoghurt N : dahi (—)
yolk N : kesaraŋ (S05.971)
young : ʤaʊa:n; jaɳagats; p^{h}ak; p^{h}akuʧ (S12.560, S12.590, S14.140)
young man N : ʥaʊa:n ʧ^{h}akʦ (S02.251)
young woman N : ʤaʊa:n ʧimeʦ (S02.261)
younger : kaniʃʈ^{h}as (—)
younger brother N : p^{h}ak bau; p^{h}akuʧ baʦ (S02.445)
younger sibling N : boiʦ (S02.4562)
younger sister N : hoʧi ba(h)u; p^{h}ak(uʧ) riŋʥ (S02.455)
zodiac sign N : lo (—)

Subject and language index

In this index, genealogical classification details are provided for languages and language subfamilies of South Asia, as follows:

DR: Dravidian
IA: Indo-Aryan (a branch of Indo-European)
LI: language isolate
MD: Munda (a branch of Austroasiatic)
ST: Sino-Tibetan

For example, "Darma (ST)" is the Sino-Tibetan language Darma and "Western Pahari (<IA)" is the Western Pahari subfamily/branch of the Indo-Aryan language family.

Non-South-Asian languages and language (sub)families are not specified in this way, for example "Danish" and "Slavic (language family)". For obvious reasons, Kanashi, Kinnauri, Sino-Tibetan, and Indo-Aryan are not indexed, although some of the subbranches of ST and IA are, in particular the two main branches of West Himalayish, Eastern and Western West Himalayish (both Kanashi and Kinnauri belong under the latter branch).

See also the "Chapter overview" introducing each chapter.

https://doi.org/10.1515/9783110703245-010

www.ingramcontent.com/pod-product-compliance
Lightning Source LLC
Chambersburg PA
CBHW071315150426
43191CB00007B/628